Please renew/return this item by the last date sh—

So that your telephone call i—
please call the numbers a—

From Area cod—   the rest of Herts:
01923 or 0208:

Renewals: 01923 4713
Enquiries: 01923 4

KU-395-434

THE EVOLUTION OF PARLIAMENT

PARLIAMENT IN 1523.

THE EVOLUTION
OF PARLIAMENT

BY

A. F. POLLARD, M.A., Litt.D., F.B.A.

FELLOW OF ALL SOULS' COLLEGE, OXFORD, AND PROFESSOR OF
ENGLISH HISTORY IN THE UNIVERSITY OF LONDON

SECOND EDITION, REVISED
WITH APPENDICES, NOTES, AND ILLUSTRATIONS

LONGMANS, GREEN AND CO., LTD.

39 PATERNOSTER ROW, LONDON
FOURTH AVENUE & 30TH STREET, NEW YORK
BOMBAY, CALCUTTA, AND MADRAS

1926

PREFACE TO THE FIRST EDITION

THIS volume is the outcome of studies which were turned in the direction of constitutional history partly by my appointment to a chair with that title at University College, London, in 1903, and more specifically by my election in 1908 to a fellowship at All Souls' College, Oxford, on condition of pursuing researches suggested by the late F. W. Maitland. The first sketch of this essay took the form of six public lectures delivered in London in Lent Term 1913, which were expanded into fifteen lectures given on the Goldwin Smith foundation at Cornell University and elsewhere in the United States in the following spring. The manuscript was completed, save for some notes and references, in August 1915, when the increasing tension of the war put a stop to remoter studies.

During these seventeen years the history of the English parliament has attracted the labour of several learned historians, and particular acknowledgement is due to Professor C. H. McIlwain's *High Court of Parliament*, which, coming into my hands at the end of 1912, confirmed the trend of my investigations and supplied me with fresh ideas and illustrations. Another American book, Professor Baldwin's *King's Council in the Middle Ages*, published in 1914, threw valuable light on a collateral subject. But the starting-point for all of us has been Maitland's introduction to the *Memoranda de Parliamento*, which he edited for the Rolls Series in 1893, the most original and suggestive essay

v

that has ever been written on the medieval English parliament. There would have been less reason for this book, had that essay, which is still on sale in its original limited edition, not been buried in the Rolls Series, excluded from disinterment in Maitland's *Collected Papers*, and generally ignored by English instructors of youth for nearly a generation.

A student who is mainly versed in the history of the sixteenth century must, however, if he trespasses on the middle ages, be ready to face prosecution with all the rigour of medieval lore; and this volume cannot escape criticism of its lack of technical knowledge in many details. My excuse for the trespass is that, being engaged on a study of the Tudor constitution, I could not understand it without seeking answers to preliminary problems which had not been solved; and historical curiosity combined with an academic interest in politics to expand an introduction to the constitutional history of the Tudor period into an essay on the place of parliament in the past, the present, and the future of the English state. The last two chapters at least of this volume are not history; but I doubt the logic and the expedience of the contention that it is only the business of those who have not studied the past to discuss the present or the future.

The book is less a history of parliament than a suggestion of the lines upon which it should be written, and rather an indication of the research that is still required than of that which has yet been done. Few of the conclusions here tentatively outlined can be established without prolonged research by many scholars; but happily the prospect of a school of historical research is not so distant as it was. Meanwhile, I have to express my deep obligations to the fellow-workers who have attended the formal and informal meetings held at University College during the last six years to discuss various problems of historical research, and to whom I owe many suggestions, references, and corrections. A list of acknowledgements would be long and invidious, but I cannot repress a word of thanks to Miss Jeffries Davis, Lecturer in the Sources of English History at University College, whose contribution to the value of those discussions has been crowned by a card-index of references to the materials for English parliamentary history, which is available for all who care to consult it. It is not, of course, complete; and possibly its most fruitful function may be to indicate the need and value of similar registers of historical materials already printed or preserved in British archives.

A. F. POLLARD.

April 23, 1920.

PREFACE TO THE SECOND EDITION

THIS volume has been out of print for nearly two years and the demand for its reappearance has been sufficient to impose upon its author the alternatives of simply reprinting or making such revision as would entitle the re-issue to be called a second edition. The cost of setting the type afresh and lack of leisure to re-write the book suggested the easy course of a mere re-impression, and both were reinforced by the inadvisability of attempting to convert an introduction to the constitutional history of the Tudor period into a history of medieval English parliaments. On the other hand, such attention as I have been able to give to the topics dealt with herein made it difficult to reprint it without reference to the modification or confirmation which those subsequent studies have suggested. The result has been some correction of errors, some addition of facts, some notes on kindly criticism, and a rather lengthy appendix on parliamentary representation in the fourteenth century.

These fall far short of what I could have desired. I should like to have responded to Mr. Crump's invitation[1] and attempted to add that chapter " to tell what ' law ' is, and how it is related to parliament," and to have argued that, since the " king's grace " was needed to turn parliamentary petitions into acts of parliament, it is not easy to divorce it from statutes or statutes from the " law." But the chapter would have run to at least one inconclusive

[1] *History*, April 1921, p. 47.

volume; and, if I read him aright, Professor Holdsworth's seven have shown the impossibility of any definition of " law " which will meet historical difficulties.   It is, perhaps, the greatest of those " no-constants "—I had almost written *non-constats*—with which historical students have to grapple.   I should like to have ventured also upon the minor mystery of the " statute-book " and the relation between rolls of parliament and statute-rolls; but these are problems for more expert hands than those of one whose fate or fortune it has been to spend more time in facilitating the research of others than in pursuing it himself.

I have, however, been able to use for this edition some works which I ought to have used, but did not, before.   The war and even the first years of peace were not conducive to historical scholarship, and monographs published abroad during that period tended to escape the notice they deserved. But my regret at having failed to read M. Pasquet's singularly acute and lucid *Essai sur les origines de la Chambre des Communes* (1914), and Professor A. B. White's scholarly articles on that and cognate subjects [1] before I wrote this book is tempered by satisfaction that so many of my more heterodox conclusions should have been independently reached by more expert authorities.   But not even the war will excuse the inadvertence which neglected Riess's *Geschichte des Wahlrechts zum englischen Parliament* published as long ago as 1885, and his article on *Der Ursprung des englischen Unterhauses*.[2]   I need hardly refer students to Professor Rait's *Parliaments of Scotland*, published last year; and I have made no attempt to anticipate myself or others by expanding the sections of this volume which deal with the Tudor period.

[1] *American Historical Review*, xvii. 12–16, xix. 735–50.
[2] *Hist. Zeitschrift*, 1888.

Apart from two new appendices the book remains substantially what it was. Such corrections as could be inserted without disturbing the type have been made in the text and will not be noticed except by the critics and correspondents to whom they are due. Others which required some discussion have been relegated to an appendix of notes, and reference to them has been made by letters of the alphabet to distinguish them from the numeric references to the footnotes.

A. F. Pollard.

Institute of Historical Research,
  September 24, 1925.

P.S.—Since this preface was written a second edition of M. Pasquet's treatise has been published, in English and with additional notes, by the Cambridge University Press. A detailed criticism of one or two points relating to medieval parliamentary elections has also been contributed by Mr. J. G. Edwards to *Studies . . . presented to T. F. Tout* (Manchester, 1925): I hope to deal with it in the April number of *History*.

Finally, I have to thank the Society of Antiquaries and Miss Ivy M. Cooper, who has been working for some years on the topography of Westminster Palace, for the last illustration here for the first time reproduced.

LIST OF ILLUSTRATIONS

THE EVOLUTION OF PARLIAMENT

CHAPTER I

THE PLACE OF PARLIAMENT IN HISTORY

In the best-known life of one historian by another there is a passage which combines the views of two writers of genius on the modern value of parliamentary institutions. " He spoke much," writes Froude of Carlyle, " on politics and the character of public men. From the British Parliament he was firmly persuaded that no good could be looked for. A democratic Parliament, from the nature of it, would place persons at the head of affairs increasingly unfit to deal with them. Bad would be followed by worse, and worse by worst, till the very fools themselves would see that the system must end. Lord Wolseley, then Sir Garnet, went with me once to call in Cheyne Row, Carlyle having expressed a wish to see him. He was much struck with Sir Garnet, and talked freely with him on many subjects. He described the House of Commons as ' six hundred talking asses, set to make laws and to administer the concerns of the greatest empire the world had ever seen,' with other uncomplimentary phrases. When he rose to go, he said, ' Well, sir, I am glad to have made your acquaintance, and I wish you well. There is one duty which I hope may be laid upon you before you leave this world—to lock the door of yonder place, and turn them all about their business.' "[1]

---

[1] Froude, *Carlyle's Life in London*, ii. 446.

B

Cromwell himself was not infected with his biographer's contempt of parliamentary institutions, and Carlyle represents the Homeric age of historical science. Hero-worship is impatient of constitutional government, and its votaries are unfitted by temperament to measure the value of parliaments. But the critics are not confined to the ranks of archaic admirers of force, and the permanence of the British parliament itself is doubted by advanced students of modern politics. English publicists have speculated without horror on the abolition of the house of commons, and Americans have described the sovereignty of parliament as a phantom. " It may well be doubted," writes one, " whether the doctrine of Parliamentary sovereignty, in any form that means much, can long survive the triumph of democracy. . . . When the Referendum really comes, the sovereign Parliament must go. But whether for good or for evil, the Referendum, in principle at least, seems to be coming." [1] To the advocates of the referendum and the believers in the sovereignty of force must be added the bureaucrat and the syndicalist; and the life of parliament might seem to depend upon that mutual antagonism of its enemies which destroys the cumulative force of their attacks. But even extinct monsters have their scientific interest, and if it were true that parliament has run its course of public utility, that fact would make it all the easier to determine its place in history.

It is possible, however, that a re-examination of the various functions which parliament has fulfilled in the past may lead to a less pessimistic view of its future, and that the dissolution which seems so patent to some observers is no more than a transfiguration. If, indeed, we regard parliament as having been a fixed institution and apply to it architectural metaphors like foundations, corner-stones, and so forth, signs of change must need appear to be symptoms of decay. But fortunately for itself parliament has never attained that rigidity, which appeals to the artist in bricks and mortar but strikes the student of life as a proof of death; and has eluded all efforts to stereotype its con-

[1] McIlwain, *The High Court of Parliament*, p. xv.

stitution which, if successful, would have had the effect of encasing a living heart in plaster of Paris. For political institutions that stand the test of time are organisms subsisting upon their adaptability to their environment and ever changing with the conditions of their existence. Parliament is not bound up with any political theory or any transient constitution; it has been the tool of monarchs, of oligarchs, and of democrats; it has been the means of opposition as well as the instrument of government, the preventive of revolution as well as the promoter of reform. It has been, and is still to some extent, a court of law, a council, and a legislature; and its forms, which were used by medieval kings, have been found still more effective by modern ministers. Its elasticity has known no bounds in the past, and we have yet to learn that it has no value for the forces of the future. The faith of men in what can be done by act of parliament is assuredly not on the wane; and the mother of parliaments has seen her progeny spread into every civilized quarter of the globe.

Parliamentary institutions have, in fact, been incomparably the greatest gift of the English people to the civilization of the world. Civilized man has drawn his religious inspirations from the East, his alphabet from Egypt, his algebra from the Moors, his art and literature mainly from Greece, and his laws from Rome. But his political organization he owes mostly to English conceptions, and constitutional systems all over the world are studded with words and phrases which can only be explained by reference to the medieval English parliament. Other nations have had their indigenous representative systems, but they have all been abandoned or profoundly modified under the influence of English ideas; and reichstag and duma, riksdag and storthing, sobranje and meiljiss are none of them the purely native products their names would imply. Here and there the grafting has not been successful, but the failure of parliamentary institutions in semitic and negroid communities is proof, not of the defects of parliaments but of the political incapacity of those who cannot work them.

As a rule the political genius of a nation may fairly be judged by the success of its representative system.

And this is a valid criterion because parliament is the only expedient by which any degree of self-government can be combined with the organization of a national state. The cities of ancient Greece and of medieval Italy governed themselves without the assistance of parliaments because they were small enough for direct popular participation in the sovereign functions of administration, discussion, and legislation. But when the ancient city state expanded into the empires of Alexander and Cæsar, self-government disappeared, because representation had not been developed, and multitudinous peoples could not appear in person. It is a small community that can govern itself without representation. Great states can exist without parliaments, but without them their people cannot govern themselves. City states can enjoy popular self-government without representation, but they cannot expand without losing their liberty; and the threadbare theme that a democracy cannot govern an empire only holds good—like other classical gibes at democracy—of popular rule without representation. It is one of the ironies of politics that those, who have derived from the study of ancient history a prejudice against democratic government, should often be so anxious to reproduce, by means of the plebiscite and referendum, that direct and commonly thoughtless popular action which was responsible for the prejudice. For it was by the growth of parliament, which the referendum would undermine, that the incompatibility between *imperium* and *libertas* was removed, the oscillations of popular passion corrected or checked, and the ancient indictment of the schools against democracy rendered obsolete.

Parliament, indeed, has been the means of making the English nation and the English state. It is really co-eval with them both. There was, it is true, an England centuries before there was a parliament, but that England was little more than a geographical expression. It was hardly a nation, still less a state; and Edward I was the first English

king of an English people that could be described as even
partially united and conscious of its unity. The un-
blushing patriotism which discovered in Alfred the Great
the founder of Oxford university was not less historical than
the crude Teutonism which saw in the Anglo-Saxon period
the golden age of English nationality, and pictured before
the Norman Conquest a free, self-governing people, combining the vigour of primitive strength with the virtue of
radical principles. Alfred himself was a Saxon king who
was hardly made English by the conquest of half the English
kingdom of Mercia. The *fyrd* was the people in arms, but
the people were tribal folk who fought for the most part
against their Anglo-Saxon neighbours; the duty of self-
defence was a local and not a national obligation; and, so
long as it lasted, the *fyrd* could not be summoned to serve
beyond the shire unless it was paid by the king for doing
what was not considered the business of the people. Down
to the time of Henry II law was not English law, but the law
of Wessex, the Mercian law, and the law of the Danes.
Politics, too, were local and provincial; the people who
lived in England regarded themselves as West Saxons,
Mercians, or Northumbrians, and even to-day the older
natives of the Isle of Wight speak of immigrants from the
adjacent Hampshire as " foreigners." Kings could not
make bricks without straw, and the material means for
creating a national state were wanting. Roads hardly
existed, communications were scanty, and administrative
organization was undeveloped. The consciousness of
nationality, without which there can be no national state,
does not grow out of nothing; it needs substantial nourish-
ment, and its provision was beyond the means of Anglo-
Saxon chieftains.

The Norman Conquest, despite the vehement protests of
Anglo-Saxon historians, did in a real sense mark the beginning of English history; and it is no mere quibble that
reckons the kings of England *post conquestum* (*a*). Absolute
origins are not, of course, to be found in historical records,
and for them we have to go back beyond the conquest

of Britons by Angles and Saxons as well as beyond the conquest of Anglo-Saxons by Danes and Normans; and the sources of English nationality, like those of great rivers, are shrouded in glacial veils.   But the English state and the English nation have been moulded on a framework provided by Norman and Angevin rulers.   Even English liberties appeared in an alien guise,[1] and there is hardly a word or a phrase in the law and custom of the British constitution that is Anglo-Saxon in origin.   To the " liberty of the subject " the Anglo-Saxon tongue has only contributed the article and the preposition; and " vote," " franchise," and " suffrage " are all extraneous terms.   Court, council, and parliament, judge and jury, inquest and verdict, alike come from abroad; and the Englishman cannot perform a single civic or legal duty, or exercise a single political function, from parish council to parliament, without using a word or expressing a thought unknown to his Anglo-Saxon forbears. It was this vast importation that made it possible to construct our English state out of the raw material of Anglo-Saxon tribes.

The process was slow and painful enough.   The work of the Normans and Angevins was not to introduce feudalism into England, but to organize the feudal forces already at work.   This meant simultaneous construction and destruction; for the more feudalism is organized, the more it disappears.   Feudalism, it has been said, implies the negation of all that we mean by the state;[2] it involves local and class association, but national dissociation.   Villeins were bound to the lord of the manor, but almost cut off from the king of the realm and, what is more important, from the villeins of other lords.   There was little in common, because the lord intercepted communications; and this privilege of intercepting communications was the lord's franchise, his " liberty " and his " honour."   It varied in

---

[1] Cf. G. B. Adams, *The Origin of the English Constitution*, p. 3 *n.*: " the thesis of this book is that this English national constitution . . . is a direct outgrowth of the earlier feudal constitution of the State"; Pollock and Maitland, *History of English Law*, 1895, i. 63.

[2] H. W. C. Davis, *Medieval Europe*, p. 93.

degree and extent; sometimes the lord could exclude the king's sheriff, take the royal writs he bore, and carry them out himself; sometimes he could exclude the king's writs altogether. It was one of the points of Magna Carta that the king should hold no communication with a lord's villeins which might turn to the lord's disadvantage; he must neither tallage them nor hear their complaints against their lord; against him they had no *locus standi* in the king's court or before the king's judges. The franchise was a petty kingdom which its lord sought to render independent, and his notion of liberty was irresponsibility in the management of his own domains.

This sectional dissociation was no worse than the Anglo-Saxon parochialism which it replaced, and against it must be set the association enforced by the Norman kings when they insisted upon the liability of every tenant-in-chief to attendance at the king's court and in the king's army. But this form of association tended to accentuate the dissociation of class from class which became stereotyped in the continental systems of estates. In England it was chiefly marked by differentiation in matters of taxation and jurisdiction. There was no national taxation in the twelfth and early thirteenth centuries; each class paid its own peculiar kind of imposition. The military tenants rendered their feudal services and aids and occasionally paid a special tax on land called the danegeld and afterwards the carucage; the merchants paid their customs; and the villeins paid in work or in kind the dues they owed their lords. But the exactions of the period were for the most part of the nature of rent or legal fines and not of taxes; they arose from men's relations with their landlords rather than with their king. Feudal aids were only due from its tenants to the crown, and tallage was owed by villeins to their lords. It was with rent and not with taxes that Magna Carta is concerned, and it represented the greatest and most successful " tenant-right " campaign in English history.[1]

---

[1] It should be almost superfluous to refer students for this subject to W. S. McKechnie's *Magna Carta* (2nd ed., 1914).

The Great Charter was wrested from John by a momentary coalition of various classes provoked by exceptional tyranny, and its historical importance lies in its anticipation of the means by which common action afterwards checked despotic tendencies. But it required parliament to focus centrifugal forces and perpetuate common activity. Its principal value in the middle ages did not consist in the ability of its members or in the wisdom of their legislation, for parliament produced few able men before the sixteenth century, and its acts were initiated, framed, and enforced by king and council rather than by " estates." Its value was less direct but not less great; it fostered and formed a public opinion, without which there can be no self-government. By its means shire was linked with shire, borough with borough, and class with class; and the dissociation of the feudal system was brought to an end. In the absence of a vernacular literature and of all those means by which nations are to-day made conscious of their identity, the only means of producing a common feeling was by personal contact; and it was the personal intercourse of their representatives in parliament that made the Northumbrian and the West-Saxon realize their common bonds and common aspirations, and led baron, knight, and burgess to merge their social distinctions in common political action. Just as common law was hammered out in the courts at Westminster and transmitted throughout the land by itinerant justices, so a common political sense was evolved from the communion of class and locality in parliaments, and communicated by slow degrees through members to their constituencies. The infiltration was facilitated by the very defects of medieval parliamentary practice. For parliaments, while they sat for only a fortnight or three weeks, were chosen afresh two or three times a year, and members were rarely re-elected; but only residents were chosen, and it followed that far more Englishmen served as members of parliament then than now. In a borough with a small constituency, it might easily happen that almost every constituent had at one time or other been sent to Westminster. The member would not be an expert politician, but the constituency would have a high average acquaintance with Westminster politics; and in politics the general intelligence of constituencies is as important as the exceptional capacity of representatives. Probably in medieval England it was more essential that a large number of local burgesses should be brought occasionally into touch with the heart of national government, than that a few should become expert, regular, and professional members of parliament.

Parliament has thus been the peculiar means through which the English people achieved their unity and nationality, and that is perhaps the reason why the nation has always excelled in politics. There are various means by which unity has been stamped upon the peoples of the world. In primitive times and backward communities it has been simply a matter of race. Sometimes unity has been achieved through religion; and Mohammedanism has been the most successful in this respect, though for a time it seemed as though the papacy might by means of the catholic religion weld the west of Europe into a unified ecclesiastical state. The Romans impressed unity on their empire by force of arms and the genius of their law. Other peoples have owed their impression of unity to their literature or their art. But in none of these ways did the English people find their national salvation, though the Hundred Years' war and the literature of the ages of Chaucer and Shakespeare powerfully aided the growth of national sentiment. But these stimulants to communion were preceded by parliaments, and it may be doubted whether, without the financial assistance of parliaments, the Hundred Years' war could have been fought at all, and whether, without the impetus of parliaments to common thought, Chaucer would have found a public for which to write.

English nationalism cannot, indeed, be assumed before the reign of Edward I. The cry against aliens was loud in the land under Henry III, but it was raised by men who were hardly more English than the aliens they denounced.

into the hands of a national sovereign, that national liberty at last got under weigh.

It had still a stormy voyage before it. The absorption of feudal liberties by the crown gave rise to a monstrous growth in the liberties of kings, and the Stuarts went down in defence of free and independent monarchy. Freedom and independence became a common cry without becoming a common cause. King, lords, commons, and law-courts all demanded liberty; but it was their own, and not other people's liberties, of which they were enamoured, and when the crown was smothered by the Whigs, the two houses of parliament each claimed an irresponsibility as complete but not as divine as that asserted by Charles I. To report their speeches or to publish their votes was an infringement of their rights, and parliamentary privilege was the latest growth of the medieval notion of liberty. But unlike the crown and the barons, parliament was the means of reforming itself; it abandoned its irresponsibility, and transformed its exclusive liberty into its duty to its constituents. If its function has not been to make all things common, it has at least created a common liberty.

Political communism is, indeed, the keynote of parliamentary history, and the house of commons has been the essential factor in the growth of parliament. " Commons " is a form of " communes " or communities; and as early as the fourteenth century, the official handbook to parliaments lays it down that the king can hold a parliament with the " community " of his realm although no bishop, earl, or baron attends, but that without the " community " no parliament can be held, though bishops, earls, and barons, and all their peers are present with the king.[1] To express the common sense of the community has always been the function of English parliaments, and the predominance of the layman has ever appealed to the English mind. The expert has seldom been at home in the atmosphere of parliament, and from first to last its communal organization has for-

---

[1] *Modus Tenendi Parliamentum* in Stubbs, *Charters*, ed. 1900, p. 512. See below, p. 80, and Appendix III, note (*i*).

bidden its separation into "estates." Its description as "three estates" arose in the fifteenth century out of a mistaken French analogy, and the phrase was never a true definition of an English parliament. The whole conception of caste implied in the word was alien to English law and English politics; and every man's place in parliament was determined by tenure and not by status, by writs of summons and not by class distinctions. The "grades" or "estates," of which we read in the fourteenth-century parliaments, were many and not merely three in number, and they were not matters of birth. The judges are called an estate, and so are the clerical proctors; yet the one was composed of royal nominees, and the other of representatives whose birth might be noble, gentle, simple, or base. There was no distinction of caste between the baron who had a special writ and the baron who sat for a shire; both might be barons and both might be knights, and every priest was at least a "lord."[1] So far from the English parliament being a system of three estates, it was the difference between such systems and the English parliament that enabled parliament to survive and grow while every system of estates dwindled away and died. Their division into estates was fatal to their permanence and power; parliament was saved by the community of thought and action which averted social schism and made our English state.

The communion of parliaments led to the estrangement of the church in the fourteenth century and to the victory of parliament over it in the sixteenth. Convocation was not merely composed of clerics; it was also elected by them, and it represented nobody else. The commons represented the nation, except for its clergy. No organized class is long successful in English politics; whenever a class acts as a class in politics, whether clergy or doctors or manual workers, it betrays a lack of political wisdom; and the most prudent as well as the most ambitious claim of the labour party is to represent all those who work for their

---

[1] "Domine" might be used as an address almost as widely as "Sir" is to-day. See below, p. 72, and Appendix III, note (*k*).

as the means of achieving a common purpose. It was only a parliamentary government, responsible to an electorate, that could raise the funds required to foil a Louis XIV or a Napoleon and to create a British empire. Its one great disruption was due to neglect of the truth that the strength of a government depends upon its sense of responsibility to those whom it governs; and the North American colonies were lost because George III's ministers believed they could tax them against their will. The omnicompetence of the modern state has grown out of the comprehensiveness of its representative parliament, and every self-conscious political element excluded from the franchise is a source of weakness to the government.

Parliament, however, could not comprehend all the self-conscious communities within the British empire, and the responsibility of governing the overseas dominions of the crown had to be delegated to other parliaments which could react more easily and quickly to their varying demands. But the habit of self-government made England readier to admit the claims of other peoples. Imperial Rome sacrificed her provinces rather than nurse them into daughter-states; the British empire has saved its unity by multiplying its representative systems, and the mother of parliaments not only made the English state, but reproduced it in every quarter of the globe. On the lines laid down in medieval English parliaments scores of legislatures are working in the world to-day, solving similar problems of localism, racialism, and class prejudice. Parliamentary institutions have softened the animosities of French and British in North America, and of British and Dutch in South Africa, and brought inveterate enemies on the field of battle into common action in the cabinet. The force of argument has supplanted the argument of force, and in discussion and debate a common sense and a public opinion have hammered out a basis of unity and supplied the foundations of national growth. Each dominion has repeated the experience of the mother country, and passed through the various phases of constitutional evolution, from crown administration to representative institutions, and from representative to responsible government. But the lessons of history were not forgotten; and results which took the mother country centuries of painful labour to achieve, were secured by the colonies within a generation and sometimes within a decade.

The very completeness of its success has suggested the thought that the work of parliament has been done. It has created the nation and educated it in self-government; democracy, we are told, can now legislate for itself, and the middlemen of parliament are superfluous. Having subjected the expert to common sense, it should itself submit to the referendum, and abandon its sovereign rights to the man in the street. If lay judgement is valid, why defer to professional politicians? The question raises a critical issue for parliament, whose future depends on the answer. In truth there never was greater need for political experts, and democracy has just as much use for the specialist as any other political system. He is not the final arbiter, but his advice is needed none the less. The member of parliament is like the doctor of physic; the patient is foolish who tries to dispense his own prescriptions, but he can choose his medical man and even reject his advice, occasionally with impunity. The responsibility for the adoption or refusal of expert advice rests with the patient because it is he who suffers. It is the same in political matters; the community suffers from foolish advice and benefits from wise counsel; it should therefore choose its advisers, and judge them by their works. If they are good, confidence will continue; if they are bad, a change of advice will be sought. But the electors can no more do the work of parliament than the patient can do his doctor's. The people are fairly good judges of legislation after experience of its effects; but they are very bad judges of programmes. For to forecast the effect of legislation requires the deepest political insight, and is the rarest of gifts. It may be argued that the people would learn to legislate wisely from the effects of their own legislation : they might also learn the properties of the

c

CHAPTER II

FOUR ideas, at least, with respect to the foundations and functions of English parliaments have become firmly rooted in the popular mind. One is that their principal object has ever been the making of laws; another is that hereditary peerage and popular representation were indispensable elements in their original constitution; a third that they have always consisted of two houses; and a fourth that they were based on three estates. Like all conceptions that have been firmly grasped by the multitude, these impressions about the history of parliament are hardly less false than true; and it is the purport of these pages to show cause for thinking that parliaments in their infancy were much that parliament to-day is not, and little that it is; that legislation was not the original purpose of their being; that they existed before they contained any representative elements; that there was a time when, if parliaments comprehended a peerage at all, that peerage was not in parliament by hereditary or any other right than royal grace; that parliament was at first a single chamber; that there was no "house" of lords until after the close of the middle ages; that the "house" of commons was not an original part of parliaments, but yet is older than the "house" of lords; and that the notion of three estates — so far from being the fundamental principle upon which parliaments were built—was borrowed from abroad and hesitatingly applied in the third century of English parliamentary history to an institution to which it was foreign in spirit and in practice.

Most of the common impressions of parliament are, indeed, irreconcileable with the correct designation of it

placed at the head of this chapter (*c*). The words are familiar
enough to those who know their book of common prayer;
but words have become so cheap that five are often wasted
where one would suffice, and four out of these five words
are regarded as merely ornamental detail added to " parliament " for the sake of magniloquence or to improve the
rhythm of the petitions in which they occur. Why the
legislature should be called a high court is a question
which few of those, who invoke divine direction for its con-
sultations, pause to ask or seek to answer. The most
picturesque method of attempting to solve the riddle would
be to visit that gilded ruin of the great council chamber
of parliament [1] which we call the house of lords, and to
trace the processes by which the various objects meeting
our eye have come to be where and what they are or pretend
to be. The house of lords is, however, still restricted to
purposes other, though not necessarily more useful, than
historical exposition; and, relying upon those powers of
visualization which every reader is bound to cultivate,
we must undertake in imagination a sort of geological and
archæological survey of that chamber, with the hope that
in our excavations we may light upon a fossil here and there
which may enable us to reconstruct an earlier, and in this
case less glacial, period of its history.

The first object to arrest our attention will be the throne,
a symbolic and material reminder of the facts that the king
is legally present in every court throughout the British
empire, and that every act of parliament is technically an
act of the king in parliament, just as every order in council
is an order of the king in council. The physical appearances
of the king in parliament have, it is true, grown so rare and
become so purely ceremonial that we may pardon our own
forgetfulness of the incongruity between our theory of the
house of lords as a chamber consisting of peers on the
one hand, and on the other the actual presence of the
king, who has no peer in his own dominions and yet is the
only person—except the lord chancellor — entitled to sit

[1] See below, pp. 72–3, 98, 291, 300.

in the house of lords without a summons. Nevertheless, it is not long since the sovereign was personally considered so essential to parliament that a demise of the crown instantaneously put an end to a parliament and rendered its further proceedings an empty form. Earlier still, in the reign of Edward III, and again in that of Henry VI, it was a matter of anxious debate in parliament and in council whether parliament could transact any business whatsoever without the corporal presence of the king. Clearly it required more than peers to make a house of lords.

Not less interesting, from our present point of view, than the presence of the king upon his throne, is the more frequent presence of members of the house of commons who are privy councillors upon its steps. But their mere presence in the house of lords, at the opening of parliament or during the progress of an important debate among the peers, is not so significant as the fact that they cannot be excluded. When a peer listens from the peers' gallery to a debate in the house of commons, he is there on sufferance; and any member can, by " spying strangers," have the peers excluded. That, we shall find, is a relic of the time when the house of commons was no part of parliament, but a more or less secret debating assembly, of the proceedings of which parliament had no cognizance until they were reported to it by the Speaker. The right of privy councillors to be present at the lords' debates illustrates the fact that the house of lords is the ancient parliament chamber of a great council which comprised other elements than peers. We are told, it is true, that the throne is not technically in the house of lords; but assuredly it is in parliament, and we are deceiving ourselves by this explanation unless we realize that within the parliament chamber there has been drawn, first an invisible line, and then a visible rail to give substance to the theory, separating the peers from some newer, but also from some older and more essential, elements of parliament.

Another object which we are told is not technically in the house of lords is the woolsack, although an act of 1539 declares specifically that it is " in the midst of the parliament chamber."[1] On it sits the lord chancellor whose presence and whose functions are as incongruous as the king's with our current notions about the house of lords. It is true that since the reign of Queen Anne the lord chancellor has always been made a peer if not already one before his appointment. But this practice has been simply one of giving him a coat of hereditary paint to make him look like his surroundings. Historically, there was no reason why the lord chancellor should be a peer; he requires no writ of summons, and, in fact, as lord chancellor, he receives no summons. It was he who summoned every one else either by special or by general writs issued out of chancery; he had no need to summon himself; he was there *ex officio*. Every schoolboy knows that Sir Thomas More was chancellor and that he never was a peer, although as chancellor he presided over the house of lords, and took the leading part in its proceedings. The same functions were performed throughout Elizabeth's reign by Sir Nicholas Bacon, Sir Thomas Bromley, Sir Christopher Hatton, Sir John Puckering and Sir Thomas Egerton, who were no more peers than Sir Thomas More; and down to 1705 the lord chancellor or lord keeper, whose power had been declared equivalent to the lord chancellor's by an act of 1559, was as often as not a commoner. In the earliest periods of parliamentary history the lord chancellor had usually been a bishop; but in 1340 Sir Robert Bourchier was appointed, who was neither a bishop nor a baron,[2] and he had successors in Sir Robert Parning, Robert de Sadington, John de Ufford, Sir Robert Thorpe, Sir John Knyvett and others, who performed the chancellor's functions without being summoned, as peers or in any other capacity, to parliament. Down to the present day a new lord chancellor takes his seat on the woolsack before he becomes a peer.

These chancellors sat in the high court of parliament

---

because they were judges or councillors; and other judges
had their places beside them. A judge is still addressed as
" my lord " because the high court of justice in which he
sits is, in spite of its removal from Westminster Palace to
the Strand, an historical part of the high court of parliament, of which the judges were lords. They still are
summoned by special writ to the house of lords, as are
the law officers of the crown and masters in chancery, and
as were the serjeants-at-law until the order of the coif fell
into abeyance. It is true that for many years these writs of
summons to king's councillors learned in the law have not
been obeyed, but their issue to all the legal luminaries of
the country proves that the constitutional theory of the
second chamber is different from the modern practice and
conceptions of the house of lords. Finally, a small detail
of parliamentary usage will serve to emphasize the point :
in both houses of parliament, an examination of the *Journals*
in the sixteenth century will show that the word used to
indicate the passing of a bill is *judicium ;* every act of either
house, public or private, was in fact a judgement, because a
parliament was a court. Indeed, had it not been a court,
it might never have become a legislature; for, as we shall
see, legislation is not a natural product of juvenile states,
and it only develops slowly out of judicial functions.

We can now approach, with some hope of understanding
its purport, the earliest definition of an English parliament.
It occurs in the work of Fleta, a pseudonymous author who
wrote in the time of Edward I or Edward II ; and it runs as
follows : *habet enim rex curiam suam in consilio suo in parliamentis suis.*[1] To the modern eye with its prejudice in favour
of the constitutional separation of powers, this description
appears to involve a strange confusion of functions. In
" curia " we have the judicature, in " consilium " the
executive, and in " parliamenta " the legislature; and they
are all here rolled into one. In substance this is true,

---

[1] *Fleta*, lib. ii. c. 2 ; Maitland, *Memoranda de Parliamento* (Rolls Ser.),
p. lxxxi; Pollock and Maitland, i. 179 *n.*; Baldwin, *King's Council*,
p. 308.

though the point of view is misleading. It is not that three constitutional functions have been merged in one; it is that the comprehensive functions of a medieval parliament have not yet been specialized and differentiated; and we are dealing with a sort of constitutional protoplasm out of which will in time be evolved the various councils of the crown, the houses of parliament, and the courts of law. There are dangers enough in applying the analogies of physical science to the development of political institutions. Nevertheless historical study has to accomplish an intellectual revolution comparable to that achieved by biologists when they broke down the idea of the fixity of species and substituted that of evolution. The separation of powers, upon which many modern constitutions have been established as though it was an immutable principle of politics, only represents a stage in constitutional growth; and we cannot understand English constitutional history, with its struggles between crown, parliament, and courts of law, unless we realize that all are descended from a single ancestor and are disputing over their respective shares in an inheritance which all had once enjoyed in common.

Further instruction can be derived from Fleta's statement by a closer examination of its terms. What does he mean by *curia?* what was the *curia regis* of the twelfth and thirteenth centuries? Perhaps we may understand these questions better by asking a third, what is *the* court to-day? Of course there are courts of many kinds; but *the* court *par excellence,* the court which requires no adjective, is the court which has its activity recorded under that simple heading in the court circular. It has no fixed habitation, no definite functions, no elaborate organization, no indispensable member except the king. It is not a building, it is not even a place; it exists wherever the king officially is or is deemed to be; it is the royal presence, actual or implied. The view is at least tenable that the *curia regis* meant nothing more; and one might guess that a medieval clerk would translate our phrases " the crown in council " and " the crown in parliament," not by *rex in concilio* and *rex in parliamento,* but by *curia regis in concilio* and *curia regis in parliamento.* We actually have the phrases *curia regis ad scaccarium, curia regis in cancellaria,* and *curia regis de banco;* and none of them can imply much more than the theoretical presence of the king in these courts by means of specialized representatives. *Curia regis* is the medieval latin for what we call the Crown.

This theoretical presence pervades every court throughout the British empire at the present time, and it is an attribute of the modern sovereignty of the crown that no one can hold a court except its representatives and delegates. Feudal theory and practice, however, permitted franchises which enabled many a baron to hold courts of his own. But the same vagueness attached to the meaning of *curia,* whether it was a baron's or a king's. It simply implied a presence and commonly it was the vicarious presence of a steward. We look in vain for any definite organization of the original *curia regis;* it kept no rolls until Henry II had made it a court of law,[1] and no list of members or record of proceedings has been discovered. We have to fall back upon a nebular hypothesis, but in time this subtile presence will take a definite form, or rather many definite forms, and our constitutional system will, by a process of differentiation and consolidation, come to resemble our solar system and comprise a number of planets, deriving their vital energy from *le roi soleil,* with orbits and circuits of their own, sustained by the central power of sovereignty. Nothing, indeed, seems to be a *curia,* unless this individual presence is implicit; and if the term was applied to the courts of the franchises and of the shires, it was because the franchise came from the crown, and the king was as much present in the persons of his sheriffs in the shire courts as he is in all our courts to-day. The courts christian implied a jurisdiction, which came also from above; and a court is not a popular institution.[2]

[1] The *rotuli curiae regis,* which exist from 5 Richard I to 56 Henry III, consist of records of the still undifferentiated king's bench and common pleas. From 1 Edward I they are divided into *coram rege* and *de banco* rolls.
[2] *Curia* seems to be less readily applied to the shire than to the hundred-courts, perhaps because the latter were oftener in private hands.

No one is therefore indispensable to a court except its lord and such of his officials as are required to transact its business. The lord's men owe suit at his court and are liable to be summoned; but they have no grievance and no remedy if he dispenses with their presence. They cannot, indeed, be tried except in his court; but that privilege does not give the individual vassal any right to participate in the trial of his peers. The presence of a single peer, when the French king's court tried a peer, was held sufficient to give the court jurisdiction, and a similar rule obtained in England when a peer was tried in the court of the lord high steward; the peers were there as a jury to establish the facts and not to give sentence.[1] Their rights were subject to the same limitations as the Englishman's right to trial by jury to-day. He cannot be condemned without trial by jury, but he has no right to be summoned to serve on any particular jury, or indeed on any jury at all. His service is a matter of duty and obligation, a liability but not a right; and this general principle pervaded the *curia regis* and its derivative institutions.[2] The baron's notion of liberty was not that he had a right to attend the *curia regis* and interfere in the king's affairs, but that the king had no right to invade the courts of his barons and prevent them from doing what they thought fit with their own. They only valued attendance as a means of checking a king who transgressed their franchises, and Magna Carta was designed to secure the local independence of barons rather than the national responsibility of kings. The king, when he holds his court, is not therefore bound to summon any particular persons to assist him; and the phrase *curia regis* merely implies the king's official attendance for certain important causes, mainly judicial in character.

The king's council is perhaps by Fleta's time a more

[1] Luchaire, *Institutions Françaises*, p. 561; Vernon-Harcourt, *His Grace the Steward and Trial by Peers*, p. 302.
[2] The writ of summons to parliament is a *mandamus*; cf. Elsynge, *Modus*, p. 19, " next to the title is considerable the form of the *mandamus*, how it is to the lords spiritual, and how to the lords temporal and the judges and others of the king's learned council."

definite organization ; but this definiteness has probably been exaggerated, and it is not at all clear whether Edward I had one, two, or three different kinds of council. It has been usual to assume at least a plurality of councils; but Maitland confessed his inability to discover more than one.[1] The subject is obscured by the absence of both the definite and indefinite articles from the Latin language, and by the indifference with which medieval clerks and chroniclers wrote *concilium* or *consilium*. Attempts have been made to distinguish the two, but without much success; and we may usefully bear in mind the warnings that while English medieval clerks wrote in Latin, they generally thought in French,[2] and that, if we wish to interpret aright their Latin words, we must ascertain the French equivalent. Now the French have only one word, *conseil*, for the Latin *concilium* and *consilium*, and for our " council " and " counsel "; and it is by no means improbable that where we see " council," the medieval scribe was only thinking of " counsel." When the draughtsman of Magna Carta says that extraordinary aids are not to be levied *sine communi consilio*, and that *negotium* . . . *procedat secundum consilium eorum qui præsentes fuerint*, it is clear that by *consilium* he means " counsel "; and it seems rash to assume that, when he goes on to prescribe the machinery *ad habendum commune consilium*, he means " for the purpose of holding a common council," and not " for the purpose of obtaining the common counsel " or consent.[3] The common council may perhaps be eliminated from the list of Edward I's advisory bodies.

Nor is it easy to adduce contemporary and official evidence for the existence of a *magnum concilium* in Edward I's reign, and it is tempting to take shelter behind Maitland's authority, and assume the singleness of Edward's councils. Nevertheless a *magnum concilium* had made itself painfully evident to Henry III between the Provisions of Oxford and the battle of Evesham. It had, indeed, stepped into

---

[1] *Memoranda de Parliamento*, Rolls Ser. Pref., p. lxxxviii.
[2] Prof. Tait in *English Hist. Rev.*, xxvii. 720–8.
[3] Moreover, *tenere* and not *habere* is the proper word for " holding " a court.

the shoes of a "mycel-gemot" in the time of William
the Conqueror; and it is clear that, while there may have
been only one council, it was quite possible to give it a
varying constitutional complexion and personal composition.
The council dear to Edward I was no doubt a royal council
without any other adjective, a council dependent upon the
king and representing only the monarchical principle. But
a council contemplated by the barons under a weak and
obstinate sovereign would be rather a *magnum concilium*,
a king's council "afforced" by a number of magnates,
representing the barons, and embodying their alternative to
monarchical government. At least it is certain that while
we can find little about a *magnum concilium* under Edward I,
we can read a great deal about it under Henry III and
Edward II. An incompetent king generally means an
incompetent council; and when the king's council is
incompetent, it has, like an inadequate jury, to be
"afforced." [1]

The council, if there was only one, was obviously an
elastic institution, as vague in its composition and as
indefinite in its rules of procedure as was the cabinet in the
first quarter of the eighteenth century. Like most important
English institutions it proceeded from the crown, but was
not created. As the cabinet was merely a meeting of "the
king's servants," the council was merely a meeting of the
king's counsellors; and there were no fixed rules determining
who these servants and these counsellors should be. No one,
whatever his baronial or episcopal rank, had any inherent
right to be a counsellor of the king. At least, this is the
theory of the council under Edward I. Doubtless that royal
theory was not the conception which underlay the barons'
attempts to make an instrument of government out of a
magnum concilium ; but it passes the wit of man to construct
a logical basis for a *magnum concilium* like that indicated in
the Provisions of Oxford. William I's *magnum concilium*,

---

[1] This chapter was written early in 1913. Since then Prof. Baldwin's
King's Council has greatly strengthened the case against the existence
of a multiplicity of councils.

preserved in the lords' house in parliament." This still remains true in parts; we have never completely divorced the king in council from the king in parliament, the executive from the legislature. It is because the king's council is embedded in his parliament that the king's throne is in the house of lords, that the chancellor is present *ex officio*, that judges, law officers of the crown, and secretaries of state sit on the woolsacks as late as the sixteenth century, and that the act of 1539 prescribes places for the council in the house of lords, whether they are peers or not.

We must not, however, when vagueness attaches to *curia* and *concilium*, look for definiteness in the use of *parliamentum*. While Fleta speaks of *consilium* in the singular, he speaks of *parliamenta* in the plural. Councils had ceased to be occasional assemblies, and had become a habit. Parliaments are still in the occasional stage of development in which the plural is more appropriate than the singular because there is no continuity between one parliament and another, and each may have its own individual constitution. The word has been traced as far back as the reign of Henry II.[1] It was certainly used in France in 1239,[2] by Matthew Paris about 1240, in

[1] The earliest instance I have found of the use of the word occurs in the phrase *en sun plenier parlement* of Jordan Fantosme, who wrote towards the end of Henry II's reign (*Chronicles of Stephen, Henry II, and Richard I*, Rolls Ser., iii. 226). Bishop Stubbs uses it, inadvertently I think, of an assembly held at Gaitington in 1189, but it does not occur in the authorities he cites (*Introductions to the Rolls Series*, ed. Hassall, p. 407). In 1244 Alexander II of Scotland was granted a safe-conduct "in coming to meet the king or his council in Northumberland . . . and so long as the parliament there shall last," and on August 15 following the sheriff of Northumberland was ordered to pay various sums for crops trodden down on account of "the parliament" held between the king and the king of Scotland (Bain, *Cal. of Docs. relating to Scotland*, i. Nos. 1647, 1651–2, 1658; Henry III was represented at this "parliament" by Richard, Earl of Cornwall). Here *parliamentum* means no more than a parley; and in this sense the word was used as late as the sixteenth century. In 1539 it is applied to the meeting between Charles V and Francis I (*L. and P.*, XIV. ii. 649), and in 1542 to one between Charles V and the Pope (*ibid.*, xvii. 1103; *State Papers*, ix. 219). Any kind of consultation might be called a parliament: according to Sir Robert Cotton abbots held their parliaments (*Cottoni Posthuma*, p. 44); so did the Inns of Court, and the Stannary Court (Cowell, *Law Dictionary*, ed. 1727 s.v. "Parliament"; *Trans. Devon. Association*, xi. 302; 4 Henry VIII c. 8). See also note (*d*).

[2] Luchaire, *Institutions Françaises*, p. 562.

the Provisions of Oxford of 1258, and officially from 1275 onwards.[1] But its meaning had not crystallized into its modern sense; and the difference between the English *parliament*, the French *parlement*, and the Italian *parlamento* [2] indicates the vagueness of an original conception which could specialize in such various directions. It is clear that it implied no sort of representation, because representation was never a feature of the French *parlement* or the Italian *parlamento;* and even in England the word is used before burgesses or knights of the shire had been summoned to meet the council at Westminster. As late as 1305 an assembly can still be not only a parliament but a " full " parliament after every one—earls, bishops, barons, as well as knights of the shire and burgesses—except members of the council has been dismissed. " Full " may, indeed, be one of those mistranslations of Latin due to forgetfulness of the fact that the Latin word is itself a translation from the French. *In pleno parliamento* stands for *en plein parlement;* but when a Frenchman says *en plein air*, he means in the *open* air, and when the famous Star Chamber act of 1487 prescribes that amercements shall be assessed " in plain sessions," it means in open sessions; indeed, they are called " open sessions " in another act of Henry VII.[3] A full parliament or a full county court may be only an open parliament or court, and may imply the publicity of its proceedings rather than the amplitude of its composition (*e*).

However that may be, the application of the phrase *plenum parliamentum* to an assembly consisting solely of councillors suggests that a session of the king's council is at first not merely, as Maitland has said, the core of every

---

[1] See below, p. 48, and Pasquet, *Essai*, pp. 3–4, 60–2, 69.

[2] " The sitting Signoria had the power of summoning a Parlamento, or gathering of the whole resident population of Florence." (Armstrong, *Lorenzo de Medici*, p. 29.)

[3] 19 Hen. VII, c. 14. See my note in *Engl. Hist. Rev.*, xxx. 660–2 This phrase is constantly used in the " Rolls " of the purely legal sessions, and has no reference whatever to the presence of specially summoned barons or generally summoned representatives. Cf. *Rot. Parl.*, i. 19*b*, 32*b*. In *Rot. Parl.*, i. 179 we have " in pleno scaccario." Moreover, when fullness is meant we have *pleinière parlement* (*Rot. Parl.*, ii. 232 *b*) which corresponds to the French *cour pleinière*. Cf. Selden, *Judicature*, p. 105.

D

parliament, but the whole parliament, and that the addition
of earls, prelates, barons and popular representatives, while
it added to the taxing powers of the assembly, added nothing
to the judicial and legislative authority wielded by the
council in parliament; and it has often been remarked that
the great legislative enactments of Edward I were not even
promulgated in a representative assembly. Nor did this
legislative capacity of the king's " council learned in the
law " cease in the thirteenth or fourteenth century. It
is true that enactments were to an increasing extent submitted to the representative body for ratification; but as
late as the sixteenth century the year books of Henry VII's
reign show that the main principles of his legislation were
formulated by the judges in common session before submission to either " house " of parliament;[1] and in Henry
VIII's reign it was the custom of the lords in parliament to
secure copies of bills introduced in the house of commons
and take the opinion of the judges upon them before they
were sent up from the lower house.[2] " Do not gloss the
statute," remarked the chief justice to counsel in 1305. " We
understand it better than you, for we made it." [3]

Parliament, therefore, in its judicial and legislative aspect,
seems to be at first simply a talk or parley of the council
in full session. Soon, of course, it comes to be used of
parleys between the king in council and other constitutional
elements. By the Provisions of Oxford twelve elected barons
are to meet the king's council at three parliaments a year.
Simon de Montfort " afforces " the elected barons with elected
knights of the shire and burgesses; and the growing financial
needs of the crown promoted frequent recourse to these
representative elements which alone could produce an
adequate financial supply. But this financial business was
not the original nor the most frequent cause of parliaments;

[1] Cf. Vinogradoff, " Const. Hist. and the Year Books " in *Law Quarterly
Rev.*, July 1913.
[2] *Letters and Papers, Henry VIII*, XII i. 901 [39, 40]; *English Hist.
Rev.*, v. 568.
[3] *Year Books* 33-5 Edward I (Rolls Ser.), p. 82; McIlwain, *High Court
of Parliament*, p. 325; Baldwin, p. 314.

and a perusal of the earliest " rolls of parliament " reveals activities of a different and comprehensive character. Nothing, indeed, is more striking than the multifarious nature of the business there recorded. Page after page reads exactly like the register of the privy council of the sixteenth century; [1] there are minute details of the provision to be made for the wars in Wales or on the Scottish borders, for Edward III's campaigns in France, for the regulation of prices, and for the administration of justice.[2] The records deal, in fact, with the doings of a body which is at once executive, judicial, and legislative; and the presence of the council in the parliament is patent in its rolls.

Mainly, however, the business of Edward I's parliaments is to deal out justice. The title-page of each of the printed volumes of the *Rotuli Parliamentorum* indicates its contents as consisting mostly of *petitiones et placita ;* the *memoranda de parliamento*, which will ultimately expand into Lords' and Commons' Journals, when the *petitiones* have been for the most part referred to other courts and the *placita* heard elsewhere, occupy but little space. It is not until late in Edward III's reign that we get a regular series of *rotuli parliamentorum ;* and some of the contents of the printed " Rolls of Parliaments " are suspiciously like the *coram rege* rolls of the king's bench which had hardly in Edward I's reign been differentiated from the king's council. The purpose of parliaments is judicial : " whereas " runs an ordinance of the Lords Ordainers in 1311,[3] " many folk are delayed in the king's court because the defendants allege that the plaintiffs ought not to be answered in the absence of the king, and many also are wronged by the ministers of the king, which wrongs they cannot get redressed without common parliament,[4] we ordain that the king hold a parlia-

---

[1] There are half a dozen entries of this character on the first page of the first volume of the printed *Rotuli Parliamentorum*.
[2] *Rotuli Parliamentorum*, i. 295, 350-1, ii. 108-11, 114-16.
[3] *Ibid.*, i. 285 (29).
[4] " Sans commune parlement " has fortunately not been used to prove the existence of a " Common Parliament," like a Common Council, distinct from other assemblies. The phrase clearly indicates the nature of the parliaments.

ment once a year, or twice if need be, and that in a convenient place. And in the same parliaments shall pleas that have been delayed and pleas about which the judges differ be recorded and determined, and in the same way the bills which shall have been handed into parliament." This ordinance was made in answer to a complaint that the commons, who came to parliaments to seek redress for grievances which could not be remedied by common law or by any other way than special process, found no one to receive their petitions as they had done in the reign of Edward I.[1] Primarily a parliament is a high court of justice.

In this sense the origin of parliaments must be traced back to Henry II rather than to Simon de Montfort or Edward I. If Henry had not made the king's court the matrix of England's common law, neither Simon nor Edward could have made it the matrix of England's common politics; for a foundation of common law was indispensable to a house of common politics. Henry had made the courts, held in his palace at Westminster, the common resort for all his subjects above the rank of villeins.[2] By inviting and attracting thereto men from all quarters of England, he had given them a common framework for their ideas of law and liberty. He had made escape from local trammels and recourse to a national fount of ideas a habit with his people. Even during the troublesome reign of Henry III, the king's court increased the number of forms of writ or judicial process from sixty to over four hundred and fifty;[3] and every new process was a fresh nerve developed between the monarchy and its subjects, a fresh means of linking the brain with the body of the community.

That the main function of Edward I's parliaments is to continue and expand the work of Henry II's *curia regis* will appear from the briefest indication of their procedure. The first step towards the holding of a parliament, after its

[1] *Rotuli Parliamentorum*, i. 444.
[2] " Le paleys soleit le plus frank leu d'Engleterre " (*ibid.*, i. 155).
[3] Maitland, *Collected Papers*, ii. 155 ; cf. *ibid.*, ii. 476.

summons had been decided, the writs issued, and the representatives, if any, elected, was to make public proclamation in the great hall of Westminster Palace (for Westminster Hall was the " aula " in which the king, like every feudal lord, held his court), in the chancery, in the court of common pleas, in the exchequer, in the guildhall, and in Westcheap that all who wished to present petitions at the approaching parliament should hand them in by a certain date.[1] " Thereupon," we are told by William de Ayremynne, the clerk of chancery appointed by Edward II to keep the *memoranda* of the parliament of Lincoln in January 1316, " the chancellor, the treasurer, and the justices of either bench were ordered to draw up in writing a brief statement of the suits (*negotia*) pending before them (*in suis placeis*) which could not be determined out of parliament, and refer them to parliament so that right might be done therein." [2] Receivers and triers of petitions were next appointed. The receivers were merely clerks in chancery; the triers were more important persons, at first mainly judges, afterwards prelates, earls, and barons. Their functions have not been precisely ascertained. Sometimes they were called " hearers " of petitions, and their commission authorized them to " determine " as well as to " hear "; but whether a hearing and determination by them *in* parliament amounted to a hearing and determination *by* parliament is a matter of doubt.[3] It is well, perhaps, to remember that parliament is not yet an institution or a body, but only a " parley," that *parliamentum* and *colloquium* are interchangeable terms, and that while the king in his council in parley may

---

[1] *Memoranda de Parliamento*, p. lvii.; *Rot. Parl.*, i. 182.
[2] *Rot. Parl.*, i. 350.
[3] McIlwain, *The High Court of Parliament*, pp. 198–202. The relation of the " auditores " to the council is also obscure. In 1314 we read of " responsiones petitionum Angliæ per auditores earundem factæ in parliamento " as though the " auditores " determined the petitions and not the council as a whole. But the form of answer is always " responsum est per consilium " (*Rot. Parl.*, i. 314). Probably the contradiction is only verbal. *Consilium* was then no more executive than *parliamentum*. The executive consisted of the agents of the crown, the chancellor, privy seal, and so forth; and *auditores*, appointed by the king, expressed the counsel taken on parliamentary petitions.

parliament as meaning a supreme court of appeal. It
acted more often as a court of first instance than as a court
of error.[1] " High " was perhaps used in the sense in which
we speak of highways in distinction to byways, and of the
high seas in distinction to the narrow seas. The high seas
are called high because they are open and common to all,
and a parliament is called a "high" court because it is
le plus frank leu d'Engleterre, the most open and free
of all English courts. Possibly the freedom of parliament
implied some immunity from the law's expense as well as
from its delays.[2] Certainly in courts like the later Star
chamber and court of requests, which inherited some of
the traditions of the high court of parliament, justice was
freely administered; and there may have been some ex-
travagant hope that the promise of Magna Carta that justice
should not be sold meant that no charge would be made for
its administration. That was doubtless a fond delusion;
fees were required for royal writs [3] and other legal expenses,
but it seems that no charge was made for the expedition
of suits in parliament.

However that may have been, parliament was only a
court of appeal in the sense that the house of commons
or of lords is a court of appeal from its committees. The
several courts of the *curia regis* were in a sense its committees : in parliament the judges and council sat in
common or joint session, and there decided cases reported
to them; the whole was held to be greater than the part,
in authority and legal wisdom as well as in size. The
court held *coram rege et consilio suo ad parliamenta sua* is
greater than the court held *coram rege et consilio suo*, just
as the latter is greater than the court held *coram rege*.
This last comes to be the king's bench; from the second
comes the jurisdiction of the king's council, and from the

[1] Maitland, *Memoranda*, p. lxxxv.
[2] Prof. Baldwin has since established this supposition (*King's Council*,
p. 282).
[3] In 1348 the fee for a writ out of common pleas was 7*d.*, and out of
king's bench 6*d.*; the commons wanted 7*d.* and 6*d.* writs for 3*d.* (*Rot.
Parl.*, ii. 170).

first the supreme jurisdiction of the high court of parliament.[1] This whole, moreover, contained more than its
expert judicial parts, and the members of the council who
were not judges added to this joint session of the courts
a lay element which represented the common sense of the
high court of parliament. The influence of this lay element
upon judicial decisions is characteristic of the political spirit
of England, where parliament lays down the legal principles
upon which judges have to act. But it was certainly a
singular by-product of this constitutional maxim when the
peers in the nineteenth century reduced the judges to insignificance in the high court of parliament, and developed the
practical paradox that the competence of the lay mind to
exercise supreme judicial authority depended upon the
accident of primogeniture. The only trace, if any, of this
hereditary monopoly of supreme appellate jurisdiction in the
time of Edward I is in the presence of earls and barons,
who have as yet no hereditary right to a summons, in
parliament. " The king," to quote Fleta once more, " has
his court in his council in his parliaments, in the presence
of earls, barons, nobles, and others learned in the law,
where judicial doubts are determined, and new remedies
are established for new wrongs, and justice is done to
every one according to his deserts." [2]

Fleta's encomium may be somewhat too generous, but
there can be no doubt as to the magnitude and the importance of the judicial work of parliaments under Edward I.
Two hundred and fifty petitions were presented to the
parliament of Michaelmas, 1290, although two other parliaments had already been held that year, one in January
and another in April.[3] Five hundred have been preserved
for one of the two parliaments of 1305; so that even the
thousands which remain in the Record Office probably

---

[1] Maitland, *Memoranda*, p. lxxx; *Rot. Parl.*, i. 15, 38, 128.
[2] Maitland, *Memoranda*, p. lxxxi. Pollock and Maitland's reading of
iuris peritis for *uiris peritis* (*Hist. of English Law*, i. 179 *n.* [1]) is adopted
by Baldwin; cf. *Rot. Parl.*, ii. 1: "placita coram domino rege et
consilio suo apud Westm' in presencia ipsius domini regis, procerum,
et magnatum regni in parliamento suo ibidem convocato."
[3] *Rot. Parl.*, i. 46–65.

represent only a fraction of the petitions sent up to parliaments between the reign of Edward I and that of Richard III. They come from all sorts and conditions of men and corporate bodies, and from every quarter of the king's dominions; a king of Norway as well as a king of Scotland is found petitioning Edward I in his parliament; [1] Edward I's own daughter Mary is represented, and the king himself prosecutes his suits there by his attorneys. Earls, bishops, and barons; abbots, abbesses, and abbeys; shires, cities, and boroughs; judges, royal officials, and foreigners; merchants and Jews; the scholars of Oxford [2] and Cambridge; poor men of this and that shire or borough; and even a body of prisoners, all expect justice or favour in parliament. The petitions, indeed, are mostly from individual persons or corporate bodies; they are not the common petitions of the people of England. Nevertheless, if we assume that on an average a score of persons are interested in each petition, and in some the number would rise to hundreds, we shall see that thousands of people, many of them influential, would be concerned in the holding of every parliament, and would have legal business to transact which could not be settled elsewhere.

Here we light upon a motive for frequent parliaments upon which adequate stress has not been laid. We assume that the foundation of parliament was financial, and that its growth was due to the necessities of the king and to the control by parliament over the national purse. No one will deny that finance has played an important part in the development of representative institutions; but there are two reasons against regarding finance as the sole factor in the foundation of the English parliament. In the first place its earliest function was judicial, and financial only in the sense in which Henry I discovered that *justitia* was *magnum emolumentum*. In most of the parliaments assembled by

---

[1] *Rot. Parl.*, i. 105, 107–13, 225; Maitland, *Mem.*, p. 9.

[2] Oxford, indeed, sent a dozen petitions to a single parliament in 1305 (*Memoranda*, pp. 44–7). There is also a petition from the judges, barons of the exchequer, and clerks for the payment of the arrears of their salaries (*ibid.*, p. 49).

Edward I and Edward II, if not also by Edward III, no financial supply was asked for, and none was granted. Secondly, the frequent summons of parliaments was a measure required not by the crown so much as by its subjects. It is the barons who in 1258 demand three annual parliaments; it is the Lords Ordainers who insist upon one or more sessions a year; and it is the commons who take up the cry under Edward III. We cannot believe that barons or burghers wanted to come to Westminster in order to be taxed three times or even once a year. So far as taxation went, they would have gladly surrendered their control, if they could thereby escape the taxation. If they desired parliaments at all, it was for the justice therein dispensed, and not for the taxation therein imposed.

It was to a high court of law and justice that the taxing and representative factors of parliament were wedded; and it was this union that gave the English parliament its strength. Its absence, the divorce between French *parlements* and estates, was fatal to orderly constitutional development in France. " Whenever a separation is made between liberty and justice," said Burke, "neither is in my opinion safe." Justice and liberty were the woof and the warp out of which was woven the web of the English constitution; but the English people had to endure discipline, law, and order before they could safely afford the luxury of liberty; and the high court of parliament comes before the house of commons.

CHAPTER III

EDWARD I'S PARLIAMENTARY MODELS

ENOUGH has been said in the previous chapter to indicate the inadequacy of the view which sees in parliament nothing but the development of the principle of political representation; but before we proceed to discuss that infelicitous phrase, the three estates, which has been commonly used to describe the form that representation took in parliaments, it may be well to examine a little more in detail the various assemblies to which the word parliament was applied in the latter half of the thirteenth century. Hitherto we have generalized mainly from the proceedings of one of the parliaments of 1305, the records of which have come down to us in a completer form than those of any previous parliament. But the importance of the subject, and the efforts still being made by the house of lords to discover the first real parliament and to elaborate a principle of discrimination, by which to decide peerage claims based upon Edward I's writs of summons, justify an attempt to elucidate the meaning of the word " parliament," to illustrate the variety of its applications, and to prove the impossibility of drawing hard and fast lines. There is little to comfort the committee of privileges in this investigation; but the idea, upon which peerage-law has been grounded, that Edward I created or dreamt of creating hereditary peerages by special writs of summons to parliaments is historically so fantastic that no historian need feel compunction in adding to the difficulties which lawyers have created for themselves by their defiance of history.[1]

[1] Cf. J. H. Round, *Studies in Peerage and Family History*, 1900, and *Peerage and Pedigree*, 1910; Gibbs, pref. to 2nd ed. of G. E. Cokayne's *Complete Peerage*, p. xiii : " it is impossible to reconcile the facts of history with the Law of Peerage."

Important historical questions are, moreover, involved in the discussion, and the truth about the origin of English parliaments can never be a matter of indifference; antiquities may be ignored, but not the beginnings of political or of any other form of life. All origins are, however, obscure, not merely from the defect of records, but because they are imperceptible to contemporary observers; and it is a shallow interpretation to regard parliaments as the creation of Simon de Montfort or of Edward I, or indeed as a creation at all. It is rather a growth from roots stretching back beyond the thirteenth century to a period long before the summons of burgesses or even of knights of the shire to Westminster. The issue of Simon's and Edward's writs did not evoke a new institution out of the void; they merely grafted new buds on to the old stock of the *curia regis*, and it was the legal sap of the ancient stem that fed and maintained the life of the medieval parliament. The species, indeed, was the same, otherwise the grafting would have failed; for law is a branch of politics, and even the seed of representation was raised in a legal frame. On the other hand, Henry II had differentiated law from politics by converting the *curia regis* from an occasional meeting of turbulent barons into a regular court of expert judges; and it was the work of Edward I to reunite these divergent elements in the high court of parliament.

The obscurity of this process of reunion is darkened by nebulous terminology, and the term parliament is applied in the latter half of the thirteenth century to each of the two coalescing factors as well as to the coalition. The common denominator of such various values is bound to be small, and almost any sort of conference, in which the crown was involved, might be called a parliament. But even so general a word as " conference " may acquire specialized characteristics, and come to be spelt with a capital; to a Wesleyan Methodist the term " conference " means a definite body which meets annually and performs numerous binding acts recorded in " Minutes of Conference." So " parliament," while remaining a vague and general term to some, becomes a term of art to others, and acquires in time distinctive records. The process is common to England, France, Italy, and possibly other countries; and while the specialization of meaning takes different forms, it seems probable that in Edward I's reign, at any rate, there was greater similarity between the French " parlement " and the English " parliament " than has usually been supposed.

At any rate, the use in England did not at first imply any notion of representation or election; for when Matthew Paris first uses it to describe a meeting in 1246,[1] he enumerates its constituent parts as " prelates, both abbots and priors as well as bishops, and earls and barons," and the fact that he calls this parliament " generalissimum," implies that an even less comprehensive assembly might have been called a " parliament " with equal propriety. The word, indeed, has no special signification for him, because two years later he describes a more general assembly comprising *milites* and *clerici* as well as bishops, abbots, priors, earls, and barons, without calling it a parliament.[2] In 1251 and again in 1257 he speaks of a *magnum parliamentum;*[3] but apparently he does not think it worth while to call the gathering of 1254—" an important landmark in the parliamentary history of England," as Stubbs calls it, to which for the first time two elected knights were summoned to Westminster from each shire *vice omnium et singulorum eorundem comitatuum*—a parliament at all.[4] Other writers begin to use the word soon after the middle of the century, sometimes with, sometimes without a qualifying adjective or phrase. T. Wykes speaks of a *parliamentum baronum* in 1260,[5] the " Annals of Waverley " of a *parliamentum magnum* twice in 1265 and once in 1268,[6] and the " Annals of Winchester " of a *parliamentum omnium magnatum* in 1270.[7] " Parliament " is *vox et præterea nihil ;* there is nothing to distinguish it from other assemblies called in pursuance of the 14th article of Magna Carta requiring the special and

[1] Stubbs, *Charters*, 1900, p. 328.   [2] *Ibid.*, p. 329.
[3] *Ibid.*, pp. 330-1.   [4] *Ibid.*, pp. 375-7.   [5] *Ibid.*, p. 333.
[6] *Ibid.*, pp. 335-6.   [7] *Ibid.*, p. 337.

general summons of tenants-in-chief to give consent to extraordinary feudal aids.

The vagueness of this terminology persists in the pages of the chroniclers throughout the greater part of the reign of Edward I; and a meeting of the king with his prelates and barons may be called a parliament whether or not it also comprises knights of the shires or burgesses. But the printed "Rolls of Parliaments" which begin in 1278 (*g*) seem to reveal a different conception in the minds of the clerks and lawyers. To them these occasional meetings of tenants-in-chief do not seem to be parliaments at all; and down to the end of the century there is nothing about their proceedings in the "Rolls." There is, indeed, a complete discrepancy between the "Rolls of Parliaments" and the so-called "Parliamentary Writs" compiled by Sir Francis Palgrave as documentary evidence for the early history of parliaments. Down to 1300 the word "parliament" is not mentioned in the special writs to prelates, earls, and barons or in the general writs to the sheriffs and mayors; they are summoned to a *colloquium* or a *tractatum*, but not to parliament. The business of the gatherings to which they are called is not recorded in the "Rolls of Parliaments"; and the meetings whose business is recorded therein were not gathered by any writs that are extant. Allowance must no doubt be made for defects in the records and in their editing; but when there are between 1275 and 1298 nine assemblies summoned by "parliamentary" writs, and fifteen sessions whose business is recorded in the rolls, and when not one of the nine coincides with one of the fifteen, the discrepancy is too significant to be explained away by defective evidence. The gatherings convoked by these so-called "parliamentary" writs were not parliaments; and the meetings called parliaments in the rolls were not summoned by the writs to which the name has since been given.

The point may be enforced by an examination of the proceedings of 1290. In that year there were three "parliaments" in the sense in which the word is used by the clerks of chancery; there is no doubt about their meaning, because these sessions are repeatedly called parliaments in the records of their proceedings. One began on January 25; the second began three weeks after Easter (*i. e.* April 23) and lasted until July 8, and the third lasted for a month from Michaelmas. For none of these sessions have any writs been discovered. There are, however, writs extant summoning knights of the shires to a fourth assembly on July 15;[1] but this is not a " parliament " according to the " Rolls." Not merely are its proceedings not recorded, but its existence is ignored. Much of the business brought before the parliament of April 23 to July 8 is adjourned *ad proximum parliamentum;* and the " next parliament " is always assigned to Michaelmas, even though writs have already been issued for the assembly on July 15. The adjourned business is taken in the autumn parliament, and none of it at the July assembly.[2]

What, then, were these " parliaments " of the " Rolls," and what was the nature of their business? An answer is suggested by a complaint and an ordinance made in 1280.[3] The complaint is of the delay and inconvenience caused to the folk who come to " parliament " by the great number of petitions which might be dealt with by the chancellor and justices; and the ordinance is that only petitions that cannot otherwise be dealt with are to come before the king and his council in parliament. The business is legal, these parliaments are " parliaments of the council," their essence is royal and judicial, and there is little in common between them and the occasional gatherings of tenants-in-chief summoned by special and general writs in pursuance of Magna Carta to give counsel and consent to demands for aids. Their proceedings are naturally entered in " Rolls," the characteristic records of courts, and they deal with " petitions " and " placita." Their sessions are regular and not spasmodic; they do not depend upon the king's financial necessities; and they are held three times a year. The three parliaments

---

[1] *Rep. on the Dignity of a Peer,* i. 54.
[2] *Rot. Parl.,* i. 15–45.
[3] Maitland, *Memoranda,* p. lvi.

of 1290 are followed by three in 1291, and there is little doubt that this was the normal practice.

Its antiquity is obscure, but there is no reason to suppose that Edward I invented it. The earliest proceedings recorded in the " Rolls " do not give the impression of novelty; the complaint of 1280 suggests inveterate growth; and the multiplication of forms of original writs during the reign of Henry III would lead us to infer a rapid increase in the number of petitioners at Westminster, and the provision of means to expedite their suits. In 1190 Philip Augustus had ordered the regents he left behind him to hold three judicial sessions a year; and the parlement of Paris, like the English " parliament " of the " Rolls," was a joint session of the several *chambres* or courts of the *curia regis*, to which the name of " parlement " was given as early as 1239.[1] When the English barons in 1258 usurped the position of regents, they arranged for three " parliaments " a year, though their parliaments were to consist, not in joint sessions of royal judges, but in joint sessions of baronial councillors.

The distinction between judges and councillors must not, however, be pressed. Every councillor might partake in judicial proceedings; and these " parliaments " of the " Rolls " were joint sessions of the judges with the less professional members of the council. Prelates, magnates, *proceres*, and clerks were present as well as the justices, though probably no magnate or prelate who was not also a councillor; and in these parliaments the business, while mainly, was not exclusively, judicial. In the " post-paschal " parliament of 1290 the statute of Westminster III (*Quia Emptores*) was passed; the resolution to expel the Jews was adopted; and " so far as in them lay," the handful of magnates present granted *pro se et communitate totius regni* an aid for the marriage of Edward's sister.[2] The need for further consent was probably the reason for the summons to the knights of the shire to meet on July 15. Moreover, there was no narrow definition of legal or judicial

---

[1] Luchaire, *Institutions Françaises*, p. 562.
[2] *Rot. Parl.*, i. 25*a*, 41*a*.

E

functions; a *pax* between the Cinque Ports and Yarmouth was *recitata et recordata*—" registered " in the French parliamentary sense—in this parliament, and so were similar agreements between the bishop of Lincoln and the university of Oxford, and between " town " and " gown " in the latter city.[1] Even the taxation of those who were not represented was not yet regarded by Edward I, or by those whom the chroniclers describe as his evil counsellors, as being outside the competence of the " council in parliament "; and in the autumn of 1290 it was decided to levy a fifteenth of their moveable goods from *universi regnicolæ tam clerici quam laici, sæculares pariter et religiosi*, without the consent of any representative assembly.[2] Such exactions were, however, denounced and resisted, for in the worst days of feudalism the crown had possessed no power to levy general taxation. The aids and scutages and even the danegeld and carucages levied on tenants-in-chief were in the nature of rent rather than taxes; they were part of the " consideration " which the tenants owed to their landlord, and the mesne tenants enforced similar claims on their vassals. Arbitrary tallage was an incident of villein tenure, which was due to the lord whether he was a king or a baron. But a general tax on personal property, like a fifteenth, levied on all irrespective of their position as tenants of the king or other lords was a novelty, indicating the supersession of the feudal by the national idea, and providing scope for the maxim *quod omnes tangit ab omnibus approbetur*.

This approbation had been the normal function of the assemblies promised in Magna Carta and frequently held in the thirteenth century. It was not the function of the terminal sessions of the council, whose business is recorded in the early " Rolls of Parliaments "; [3] and so far we have had two kinds of meetings, widely differing in composition and character, but both described as " parliaments " by different authorities. One kind, which is so called by the

---

[1] *Rot. Parl.*, i. 16, 32b, 33.   [2] Stubbs, *Charters*, p. 435.
[3] The outcry raised over the imposition by the " parliament " of Michaelmas, 1290, may have helped to suggest the " model " parliament of 1295.

chroniclers, is or may be a large and tumultuous gathering of tenants-in-chief summoned by special and general writs; and while its potential size is reduced by the practice of permitting from two to four knights to represent all the lesser tenants-in-chief of the shire, it is increased by the admission of representatives of cities and boroughs which are regarded as collective tenants-in-chief of the crown. The other kind of " parliament "—so called by the clerks —is a smaller, regular meeting of the king's council, consisting of some prelates and magnates, most of the judges, and a selection of clerks, and dealing mainly with judicial business. The two bodies are summoned by different methods, meet at different times, and discharge different functions.

But during the latter half of Edward I's reign there is a process of amalgamation, and it is this amalgamation between " estates " and " parlement," rather than his addition of burgesses to the meetings of tenants-in-chief, that constitutes Edward's claim to be the creator of a model English parliament. Not that Edward I completed the process; parliament remained for centuries after his time a composite body, in which judicial and representative elements, legal and political functions were curiously blended, and it still retains the marks of its original heterogeneity. The approximation made in the reign of Edward I was confined to summoning the two assemblies to the same place at the same time and establishing a common session for certain purposes. But inasmuch as this co-operation between " estates " and " parlement " was the main constitutional difference between England and the rest of Western Europe during the later middle ages, the achievement was great enough, and requires greater attention than it has yet received. It was not determined by any large principle or any single dominating cause, but by the cumulative force of a number of small considerations; and the process of adoption consisted of gradual and almost imperceptible changes.

The principal predisposing cause of union was the fact that the crown in council was always present at both kinds of parliament, in the one to lay before the assembled tenants-in-chief and burgesses the financial demands of the government and to explain the causes of their necessity, and in the other to hear petitions, move the courts, and decide cases about which the judges differed or doubted. It would clearly be a convenience that, when the council was gathered together for judicial business *in pleno parliamento*, it should at the same place and during the same period meet the larger assembly summoned for financial and political considerations. Further, it must be remembered that according to feudal theory every tenant-in-chief of the crown was liable to suit and service at the *curia regis;* and that not merely the joint session of the courts in parliament but each individual session *ad scaccarium, in banco,* or *coram rege* was a session of the *curia*, to which any tenant-in-chief might be summoned; and therefore, although this feudal theory was obsolescent in Edward's reign, the *personnel* from which both kinds of assemblies were drawn might be regarded as potentially identical.

Nor was this identity merely potential. The councillors and judges who heard and determined the pleas and petitions in the terminal sessions of parliament were no doubt comparatively few in number; but Westminster Hall was crowded with " suitors," and " suitors " includes not only litigants but recognitors, jurors, and inquest. It is probable that in Edward's day a terminal session in Westminster Hall was more largely attended and, in spite of the fact that its attendants were not elected, more representative of all sorts and conditions of men than any gathering of the so-called " three estates." It was as a court of justice and not as houses of parliament that the palace of Westminster was called in 1302 *le plus franc lieu d'Engleterre ;* and the pleas and petitions heard before the king in council at Michaelmas 1290, provide a more comprehensive picture of national life than the meagre proceedings of the Model Parliament of 1295.[1] There London petitions for its mayor and ancient liberties, and Gloucester against the frequency and severity

---

[1] *Rot. Parl.,* i. 45–63.

of tallages levied by the "potentes villæ," and asks for an inquiry as to what had become of the proceeds; while Hampshire offers £200 to have its lands disafforested. The people of Appleby beg that they may have a water-mill built out of the 20 marks farm they pay, and offer to raise it to £20 if they may levy market-tolls like Carlisle. "Poor men" come from Norfolk, from Lincolnshire, and elsewhere, with petitions against various forms of exaction. "Plures de populo" present an awkward request for a commission to determine when the courts christian are to be bound by prohibitions and when they may proceed notwithstanding. "Multi de civitate Londonii," complain of conspiracies, machinations, and partiality in clerks and ministers of justice. Canterbury laments the encroachments of its archbishop, and London again accuses the clergy of extorting more money by their citations and excommunications than all the lay officers put together. On the other hand, the abbot of St. Mary's, York, begs to have his liberties defined "propter subtilitatem modernorum," while the Jews complain of compulsory baptism. No electoral system then in existence could have provided so varied a bill of fare for a merely political parliament; and when the law court and the "estates" coalesced, the coalition owed its popularity to the law and not to the politics in which it dealt. Recourse to Westminster Palace was a common custom before Edward I adapted it to the purposes of taxation and representation.

The main difference between the two kinds of assembly was that the presence of petitioners at the court was largely spontaneous, unorganized, and irresponsible, whereas the elected knights and burgesses came in response to official writs of summons, elected and empowered to bind their constituents. But even this distinction must not be over-drawn. The Hampshire men must have been authorized to offer £200 for its disafforestation, and the Appleby men to promise £20 a year for their market-tolls; and they must have been elected or selected by some process or other to represent the grievances or aspirations of their shires and

boroughs.   But their appearance was casual and disjointed;
and soon after accredited representatives of the shires and
boroughs began to be summoned for taxing purposes to the
presence of the king in council, the idea must have occurred
that it would be a saving of time, expense, and travel to
entrust these representatives with the petitions which the
communities desired to present for legal redress.   The idea
would, however, be impracticable unless the representatives
foregathered at court *in tempore parliamenti*.   The convenience of amalgamation was common to both the king
and his people.   It was clearly a waste of time for the
magnates, who happened to be present in council at the
post-paschal session of 1290, tentatively to grant an aid
quantum in ipsis est, and then to summon in July a
meeting of elected lesser tenants-in-chief to consider the
same proposal.   So, too, the connexion between the petitions
for redress presented to the council in parliament and the
demands for financial aid presented by the king to elected
representatives of the estates was natural; a bargain was
inevitably suggested, and the bargaining could only be done
satisfactorily if the people empowered to grant the aid were
also those in charge of the petitions.   The crown would be
less amenable to the pleas of petitioners who brought no
financial powers with them, and representatives who had no
successful petitions to carry home to their constituents would
be less responsive to the financial pleadings of the crown.
Justitia magnum emolumentum was as true in the days of
Edward I as in those of Henry I and Henry II; and justice
and finance were the two principal ingredients in the
parliament compounded by Edward I.

Edward's financial necessities, which arose from his wars
in France and Scotland and culminated in 1297, drove him
in this direction; but the compounding was not achieved
in the Model Parliament of 1295.   That assembly, which
met on November 27, was " model " only in so far as it
completed the representative character of the body summoned to give consent to the levying of taxation; and even
in that respect it may have been anticipated by the assembly

of 1275.[1] It was not " model " in the sense of exemplifying that fusion of " parlement " and " estates," of justice and finance, which was the essential basis of the English parliament. The regular terminal sessions had been concluded before the " model " parliament met; the only one in that year, of which any records have been preserved, met on August 15 and sat till the 30th; and though various parties were referred for further hearing to a following session *a die Sancti Michaelis in unum mensem*,[2] there is no reason to suppose that this Michaelmas term was prolonged beyond its normal month, so as to coalesce with the session of the " estates " at the end of November. The Model Parliament of November–December apparently received no petitions and heard no pleas; its business was merely to vote supplies; and there was no scope in it for those judicial functions which made parliament the highest law court in the land and gave it a framework and organization strong enough to save it from the shipwreck that overtook mere representative bodies everywhere else.

It was in 1298, after the crisis of 1297, that we have the first conclusive evidence of a simultaneous session of the representative and judicial bodies. Edward returned from Flanders in March; at a terminal session of the council held about Easter, it was ordained that the exchequer court should be held at York on the morrow, and the common pleas on the octave of Trinity Sunday, that is to say, on the 2nd and 9th of June respectively.[3] A week earlier, on May 25, representatives of the shires, cities, and boroughs were also to meet at York, and corresponding writs were sent to the prelates and magnates, though not, it appears, to the lower clergy. From this time onwards to the end of the reign every session of the representative body coincides with a terminal parliament of the judicature, although of course the latter are more frequent than the former, and it was long before the judicial parliamentary sessions were restricted to the brief periods during which the representatives were kept

[1] *English Hist. Review*, xxv. 231–42.
[2] *Rot. Parl.*, i. 132–42. [3] *Ibid.*, i. 143.

together. The next representative assembly was summoned
to meet at London on March 6, 1300, and it is significant
that now they are summoned in the writs " ad parliamentum "; for in March 1300 a " parliament " in the sense of
the " Rolls " was being held in the capital. Knights of the
shire were summoned to York in the following May; and
although there are no records of a judicial session held there
at that time in the " Rolls of Parliaments," there is in the
following year an interesting reference to the " male and
female " merchants and burgesses of York who had been
brought before the justices of common pleas during their
session in that city. For the well-known parliament at
Lincoln in January 1301, there are both writs summoning
representatives and " Rolls " recording judicial proceedings;
and the same holds good for the Michaelmas parliament of
1302, and the Lent parliament of 1305. No records of a
judicial session of parliament for 1306 are printed in the
" Rolls," but it is practically certain that one was being
held in May when knights and burgesses were summoned
to Westminster;[1] and records of both kinds of session are
extant for Edward's last parliament which was at Carlisle
in January 1307.

The presence of these specially and generally summoned
prelates, magnates, knights, and burgesses at the time and
place of the legal sessions has its effect upon the " Rolls of
Parliaments." This legal record is no longer confined to pleas
and petitions; and the clerk of chancery who keeps account
of these legal proceedings takes over the clerical work of
the " estates." In 1305 the presence of these intruders into
the court and their dismissal is mentioned in the " Rolls ";
in 1307 the names of those who received a special writ, and
of the proxies they appointed, are entered, and note is made
of the fact that general writs had been addressed to the
sheriffs directing the election of knights of the shire and
burgesses. All are said to have been summoned *ad parliamentum*, and their business is *ad tractandum super ordina-
tione et stabilitate terræ Scotiæ, necnon et aliis negotiis*

---

[1] There is an adjournment of a case to May 1306 (*Rot. Parl.*, i. 180a).

dictum regem et statum regni sui specialiter tangentibus.
It is true that the name " parliament " is applied in the
" Rolls " to these assemblies, not because they contain a
complete representation of " estates," but because they are
also sessions of the king's council in parliament; and they
will be called *plena* and *generalia*, not merely after all
save members of the council have departed, but when they
have not been summoned at all.   The parliament which
met on September 15, 1305, is none the less a parliament to
the keeper of the " Rolls " because it deals with only judicial
business and is not attended by any elected commons or
specially summoned magnates.   But politicians have been
admitted to parliament, and politics have been recorded on
the Rolls; in time they will almost expel the judges and
usurp the name of parliament; and the word, which is
originally used in the " Rolls " of meetings in which there
were no representatives, will be restricted to those in which
representatives will be the predominant factor.

In Edward I's reign, however, the intrusion of the
" estates " was only an episode or an incident in the life of
a parliament, an episode which might last no longer
than a few days, and rarely extended over three weeks.
On February 28, 1305, a parliament was begun; on March 21
not only the knights, burgesses, and clergy, but also the
prelates and magnates who were not of the king's council
were dismissed.[1]   But the parliament still continued: on
April 5, in the presence of bishops and other prelates, earls,
barons, justices, and other noble clerical and lay councillors,
" generali parliamento tunc existente ibidem," letters from
the pope were presented to Edward; and on April 6 the
king *in pleno parliamento* forbade his chancellor to issue
certain letters of protection.[2]   This practice continued into
the reign of Edward III.   A parliament began on Monday,
March 17, 1332; on the following Saturday the knights,
citizens, and burgesses were dismissed, but the " prelates,
earls, barons, and gentlemen of the king's council " were

---

[1] Cf. Maitland, *Memoranda*, p. xxxv.
[2] *Rot. Parl.*, i. 172, 177-9.

retained, and the proceedings *en pleyn parlement* continued in the following week.[1] It is clear that the prelates, magnates, knights, and burgesses who obeyed the writs of summons to parliament did not constitute a parliament or even make a parliament *plenum* or *generale*. They were summoned to something that was a parliament apart from their presence. The essential presence is that of the council; nothing was called a parliament from which the council was absent; parliament is, in fact, a parliament of the council, and a *plenum* or *generale* parliament was simply a general and full (or public) session of the council. Fleta knows nothing of elected representatives; they are an accretion not yet recognized as indispensable to the composition of a parliament, a sort of slip-carriage or series of slip-carriages which may be detached at any point in the journey of the parliamentary train. The essential factor is the engine of the council, which supplies the motive force and travels all the way.

The organization and business of parliament were as composite as its *personnel*, and the contents of the "Rolls" reflect the varied nature of its proceedings. Its machinery was, however, purely legal in origin, and down to this day the technical details connected with the issue of parliamentary writs and other business are suggestive of those employed in the law courts. Chancery supplied the presiding officer and the clerks of parliament, issued the writs of summons and examined the returns, provided the methods of proceeding by petition and bill, and kept the records; and at times parliament has the appearance of being nothing but chancery turned to political purposes. It was natural that the inorganic "estates" should fall under the management of the organic court of law with its regular sessions, coherent *personnel*, and expert clerks, when once the connexion between the two assemblies had been established; for the "estates" had developed no organization and no records of their own before they came into contact with the organized terminal sessions of the council; and it was not

[1] *Rot. Parl.*, ii. 64-6.

until the later development of the "house" of commons that we discover in the Speaker a parliamentary official who has no essential connexion with the law.

But there were no "houses" in Edward I's reign, and the earliest trace of the organization of "estates" apparently consists of the clerks of chancery who seem to have been allocated to the different groups of representatives to assist them in drafting their replies and perhaps to keep some record of their attendance, upon which the writs *de expensis* were issued when they were dismissed. Even this is a development of the reign of Edward III, and while separate deliberation by different groups may perhaps be inferred for that of Edward I, there is no evidence of it in the "Rolls of Parliament." All that we can say is that the "estates" were called into the presence of the council, presented petitions as individuals rather than as a corporate body or bodies, heard a statement of such of the king's intentions as he thought fit to reveal, and gave assent, perhaps by silence, to his demands for money. These brief and one-sided interviews between the council and "estates" suggested and required little organization. They did not sit together, for the commons, at least, stood in the presence of the king and council, and the attitude of Edward I was somewhat patriarchal. They probably took a less active part in parliament than the audience does in a public meeting of to-day; the council sat on the platform, and the business was cut-and-dried. The commons, at least, were summoned not to decide, but to consent to decisions; and the object of their presence was not to tie the hands of the council, but to unloose the pockets of their constituents.

This was the political business of a parliament; but its first purpose was judicial, and before the estates assembled, proclamation was always made in Westminster Hall and elsewhere that all who had petitions to present should present them by a certain date. Individual prelates, barons, knights, and burgesses may have attended to support the particular petitions in which they were interested; but there were few petitions to Edward I's parliaments of more than local or

personal import; and it is unlikely that the audience for the
hearing of others was large.   Apart from the grant of money,
and the discussion thereof, in which the commons took but
a humble part at first, the " estates " had little to do in
parliament; and it is small wonder that they were commonly
dismissed after a few days or a week or two.   Their importance as a deliberative assembly grew slowly with their gradual
realization of the fact that their individual petitions, arising
spontaneously from different localities, dealt with grievances
common to all and might well be fused into common petitions.   When that took place, parliament became a political
arena rather than a court of law; for, while individual
grievances are matters of law, national grievances are matters
of politics.   The one requires merely judicial action, the
other calls for legislation.   But this was a slow development of the fourteenth century, dependent upon the growth
of a common consciousness among the locally-minded
delegates or petitioners whom Edward I dragged or invited
into the presence of his council in parliament.

CHAPTER IV

THE MYTH OF THE THREE ESTATES

WHILE the high court of parliament was the correct and official description of the two houses in the sixteenth and seventeenth centuries, the "three estates" was the more popular and inaccurate designation applied to them in the eighteenth and nineteenth; and the phrase has become so deeply embedded in historical terminology that it is accepted as synonymous with parliament without any critical examination of its real relevance. There has, it is true, been some divergence of opinion as to whether the three estates were king, lords, and commons, or lords spiritual, lords temporal, and commons; but the former definition of the term, which was common in eighteenth-century parliamentary oratory, has been frightened even out of school-books by the contemptuous ridicule of nineteenth-century historians. The error, if an error at all, is, we shall see, not quite so flagrant as it has been represented; and in any case, it is only a detail compared with the fact that the more we realize the importance and the permanence of parliament as a high court, the less ready shall we be to accept the three estates as a complete or even a plausible indication of its essential character and constitution. Judicature is not a function of estates; and where three estates have really existed, as in France, they have had little or no connexion with *parlements*. Yet as late as the reign of Henry VII, half the time of parliament was occupied with purely judicial functions; [1] they were discharged by parliament centuries afterwards in passing

[1] The reason still given in 1485 for the appointment of receivers and triers of petitions is " ut justitia conqueri volentibus possit celerius adhiberi " (*Rot. Parl.*, vi. 267).

subsequent centuries about preserving the state, they often
meant the " status quo." The state was something established by law or by custom, something that could not or
should not be changed. Any fixed order or species might
be a state, and the word implied something fundamental
by the law of God or of nature. It was characteristic of
the ages in which men had some notion of social statics
but none of social dynamics, some desire for order but no
conception of progress.

That there was something natural, if not also divine,
in the separation of mankind into three classes seemed
as clear to medieval philosophers as it did to nineteenth-
century railway companies. The idea was as old as Plato; [1]
parliament itself in 1401 speaks of a trinity of estates; [2]
and Wycliffe writes of the " state of priests, state of knights,
and state of commons." [3] This corresponds to a common
philosophical distinction of priestly, military, and plebeian
orders, though another division was into fighters, councillors, and labourers. There is a vague similarity between
these theoretical classifications and the division into church,
lords, and commons, of which parliaments embodied a
rough representation. But it is a long step from this
analogy to the theory that parliament was organized
upon the basis of three estates; and in practice there was
little in common between the two. The first estate was
the church; but in parliaments, after the reign of Edward II
at any rate, the church is represented only by the bishops,
some abbots, and one or two priors; and they are summoned, or rather, are liable to summons, not because they
represent the church, but because they hold land *per
baroniam*, by military tenure-in-chief of the crown. [4] They

---

[1] *Republic*, ii. 370 *sqq.*   [2] *Rot. Parl.*, iii. 459b.
[3] *English Works*, ed. Arnold, iii. 184. Cf. also Hallam, *Middle Ages*,
iii. 105–6, and Stubbs, *Const. Hist.*, ii. 172 *n.*
[4] See Pike, *Const. Hist. of the House of Lords*, pp. 155–6, 219. It is
inaccurate to say that they were summoned because they held baronies,
for many who held baronies were not summoned at all. They were summoned because the king desired their counsel; and their baronies gave him
a lien on their suit and service at his court. The crown was not prepared
to abandon the bishops to the papacy, and they were expected to be royal,
as well as papal, courtiers.

are, in fact, barons as well as prelates, and Henry II had laid it down in the Constitutions of Clarendon that they were liable to suit and service, like other barons, in the king's court; and Edward III's answer to the prelates who complained of taxation in 1341 unmistakeably implies that they were summoned to parliaments because they held by barony.[1]

This view has been disputed, and a spiritual right to be present in parliament has been asserted, mainly on the ground that during the vacancy of episcopal sees, the guardian of the spiritualties who did not hold *per baroniam* received a special writ of summons like a bishop. But he received this summons because of the *præmunientes* clause it contained, requiring him, as the only person capable of so doing, to cause proctors to be elected for the clergy of the diocese of which he had temporary charge, and not for the sake of securing his personal presence in parliament. Certainly no abbot ever sat by a spiritual title, and the ground upon which many of them sought to evade the duty of attendance, was always an allegation that they held no land *per baroniam* and therefore were not liable to a summons. The force that brought spiritual and temporal lords together into one house of lords was clearly not their common membership of the same estate, for *ex hypothesi* they belonged to two sharply distinguished orders, but their common receipt of a special writ of summons based on their common tenure-in-chief from the crown. "Comme ercevesques et evesques," plead the prelates themselves in parliament in 1352, "tiegnent lour temporaltes du roi en chef et par tant sont pieres de la terre comme sont autres countes et barons."[2] If the house of lords is an estate at all, it is an artificial estate created by the action of the crown out of heterogeneous elements gathered from all the three normal estates of theory—bishops and abbots from

[1] *Rot. Parl.*, ii. 130. The prelates "qui tiegnent du roi par baronie et deyvent venir au parlement par somonse" are told that they must pay a ninth; while clergy "qui ne tiegnent rien par baronie ne ne sont pas acoustumes d'estre somons au parlement" need only pay a tenth.

[2] *Ibid.*, ii. 245. It has not, I think, been established that a guardian of spiritualties ever sat in parliament on that ground.

F

the first, earls and barons from the second, and councillors, judges, and secretaries from the third.

Nor was the second estate more satisfactorily represented in the house of lords than the first. The theory of three estates would seem to imply that each member of an estate is entitled either to be present at the estates-general in person or to vote for the election of a representative; at any rate, that was the interpretation adopted at the great assembly of the estates-general of France in 1789. But no one—save its *ex-officio* members, the chancellor, the treasurer, and so forth—has ever sat in the house of lords except in response to a special writ of summons; and the vast majority of the military tenants-in-chief received no special writ, and were represented in the house of commons. If there was ever a noble estate in England, it was unceremoniously cut by English monarchs into two unequal sections, the smaller of which was called to the house of lords, while the larger was relegated, in the persons of the knights of the shire, to the third estate in the house of commons. For the knights of the shire were barons, the *barones minores* who, according to Magna Carta, were to be summoned to give their advice by general writs addressed to the sheriff and not by special writ addressed to the individual baron (*h*). The house of lords is not an estate of the realm; if it represents estates at all it is a royally compounded mixture of fragments of estates.

Least of all is the house of commons a third " estate." It is no mere assembly of *bourgeois* like the old *tiers état* in France. Its most important and turbulent element in the middle ages consists of the knights of the shire, *barones minores, milites,* or *chivalers,*[1] as they are called, who were tenants-in-chief of the crown, who often called themselves " nobles," [2] and who belonged by the theory of estates to

---

[1] We should be inclined to regard *miles* and *chivaler* as synonymous, were it not that a knight of the shire is sometimes described as *miles et chivaler* in the " Official Return of Members of Parliament." Nor must we identify *milites* with *barones minores*, since even an earl was often a knight as well (cf. *Magna Carta Essays*, Royal Hist. Soc., pp. 46–77, 100).

[2] The " nobility " in England down to the sixteenth century included, as it did in France, the *petite noblesse.*

the second and not to the third. It was their combination
with the city and borough members that gave the house
of commons its singular strength in the middle ages and
made it unique among representative institutions. But it
was no estate of the realm; it was a concentration of all
the communities of England, shires, cities, and boroughs;
and it consisted no more than they did of a single class.
If it represented one estate more than another, it represented the second rather than the third; for the knights
of the shire were often nominated by its magnates, and the
same magnates sometimes controlled the elections for the
boroughs on their domains. Lastly, in a system of three
estates there is no natural or logical place for the large
official and legal element which we find throughout in the
high court of parliament.

These facts, or some of them, have been generally recognized by historians, who nevertheless accept the fundamental truth of the theory of three estates; and the inconsistency between that theory and the facts is explained by
the contention that the English have never been logical,
and that parliaments represented only a rough approximation to the orthodox theory. If a clerk of a fourteenth-
century parliament writes of the judges or merchants as
being " estates," or refers in a hazy way to half a dozen
or more " estates," the reference is regarded as a slip of
the pen, a loose use of the phrase, or a mental aberration.[1]
The difficulty is, however, to discover the evidence for the
norm, from which these exceptions depart. Exceptions no
doubt will prove a rule, but only if they can be proved to
be exceptions; we must satisfy ourselves that the exception
is not the rule, and so far from being able to show
that it was the custom to regard a parliament in the fourteenth century as an assembly of three estates consisting
respectively of lords spiritual, lords temporal, and commons, we cannot, I think, adduce a single instance of such

---

[1] Cf. Maitland, *Memoranda*, p. lxxxiii. We are apt to think that
" whatever upon our record makes against this belief should be explained
away as irregular or anomalous."

a description until towards the close of the reign of Henry V.

Certainly, the only known description of parliaments in the fourteenth century, the *Modus Tenendi Parliamentum*,[1] knows nothing of three estates or, indeed, of any estates at all (*i*). This tract has been commonly treated as a fanciful sketch of no authority for somewhat inadequate reasons, unless its disagreement with orthodox views be regarded as a sufficient ground for neglect. It is true that its opening statement, professing to give an account of the method of holding parliaments in Anglo-Saxon times, does not commend it to historical students; but the fact that it is of no value for Anglo-Saxon history does not disprove its claim to be considered as of some authority on the parliaments of the century in which it was written, any more than chroniclers who begin with the Creation are to be ignored when they come down to contemporary history. Its composition has been assigned to the opening years of Edward III's reign, mainly because it mentions no viscounts, marquises, or dukes, but only earls and barons among the magnates, and the first English duke was created in the person of the Black Prince in 1337. At least three of the extant MSS. date from the fourteenth century; and it seems to have been regarded early in the fifteenth century as an authoritative rather than a fanciful description. At any rate, a revised version of it was sent over to Ireland in 1418 by the privy council to inform the lord deputy of the method in which parliaments should be held in Dublin; in 1510 the clerk of the parliaments thought it worth while to transcribe the treatise and prefix it to the *Journals* he had to keep; and another copy was apparently handed from clerk to clerk of the house of commons.

[1] The best edition of the *Modus* is that by Hardy (London, 1846), from whose text Stubbs printed it at the end of his *Select Charters*. The Irish version of 1418 was first printed in 1911 in R. Steele's *Bibliography of Proclamations* (Oxford: Clarendon Press), i. clxxxviii–cxci. Numerous MS. copies of the English version were made, and in the first half of the seventeenth century it was a favourite text for parliamentary lawyers like Hakewill and Elsynge to edit. Some attention has been given to it by members of my seminar, and a preliminary survey of forty-seven MSS. extant in the British Museum was published in the *English Hist. Review*, April 1919, pp. 209–25.

Now, the *Modus*, while saying nothing about three
estates, says a good deal about six " gradus " of parliament; and these " grades " or orders are the king, the
prelates, the ecclesiastical proctors, the lords temporal,
the knights, and the commons. The Irish version of 1418
contains some important modifications of the earlier English
version; but there are still six grades of parliament, each
with its own clerk, each deliberating apart, and reporting
its answers separately to parliament. It would in any
case be somewhat arbitrary to ignore this evidence, and
such neglect becomes impossible when the general conclusion to be derived from the *Modus* as regards the three
estates is confirmed by the " Rolls of Parliament " themselves. The *Modus* gives too few rather than too many
" grades " of parliament; for the judges are sometimes
described in the " Rolls " as an estate, the " chivalers "
as another, and the merchants were summoned by writ
as a separate class in 1339 and 1340. This latter practice
was, however, prohibited, on the petition of the commons,
in 1362 and 1371; and the judges are seldom described
as an estate. That the " Rolls " should describe them as
such at all, and that they should speak of prelates, lords
temporal, knights, judges, *et tous autres estats*,[1] being
charged to deliberate one by one, is sufficient evidence that
these estates themselves, or the clerk of the parliaments
who recorded their proceedings, knew nothing of any sacrosanct trinity of estates. The most formal and authoritative
definition of " a parlement somond of all the states of the
reaume " is given by Chief-justice Thirning on the solemn
occasion of Richard II's abdication; and he enumerates
them as : (1) archbishops and bishops; (2) abbots, priors,
and " all other men of Holy Church, seculars and regulars";
(3) dukes and earls; (4) barons and bannerets; (5) bachelors
and commons, who are divided into two sections, those
" by south " and those " by north." He also refers to
" the state of kyng," and, besides the " states," to " all
the people that was ther gadyrd by cause of the sommons

---

[1] *Rot. Parl.*, ii. 278, iii. 100.

forsayd," by whom Richard's renunciation and cession "ware pleinelich and freilich accepted and fullich agreed." [1] Even when we do come, in the first year of the fifteenth century, across an allusion in the " Rolls " to three estates, they are not the three of constitutional orthodoxy; and it is as a trinity of king, lords, and commons that the last-named describe the three estates in their address to Henry IV in 1401.[2] If the commons had enjoyed the advantage of reading our modern constitutional histories, they might have avoided this " error," into which Burghley fell in 1585 [3] and Charles James Fox and thousands of others in the eighteenth century.[4]

It is in 1421 that we get the first official reference to parliament as consisting of *tres status, videlicet, prelatos et clerum, nobiles et magnates, necnon communitates dicti regni;* [5] and the circumstances of this reference suggest an interesting explanation of the introduction of the phrase into English parliamentary usage. The Peace of Troyes had been concluded between Henry V and Charles VI of France, and every formality was to be observed which might render it and the union of the two crowns binding. The peace was accordingly to be sworn to by the three estates of the two realms. It had been signed in France, where there really was a system of three estates, and the advantages of uniformity suggested the employment of identical phraseology when the treaty was sent over to England for confirmation. From this time the phrase comes slowly and doubtingly into English official and popular use.[6] The process was eased by the contact of the English government with systems of three estates in its French

---

[1] *Rot. Parl.*, iii. 424; Hughes, *Chaucer's England*, pp. 293–4.

[2] *Ibid.*, iii. 459b; Stubbs, ii. 172 n.

[3] D'Ewes, *Journals*, p. 350; Bishop Aylmer has the same definition (*An Harborowe for Faithfull Subjects*, 1559, H. iii.); and so has Bishop Gardiner (Foxe, *Acts and Mon.*, vi. 51).

[4] Lecky, *Hist. of England*, 1892, iii. 388 n.; B. Whitelocke (*Notes on the King's Writ*, ed. 1766, ii. 43) takes the same view.

[5] *Rot. Parl.*, iv. 135, v. 102–3. Even this adds "clerum" to the conventional "lords spiritual."

[6] *Ordinances of the Privy Council*, ed. Nicolas, v. 297, vi. 71; *Rot. Parl.*, iv. 420, v. 128, vi. 39, 424, 444.

provinces; and the privy council speaks of the three estates of Guienne before it speaks of the three estates of England or Ireland.[1] Englishmen, however, seemed to be conscious of the false assimilation, and the phrase " provincial estates" was never apparently applied to the assemblies of the so-called English palatinates. Fortescue will not call parliament three estates; he cautiously remarks that the three estates of France " when they bith assembled, bith like to the courte of the parlement in Ingelonde "; and Commines will only say of Edward IV's parliament that it *vault autant comme les trois estatz*.[2] And the phrase in its older and vaguer sense continued in vogue. Bishop Stillington, in 7 Edward IV, calls the lords spiritual, lords temporal, and commons the three estates of the realm, but speaks of a royal estate over them all.[3] The council talks in 1440 of the " estates of holy church," just as in Edward I's reign the " Rolls" speak of *tous ces estats de prelacie*.[4] In 1491 Henry VII, in a proclamation, speaks of being informed " by the estates and nobles "; in 1497 Perkin Warbeck refers to Henry's projected flight " in person with many other estates of the land "; and in 1513 the commons desire " the great estates, peers and nobles of this realm " to grant adequate taxes. A chronicler of Henry VII's reign gives the following illustrations of the persistent indefiniteness of the phrase : " there stood the king, queen, and many great estates of the realm . . . the said estates took their horses and chairs, and so rode to Richmond," and again, " considering the great and notable court that there was holden, as first the king, the queen, my lady the king's mother, with my lord of York, my lady Margaret, and divers other estates." [5]

---

[1] Nicolas, v. 161.

[2] Fortescue, *Governance of England*, ed. Plummer, pp. 113, 195.

[3] Fortescue, p. 127, also says that the King's estate is the highest estate temporal on earth. So James I says the "state of monarchy is the supremest thing on earth." (Prothero, *Documents*, ed. 1898, p. 293.)

[4] *Proceedings of the Privy Council*, v. 88, 148; *Rot. Parl.*, i. 219.

[5] Steele, *Proclamations*, i. No. 17; my *Henry VII*, i. No. 108; Kingsford, *Chronicles of London*, pp. 222, 245, 253, 263; *Lords' Journals*, vol. i. p. xxvi.; cf. *L. and P.*, 1539, i. No. 858, "states doth daily assemble against the parliament." See Appendix III, note (*j*).

The impression produced by this divergence and vagueness in the use of the word " estates " [1] is borne out by what we know of the medieval organization of parliaments. Fleta is apparently unaware of their existence; to him parliaments are sessions of the king's council in the presence of earls, barons, nobles, and other learned men; in 1305 a parliament can still be a " full " parliament when all but the councillors have withdrawn; and as late as the reign of Henry VI the lords can be described as being " in full parliament " without any other assessors.[2] Even when other elements, nominated and elected, come to be recognized as normal if not essential additions to the council for parliamentary purposes, they are not regarded or organized as three estates. They meet and transact their public business in a single chamber, the *camera magni consilii vocata le parlement chambre*, otherwise known as *la chambre blanche pres de la chambre peynte*,[3] or else in that Painted Chamber, sometimes called the chamber of Edward the Confessor, where, down to the nineteenth century, conferences between the lords and commons continued to be held.[4]   In this council chamber, which came

[1] This absence of definite estates is illustrated by a corresponding absence of, or vagueness in, the designations now used to indicate differences of status.   Originally *baro* simply meant a man; the *barones majores* were the king's greater, and the *barones minores* his lesser, men.   In the fourteenth century, while a tenant by barony might be described as " baro " of such and such a barony, just as we may describe so-and-so as lord of the manor of this or that place, the word " baro " was no more used as a title of honour than lord of the manor is to-day.   There was nothing in his designation to distinguish a " peer " from a knight; the knight may have been a lesser baron, but his inferiority was expressed in the extent of his holding and his lack of a special summons, and not in his mode of address; and the baron might or might not be a knight. " Dominus " and " Sir " were titles they shared alike, and they shared them both with priests; it was not until after the Reformation that " Dominus " and " Sir " were replaced by " Reverend " as the normal prefix to a cleric's name.   " Dominus," moreover, as applied to a priest, was inferior to " Doctor " and even " Master," and seems to have been applied regularly to those who had taken no University degree or none higher than that of Bachelor, a custom still retained at Cambridge (*k*).

[2] *Proceedings of the Privy Council*, iii. lxi. : Nicolas interprets the phrase as meaning " a full meeting of peers."   But there are other lords than peers : "lords of parliament " would be more correct.

[3] *Rot. Parl.*, ii. 225, vi. 232.

[4] May, *Parliamentary Practice*, p. 496.

to be called the parliament chamber because the council parleyed there, lords and commons still assemble as one gathering before the throne to hear the king's speech, the prorogation or dissolution of parliament, and the royal assent to legislation, although the historical origin of the chamber is effectually concealed beneath its modern name of the house of lords. Edward I knew no more of two houses than he did of three estates; and in his reign and in those of his son and his grandson, all the formal work of parliament is done in common session. It is only the work thus done in common, and perhaps in public, that is officially recorded in the " Rolls of Parliament." Such are the " acts " of parliament.

This common session, however, while convenient and even indispensable for the formal proceedings of parliament, was no less inconvenient for its real work of deliberation and discussion. Only rigid rules of procedure, the result of six centuries of elaboration, enable a body so homogeneous as the present house of commons to transact any business at all; in the assemblies which the first two Edwards called few rules of procedure had yet been evolved, and the gatherings, whether they consisted of six grades or of three estates, were too heterogeneous to act in common. If the king extracted any response at all to his demands for money or requests for counsel, it would be a babel of tongues. Intelligent answers could only proceed from previous consultation; and the exigencies of consultation required some sort of organization. The accepted theory is that this organization took from the first the form of two houses or three estates; the *Modus Tenendi Parliamentum* speaks, on the other hand, of six grades, assigning to each a clerk, whose function was presumably to reduce the resolutions of his " grade " to writing, and possibly to keep some record of its proceedings. The " Rolls of Parliaments " do not support either theory in its entirety; they refer vaguely to an indefinite number of " estates "; but never, I think, to more than two clerks. One was the clerk of the parliaments, who sat in the parliament chamber, and still sits in the house of lords;[1] and the other was the clerk of the *domus communis*. There may have been more; the proctors of the clergy doubtless had a clerk of their own, who might also be a clerk of convocation, and the different answers sometimes returned by the knights and the burgesses imply separate deliberation and possibly separate clerks to record their results. But if the picture drawn in the *Modus* ever represented actual practice, that practice was greatly modified during the fourteenth century; and by a process of elimination and amalgamation the six grades were reduced to three or two.

In the first place, the clerical proctors preferred to give their answers to the king's proposals in convocation, and absented themselves from the parliament chamber, though their right to petition the king in parliament remained, and in Richard II's reign, the appointment of Thomas Percy as clerical proctor, to assent to the proceedings against the Appellants, paid homage to the doubtful theory that clerical consent was necessary to their validity.[2] This abstention eliminated one of the six " grades " of the *Modus*. Another disappeared with the amalgamation of the knights and burgesses, and a third with the merging of the specially-summoned barons and prelates under the common designation of " seigneurs " or " lords " of parliament. The process was thus complete by which parliaments came in appearance to consist of two houses and of three estates. It was due, however, not to any preconceived ideas about the value of a bi-cameral legislature or of a threefold system of estates, but to the operation of royal writs and political convenience. It was the custom of the king's chancery, in issuing special writs of summons, that differentiated the lesser from the greater baron, the " peer " from the knight

---

[1] His present postal address, " Clerk of the Parliaments, House of Lords," is in itself an item of historical evidence. The use of the plural, " parliaments," and the juxtaposition of the two terms, point the contrast between the medieval and the modern view of his position.

[2] *Rot. Parl.*, iii. 348, 356. There is no evidence of the actual presence of the well-known Thomas Haxey in the parliament of 1396; he seems merely to have sent up a bill to the commons upon which they acted (*ibid.*, iii. 339).

of the shire, and one abbot from another. As early as the
reign of Edward III there was a list in existence of twenty-
eight abbots whom it was not customary to summon by
special writ,[1] and this custom made some of them lords of
parliament and left others out in the cold. It was political
convenience that led the knights of the shire to coalesce
with the burgesses, and induced the clerical proctors to
confine themselves to convocation.

Both the process of coalition and that of elimination
would have been impossible had there been any marked
division of estates. The mere fact that the knights of the
shire could separate from the other barons and throw in
their lot with the burgesses proves that the lines of demarcation were not deep or fundamental. There was, indeed,
a sharp distinction between the freeman and the villein;
but that had nothing to do with parliamentary organization.
The villein had no " estate " in anything, and nowhere did
he constitute an "estate" of the realm. He had no status
or *locus standi* in the king's court, except in so far as he
was protected by the king's claim to criminal jurisdiction,
and therefore none in the king's high court of parliament.
The other clear distinction in English medieval society was
between layman and clerk; but that, too, soon ceased to
influence parliamentary organization, because the proctors
ceased to attend, and in the " upper house " or great council
in parliament the common receipt of a special writ over-
rode the distinction between spiritual and temporal; the
peers did not act as two estates, but as counsellors of the
crown.

This had an all-important effect upon the course of
English constitutional history, and saved the country on
more than one occasion from formal revolution (*l*). If the
necessary assent of the lords spiritual and temporal to legislation had involved the independent assent of a majority
of each " estate," many a change constitutionally carried
out could only have been effected by revolution. As it
was, spiritual votes could help to carry temporal reforms

[1] Pike, p. 349; see below, p. 99.

in the teeth of a majority of temporal peers, and temporal votes could carry religious reforms in spite of spiritual peers.[1] The bishops and abbots protested against the statutes of provisors and præmunire; they were none the less law for that, and the prelates did not pretend that their protest had the effect of a royal veto. A majority of spiritual peers did, indeed, vote for Henry VIII's and Somerset's ecclesiastical changes; but with Warwick's accession to power and the adoption by the government of definitely protestant proposals, this ecclesiastical acquiescence disappeared, and the crisis came in the first year of Elizabeth. Every spiritual peer present voted against her act of supremacy and her act of uniformity, and the latter was only carried by a majority consisting of twenty-one temporal peers over a minority consisting of eighteen spiritual and temporal peers. By no conceivable stretch of language could it be contended that the spiritual " estate " had consented to Elizabeth's settlement of religion, although the notion of three estates had by this time made sufficient way to countenance the theory that the assent of each was indispensable to the validity of legislation. If this was the true theory of the constitution, then, indeed, the acts of supremacy and uniformity were not merely unconstitutional, but illegal; in fact, they were no acts at all, and the courts should have refused to carry them out. But it was not, and never had been, the true theory of the constitution, because parliaments had never consisted of estates at all. Nor was it possible to escape from the dilemma by the hypothesis that a majority of two out of the three estates could over-ride the third; for in that case the lords spiritual and temporal could always have legislated in defiance of the commons, but in Henry VII's reign the judges had laid it down that even for an act of

---

[1] It has often been contended that Elizabeth's ecclesiastical settlement was unconstitutional because it was carried against the votes of the spiritual peers; but the same theory would invalidate temporal measures carried by episcopal votes, except on the assumption that ecclesiastical affairs were the concern of ecclesiastics alone, but state affairs were the common concern of laymen and ecclesiastics.

attainder, an almost purely judicial function, the co-operation of the commons was essential.[1] The theory of the three estates would, in fact, if there had been any substance in it, have stereotyped and petrified the constitution in the middle ages. But Englishmen's political instinct has always been sounder than their scholarship or their logic; and constitutional progress has not been seriously impeded by the theories of constitutional historians.

It is, indeed, hardly too much to say that parliament, so far from being a system of three estates, is the very negation of the whole idea. A system of estates is built upon the principle, not of national, but of class representation; it suggests that a nation is not one, but three states, each with an independent will of its own, and each entitled to veto national progress. It was by no accident that the first step in the first French Revolution was the fusion of the three estates into one National Assembly. The difference between English and French development was that in France the fusion was instantaneous and therefore caused an explosion, while in England it was a gradual transformation spread over centuries. The reduction of the six " grades " of the *Modus* to two or three was an illustration of the process, and a proof of the elasticity of the English political and social system. There were no fixed gulfs between the different grades which the royal authority could not bridge. If the knights deliberated apart from the magnates, it was not because there was any social barrier between them, but because the crown directed them to deliberate with the commons; and conversely it directed the prelates and magnates to consult together.[2] The crown, too, could issue a special writ of summons to a knight and thus convert him into a magnate; and by a

---

[1] See my *Henry VII*, ii. No. 14.

[2] *Rot. Parl.*, ii. 135. This explicit direction of the crown in 1343 implies that prelates and magnates, knights and burgesses might have otherwise, and probably had previously, deliberated apart and returned separate answers; and if, with Mr. Pike, we assign the *Modus* to the second quarter of the fourteenth century, this direction would tend to strengthen the credibility of its division of parliaments into six grades.

writ of distraint could make an esquire into a knight. The most permanent factor in the English medieval representative system consisted of the knights of the shire, and they represented, not an estate, but the shire courts of the realm. "Status," indeed, entitled no one to any position in medieval parliaments; their composition and their organization were alike determined by royal writs and royal directions. Even to-day it is a royal writ, and not hereditary right, that entitles a peer to sit in the house of lords; and it was a royal writ that entitled a borough to elect a member of the house of commons. It is true that through judicial decisions in one case, and through statute law in the other, the crown has lost the power of refusing a special writ of summons to the eldest son of a peer or a general writ to a borough; but without the writ the peer's heir could not take his seat and the borough could not elect, and the modern form is the relic of a medieval power.

Nor is it without significance that the English was the only representative system called a parliament, or that other nations, when they set about imitating English institutions, abandoned the name of estates. Emphasis has, in fact, been continually laid by constitutional historians upon the differences between English and foreign representative systems; but it is singular that they should have sought to fix upon the English parliament a designation appropriate only to those estates from which its difference is so clearly marked. Estates-general could only vote taxes and petition for redress; they could not impeach, or pass acts of attainder, or enforce the responsibility of ministers. For they were not a court of law, and it was from its armoury as the sovereign court that parliament drew the weapons it used with most effect against the crown. Its procedure by bill was borrowed from chancery, its powers of judicature were inherited from the *curia regis*, its acts have always been " due process of law"—a character which American judges have denied to acts of the American congress; for that is not a parliament or a court.

The ineffectiveness of estates-general arose from the fact

that they were nothing but a body, or bodies, of representatives. They were not numbered among the " cours
souverains " of France, and the judicial functions performed by the English parliament were left in France to
the non-representative *parlements*. The use of impeachment and acts of attainder in England from the fourteenth
to the eighteenth century may have involved injustice to
individuals, but it was of inestimable service to English
constitutional progress that the judicial review of state
offences should have been preserved for the English representative assembly by the fact that it was a parliament
rather than a system of estates. It was hardly of less importance that the representative elements themselves, when
added by Simon de Montfort and Edward I to the king's
council in parliament, should have appeared in a juridical
guise. Every suitor to the county court in which members
were returned to the house of commons was an actual
juror; the elector was present at the election primarily
because he had to attend the court for judicial business.
And the legal capacity clung to their representatives; if
the lords in parliament were its judges, the commons,
says Prynne, were " informers, prosecutors, grand jury-
men." " Through all their history, too, the Commons have
remained ' the Grand Inquest of the Nation.' Judges and
inquest the two Houses were before they were joined;
Council and Grand Inquest they remained; and this conception of their origin, their character, their duties, and
their privileges serves in a large measure to explain throughout the history of Parliament not only the claims of one
House against the other, but also their common claims as
the High Court of Parliament." [1]

But while parliament consists, in its judicial aspect, of
judges and inquest, it is in its political aspect a meeting
of council and community. Members of the upper house
have properly claimed to be historically the counsellors of
the crown, although hereditary right was not the original
basis of their title to give counsel to the crown; and

[1] McIlwain, *The High Court of Parliament*, pp. 186-7.

historically the house of lords is the king's council in parliament. No quorum was, however, required to give validity to the action of a royal council; because its function was to advise, and the act was always the king's. Thus the *Modus* goes so far as to say that even though every specially-summoned magnate absented himself from a meeting between the crown and the community, the meeting might still be a valid parliament. The two essential factors were the crown and the community, that *communitas communitatum* which came to be called the house of commons. If this seems modern, it is also medieval doctrine; and the conservative value of history is that, when properly understood, it helps us to see how reform succeeds not by innovation, but by the renovation and expansion of the principles and practice out of which the constitutional fabric has been made. If parliaments had ever been based on a foundation of three estates, our constitutional development would have encountered that dilemma of stagnation or revolution which sooner or later has confronted every representative system founded on class divisions. It was a happy fate for England that its parliaments were dominated by elements, ideas, and a procedure emanating from the *curia regis* until after its estates had been merged by the growth of national feeling into a single state.

CHAPTER V

THE FICTION OF THE PEERAGE

In speaking of the " fiction " of the peerage, no allusion
is intended to certain sumptuous and annual publications,
the genealogical contents of which might fairly entitle them
to that description.   Nor is it meant to deny that a work of
fiction may be good as well as bad.   Fictions, and especially
legal fictions, have played a great and sometimes a beneficent
part in English constitutional history.   The presence of the
king in every court and every parliament in the empire is
a useful fiction; the dogmas that " the king never dies "
and can do no wrong, are others of no less value.   By means
of fictions judges have made law, and there is a considerable
element of truth in the claim that on some occasions national
legislation by the judges over-rode the class legislation of
parliaments.[1]   At times the fictions of the courts have been
strong meat, and the identification of Cheapside with " the
high seas," which was once effected in a court of law to bring
a case within its jurisdiction, marks perhaps the limit to
which the process should be carried.[2]   But the house of
lords is the highest court of law for civil jurisdiction in the
British Isles, and it is natural that there legal fictions should
have winged their highest flight.   Certainly no legal fiction
runs counter to more historical fact than the rule of the house
of lords that a special writ of summons to the Model Parliament of 1295 entitled its recipient and his successors to
an hereditary peerage, and consequently to a special writ of
summons to every succeeding parliament until his lineage

[1] T. E. Scrutton, *The Land in Fetters*, p. 76.
[2] McIlwain, p. 266.

was extinct; and that if a commoner can to-day prove himself to be the eldest male descendant in the eldest male line of any one who has since 1295 been specially summoned to and taken his seat in a parliament, he becomes thereby entitled to a peerage of the United Kingdom and his blood is ennobled for ever.

Before we proceed to examine this tissue of legal fiction and its bearing upon the history of parliament, it may be well to enter a plea on behalf of the committee of privileges which advises the house of lords on peerage cases. Every one of the distinguished lawyers who constitute that court is perfectly aware by this time that this rule is based on a mass of historical falsehood; he will none the less be bound in conscience to enforce it as the law. For the law takes little cognisance of historical fact until the fact has been interpreted by the law; and then the interpretation becomes both fact and law. Once the interpretation has been accepted, the historical fact or fiction upon which it was originally based becomes irrelevant; and no amount of historical investigation can affect the law. It is the law of the land that any one who proves himself the heir of a magnate of 1295 is entitled to a peerage. Not even the crown can debar him from it; and the court is bound to enforce that law. It is also apparently bound to do far greater violence to historical truth, to interpret historic facts of the fourteenth century in the light of a law that was not evolved till the seventeenth, and to assume that when Edward I or Edward II summoned a man by special writ to a parliament he intended to create an hereditary peerage. From the point of view of the court it is entirely irrelevant to prove that Edward I would not have known what the phrase " hereditary peerage " meant, that he never created or intended to create one in his life, that scores of barons summoned by special writ to one parliament were not summoned again, and that no one for more than a century after Edward I's death dreamt of claiming a right to a peerage at all.

All this would be merely historical fact; to impress the

court one must show that this historical fact had been interpreted as law. It is fortunate for the peerage that the house of lords can take no cognisance of historical fact which conflicts with its own judicial interpretations. If the house of lords says a commoner is a peer, he is a peer, however inadequate or erroneous its reasons may have been. A peerage adjudged to a claimant on the strength of a forged pedigree is not forfeited by the subsequent proof of the forgery. A peerage adjudged to the heir general on the strength of the presumption that it was created by writ of summons is not forfeited by the subsequent discovery of letters patent limiting its descent to the heirs male; for no writs of error lie against the house of lords, interpretation supersedes the fact, and the law is superior to history. This, indeed, is common sense; *quod non fieri debuit, factum valet*. Much of the law of England might disappear altogether if its legality depended upon the historical accuracy of the claims to peerage possessed by those who voted for it; and the legal foundations of the English church itself would no longer be secure if the validity of Elizabeth's act of uniformity could be shaken by attacking the pedigrees of three of the peers who constituted the majority in its favour.

We are not, however, here concerned with the legal validity of the lords' decisions, except to point out that the law of the peerage is not historical evidence, and that judicial theories are as irrelevant to historical investigation as historical fact is to legal decisions. The lawyer is bound by judicial decisions which are more important than evidence; the historian is free. A judge can make law in a sense in which the historian cannot make history. It might indeed be contended that historians have been responsible for not less fiction than the courts of law; but there is a difference. The fiction of the courts becomes a binding law; the fiction of the historian only entertains the student. It is only when history is merged in theology that pontifical utterances are considered decisive of historical problems. It is not the historian's function to wear the black cap or to speak *ex cathedra;* his opinion constitutes neither a sentence nor a dogma, and there are no penalties for contempt of court.

The fictions of the courts and of the crown are much more serious matters. *Solus princeps*, runs a legal maxim, *fingit quod in rei veritate non est;*[1] supreme capacity for fiction is an attribute of sovereign power. Sometimes it seems more like the last resort of weakness, and some of the fictions of the crown have proved an ever-present help in time of trouble. Such were the rules that an allegation of the crown could not be traversed, and that only those things were " records " which the crown could call to mind. The memory of the crown became the evidence for the fact. But it had in time to share its privileges with the peers and to acquiesce in the distribution of its sovereign power; and peerage law is not a fiction of the crown, but the invention of the house of lords.

None of the lords' decisions have, however, summed up quite so briefly so much absurdity as the popular ,phrase " blue blood." It would hardly be worth while examining the fantastic implications of this expression of the theory of peerage, had it not been seriously defended by the latest historian of the house of lords, who writes with intimate knowledge of many aspects of peerage history. " The doctrine," says Mr. Pike,[2] " is no absurdity at all, but one which is perfectly intelligible, perfectly consistent with itself at all points, and as scientific as anything to be found in medieval or modern literature." Neither medieval nor modern literature is perhaps the place to look for science, and it may be that this pronouncement is not intended to be so portentous as it appears. The obvious criticism, that the blood of the younger sons of a peer is just as blue as that of their eldest brother, and yet does not make them peers, is met by the explanation that the doctrine of blue blood, properly understood, does not mean that blueness of blood in itself made its fortunate possessor a peer, but makes him capable of inheriting a peerage. This may be

[1] Maitland, *Collected Papers*, iii. 310.
[2] *Const. History of the House of Lords*, pp. 141 *sqq.*

comforting to a considerable number of Englishmen; for
there are some thousands of living descendants of our kings; [1]
and there must be hundreds of thousands descended from
the younger sons of peers. They are commoners none the
less, and the blueness of their blood gives them no legal
or political distinction whatsoever. If this is all that is
meant by this perfectly scientific doctrine, it has nothing to
do with peerage. For there is no mistake about a peer;
the legal and political distinctions between him and a commoner are clear and sharp enough, and they can be acquired
without any pretence to blueness of blood. Moreover, in
the middle ages the husband of a peeress in her own right,
although himself a commoner, was often summoned by
special writ to parliaments. Mr. Pike himself quotes the
case of Ralph de Monthermer, who was summoned as Earl
of Gloucester and Hereford in the right of his wife, but lost
to her son the right to be summoned when that son came
of age.[2] He seems to have enjoyed that strange anomaly,
a temporary lease of blueness of blood ! Into such vagaries
can people be betrayed by mixing a physiological term like
blood with law and politics. Titles to peerage have been
decided, not by blueness of blood, but by royal writs and
judicial decisions. If it pleases people to think that their
blood was turned blue by a writ of summons or letters
patent, and made red again by attainder, there is no harm
in the superstition; but it need not concern the student of
the history of the peerage.

There are two serious problems to be considered. Firstly,
what is " peerage," and how did it develop ? And secondly,
how did it come to enjoy its present position in parliament ?
The two are distinct questions, for there is no necessary
connexion between peers and parliaments, at any rate not
in the modern sense of the peerage. But the word itself
has passed through the whole gamut of meaning, from its

---

[1] See Joseph Foster, *The Royal Lineage of our Noble and Gentle Families*,
1883.
[2] Elsynge, *Modus*, pp. 39, 55; Pike, *Const. History of the House of Lords*,
pp. 70-2. He was subsequently summoned as Baron Monthermer in his
own right.

etymological sense of " equal " to its modern implications of privilege. In the earliest Anglo-Norman legal terminology it simply denoted equality. Co-heiresses were said to be *pares* in respect of their father's inheritance, because all inherited equal shares; a villein was described as the " peer " of other villeins holding of the same lord. There were, in fact, all sorts of peers; we read of " peers of the county," and " peers of the borough "; Valenciennes had twelve peers, so had Lille, and Rouen had a hundred in the time of King John.[1] The *Modus Tenendi Parliamentum* implies that every member of a parliament was a peer, by dividing the whole assembly into *sex gradus parium*, clerical proctors, knights, and burgesses, as well as prelates and magnates.

But even before the Norman Conquest a limitation begins to be attached to the meaning of " peer " on the continent, a limitation arising out of its frequent association with the words *judicium* and *judicare*. Under Charles the Bald in 856 and Conrad the Salic in 1037 we find it stated that men are to be judged *per pares suos* or *secundum judicium parium suorum;*[2] and in England from Henry I to Magna Carta we have constant references to the principle *quisque judicandus est per pares suos et ejusdem provinciæ.* Peer, baron, and judge come to be used as almost synonymous terms, though where a vassal speaks of his " peers " the king speaks of his " barons," because the king has no peer in his kingdom. By this time only those are peers who are equal to judgement, and this excludes the majority; *villani vero*, Glanvill tells us, *non sunt inter legum judices numerandi.*[3] This is the meaning of " peers " at the time of Magna Carta. The idea that *judicium parium* in that famous document meant trial by jury has been too often exploded to need further comment.[4] But it is material to our purpose to point out that judgement by one's equals meant that one was not to be judged by inferiors; it did not in the least mean

---

[1] L. Vernon Harcourt, *His Grace the Steward and Trial by Peers*, pp. 226-7.

[2] *Ibid.*, pp. 205-6.

[3] *Ibid.*, p. 207.

[4] Cf. McKechnie, *Magna Carta*, 1905, pp. 158-63, 456-8.

that one was not to be judged by superiors.[1]   Our criminals
are not the peers of our judges; and every lord of a manor
could judge his villeins.

The " peers " are thus already a privileged class; they
possess the right to be judged by their fellow-vassals in the
king's court, and the right to judge their villeins in their own.[2]
They are also becoming hereditary, for these privileges are
always attached to the tenure of land, and the tenure of
land, though at first a mere life interest conditioned by service,
grows more and more into irresponsible property.   This
process was accelerated by the creation of strict entails
under Edward I.   Estates now passed from father to son by
right of heredity, and with the estates the privilege of exercising judgement, which seems to be the essential factor in peerage.   By the end of Edward's reign England may fairly be
said to have had an hereditary peerage.

But this peerage has as yet little to do with parliament.
There are many hundreds, possibly thousands, of these
" pares," but Edward I summons less than a hundred magnates by special writ to parliament.   Those who sit in
parliament have no hereditary claim to do so.   The word
" peer " does not occur in the " Rolls of Parliaments " for
his reign, and it is not mentioned in his writs.   It does not
entitle any one to a special writ of summons, though
probably every " peer " was either summoned in person or
included among those from whom the sheriff required
obedience to the general writs.   But the " peers " still
numbered their thousands, and included the lesser as well
as the greater barons.   It is clear, however, that the process
of limitation, begun by the restriction of " peerage " to those
who could " judge," was proceeding apace in the thirteenth
century; and the problem is to bridge the gulf between the
numbers of " peers " entitled by Magna Carta to judge and
be judged by their equals, and the smaller but still indefinite

---

[1] " Assisiæ vero tenentur per barones et legales homines.   Par per
parem judicari debet; barones igitur et milites, legis statuta scientes et
Deum timentes possunt judicare unus alium et subditum eis populum;
rustico enim non licet, vel aliis de populo, militem vel clericum judicare"
(Glanvill; cf. Pollock and Maitland, i. 173; Vernon Harcourt, pp. 207,
214; *History*, April, 1920, pp. 33–5).

[2] Elsynge, *Modus*, p. 9.

number of "peers" who develop into a parliamentary force under Edward II. The question is closely connected with the change in the *magnum concilium*. By what process were the thousands of tenants who are presumed to have gathered on Salisbury Plain in 1086, reduced to the "magnates" who gathered at Oxford in 1258? Or, in other words, how was the line drawn between the greater barons entitled by Magna Carta to a special writ and the lesser barons summoned in general through the sheriff? For it is clear that the term *pares* tends to be restricted to the greater barons; and the same question might be put in yet another form: what is the social and legal difference between one who holds a barony and one who simply holds by barony, or between one who holds *per baroniam* and one who holds *per servitium militare?* The answer to any one of these questions should supply answers to all the others; for the holder of a barony receives a special writ of summons, becomes a magnate and then a modern peer. Even those who hold, not *baronias integras*, but *per baroniam*, are liable to the summons; for, whatever "barony" may have been, it implied a special jurisdiction and a special obligation to the crown which conferred it.

Now it is obvious that the thousands who took the Sarum oath to William the Conqueror did not all hold baronies, and it may be doubted whether any definition of a barony had yet been evolved.[1] But they were all the king's men, his barons, and they held their lands in chief by military service. The lands might be great or they might be small; the extent would not affect the nature of the tenure, but it would affect the political value and importance of the tenant. Before long there is a distinction between barons and knights;[2] both hold by the same military tenure-in-chief, but some are the king's barons, while others are only

---

[1] Cf. Elsynge, p. 51.

[2] The term "miles" or "knight" is here used in its feudal sense, in which it implied tenure by military service. Later on, in the days of chivalry, it became a *nomen et honor*, conferring a military and social distinction without any reference to the tenure of land, just as, in still later days, "peerages" came to be created without any reference to tenure-in-chief of the crown. Barons were even knighted, so completely did the later idea supersede the feudal principle.

knights.   Later there is a further distinction among the
barons themselves; some are greater and some are less, and
the lesser barons are lost among the knights.   By the time
that the *Modus* is compiled, a rule has been elaborated by
the king's exchequer to distinguish barons from knights;
the baron is the holder of a barony, and a barony is thirteen
and one-third knights' fiefs.[1]   Now a knight's fee is calculated
at five hides, and if a barony was thirteen and a third times
as much, it was two-thirds of a hundred hides.   It is
merely a guess that such an extent of land may have
entitled a barony to be regarded as a private hundred
possessing the jurisdiction usually connected with that unit
of organization.   But it does not appear entirely fanciful to
conjecture that the individual holder of extensive lands was
regarded as being entitled to special immunities, such as
the right to exclude the sheriff from his barony, and exemption for himself and his tenants from attendance at the shire
court, just as individual boroughs in later times achieved
the status of counties.   These and greater privileges had
been granted to the earlier " honours," but from 1176, when
Henry II insisted that no "honour" should exclude the royal
judges, there is said to have been little distinction between
an " honour " and a barony; and it is probable that these
two kinds of " liberty " or " franchise " approximated.
For baronies tended to be reduced in number and increased
in size and dignity.   Some fell into abeyance between
co-heiresses; others were accumulated in single hands by
marriage and inheritance.   The process which concentrated
five earldoms in the hands of Thomas of Lancaster operated
also in the case of baronies.

Now, while the grant of immunity from the shire court
would not prevent the baron from attending if he chose,
frequent complaints in the thirteenth century of the difficulty
of holding shire courts owing to the number of " liberties "
granted by the king [2] indicate that voluntary attendance

---

[1] Stubbs, *Charters*, 1900, p. 503.

[2] In the " Petition of the Barons," presented at Oxford in 1258, they
complain of the difficulty of taking grand assizes owing to the numerous
exemptions granted to knights by the king (§ 28), while they (§ 17) attack
the sheriffs for requiring the personal attendance of the earls and barons.

was rare; and a rough division of labour and liability seems to have been in practice established. Lesser barons, who had to attend the shire court, were only summoned by a general writ to Westminster, the practical effect of which was probably a licence to stay away, and afterwards they were permitted to excuse themselves by sending a couple of representatives. But the greater barons, who escaped the duties of the shire court, were at least liable to a special writ of summons to parliament; and it is probable that the divergence between knights and barons which had so powerful an effect upon the organization and growth of parliament, had its root in an earlier separation in the shires. The barons held aloof from the local business of the people, while the knights busied themselves with its conduct; and habits of co-operation and of management contracted in the shires were perpetuated in the national business of parliament.

Whatever its cause and method of operation, this discrimination between greater and lesser barons effected a change in the *magnum concilium*. If that name is properly applied to the concourse on Salisbury Plain, the adjective clearly applies to the numbers who attended, and not to their individual greatness. For baron at first means nothing but " man "; and *baron et femme* is the regular Norman-French for " man and wife." But in process of time the *magnum concilium* became a small gathering of great men rather than a great gathering of small men. Greatness, not tenure-in-chief, constitutes the right or the liability to a special writ of summons to the *magnum concilium*, which in the reigns of Henry III and Edward II seems to have been a council of magnates. It is significant that during the interval of Edward I's strong rule, the adjective disappears from the council. His council is a royal and not an oligarchic council; its personnel depends upon royal writs and not upon feudal privilege, and attendance is a matter of obligation and not of right. But the idea of right has grown up in resistance to the centralizing policy of Henry II, the tyranny of John, and the alien misgovernment of Henry III; and it is only for a time that Edward I can check the aristocratic claims of the greater barons to limit the royal authority and participate in the control of national affairs. The contest centres round the council, its composition, and its powers. Is it to be a council of magnates based on baronial rights, or a council of royal advisers dependent upon the crown? This is the issue between Edward II and Thomas of Lancaster, and it is during that struggle that peerage makes its *début* as a constitutional force in parliament.

Naturally it sought to base itself upon precedent, and the *judicium parium* of Magna Carta formed a considerable part of the political stock-in-trade of the baronial party. They appealed to it as to fundamental law, which bound the high court of parliament itself; a judgement or act which contravened Magna Carta was regarded as *ipso facto* void.[1] But every political party falsifies history in its appeal to precedent, and the *judicium parium* of Magna Carta was magnified and transformed under the stress of political exigencies into a new political principle. Its germ may no doubt be found in Magna Carta, and even in 1215 there may have been more in the minds of the barons who talked about judgement by peers than its purely legal application. Without plunging into the vortex of the discussion, which has vexed courts of law as well as historians, about the meaning of *vel* in the famous phrase of Magna Carta,[2] *per judicium parium suorum vel per legem terræ*, we may perhaps indicate a preference for the disjunctive interpretation, and hold that in the minds of the barons there was a clear and important antithesis between *lex terræ*—the custom of the country—and *judicium parium*—a more or less novel royal expedient or baronial safeguard.[3] Henry II had invented or applied

---

[1] Edward I's *Confirmatio Cartarum* declared void all future judgements against Magna Carta, and the declaration was repeated in Stat. 42 Ed. III, c. 1 (1368).

[2] Cf. McKechnie, *Magna Carta*, pp. 442–3; Vernon Harcourt, p. 224; Pollock and Maitland, i. 152 *n.* It may not be presumptuous to remark that *vel* is always disjunctive, but that sometimes it differentiates things and sometimes only words. That does not, however, help us with *judicium parium vel lex terræ*, because the whole dispute is whether those are two different things or merely two descriptions of the same.

[3] While *lex* is the custom of the country, a *judicium* is a particular sentence or "doom," and "doom" is perhaps the best translation; doomsday is the day of judgement. The ordeal and trial by battle were parts of the *lex*, but the result of any particular ordeal or combat would be a *judicium*, a *verum judicium Dei*.

to England a number of new-fangled legal methods which were certainly no part of the customary law of the land; and one at least of the motives of Magna Carta was to protect the barons against the abuse, if not also against the use of Henry II's expedients. The ancient laws or customs the barons did not impugn, but they would have none of these novel *judicia* except with their consent. The crown was not to be free to devise judicial methods and enforce them by judges who were no better than royal servants; if there were to be innovations, the barons must consent to their institution or at least participate in their application.

A case in the reign of Edward I may illustrate their point of view. A baron objected to the king's judges that they were not proceeding against him *per legem terræ ;* the judges admitted the fact, but thought it no bar to their action. They were proceeding by royal mandate, *per speciale mandatum regis*, we might say in later legal language.[1] It was to bar such proceedings that the principle of *judicium parium* expanded with the growth of royal jurisdiction. The crown was ever pronouncing new decisions, and chancery devising novel writs.[2] These things were no part of the *lex ;* they were therefore not to be done except *per judicium parium.* Even acts of parliament were not *leges*, but the *judicia* of a court. The law was begetting politics, and the privilege of peerage overflowed from the one sphere into the other. The invasion was all the more easy because the frontiers had not yet been fixed; a resolution of the king in council to make war on a vassal was a *judicium super eum ire*,[3] and every legislative act was also a *judicium. Judicium parium* was a principle that might be applied in every sphere of public affairs, and the veto of the house of lords has a pedigree stretching back to Magna Carta.

But the more widely the principle was extended, the

[1] Vernon Harcourt, pp. 281, 301; but the phrase is used in Edward III's reign (*Rot. Parl.*, ii. 266).
[2] Maitland (*Collected Papers*, ii. 155) mentions the existence of 471 different kinds of original writs in Edward I's reign, compared with fifty or sixty in 1227.
[3] At least so says Vernon Harcourt, p. 248.

narrower grew the class which benefited by its operation. The *pares* of Magna Carta may have been few compared with the total population, but they were a multitude compared with the peers by whom and in whose interests Edward II was to be deprived of royal authority. The reign of Edward I was treated as an interlude, and the barons reverted to the inter-regnum of the Barons' Wars. But they had no Simon de Montfort among them, and showed no desire to share their counsels with knights of the shire or burgesses. They had, however, some notions of their own which had not occurred to authors of the Provisions of Oxford; and it is at this crisis that we first read about peers " de la terre " used in a sense somewhat nearer to its modern signification than the *pares* of Magna Carta.

The phrase is stated to have first been used in 1322 in the charges of " the prelates, earls, and barons, and the other peers of the land and the commons of the realm " against the two Despencers.[1] But there is an earlier instance of the use of the phrase in the indenture drawn up between Edward II and Lancaster at Leake in August 1318.[2] This agreement provides for the attendance at council of two bishops, one earl, a baron, and a banneret of Lancaster's household, on Lancaster's behalf, and stipulates that if the earl's representatives disagreed with any resolution of the council, *soit tenuz por nient et adresce en parlement par agard des pieres, et totes choses convenables soient redressez par eux.* The later reference lays a good deal of stress on the *pieres de la terre;* the phrase occurs five times in the document. Judgement by peers is no longer a mere protection against the legal innovations of the crown; it has been erected into the principle that they are to judge the acts of the crown and its ministers. Impeachment already looms upon the horizon.

[1] Pike, p. 157, citing the Close Roll of 14 Edward II, membrane 14, printed in *Statutes of the Realm,* i. 181-4. The fourteenth year of Edward II, however, ran from July 1320 to July 1321.

[2] *Rot. Parl.,* i. 453-5. The entry runs "escrit a Leek le ix jour d'Augst l'an du regne du dit Roi Edward duzieme," and it was read and examined at the York parliament of Oct. 1318. The entry is printed in the *Rot. Parl.* from the Close Roll of 12 Ed. II, m. 22 dorso.

This use of the word " peers " in the reign of Edward II is limited to the Lancastrians; no royal clerk or royalist partisan seems to employ it, and it obviously expresses a political theory held by the opposition. Its adoption by Lancaster in the proceedings against the Despencers recalls the insistence by the Lords Ordainers upon the " baronage " in their attacks upon Gaveston.[1] Peerage is a principle used to support the magnates in resistance to the crown, and *par agard des pieres* takes in 1318–22 the place of the *par agard del baronage* of 1311. It was naturally selected by the opposition because the " peers " had grown to be independent of the king; they could hardly pretend to independence so long as they were tenants-at-will of the crown and called themselves barons. But hereditary tendencies culminating in strict entails had rendered the lords of the land secure; and lords, seigneurs, barons, and peers of the land come to be used as synonymous terms to express a landed aristocracy striving for political supremacy. Their claims reach their high-water mark in the ordinances of 1311. The king is not to leave the realm, declare war, appoint judges or ministers, keepers of castles or wardens of ports without the assent of his baronage; and the royal authority is put in commission among the " peers."

But we are still some distance from the modern peerage, and even when clerks of chancery are constrained to write of peers in Edward III's reign they leave a very vague impression of the meaning of the word. That it was not the modern meaning is clear from the most cursory inspection of the " Rolls of Parliaments " wherein the clerk often writes of " prelates, earls, barons, and their peers," but never limits the peers to prelates, earls, and barons.[2] The vagueness of the phrase is illustrated by the fact that it was possible for a not unlearned clerk of the parliaments in the seventeenth century to maintain that the peers of the realm were not the earls or barons, but the bannerets, who were not infre-

---

[1] *Rot. Parl.*, i. 281 ff.
[2] Cf. *Rot. Parl.*, ii. 53 : " Lesqueux countes, barouns, et peres," and " peres, countes, et barouns."

quently summoned by special writs to parliament.[1] This introduces an unwarrantable precision into the terminology of the fourteenth century, but there is no doubt that bannerets were included in the category of those who are described as peers of the prelates, earls, and barons. Earls and barons were peers, but others were peers as well,[2] and the clearest indication of who these others were is afforded by the grant, in January 1339–40, of a tenth to the king by the earls and barons for themselves and for their peers of the land who hold by barony.[3] Just as in Anglo-Saxon times there were men who were " thegnworthy " without being thegns, so in the fourteenth century there were men who, without being earls or barons, were their peers. From a passage in the *Modus* we might infer that this line of peerage was determined by the possession of thirteen and a third knights' fees;[4] but the inference would not be safe. There are instances of men possessing less than a single knight's fee being summoned by special writ to parliament, and before long Richard II will create peers by letters patent without any reference to the lands they hold. In any case this peerage constituted a liability rather than a right; and just as the tenure of a ha'porth of land, as Bracton says,[5] by military tenure rendered the tenant liable to feudal incidents, so it rendered him liable to a special writ of summons to the king's high court. It gave him no right to such a summons; but if it were sent, he could not disobey unless he could prove that he held no land *per baroniam*.[6]

[1] H. Elsynge, *The Manner of Holding Parliaments*, ed. 1768, pp. 43–8, 79. Selden (*Judicature in Parliaments*, p. 159) writes of earls, barons, and " baronets " assembled in the parliament of 1386; and the roll of 1513 has " every other baron, baronet, and baroness " (*Lords' Journals*, i. p. xxvi.), where baronet seems to be the eldest son of a baron. For other uses and the confusion of banneret and baronet, see *N. E. D.*

[2] Earls, barons, and peers are all summarily referred to (*Rot. Parl.*, ii. 53) as " lesdits peres."   [3] *Ibid.*, ii. 107.

[4] Stubbs, *Charters*, p. 503 : " item summoneri et venire debent omnes et singuli comites et barones *et eorum pares*, scilicet illi qui habent . . . tresdecim feoda et tertiam partem unius feodi militis." The poet Spenser thought these *pares* of the earls and barons were baronets; see *N. E. D.*, s.v. " Baronet."   [5] Pollock and Maitland, i. 257.

[6] *Rot. Parl.*, ii. 132, 139. Nevertheless, recipients of special writs of summons did occasionally claim exemption on the ground that they held, not a barony, but only *per baroniam*.

There were, therefore, many peers, but not every one who called himself a peer was called to parliament. Nor is the word officially used as a normal description of those who received a special writ of summons. Its correct employment is with reference to judicial proceedings, to trial by peers of their equals. It is then that the peers most insist on their peerage; as peers they are there in the king's high court for judicial purposes only. When political matters are under discussion, it is not as peers that they act, but as lords of the council in parliament, and they are described as prelates, earls, barons *et autres grantz* or magnates. The king still holds his court in his council in his parliaments; its duties are multifarious, and so are the parts of its members. When they sit in judgement they act as peers, when they advise the crown in matters of administration they are councillors, and in time both these functions will be obscured by their third capacity as legislators. This is not the view of the " peers " themselves. In their own eyes they are peers above everything; and in all their petitions, whatever their purport, they call themselves " peers." They speak of the statutes made by the king, peers, and the commons;[1] they demand that the chancellor and the treasurer should always be " peers." They won in the end, but it is not until after the close of the middle ages that " peers " became a regular term for the lords in parliament; and it never became a correct and exhaustive description of those who sat in the house of lords.

Nor did the use of the term in the least imply that even when trial of peers was the business of parliament, any peer had a right to be present. Some peers must participate in order to make the trial a trial by peers; and presumably all the " peers " who had received a special writ to a parliament were entitled to sit when parliament tried a peer. These peers gradually, too, asserted the principle that no one who was not a peer, even though he had received a special writ, was entitled to judge a peer. The prelates ceased to take part in judicial proceedings, not so much

[1] *Rot. Parl.*, ii. 140.

perhaps because their " peerage " was doubtful as because their holy orders forbade the shedding of blood; and the trial of peers in parliament was always on capital charges. The exclusion of the judges, or rather their reduction to the position of assistant advisers without a vote, substantiated the old claim of the barons that the king's judges and barons of the exchequer were not their peers and could not judge them. But the old claim was vastly extended; and the inferiority of the judges, admitted when the lords sat to try their peers, was also enforced by degrees when the lords sat in their other capacities, as a council and as a house of parliament. The fact that the judges could not perform one of the functions of the king's court in his council in parliaments was eventually held to debar them from performing the others; and ultimately the principle that a man should only be tried by his peers was distorted into the notion that peers, and peers only, could vote in the house of lords. By a like perversion the trial of men by *their* peers sometimes became their trial by *the* peers. This was not an infringement of Magna Carta, because none of its clauses forbade trial by one's superiors. The peers' jurisdiction, too, was limited to crimes against Magna Carta.[1] But even with this limitation their claim was a usurpation. It is true that in 1330 they protested that as peers they were not bound to try Simon Burford, who was not their peer. Yet as " judges of the parliament " they, with the assent of the king, sentenced him also as a traitor.[2] This, they admit, was against the law, and ultimately it was established that the participation of the commons as the grand inquest of the nation was essential to the trial of commoners by the peers and to their condemnation by act of attainder.[3]

[1] In 1311 the Ordinances also included the Confirmation of the Charters and the Ordinances themselves among the laws, the breach of which was to be tried by the barons in parliament; and in 1341 the peers wanted to include the " liberties of holy church " and the Charter of the Forests (*Rot. Parl.*, i. 285, ii. 126).

[2] *Rot. Parl.*, ii. 53*b*.

[3] *Year Book*, 4 Henry VII, p. 18 : " en le parlement le roy voule que un tiel soit attaint et perde ses terres, et les seigneurs assentent, et rien fuit parle des comons. Purquoi touts les justices tenent clerement que ceo ne fuit acte. Purquoi il fuit restore," etc.

H

We are still, however, far from a house of lords in the reign of Edward III, and the lords of parliament are still for the most part lords of the council. But the reign of Edward II had permanent effects upon the constitution, and Edward III never reduced the magnates to their insignificance under Edward I. The " Rolls " are replete with references to the *magnum concilium*, which has entrenched itself in the heart of parliament, and the " council" which the king holds in his parliaments is now the *magnum concilium;* the *camera magni concilii* has become the "parliament chamber." The process is very obscure, but one or two points emerge. It is clear that the magnates have mastered the council. In 1315 parliamentary pleas are held *coram magno concilio*, and answers are given *coram rege et magno concilio*, instead of *coram concilio*, as in the reign of Edward I. In the following year the chancellor, judges, and other members of the council report to the king *quod non audebant dictum negotium diffinire nec eidem domino regi super hoc consulere sine assensu magnatum de regno propter difficultatem et raritatem negotii supradicti;* and they recommended its reference to either a parliament or a *convocatio magnatum de regno*.[1] " Great councils " continued to be summoned for centuries after the organization of the Model Parliament, and they were a favourite expedient with the Lancastrians.[2] But here we are concerned with "the king's great council in parliament"[3] which gave its name to the "parliament chamber," and eventually became the house of lords.

That it is still primarily a king's council is clear from the facts that no principle upon which a " peer " could claim a right to be summoned had been established. Indeed, there seems to be no instance in the middle ages of any one claiming a right to be summoned at all; and it cannot be

[1] *Rot. Parl.*, i. 354a.
[2] See Nicolas, *Proc. of Privy Council*, i. 17, 102, 144, 156, ii. 85–9, 156, iv. 105, 185–6, 225, v. 64, 108, vi. 214, 290, 298, 333, 339. Their object was often probouleutic, such as to decide whether or not a parliament should be called. But in the fifteenth century they were not confined to magnates; about half the prelates, earls, and barons summoned to parliament were usually summoned to a great council, but sometimes they were reinforced by half a dozen knights or esquires from each county (*ibid.*, i. 156).
[3] *Ibid.*, iv. 185.

too often emphasized that even to-day peerage does not
in itself constitute a right to sit and vote in the house of
lords; it has been held to constitute a right to a summons,
but it is the writ of summons that constitutes the title to
sit and vote, and in the middle ages the issue of this writ
was a matter within the discretion of the crown. The
reason why some abbots sit and others do not is simply
that it has become the custom of chancery to summon one
and not the other. The abbot who is not summoned never
dreams of claiming a summons; he has no right to a summons,
and a baron is in the same position. A mere glance at the
number of those who were summoned at different times
will show that the receipt of a writ depended upon the discretion or caprice of the crown and not upon hereditary
right.[1] To the parliament of 1295 Edward I summoned
forty-one barons, to that of 1300 he summoned ninety-nine.
To the parliament of 1321 Edward II summoned ninety, to
that of 1322 he summoned fifty-two. To the parliament
of 1333–4 Edward III summoned sixty-three barons, to
that of 1346–7 he summoned only thirty, but to that
of 1347–8 he summoned fifty-six. No natural cause
like that of death will explain these violent fluctuations;
and the barons who received a special writ of summons
under Edward I and Edward II were not reduced to half
their number by extinction of their heirs. Whatever the
house of lords may, in defiance of history, have made law
in the nineteenth century, there was no idea in the fourteenth
or fifteenth that a baron summoned to one parliament must
needs be called to another, or that a writ of summons created
a " peerage " transmissible by descent. A peerage, indeed,
is not a term which a medieval lawyer would have understood; [2] he knew that an earldom meant an office, the tenure
of which always involved a special writ of summons to parlia-

---

[1] Palgrave's published *Parliamentary Writs* only cover the reigns of
Edward I and Edward II, but his MS. lists, preserved in the Public
Record Office, go on into the fifteenth century; cf. Maitland, *Memoranda*,
p. xxxv; and Pike, pp. 96–100. For later lists of "peers" summoned see
47th *Report of the Deputy-Keeper of the Records*, pp. 79–83.
[2] Murray's *N. E. D.* gives no instance earlier than 1671 of the use of
the word to indicate a dignity; nor is "the peerage," meaning the body of
peers, found before 1454.

ment; he believed that a barony meant the tenure-in-chief of an amount of land, or more probably rights of jurisdiction, if not an office, which involved at least a liability to that summons. But in the reign of Charles II it was decided that the tenure of a barony did not involve the possession of a " peerage " or a right to a special writ of summons to parliament; [1] and assuredly no such right existed in the middle ages. There were many heirs in Edward III's reign of barons summoned by special writ to parliament under Edward I or Edward II, who received no writ of summons themselves and never thought of claiming it as a right.[2] The law of " peerage " is a modern monument of legal fiction. At the end of the middle ages Fortescue talks enough about lords spiritual and temporal, but he never calls them peers, and the word does not occur in the " Rolls of Parliaments " for the reign of Henry VII, or in the " Journals " for several succeeding reigns. Nor does Sir Thomas Smith, who wrote under Elizabeth, use the term. Peerage had been a juridical concept in Magna Carta; under Edward II it was turned by a limited class to political purposes; but the vogue of hereditary peerage as a foundation of the constitution is a modern growth born of antagonism to Stuart and then to democratic principles. To Fortescue the barons are not an independent " peerage," but councillors of the crown, bound to give advice when asked, but not entitled to enforce it.

It is easy, too, to exaggerate the meaning of *natus* in Fortescue's statement that the lords are *consiliarii nati* to the king; for he expressly includes lords spiritual as well as temporal, and every archbishop of Canterbury and of York was *legatus natus* of the pope. It is clear that a lord spiritual was not a councillor of the crown, nor the archbishop legate of the pope, by hereditary right; and Fortescue's statement that the lords are councillors " by

---

[1] Cruise, *Dignities*, 2nd ed., p. 66; the question was not, however, finally settled until the Berkeley peerage case in 1861; see below, p. 307 *n*.

[2] For instance the Ughtreds (*D. N. B.*, lviii. 16*a*), Umfravilles (*D. N. B.*, lviii. 23*b*), Dynhams (G. E. C.'s *Complete Peerage*, ed. Gibbs, iv. 371–9). Not a few of these " peers " of modern theory acted as sheriffs or sat in the house of commons.

reason of their baronies and estates," clearly implies that they are councillors in virtue of their feudal relation to the king and not of their blood relation to their ancestors. The barony, indeed, has become hereditary, but the bishopric has not, and the bishop or archbishop is just as much *consiliarius natus* or *legatus natus* as the baron. The right or the duty to give counsel seems to be innate in the dignity rather than in the individual or in the blood; the spiritual lord ceased to be *consiliarius natus* when he resigned his bishopric and the temporal lord when he lost his barony. Ralph de Monthermer became *consiliarius natus* when he married the Countess of Gloucester and ceased to be such when her son came of age.

Nevertheless, the barons, who in the reign of Henry III had merely claimed to be the king's " natural " councillors, as distinguished from unnatural aliens,[1] begin in time to claim, as " hereditary " councillors, an indefeasible right to a seat in parliament. The mere routine of chancery clerks tended to stereotype a list of barons to whom a special writ was sent. It was easier for officials to address the writs as before than to pick and choose. They could hardly vary the list of barons or abbots, whom it was usual to summon, on their own authority; and even the strongest kings developed a respect for chancery forms. Chancery, too, was further removed by the growth of the privy seal from the caprice of the crown; and when a Tudor required the absence of a lord from parliament, it was secured, not by withholding the writ of summons issued under the great seal of chancery, but by a more intimate injunction, under the privy seal or signet, not to obey it. From the third Edward to the third Richard, however, kings were concerned to secure the presence rather than the absence of their councillors in parliament. A crowded council betokened a vigorous government, and the lack of Lancastrian governance was betrayed by the absence of lords from the council in and out of parliament. Richard II imposed heavy fines on

[1] An alien, even though he held an English earldom, was not a *consiliarius natus* of the crown; see below, p. 273 *n.*

absentees,[1] and the dwindling number of barons summoned
to parliament was due to the inability of the crown to enforce,
and to the reluctance of the lords to meet, the obligation of
suit and service at the king's high court.   In 1433 the
crown could only extort even from its chief councillors an
undertaking to attend the council *non tamen continue sed
saltem tempore curiae*.[2]   Their ambition was not to sit as
lords of council or of parliament at Westminster, but to
rule as princes in the provinces; a special writ of summons
to parliament added nothing to the prestige of a Neville or
a Percy, and threatened an irksome distraction from more
local and more congenial occupations.

It was not for the writs of summons attached thereunto
that these lords of misrule sought dukedoms, marquisates,
earldoms, viscountcies, and baronies, but for the lands, pen-
sions, and other grants which accompanied the conferment
of these dignities.[3]   A seat in parliament only became an
object of ambition when parliament itself became a seat of
authority; and in the fifteenth century a writ of summons
was merely a disagreeable incident to baronial dignity.   It
was, however, becoming hereditary because strict entails
had made baronial tenure hereditary, and writs of summons
had become attached by custom to greater baronies.   This
association seemed to the crown to portend a baronial
tyranny; it tended to restrict the king's choice of counsellors,
because no one could be disseised of his barony save by the
judgement of his peers, and the *personnel* of the king's great
council was thus determined by them and not by the sovereign
they were to advise.[4]   The more rigid the custom grew of
sending writs to the earls and greater barons, the less scope
there was for the crown to summon others outside the limited

---

[1] Pike, p. 237.   [2] *Rot. Parl.*, iv. 446.
[3] It was the rule then for aspirants to receive and not to make
payments for their dignities.
[4] The loss of control over the great council was one of the causes which
led kings to develop a privy council immune from the limitations of baronial
and hereditary tenure, in somewhat the same way as the independence
of chancery, due to the growth of tradition and custom, led them to
devise the more intimate and personal machinery of the privy seal and
signet.

circle of territorial magnates. Richard II was naturally the first to find this limitation intolerable, and it was probably to escape it that he began the practice of creating barons and other peers by patent without reference to the lands they held. This practice saved the crown from a danger similar to that which was threatened by the peerage bill of 1719; it could create peers without being limited in its choice to the holders of great estates.

But the association of land tenure, and consequently of the hereditary principle, with peerage had been too long established to be eliminated; the baron created by patent was usually granted lands to support his dignity, and even to-day, when he is less fortunate, he commonly takes a territorial title. Nor did the creation of peers bring lasting advantage to the crown: the new peer might be subservient to his creator, but his descendants had no such attachment to his creator's successors. The patents of Richard II and his successors asserted the principle of heredity against the implications of the writ of summons, for they were made out to the recipient and his heirs male, whereas writs of summons ignored the recipient's heirs altogether, and the transmission to heirs general has been a matter of judicial fiction. But the notion of councillorship is emphasized by the limitation of patents to heirs male. Lands might descend to females, but only males could counsel the crown. Nor is it certain that the creation of a barony, viscounty, marquisate, or dukedom by letters patent committed the king, and still less his successors, to the perennial issue of parliamentary writs of summons to the newly-created peer and to his heirs. Kings were jealous of circumscribing their discretion; even a statute, it was contended as late as the seventeenth century, made by one king did not bind his successors.[1] Letters patent were certainly not more binding than a statute, and they contained nothing about writs of

---

[1] Prothero, *Select Documents*, ed. 1898, p. 340. Baron Clarke's argument in Bates' case: "The statute (45 Ed. III, c. 4) extends only to the king himself, and shall not bind his successors, for it is a principal part of the crown of England, which the king cannot diminish."

summons, the right to which was by later generations read into the patent of creation.

These patents did, however, create hereditary dignities[1] to which a writ of summons to parliament came in common practice to be attached; and the development or perversion of the king's council in parliament into an hereditary house of lords is mysteriously connected with the growth of heraldry, which characterized the decline of the middle ages. The incorporation of the College of Arms by Richard III, the passion for pedigrees, the heralds' visitations, and the granting of arms (when they were losing their practical value) were all manifestations of a social evolution, the political and constitutional effects of which have not been properly explored. There is no mention of Garter king-of-arms[2] in any version of the *Modus Tenendi Parliamentum*, not even in that which the clerk of the parliaments prefixed to the *Journal* for 1510; but he figures largely in the pictures of parliament which date from the sixteenth century, and his functions were important. He preceded the newly-created peer when he came to take his seat, and presented his letters patent;[3] and Burghley once moved Garter's appointment to a committee of lords to determine questions of precedence.[4] Pedigrees, too, were recorded on the first writs of summons issued to peers on succession, and came to be regarded as an indefeasible title to the writ. The obsequiousness of the lords in parliament after the Wars of the Roses and the reduction of the prelates by Henry VIII blinded the Tudors to the growth of a strictly hereditary peerage which ultimately turned the tables on the crown.

The vogue of the phrase " hereditary peerage " involves,

---

[1] I have some doubts about the correctness of this customary phraseology. The dignity was created by the crown, and the letters patent were, like proclamations, merely the evidence of the fact and not the fact itself. The act was, moreover, often done by the crown in parliament; and it seems to have been merely an accident that these acts did not permanently become acts of parliament.

[2] First created, it is said, by Henry V.

[3] Elsynge, pp. 6, 8, 97–8.

[4] Townshend, *Historical Collections*, p. 83. The intrusion of Garter king into the high court of parliament is a portent of the subversion of the king's great council in parliament by the modern peerage.

however, some confusion of thought. The essence of the house of lords is not that it is based upon the principle of heredity like the old nobility of the continent, but upon the principle of primogeniture, which as the foundation of a legislative chamber was peculiar to England. There is a great deal of physiological truth underlying the current phrases about " good old stock," " in the blood," and so forth; but hereditary virtues have a trick of eluding eldest sons. There have been many illustrious sons of illustrious sires in English history, but they have rarely been the eldest. Queen Elizabeth was served by two great Cecils, and George III by two great Pitts; but the first Earl of Salisbury was not the eldest son of the great Lord Burghley, nor was William Pitt of the Earl of Chatham. Three of the five Tudors were among the greatest of English sovereigns, but not one of the three was the eldest son or eldest daughter of a king. A house selected from the sons of peers would have been an abler body than the house of eldest sons, and more hereditary virtue has enriched the house of commons than the house of lords. Primogeniture was given its peculiar and exclusive privilege in order to keep fiefs intact, and not from any belief in its efficacy in the transmission of wisdom. The special writ of summons became attached to great hereditary baronies because the consent of their holders was essential to the financial success of the king's proposals in parliament; and the principle of primogeniture was communicated from the barony to the special writ of summons.

The growth of this principle led to the depression of the simple councillors in parliament, and as early as Edward III's reign the judges were denied a vote, though not a voice, in the high court of parliament in which they sat. They become assessors or advisers; and while Sir Thomas More, as chancellor, presided over the lords' deliberations, participated in their discussions, and adjourned their sessions from day to day, he had no vote in their determinations. It was not, however, until comparatively modern times that the hereditary element became predominant in the house of lords. Down to the dissolution of the monasteries the non-hereditary spiritual peers constituted a majority; and until a considerably later period the bishops and newly-created peers outnumbered those who owed their writs of summons to heredity. There were sixty temporal peers when James I ascended the English throne; but he created fifty-four, and the bishops numbered twenty-six; and the eldest sons of peers had barely attained a majority in the house of lords when the Long Parliament abolished it as a dangerous and unnecessary institution. The house of lords, as it is known to-day, is the outcome of the Restoration.

CHAPTER VI

THE GROWTH OF THE HOUSE OF COMMONS

ALTHOUGH the " commons " were the last of the elements
to arrive in the thirteenth-century parliament, they have
suffered less subsequent change of position than the crown,
the judges, or the lords. The presence of the crown has,
except in theory, been limited to ceremonial occasions; most
of the judges of the high court have been excluded altogether;
and the lords of the council in parliament have been converted
into an hereditary peerage. The " commons," however, have
remained in many essentials what they were in the reign of
Edward III, when they shared with the crown the privilege
of being one of the two indispensable elements in a valid
parliament.[1] Then, as now, the essence of parliament was
parley between crown and commons, the government
and the governed. There were other factors than the
crown in the government, and other " estates " than the
commons among the governed; but they were minor ingredients. The distinguishing feature of the English parliament
is the junction it made between government and the people.
Not that the house of commons was ever that house of the
common people which it is sometimes supposed to have been.
For " commons " means " communes "; and while " communes " have commonly been popular organizations, the
term might in the thirteenth and fourteenth centuries be
applied to any association or confederacy.

Common action was, however, commoner among the
common people, because they had greater need than indi-
vidualistic barons of union for self-protection, and it was

---

[1] *Modus Tenendi Parliamentum* in Stubbs's *Select Charters*, p. 512.

only under the pressure of exceptional royal tyranny that barons borrowed the methods of association from the humbler townsfolk who first put the fear of " communism " into the hearts of privileged classes. A " commune," wrote a horrified monk of St. Swithun's when John, in the absence of Richard I, granted common self-government to London, *est tumor plebis, timor regni, tepor sacerdotii*,[1] which might be flippantly rendered in the vernacular, " a commune swells the people's head, terrifies royalty, and makes the clergy lukewarm." It was a popular conspiracy, and the chronicler doubtless had in mind those formidable communes of northern Italy which had humbled the pride of an emperor at Legnano. Monarchy in England was made of stouter stuff than the Holy Roman Empire ; but, if Richard of Devizes could have foreseen that " commune of communes," as the house of commons was called two centuries later, his prophetic soul might also have foreboded 1649 and 1688, when the commons became indeed a terror to royalty, and perhaps other occasions, both later and earlier, when they " put the clergy in a stew."

But the " communes " or " communitates," which gave their name to the house of commons, were lawful and orderly, comprehensive, but not democratic associations. They were simply the shires or counties of England, and the full county courts in which the knights of the shires were chosen did not include the " common " people. For villeins were not legally qualified to perform the judicial functions for which the courts were held. They did not attend as " suitors of the court," and they were only represented in the sense in which the lord of the manor was held to represent his tenants without any choice or election on their part. Even the freeholders who possessed less than a 40s. freehold were excused in the reign of Edward I ;[2] and excuse from attendance to unpaid and unpopular duties meant absence. The

---

[1] Richard of Devizes, p. 53.

[2] *Rot. Parl.*, i. 116; the statute only applied to the county courts, and not to the assizes held by the king's justices in cities, boroughs, and other market towns. The exemption of 1294 became the exclusion of 1430.

duty was even attached to particular tenements rather than to their holders, and instances are known in which suit at the county court was imposed as a condition of the lease or grant of land.[1]

This suit at the county court was, of course, required for the administration of justice, and it is important to remember that not only the members of parliament, but the electors as well, were primarily jurors, and only incidentally electors. Justice was the regular monthly work of the county court, the election of members of parliament was an occasional addition to the duties of those who were already present to exercise jurisdiction. The house of commons, as well as the house of lords, grew out of the legal system, and the politics of parliament were the outcome of its law. It was in this legal atmosphere that representation had its birth, and the county court is the foundation of the house of commons. Representation was not the offspring of democratic theory, but an incident of the feudal system.[2] Suit and service were due from all; but, we are told in the *Leges Henrici Primi*, if the lord or his steward will go to the county court, his presence will "acquit" the tenants on his domain.[3] If neither lord nor steward is present, there must come the priest and the reeve, and four best men of the township on behalf of their fellows. The boon of representation is not in election to serve, but in the licence to stay away; it consists in the immunity obtained through the vicarious service of others, and centuries elapse before the service becomes a privilege and the burden an object of envy and a source of pride. In the twelfth and thirteenth centuries the difficulty is to enforce the attendance of representatives; medieval "liberties" were nearly fatal to representation and to the county courts, for the most cherished liberty was that which excused the lord and his tenants from the hundred and county courts, and gave them jurisdiction of their own.

But, scanty and reluctant though the attendance may

---

[1] Maitland, *Collected Papers*, i. 458.   [2] See below, p. 153.
[3] Stubbs, *Select Charters*, ed. 1900, p. 105.

have been, the court was the legal embodiment of the shire; everything it did was the deed of the shire, and except through it the shire did nothing. Its verdicts were the final verdicts of the shire; [1] there were no imperative mandates from below, no limitation of powers, and no referendum; its representative character was complete. It was the *communitas*, and not a mere " estate." Bishops, earls, and barons, as well as knights, were expected to attend in person or provide their representatives,[2] and all were " peers of the county." [3] " Peers of the realm " did, indeed, secure exemption after a while—not as a class, but as individual recipients of royal grants and charters—and the ground of their exemption was perhaps their liability to a special summons to more arduous business at Westminster. But the exemption was not a prohibition; they could attend if they liked, and it is probable that the magnates who in later centuries intervened in the nomination of members of parliament in the shire courts, were not exceeding their legal rights. It was only a resolution of the house of commons that forbade a peer to concern himself with parliamentary elections.

Here in the shire courts was acquired that habit of common action, and here was laid that foundation of public opinion, upon which the house of commons was based. It may be that undue stress has been laid upon the fact that, while Simon de Montfort summoned the citizens and burgesses to his parliament by writs addressed direct to the cities and boroughs, Edward I sent the writs through the sheriffs and had the returns made in the shire courts. It was, indeed, more than a question of mere machinery, for the common return of knights of the shire and burgesses in the same shire courts emphasized a community which was retained in the house of commons. But the links were forged at an earlier period, and were made of stouter stuff than sheriffs'

---

[1] Maitland, *Lectures on Constitutional History*, p. 43.
[2] *Leges Henrici Primi*, Stubbs, *Select Charters*, p. 105.
[3] This phrase occurs frequently in the fourteenth century, and probably means the " judges " of the county court as defined in the *Leges Henrici Primi*, c. xxix., Stubbs, *Select Charters*, p. 106.

writs. The knights who failed to obtain baronial exemption from attendance at the shire courts recouped themselves by managing the business of their humbler neighbours in the shires. It was they who prepared the agenda for the fiscal and judicial visits of the justices in eyre, consulted with the townsfolk and small freeholders in attendance at the court, and negotiated their affairs. They had their reward in a leadership, lost by the peers of the realm through their privileged abstention from the county courts, and won by the knights who continued at Westminster the popular co-operation they had learnt in the shires.

Nor is there any reason to suppose that this presentation and conduct of popular business by the knights was limited to the county courts in the thirteenth century before the formal election of members to parliaments or great councils. Henry II had thrown open the doors of the *curia regis* to suitors of all sorts—save villeins pleading against their lords; and nothing in the records of Edward I's parliaments suggests that the regular invitation to suitors, with which a parliament always began, was a novelty. Suitors had been in the habit of coming to Westminster from the county courts before the days of Simon de Montfort and Edward I; and it is almost certain that knights from the shire did a good deal of representative legal business at Westminster before they were summoned thither by writs. The writ to the sheriff, the election in the shire court, and the indenture between the sheriff and the elected knights merely made formal and regular the spontaneous habit of representation of counties by knights at the king's high court; and the intervention of chancery, with its formal writs and returns, was, no doubt, intended to render the words and deeds of the representatives more binding upon their constituents. They were to come, not merely with such varying powers as different counties might at different times choose to give them, but with full power to commit all the counties alike to approval of whatever proposals the king and his council might lay before them; and in Edward I's parliamentary writs there was implied, not only a theory of government by consent, but also the authority of representatives and the tyranny of majorities.

Similarly there are grounds for believing that cities and boroughs had been represented at Westminster before Simon de Montfort issued his writs,[1] and that the petitions from towns which abound in the earliest " Rolls of Parliaments " had not sprung up in a generation; and again, all that Simon did was to systematize, and perhaps turn to political and party purposes, a habit of representation that had long obtained in the redress of grievances and the administration of justice.   The itinerant justices did not exhaust the judicial business of the counties or the judicial powers of the king's court.   There was always the reserve at Westminster; to tap justice at its source the counties had to appear by their representatives in the *curia regis*, and the original purpose of parliament, as declared on countless occasions throughout the fourteenth century, was by means of a joint session of the courts to redress delays and determine cases in which the judges were in doubt.

Out of this attendance of representatives of the shires at the *curia regis* grew in time the share of the house of commons in the judicial work of the high court of parliament. They were not, it is true, judges in parliament, but they were the grand jury of the nation; the lords could try no commoner except on their impeachment, and their presence was essential at various stages in the proceedings.   The separate representation of cities and boroughs was, no doubt, due to the varying degrees of immunity from the jurisdiction of the shire courts which they enjoyed.   But no city save London seems to have secured total exemption from the shire system before the fourteenth century, and there must therefore have been a local basis of co-operation between town and county, which facilitated co-operation between their representatives in parliament.   The co-operation was not, however, complete at first; as late as the reign of Edward III knights and burgesses act independently, and seemed not unlikely to form

---

[1] *Rotuli Chartarum*, Record Comm., pp. 57, 65; Pike, p. 337.

separate "estates." [1] Their ultimate amalgamation was due to the exigencies of parliamentary organization.

The house of commons was not, in fact, created either by Simon de Montfort or by Edward I. Representatives of shires, cities, and boroughs attended the king's court at Westminster for judicial and financial purposes before either Simon or Edward issued their famous writs. They came, indeed, sporadically and not as a body of men; but their organization into a "house" of commons required a great deal more than the simultaneous summons to shires and boroughs issued by Simon and Edward. It grew up during the fourteenth century, and its growth is slow and obscure. The "Rolls of Parliaments" tell us little about the house of commons, because they are only concerned with what is done in parliament, and technically the discussions and other domestic business of the house of commons are not transacted *in* parliament at all. Down to this day the commons' debates are beyond the ken of the clerk of the parliaments, an official who sits in what has come to be called the house of lords. In the fourteenth century they were held in the refectory or the chapter house of the abbey of Westminster; and as late as the reign of Henry VII the commons only "appear" in parliament when they come to hear the opening speech, to present their Speaker,[2] or to announce by his mouth the decisions they have reached on the business submitted for their approval. Consequently it is on these occasions alone that they figure in the "Rolls of Parliaments" kept by the clerk of the parliaments, who sits in the parliament chamber of the palace. It is true that early in Edward III's reign an "under clerk of the parliaments" has been told off to attend to the domestic business of the commons, and ultimately he becomes the clerk of the house of commons. But his duties were apparently to draft the

---

[1] As late as 1523 they took separate action (Hall, *Chron.*, p. 657).

[2] The obscurity which covers the origin of the Speakership and early development of the privileges of the commons is due to the total absence of any record of the domestic proceedings of the house of commons in the chapter house until its *Journals* begin in 1547. The entries in the "Rolls" only relate to decisions after they have been reached by the house and are reported in parliament by the Speaker (see *History*, iii. 33–5).

I

common petitions of the house, and possibly to keep some record of attendance, upon which the chancery founded its writs *de expensis*, entitling members to recover their wages from their constituents. No other trace of his activity has been found; it is improbable that any *Journal* of the house of commons was kept before 1547.[1] If it was, it has been lost, and in any case its contents were not incorporated in the " Rolls," which ignore proceedings taken outside the parliament chamber.

Another cause of obscurity in the history of the house of commons arises from the indeterminate character of the terminology employed in the " Rolls." By the end of the fourteenth century the term *communitates* or *communes* implies both the knights of the shires and the representatives of the cities and boroughs; but this usage expresses the result of a gradual amalgamation, and before 1350 the word is used in different senses. *Le commun* is used in 1258 of a clique of barons; in 1259 *communitas bacheleriæ* describes a "cave" of aristocratic forwards. In 1340 *les communes de la terre* is the phrase employed to distinguish the knights of the shires from the representatives of the cities and boroughs. In 1343 we have *les chivalers des countez et communes*, where *communes* seems to mean the town members as distinct from the knights of the shire; but in the next line we have *prelatz, grantz, et communes*, where both are apparently included in the common designation, and later on the same page we have, *les chivalers des countees et les autres communes*. Similarly in 1332 we have a distinction between *les chivalers des countez* and *les gentz du commun*.[2]

Beneath this confusion of terminology it is not possible to detect any real house of commons consisting of a combination of knights and burgesses. It should be remembered that many knights of the shires were not *chivalers*, and

[1] See *Trans. Royal Hist. Soc.*, 3rd Ser., viii. 27.
[2] *Rot. Parl.*, ii. 65a, 112, 136; cf. Tout, *Edward II*, p. 89. In 1352 we have reference to "longe trete et deliberation eues par les communes ove [avec] la communaltie, et l'avis d'ascuns grantz a eux envoiez " (*Rot. Parl.*, ii. 237b).

that many barons summoned by special writ were. There was no social designation to distinguish the lesser from the greater baron; either might be a *chivaler*, either was a baron, and either was *nobilis*—a quality attributed to knights as late as the fifteenth and sixteenth centuries. Out of a list of twenty-four knights present at the parliament of 1305, ten had received a special baronial summons. The sole distinction between knights and barons was drawn by royal writ of summons, and it is significant that when, at the parliament of Lincoln in 1301, we find the earliest notable instance of the parliamentary activity of a knight of the shire, that action is taken by Henry of Keighley, as the mouthpiece of the barons, and not as a leader of the commons. It is probable that for a generation after 1295 the influence of the " communes " in parliament was simply that of the lesser tenants in chivalry. What general legislation there is affects them only, and they act as a knightly estate rather than as a house of commons.

Nor must their parliamentary importance be exaggerated. There is hardly a parliament of the first half of the fourteenth century the opening of which had not to be postponed owing to defective attendance. But the defect is always due to the absence of prelates and magnates, and never to that of knights or burgesses; and it is more probable that such absence was not regarded as a fatal defect in a parliament than that it never occurred. The summons of knights of the shire and burgesses does not prove their attendance; and when, later on, measures are taken to compel attendance at parliament, they are applied to magnates long before they are enforced upon knights of the shire or burgesses. The summons was all that was needed; according to the *Modus* a total absence of magnates did not invalidate a parliament, provided they had been summoned; and even Magna Carta had laid it down that the absence of those who abstained was not to frustrate the counsel of those who attended. Absence, following upon due and lawful summons, gave consent as effectively as silence on the part of those who were present. In the parliament of September 1332 a tenth was imposed on cities and boroughs, although the only consent recorded is that of the prelates, earls, barons, other magnates and knights of the shire who granted a fifteenth; [1] and, although the election of burgesses to that parliament is recorded in the *Official Return*, no trace of their presence is found in the " Rolls." That some burgesses as well as some knights of the shire did attend this and other parliaments, their presence in which is not mentioned in the " Rolls," is probable. But it seems clear from the writs *de expensis* that election did not mean attendance, and that the large number of elections recorded in the *Official Return of Members of Parliament* may convey an exaggerated impression of the importance of the commons in parliament.[2]

The treatment of the commons by the crown during the first years of Edward III's reign was not, in fact, calculated to encourage attendance. In March 1332, for instance, the commons met on Monday the 17th; five days later they were told that their petitions had neither been received nor answered, and that they might go home, the king promising to call another parliament to deal with such business. This he did in September; but as soon as money had been granted, the other estates, though not the burgesses, were asked to advise the king whether he should deal with petitions or go north to deal with the Scots. He was advised to deal with the Scots, and the commons had to be content with a gracious promise to deal with their petitions at a convenient season. The third parliament for that year met at York on December 4, but only five prelates attended; the requisite lords and lawyers failed to appear, petitions could not be answered, and parliament was prorogued until January, when again it met at York.[3] A journey to Westminster was then a matter of weeks; a journey to York was worse for most of the members. Cornwall returned ten members to the parliament of March, and fourteen to that of September; but it is not surprising that only two of the ten were found among the fourteen, or

---

[1] *Rot. Parl.*, ii. 66.
[2] Cf. Tout, *Edward II*, 1914, pp. 89-90, 104. See below, Chapter xvi.
[3] *Rot. Parl.*, ii. 64 ff.

that no returns at all have been discovered from Cornwall to the parliaments of December and January.[1] It needed the Hundred Years' war, with its financial embarrassments, to render the crown more respectful and the commons readier to make better use of the parliamentary organization which had been slowly developing since the days of Edward I.

No precise dates can be assigned to the steps in that progress, and it has been further obscured by antedating the definiteness of parliamentary institutions. All talk about two houses of parliament in the fourteenth century is clearly beside the mark, and it can hardly be too often repeated that the earliest reference to a " house of lords " occurs in the reign of Henry VIII. Edward I was as ignorant of two houses of parliament as he was of three estates, and his Model Parliament consisted of a single chamber. Nor can we obtain an accurate view of Edward's parliaments so long as we regard them as being primarily legislative assemblies. The king summoned them to secure supplies, and members attended to seek redress for their grievances. But the petitions they presented would practically all be now called private bills; they were not collective petitions and were not preferred by corporate action. Of the five hundred petitions presented at the parliament of 1305, five only deal with matters of public concern, and of these five three affect feudal tenants-in-chief alone. Ninety-nine hundredths of the petitions are individual requests for legal relief, for royal favour, or for redress of private wrongs, and they called for no common action among the petitioners.[2]

An appreciation of the significance of this fact is essential to any understanding of the Edwardine parliament. There could be no house of commons so long as this condition continued, for such an institution could only grow out of common action. Again, this fact alone would indicate that

---

[1] *Official Return of Members of Parliament*, s. aa.

[2] This computation was made from the petitions for 1305 in Maitland's *Memoranda de Parliamento*. Palgrave in giving evidence before the Committee on Public Petitions in 1832 reached a similar conclusion from his knowledge of the whole medieval period: " I should state that ninety-nine out of every hundred petitions presented by individuals related to individual grievances " (*Parl. Papers*, 1833, xii. 20).

when they present their petitions *les unes sount ajournes devant le roi, et les autres devant le chancellier, dount nul issue n'est fait.*[1]   Reference to the king's bench—*coram rege*, to chancery, and to other courts, was, we have seen, the regular method of dealing with petitions in parliament; it has now become a grievance for which a remedy is sought by the commons and promised by the crown.   The remedy is not prescribed in 1325, but it appears in 1327 in the demand of the commons that their petitions may be made statutes in parliament and held good.[2]   This demand would only apply, as a rule, to common petitions : the individual petitions would continue to be referred to the various courts; but the common petitions come to be taken first, to be answered in parliament before the "estates" go home, and to be enrolled as statutes.

The common petition is thus the root of the house of commons as a separate legislative assembly.   Institutions in the middle ages are not made, they grow; the common petition required common deliberation, common action, and perhaps even a common clerk; the common action became a habit, the habit an institution, and the institution a house. Such processes, especially in their initial stages, are not recorded; but in historical as well as in physical science we have to deal with many developments of which we possess no records, and the fact that they were not recorded does not prove that they never occurred.   There is ample evidence that no house of commons existed in Edward I's reign, and ampler evidence that it did exist in that of Edward III; and it is our business to infer from such knowledge as we possess the means by which it developed.   This requires a little imagination, but without any undue stretch of fancy, one or two guesses may be hazarded with regard to the growth of parliamentary procedure early in the fourteenth century.

The king in council clearly met the lords and commons in parliament in common session, when the chancellor or some other member of the council, usually a judge, explained to the assembly the purport of its summons and the requests

[1] *Rot. Parl.*, i. 430.   [2] *Ibid.*, ii. 10, 12.

PARLIAMENT IN 1585.

for assistance and advice that would be laid before it. The advice was mainly a matter for the lords, the assistance for the commons. There is reason to believe that from Edward I's time the king's council sat in the midst of this assembly on four woolsacks (of which only one remains) facing one another, and that Fleta's phrase about the king holding his council in his parliaments has a literal and material, as well as a figurative meaning : no one would have arranged the four woolsacks in that way unless their occupants were normally engaged in confidential deliberation. Outside this inner ring there sat, to the right of the throne, the spiritual lords, and to the left the temporal lords, and facing the throne there stood the commons. To them the demand for aid would be particularly addressed, and then the problem of how and what to answer would arise. Probably there would be a division of opinion, and possibly discordant murmurs ; courageous commons at the back might urge in whispers to their colleagues in the front the exorbitance of the king's demands and the necessity of refusal ; timid members at the fore might tell their daring but half-concealed advisers at their back to speak for themselves ; and then, amid the muttering and murmuring, the chancellor or other member of the council might suggest that not much progress was being made, and that the commons should go and talk it over among themselves, and then come back with an intelligible answer. On some such occasion it must have been suggested that they should choose some one of their members to be their Speaker, and that his answer, whether representing unanimity or but a small majority, should be considered equally binding upon all. The commons then trooped out of parliament to discuss in some more private place their domestic differences. They only reappeared in parliament when they had reached a resolution which was reported by the Speaker ; and he alone had liberty of speech in parliament.

This procedure was probably not limited to the commons : each estate deliberated apart and outside parliament, and at first the knights of the shire and the burgesses occasionally, if not regularly, deliberated apart from one another. There are instances of the lords deliberating apart from the council in parliament, though in the end the lords remained with the council in parliament to form the house of lords. The clergy went off to convocation, and it soon becomes impossible to distinguish between assemblies of the clergy summoned by the archbishop for ecclesiastical purposes and assemblies of the clergy summoned by the king for temporal objects. Logically, of course, there was a fundamental distinction between the two : the clergy summoned by the archbishop consisted only of the clergy in his province; the clergy summoned by the king consisted, or should have consisted, of clergy from both provinces alike. But in this respect the church proved stronger than the crown, and the provincial organization of the one prevailed against the national organization of the other. Instead of uniting to form a clerical estate in parliament, the clergy of the two provinces preferred to transact their temporal business, such as voting taxes, in their two provincial convocations, and to abandon parliament except in so far as they were represented there by prelates who held baronies of the crown and failed to escape the liability involved therein.

Where the commons conducted their domestic deliberations when they first departed from parliament, is not known; but in Edward II's reign they seem to have met in the refectory of Westminster Abbey, a place outside the jurisdiction of the chamberlain and other palace and parliamentary officials. Soon they took to meeting in the chapter house, which enjoyed similar immunity; their presence there is recorded in 1352, and by 1376 the chapter house is already described as their ancient place of meeting.[1] This departure is the first step in the so-called separation of parliament into two houses; but that separation has never been complete, and the house of commons was formed, not so much by separation from the house of lords, as by the amalgamation of knights and burgesses. There are still many forms which indicate the unity of parliaments, and those forms were realities long after the fourteenth century. The discussions in the chapter house were not, strictly speaking, transactions in parliament at all, and the gather-

[1] *Rot. Parl.*, ii. 237, 322; cf. "*History*," iii. 34.

ings of commons, clergy, lords, were more like committees than houses of parliament. Then, as now, no act of parliament could be made or done outside the parliament chamber; then, as now, the presence of the Speaker and commons was required at the passing of every bill,[1] at the opening and prorogation of every parliament. Parliament still acts as one body, and not as two houses, in all its solemn functions, but in the fourteenth century the " houses " had neither been organized nor reduced to two. The " committees " were the various estates in parliament, who as late as 1381 are referred to as " prelates, temporal lords, judges, knights, and all the other estates." It is the "knights and all the other estates "[2] who migrate to the chapter house and become in time the house of commons.

The judges remained, naturally, in the parliament chamber with the council, of which they were an integral part. For some time and to some extent the spiritual and temporal peers deliberated apart from the council in parliament and from one another.[3] But baronial tradition and influence proved too strong for the king in parliament; and while outside parliament the council became " privy " and remained royal, inside parliament it became " magnum," and from about the middle of the fourteenth century, whenever we read of the king's council in parliament the king's great council is meant.[4] In time the peers monopolize the position of " consiliarii " in parliament, reduce the other councillors, such as the judges and even the chancellor, to the status of

[1] It was a demand of the commons in 1348 that their petitions should be answered and endorsed " en parlement devant la commune " (*Rot. Parl.*, ii. 165).

[2] Probably the clergy were not included in this vague reference, having already before 1381 practically severed their connexion with Parliament.

[3] See, for instances of separate deliberation of spiritual and temporal lords, *Rot. Parl.*, ii. 64*b*, 66.

[4] This is one of the points Prof. Baldwin has not elucidated, and it remains obscure. As late as 1433 there was a " king's great council in parliament " as well as a " king's great council out of parliament " (Nicolas, *Proc. of Privy Council*, iv. 185–6); the latter contained nominated knights of the shire (*ibid.*, i. 156, vi. 339). Probably a "council " was not even yet regarded as a definite body of men, but rather as a conference without any specification of personnel. The personnel would be specified by the writs of summons and not by the name of the meeting to which they were summoned. It is doubtful whether we should think of definite " bodies " until we can properly talk of " corporations."

voteless advisers, and eliminate all trace of separate consultation of peers apart from councillors.   The lords, therefore, instead of leaving the parliament chamber to deliberate
by themselves as one or two estates, remained with the
council as advisers of the crown.   It is thus that the
petitions of the commons are enacted with the advice and
consent of the lords; for the lords are the lords of the
council which they have invaded.   They sit in the parliament chamber, they transact all their business there, and
they are not called a "house" until the sixteenth century.

The knights of the shire and the burgesses were thus left
to retire alone for joint or separate discussion and resolution.
Their co-operation has been commonly regarded as the
outcome of a deliberate determination of the knights to throw
in their lot with the burgesses rather than with the lords;
but this view presupposes too great an influence of the
burgesses in parliament.   There is hardly a definite trace of
parliamentary action on their part before 1340, while there
are many occasions on which the knights were consulted without any reference to burgesses at all.[1]   It would appear that
the knights had already established the habit of independent
deliberation, and that the fusion of the county and civic
representatives was rather due to the burgesses attaching
themselves to the knights.   No doubt there must have been
a reciprocal willingness on the side of the knights, and it is a
peculiar and remarkable feature of the English constitution
that the knights, in spite of their social and political bonds
with the barons—such as common military tenure-in-chief
and common ideas of chivalry—should have found it easier
to work with burgesses than with barons; indeed, it would
not have been possible but for the shrinking of the baronage
into the peerage.[2]   The fusion of knights and burgesses was,

[1] E. g. Rot. Parl., ii. 66.
[2] This, in its turn, was largely due to the success of the crown in insisting on the writ of summons as the qualification for attendance at parliament.   If parliament had really been a system of estates, and the
second estate had elected its representatives, the lesser barons would
doubtless have continued to co-operate with the greater.   But these
greater barons were summoned by special writ, which gave no opportunity
for election and removed them from the control of the lesser.

however, a slow process, the steps in which might be traced in some detail in the " Rolls of Parliaments "; possibly the Good parliament of 1376 exemplified the firstfruits of amalgamation. In any case, separate consultation of knights and burgesses grew rarer, while their joint deliberation in the " domus communis " grew more regular and well defined.

This growth required some organization, and during the fourteenth century the development of the house of commons gave rise to the speakership and clerkship of the house. The *Modus Tenendi Parliamentum* speaks of each of the five " gradus " of parliament having its own clerk;[1] but the fusion of estates reduced the number of clerks to two, or three if the clerk of convocation be included. The clerk of the parliaments was, as he remains to-day, the official responsible for the records of the transactions of the estates in common session in the parliament chamber, now called the house of lords; his assistant, the second clerk, was told off to do the clerical work of the knights and burgesses, and became the clerk of the house of commons.[2] He kept no journal in the modern sense of the word, though he may have kept in the fifteenth, and certainly kept in the sixteenth century a book in which he entered the attendance of members.[3] But his principal work was to draft the answers of the commons to the king's demands, and to reduce to writing common petitions or bills based upon the discussions in the house. The individual petitions which members brought up with them were, no doubt, drafted locally, but to combine them in common petitions or to draft fresh ones after deliberation required a clerk of the house.

---

[1] There is no direct trace of the action of these five clerks in the " Rolls "; possibly the *Modus* refers to the period before the " Rolls " become anything like a full record of parliamentary proceedings.

[2] The so-called clerk of the house of commons is still described in his patent of appointment " Under-Clerk of the Parliaments appointed to attend the House of Commons " (*Report on Establishment of H. of C.*, Parl. Papers, 1833, xii. 15).

[3] In the fourteenth century the attendance of knights and burgesses was so little necessary that no means of compulsion were employed, the only penalty being loss of wages. Richard II tried to compel the attendance of barons, but compulsion was not regularly applied to burgesses until the sixteenth century; see below, chap. xvi.

The other official was the Speaker, so called because he
" spoke for " [1] the commons in parliament and alone enjoyed
liberty of speech in the parliament chamber.   This, of course,
was an entirely different liberty from that with which it has
been confused, the liberty of individual speech on the part of
members in the " domus communis," which was not in
parliament at all. The medieval claim made by every
Speaker at the beginning of every parliament was for himself
alone, and referred to transactions in the common sessions
in the parliament chamber. There each prelate, baron,
or councillor might speak, but no member of the commons
save the Speaker, and this is the rule to-day. He could only
speak as the mouthpiece of the commons, and the principal,
indeed, the only, liberty he claimed for a century, was that,
if he misreported or misrepresented any resolution of the
commons, he might withdraw or correct what he had said.
The entirely different claim to freedom of speech on behalf
of individual members in the house of commons was not
added to the Speaker's repertoire until the reign of that
great architect of parliament, Henry VIII.[2] With regard
to those other functions of the Speaker which have eclipsed
his original reason for existence, their growth is wrapped
in darkness. No records whatever have survived of the
domestic proceedings of the house of commons earlier than
1547, and we have no information about the steps by which
the Speaker became chairman of the house and by which his
authority was developed. Sir William Trussell was apparently
Speaker in 1343,[3] but he and his medieval successors only
appear on the record when they have left the *domus communis*, and come at the head of their fellow-members before
the lords and the council in the parliament chamber.

---

[1] " Prolocutor " is his earliest official title.

[2] In 1477, for instance, the Speaker asks for " omnes ac singulas alias
libertates et franchesias quas aliquis hujusmodi Prolocutor perantea
melius et liberius habuit."   The petition is for himself, and not for other
members of the House (*Rot. Parl.*, vi. 167).   In 1482 the Speaker, John
Wood, omitted the petition for these " alias libertates " (*ibid.*, vi. 192;
cf. iv. 420, 482).

[3] *Ibid.*, ii. 136 *b* : " et puis vindrent des chivalers des counteez et les
communes et responderent par Monsieur William Trussell."

But the mere existence of the Speaker is evidence of a corporate feeling and organization, which was totally lacking in the reign of Edward I but grew out of a subsequent half-century of common deliberation and action. Then knights and burgesses had only been present at Westminster as individual petitioners on behalf of their constituents; and it is even doubtful whether they voted grants collectively or by separate bargain with the crown. In the reign of his grandson they are a coherent body of national legislators. The " common " petition has been developed, backed by the hint of a common resistance to taxation; and in 1340 half a dozen citizens and burgesses, as well as a dozen knights, are elected by their fellow-members to join with certain prelates, earls, and barons to try and examine the petitions presented in parliament and put them into statutes which shall be perpetual.[1] This is the method by which the commons asserted legislative power. They never claimed a right to initiate legislation; and much industry has been wasted in attempts to fix the date at which the commons asserted their right to legislate. They do not possess that abstract right to-day. The crown alone enacts legislation in parliament; the commons merely petition, and the right of petition has existed since the days of Henry II. The process of development was more subtle than any declaration of right. The individual petition was gradually turned into the common petition of the house, and then backed by the control of the purse, and the so-called right to legislate consists in the commons' power of making government impossible if heed is not paid to the petitions they have the right to present.

The change from the individual to the common petition was fundamental. The high court of parliament was converted into a legislature, and its judicial function obscured by its legislative activity. Common petitions lead us out of the realm of common law into that of common politics; for the individual wrong is a matter of law, the common grievance is a question of politics. Common petitions could

[1] *Rot. Parl.*, ii. 112.

not be settled in court, and the remedy for their reference to chancery, king's bench, and so forth, of which the commons complained in 1325,[1] could only be found by their enactment as statutes in parliament *devant la commune*. Common action is the cause, as well as the result of community of feeling, and the *communitates* become the *communitas communitatum*. By that process the locally-minded representatives of heterogeneous communities are welded into a house of commons, and in that house, more than anywhere else, the " estates " are made into the state.

This growth of common petitions, and the absorption of the commons in their prosecution, diminished the share of the commons in the judicial work of parliament, made parliament itself less of a high court, and fostered the ultimate but incomplete differentiation between our high court of parliament and our high court of justice. Individual petitions were more and more neglected by the commons; they insisted upon answers being given to their common petitions in parliament before they dispersed, but they would not wait for answers to individual petitions. These were more and more referred to the council at the end of the session,[2] if they had not already been answered, and this reference entitled the council to endorse its answers *per auctoritatem parliamenti*.[3] Answers to such referred petitions were also entered on the " Rolls of Parliaments," although not given until after the dismissal of the estates,[4] and although the duration of a parliament was coming to be regarded as limited to the session of the estates. For, while as late as the beginning of Edward III's reign a parliament might continue after the dismissal of the commons,[5] the concen-

---

[1] *Rot. Parl.*, i. 430.

[2] *Ibid.*, ii. 243; Nicolas, *Proc. of Privy Council*, ii. 307, v. p. xi.

[3] Cf. Elsynge, *Modus*, pp. 294–7, and below, p. 328 *n.* It was this reference of petitions to the council *per auctoritatem parliamenti* that really gave the council in the Star Chamber its statutory sanction, and not the Act of 1487, which apparently has nothing to do with the Star Chamber (*English Hist. Review*, Oct. 1922, pp. 520–7, 539).

[4] *Rot. Parl.*, ii. 304, iv. 334, 506.

[5] E. g. *Rot. Parl.*, ii. 65*b*. After the knights, citizens, burgesses and clergy had been given leave to go home (Saturday, March 21, 1331–2) on condition that the prelates, earls, barons, and councillors remained, proceedings continued " en pleyn parlement " on the Monday.

tration of attention upon common petitions led, before the end of the reign, to the adoption of the idea that the presence of the commons was essential to the continuance of a session of parliament. Out of this habitual reference of individual petitions by parliament to the council grew, in the latter half of the fourteenth century, the extensive jurisdiction of the council and indirectly of chancery, to which the council in turn referred the bulk;[1] and the specialization and differentiation of the functions of parliament began. In Edward I's reign all sorts of business had been transacted in parliament; the regular reference of individual petitions to the council and to chancery tended to develop the council's jurisdiction and to restrict parliament to legislation.

This division of functions likewise tended to limit the council's power of legislation. The means by which the commons secured[2] the enactment of their common petitions have already been indicated; it cost a longer and severer struggle to limit the council's power of legislation and enforce the necessity of parliamentary consent. Edward I's great legislation had been promulgated in assemblies which, if called parliaments, did not contain the estates, and the presumed recognition, in 1322, of the need for the consent of the commons to legislation has been exaggerated.[3] In 1327 we find a distinction made between statutes and other forms of legislation, and the idea is that a statute should be perpetual, while enactments of a more temporary character were expressed in letters patent.[4] But the differentiation between those petitions, or parts of petitions, which were to be made statutes and those which were to receive less solemn authorization was left to the council or to the judges as late as 1422, when the clerk of the parliaments was ordered to read to the council the acts passed at the late parliament, and then submit them to the two chief justices, who were to decide

---

[1] Cf. Baldwin, *King's Council*, pp. 241 *sqq.*
[2] Their success was, of course, only partial; the crown's power of veto was only limited by political expediency; it has never been limited by law except during the Long Parliament.
[3] See below, pp. 241-2.
[4] *Rot. Parl.*, ii. 12, 113.

K

which of them were statutes. These were to be proclaimed; the other " acts " were to be handed over to the clerk of the council, though all alike were to be enrolled, as was the custom, in chancery.[1]   It was not till the sixteenth century that the crown lost the power of amending and modifying bills passed by both houses of parliament.   In the fifteenth century the practice was extended, if not also begun, of drafting petitions in the form of acts, and we have frequent references to a bill or petition " in se formam actus continens "; but Henry VII himself, and even Elizabeth, occasionally took the liberty of adding provisos to, or otherwise modifying bills before signifying the royal assent.[2]   There are three stages in the history of legislation : down to the reign of Edward I it is the act of the crown; then it becomes the act of the crown in parliament, and finally the act of parliament.   At the end of the middle ages it is only in the second of these stages, and side by side with its power to legislate in parliament the crown possessed a concurrent right to legislate by ordinance independently of parliament, a power which had never been defined.

The original function of parliament as a gathering in which, according to Fleta, " judicial doubts are determined and new remedies are established for new wrongs, and justice is done to every one according to his deserts," tends thus, by the end of the fourteenth century, to be limited to the second object of enacting new remedies for new wrongs; and this restriction of function led to a restriction of its frequency. To the council and chancery parliament itself referred most of its business, and they sat throughout the four legal terms of the year.   As early as 1348 it was ordered that individual petitions should be addressed to the chancellor and common petitions to the clerk of the parliaments.[3]   Parliament need no longer meet thrice a year, as in Edward I's reign; and indeed, quite apart from this judicial transformation,

---

[1] Nicolas, *Proc. of Privy Council*, iii. 22.

[2] E. g. *Rot. Parl.*, vi. 275, 412, 460; my *Henry VII*, ii. 16–17; D'Ewes, *Journals*, p. 341b.   Bills drawn up in the form of an act were apparently drawn on parchment (*Rot. Parl.*, vi. 288, 331).   See Appendix III (*m*).

[3] *Rot. Parl.*, ii. 201.

there were other causes tending to the infrequency of parliamentary sessions. The more popular and important an assembly it grew, and the greater the attendance of commons
and the length of their sessions, the less practicable it became
to hold three general elections and three sessions a year.
Accordingly the three sessions a year of Edward I's time are
reduced to about three in two years in Edward II's, to one
a year in the middle of the fourteenth century, and in the
fifteenth century to one in two, three, four, or even five
years. This progressive rarity of parliaments is not due to
the tyranny of kings, for it proceeds independently of the
dynasty or particular monarch; it is due to a fundamental
change in the character of parliament, to the specialization
of functions previously performed by a rudimentary organ,
and to the transference of most of the original work of
parliament to the council and to chancery.

CHAPTER VII

PARLIAMENT AND NATIONALISM

THE loss of original functions through the transformation of parliament from a high court into a legislature diminished its usefulness and the reasons for its existence; and, pending the development of fresh grounds of action, parliament in the fifteenth century seemed to be treading the downward path of continental estates. Its sessions grew ever less frequent; from three a year they sank to one in every four or five years; and intervals of seven years under Henry VII and Wolsey, and of eleven under Charles I, might have been the prelude to a silence as prolonged and profound as that which fell upon national representation in France. Parliament itself showed no desire to insist upon its continuance. After the reference of most of its judicial work to the council, the need for supply alone made it indispensable to the crown; and if parliament had succeeded in enforcing its persistent demand that the king should " live of his own," it would have rendered its own existence superfluous. Nothing but compulsion on the part of the crown could get a parliament together; and as late as the sixteenth century ministers were wont to apologize to parliament for its summons. " What," asked Sir Thomas Smith in 1560, " can a commonwealth desire more than peace, liberty, quietness, little taking of their money, few parliaments? " [1]

The reluctance of parliament to assume responsibility was as marked as its unwillingness to meet, its haste to get home, or its anxiety to escape taxation; and the impotence that was the result of this slowness to serve might well have

[1] Strype, *Life of Sir T. Smith*, p. 192. Sir Nicolas Bacon in January 1563 claimed in parliament credit for the queen on the ground of her reluctance to burden the country with it (D'Ewes, *Journals*, p. 61).

explained its disappearance at the end of the fifteenth
century. It had failed alike to check tyrants and to support
constitutional kings. Good resolutions were the limit of its
capacity, and they were short-lived. No parliament had
offered successful resistance to the crown, and the troubles
of Richard II, Henry VI, and Richard III came from other
quarters. While parliaments were ever in opposition, rebellion and rival claims to the throne were always required to
effect a change in government or in policy. In spite of the
vaunted constitutional experiment of the Lancastrians, constitutional methods were, to the end of the middle ages,
powerless to effect constitutional government. So far from
the constitution being in all essentials complete in the reign
of Edward I, it lacked the elementary means of working at all
and was periodically being superseded by battle and murder.
The constitutional ideal which Sir John Fortescue depicted
at the close of the middle ages had little more relevance
to the practice of his day than More's *Utopia* had to the
government of Cardinal Wolsey.

The great service which parliaments rendered in the
middle ages was not, in fact, to make England a constitutional state, but to foster its growth into a national state
based on something broader and deeper than monarchical centralization, to make national unity a thing of
the spirit rather than a territorial expression or a
mechanical matter of administration, to evoke a common
political consciousness at Westminster and then to pro-
pagate it in the constituencies. The value of parliaments
consisted not so much in what members brought with them
as in what they took away. Nationalism in the middle ages
came nearer to Napoleon III's *la volonté de chacun* than to
Rousseau's *la volonté générale*, and it was in and through
parliaments that local and social prejudice was merged
in a common sense. Every Englishman of to-day feels
and realizes his nationality to some extent; the degree is
a matter of individual imagination, education, and interest.
Generally speaking, his attachment to his country over-
rides every other affection except, perhaps, his devotion to

himself and his family and in some cases his addiction to his religious or moral faith.   But in the middle ages we are dealing with men whose nationalism came comparatively low in the scale of their affections.   Men of the highest mind and character agreed with Archbishop Winchelsey that the loyalty they owed the pope came before the loyalty they owed the king.   Barons were, as a rule, more devoted to their class than to either pope or king; the ordinary burgess or squire valued his local affinities more than his national bonds, and to the villager the parish was his world.   When he threw himself upon his country—*posuit se super patriam*—his country consisted of his neighbours, and every one else was a foreigner.   These symptoms are not yet extinct, and in very recent years a protectionist speaker was told by his Devonshire audience that it was not the " foreign " foreigner they disliked, but the Somersetshire foreigner; a similar feeling may even be traced with regard to the Mercians in the works of the vigorous West-Saxon who wrote the *History of the Norman Conquest.*   The difference between modern and medieval Englishmen's patriotism is one of degree; in the middle ages locality preceded the nation, and it was through parliaments that the order was reversed.

The nation, like the child, began its education with what the Germans call *heimatkunde.*   Intimate things were the first its mind could grasp.   By the thirteenth century the normal range of the average freeman's imagination comprehended the shire, and his public activities were organized on that basis.   He had to bear arms in the *fyrd*, but the *fyrd* could not be summoned to fight outside the shire except at the king's expense.   He had to serve as a juror, but he could not be empanelled or forced to plead as a suitor beyond the county boundary.   The county was his country, and both the political and the verbal distinctions between the terms are of modern growth.[1]   Men fought as shires and

---

[1] Cf. R. Brunne, " the cuntre of Dorseth " (*c.* 1330), Caxton, " the countre of Leycester " (1480), Fitzherbert, " Leycestershyre, Lankesshyre, Yorkeshyre, and many other countreys " (1523) (*N. E. D.*).

thought as shires and judged as shires; they did nothing
as a nation, and it is grotesque to speak of " England "
doing anything at all before parliaments appeared, because
there was no " England " capable of doing it. During the
Norman period " England " suffers, but does not act;
Henry II does much, but he spends nine-tenths of his reign
abroad and represents France rather than England. The
importance of Magna Carta consists, not in the nature of
its provisions, but in the co-operation by which it was
achieved. The movement against John was, however,
spasmodic and feudal rather than popular, and the opposition
to Henry III was also mainly baronial. It was not until
Simon de Montfort and Edward I popularized parliaments
that England became really conscious of itself and acquired
the means of national action. Even then the action must not
be exaggerated; there was no will on the part of the English
people to determine or direct a national policy, and it was
little more than a formal expression of national acquiescence
that Edward I sought in parliaments. Consent, and not
direction, was the object of its summons; and its importance
lay in its unity, in the absence of rival parliaments and of
provincial estates.

There are many aspects of this unity of the English parliamentary system. An attempt has already been made to
indicate the significance of the fact which distinguished every
English parliament since Edward I from all continental
systems of estates, namely, the fact that it was not merely
a *parlement* nor a system of estates, but both a court of law
and a representative assembly, at once a judicial, a legislative, and a taxing body. This was perhaps the most fundamental element in the unity of parliament, but another was
hardly less essential to its national character, and that was
its comprehensive scope. Popular representation by itself
has never been incompatible with monarchical despotism :
provincial estates with representation of the *tiers état* continued in many parts of France throughout the *ancien régime*
down to the Revolution of 1789. They continued in the
Spanish-Austrian Netherlands throughout the same period,

and while Philip IV denounced estates-general as fatal to the principle of monarchy,[1] he and his successors permitted the innocuous continuance of provincial representation. The most despotic of German princes were equally complaisant, and even Von Ranke expressed a preference for *Landtag* over *Reichstag* which helps to explain the failure of the German empire to achieve responsible government. This monarchical predilection for provincialism is merely an expression of the despotic maxim *divide et impera,* and it illustrates the fact that provincial estates were not merely harmless to autocracy but dangerous to national self-government; they were, in fact, the principal enemy of estates-general, because by diverting to local objects the desire for self-government they weakened the strength of national co-operation. Nowhere did provincial estates, or estates-general where provincial estates existed, succeed in their resistance to the growth of monarchy in the sixteenth century.

The unity of the English parliament has been unchallenged for so many centuries that it requires some effort to realize the medieval danger of provincial estates. Yet the forces and temptations leading to such a developement were by no means inconsiderable. England before the Norman Conquest was rarely united under a single crown, and even when it was, expedients were occasionally adopted, like Cnut's four great earldoms, which were hardly less fatal than actual dismemberment to national unity. Long after the Conquest the divergences between England north and England south of the Humber were sufficiently strong to make their separation a possible contingency. It was a recognized line of administrative division throughout the middle ages, and as late as Elizabeth's reign northern catholics dreamt of an independent kingdom, or of dependence on the Scottish rather than on the English crown. The Pilgrims of Grace demanded a parliament at York, and Mary thought of removing her government thither for shelter and sympathy.

---

[1] "Les États généraux sont pernicieux en tout temps et dans tous les pays monarchiques sans exception " (Pirenne, *Hist. de Belgique,* iv. 401).

It was only by the hundred years' labours of the council of the north that the conservative counties north of the Humber were really made one with the rest of England. Further, there was the ecclesiastical model; and if parliament was moulded so closely upon the organization of the church as has sometimes been supposed,[1] there would have been two parliaments in the English state, as there were two convocations in the English church. Had the state imitated the church and constructed two parliaments in England, or had the church imitated the state and gathered its forces into one national assembly, the history of both church and state in England would have been fundamentally different.

Edward I did, during one misguided moment in 1282, set the perilous precedent of a double parliament, one for the north, meeting at York, the other for the south, meeting at Northampton. That neither he nor any of his successors followed this evil example was due to a number of causes connected with general English history. The unity of England is primarily the effect of the unity of its monarchy. Fortunately the Danish wars destroyed all royal houses save that of Ecgberht; Alfred the Great was not, like Hugh Capet, elected king by a group of rival princes, whose descendants might claim to be peers of the crown. Harold's usurpation might, if successful, have divided England as France was divided; but the most unruly feudatory of the French crown restored unity to England by the Norman Conquest. To the Conqueror there was little difference between West Saxon, Mercian, and Northumbrian; he had no more local prejudices than the Indian civil servant, who is making India a nation by the same steady application of common principles of government to diverse peoples as that by which the Norman baron and Angevin lawyer reduced to some appearance of uniformity the tribal perversities of their heterogeneous subjects.

Not only was monarchical unity secured, but all traces of the kingdoms over which rival houses had ruled were

[1] Cf. E. Barker, *The Dominican Order and Convocation*, 1913.

obliterated.   When the West-Saxon kings acquired Mercia, Northumbria, and East Anglia, those realms were not retained, as Brittany, Normandy, and other French fiefs were, as administrative units.   They were split up into shires controlled by the central government, and not permitted any provincial *parlements* or estates.   Even in the most turbulent periods of English anarchy, the over-mighty subject had to rely upon scattered domains.   A Geoffrey de Mandeville, a Thomas of Lancaster, or a Richard of York might wreck a government and overawe, or even seize, the crown; but they could not dismember England, because they could acquire no such consolidated fiefs as those upon which dukes and counts in France, Germany, and the Netherlands built their independence of national authority.   The shires saved the unity of medieval England because they were controlled by the crown and did not foment provincial independence. They were the largest subdivision under the crown, and the great majority of them were given no earls.   A dozen is the maximum number of medieval earls against thrice that number of shires.   Two-thirds were directly under the crown, and even in those which had earls the king maintained a sheriff who took two-thirds of the proceeds of jurisdiction, leaving but one to the earl.   It is the sheriff, and not the earl, who dominates the shire, and thus links the shire to parliament, instead of leaving it to develop feudal autonomy and provincial estates under the earl. The " palatinates "[1] which approached most nearly to the provincial organization of the continent were few, and were restricted to the borders.   The rest of England was " shired," and this " shiring " did for the unification of England what the breaking up of the French provinces into departments achieved for the unity of revolutionary France.

The shire-organization, being the work of the central government, was naturally made the means of the development of common law and of parliament.   It was in the

---

[1] The word is rarely used in the middle ages, though Anthony Bek claimed in 1293 to hold as a *comes palatinus*.   The title *Registrum Palatinum Dunelmense*, which Sir T. D. Hardy prefixed to the four volumes he edited for the Rolls Series, was invented by him.

county courts that the royal judges appeared and applied the practice of the *curia regis ;* it was the sheriff who carried that law into execution. It was there, too, that all elected members of parliament were returned; for the citizen and the burgess, though elected in his city or borough, was returned by indenture made with the sheriff in the shire court. The sheriff, as the local agent of the central government, received and returned the writs that emanated from the same monarchical authority. The members came to Westminster not as sent from sovereign constituencies, but as summoned by a sovereign lord; they attended not as delegates with imperative mandates to do what their constituents told them, but as the unfortunate and unwilling persons selected by their fellows to carry out the requirements of the crown. Their powers came from above and not from below, and their position was nearer to that of those persons selected for service under Militia Ballot Acts than to that of plenipotentiaries. Parliament in its origin had less to do with the theory that all power emanated from the people than with the fact that all people held their land directly or indirectly from the crown, and were bound by a corresponding obligation to obey its writs of summons and carry out its behests. It was the crown that put *ad faciendum* in their writs of summons, and it was the business of the crown they had to transact.

The crown by means of parliaments thus imposed a bond of unity upon the shires, and it was probably because there was only one *curia regis* and one king's council that there was only one parliament. Fortunately for England her administrative unity was achieved before her popular representation. Even so, had parliament been merely a system of estates, and had its original business been the granting of taxes, local patriotism might have insisted on local parliaments, where men could grant what they had to grant without a troublesome journey to Westminster. But their business was with a single series of national courts of law, king's bench, exchequer, and common pleas, sitting in common session. On occasion, at great inconvenience, this session was held elsewhere than at Westminster, and wagons of records and other essentials wended their way to Nottingham, York, or Carlisle. But the greater grew the bulk of these records and the more specialized the machinery of government, the more serious was the inconvenience of migration, and except in 1282 the experiment of a divided parliament was never tried.

Englishmen from every shire were therefore brought together, generally at Westminster, once or more every year. It was not less important that they were gathered from various classes, and almost coerced into common deliberation on common objects; for division between class and class is not less fatal to national unity and self-government than division between province and province. Assuredly it was social rather than local separatism that explains, if it does not also excuse, both the weight of Bourbon despotism and the savagery of the French Revolution. For when class cannot act with class, no public opinion is possible and therefore no self-government; the necessary result is a common despotic authority, and when that despotic authority falls before revolution, the only check is removed from class hatred, which arises from lack of co-operation, and, in its turn, breeds suspicion and distrust. Every class in France during the first French Revolution was ready to believe that it was betrayed and that other classes were bought with Pitt's gold, because all classes in France were strangers to one another. Similar accusations, even if made, have seldom been believed in England, because all classes know something about one another; and that knowledge has come from centuries of co-operation between diverse classes in local and national government. It was not for nothing that the shire court was called a community, and the house of commons the community of communities. The house of commons is not, indeed, and never was, a haven of peace; feeling runs high and language is tempestuous; but when one leader accuses another of having no principles, it is not because they belong to different classes or have different codes of honour, but because they belong to different parties and have to observe the conventions of party conflict. The gulf is easily closed at times of crisis and easily passed by individuals whenever they feel disposed.

The absence, or rather the confusion of class distinctions, which dates from before the Norman Conquest, was confirmed by parliament. The "estates" of which we read in its "Rolls" had little of caste rigidity; the judges, for instance, are called an estate, but in England judicial office never became hereditary, as in France, and such great offices of state as did become hereditary soon lost their importance. Prelacy also is called an "estate," but prelacy, like the judiciary, was always a career that was open to talent. Nor was there any demarcation of birth between the knights and bannerets, who sat in the house of commons, and the barons, who sat in the house of lords. Elected knights and bannerets were often "chivalers" and were commonly called nobles; there were "barons" of the Cinque Ports and of the exchequer who were not "peers of the realm," and the distinction between the "nobility" and the gentry of England in the fourteenth century was as vague as is to-day the meaning of gentleman. Even the serio-comic distinction, made by the College of Arms between those who have inherited or bought the right to bear arms and those who have not, had not been invented. Co-operation and community of sentiment were thus comparatively easy; and the separatist tendencies of deliberation by "estates" were checked by the common action which followed it in the parliament chamber. In 1332 we read, for instance, that the estates first answered separately *et puis tous en commune ;* [1] and although acts of parliament are now made law by the royal consent given in what has come to be called the house of lords, the presence of the Speaker and some of the commons, which is always required, still bears evidence to this common action of all the estates. It was in parliament that differences of local and class sentiment had to be accommodated

[1] *Rot. Parl.,* ii. 67.

and fashioned into a national determination; and the result was effected more and more by mutual interchange of views, less and less by the arbitrament of a superior authority. Far more of the work of parliament was done by conference in the Painted Chamber or elsewhere than was the case after the amalgamation of the various estates and the severance of parliament into two houses.

The fluidity of medieval ideas about " estates " facilitated the unifying work of the crown in parliament. Their number and the vagueness of their delimitation, which depended more upon royal writ than upon any question of status, hindered the adoption of the continental theory, that the assent of each estate was essential to legislation. It is true that phrases expressing the assent of the lords spiritual and temporal and the commons in parliament assembled came to be customarily used in acts of parliament; but it is certain that their employment had not become essential by the end of the fifteenth century, and a great deal of legislation was passed as late as the reign of Henry VII without any further testimony to its legality than the fact that it had been enacted by the king in parliament.[1] Moreover, the " assent of the lords spiritual and temporal " did not mean their several assent, and the validity of the statutes of provisors and præmunire, as well as of Elizabeth's acts of supremacy and uniformity, depends upon a repudiation of the theory that the assent of the lords spiritual was requisite for such legislation. For no other " estate " has the claim ever been made. The assent of the lords was sought, not because they were one or two " estates," but because they were *consiliarii nati* of the crown. The assent of the commons was claimed as necessary not on the ground that they were an estate, but because they were the *communitas communitatum*.

---

[1] Cf. my *Reign of Henry VII*, vol. i. p. xxxii, iii. 199–200. A more scientific study of the development of legislative forms is badly needed. Even the editors of the *Statutes of the Realm* have sometimes preferred one MS. of a statute to another, on the ground that it embodied modern legislative phraseology, although that fact is evidence of its later date. The stereotyping of this phraseology has been considerably ante-dated, and the constitutional importance of the middle ages has been magnified by attributing to them not a little modern achievement.

Taxation was, of course, a different matter. For the ordinary revenues of the crown, such as feudal aids, regular customs, and so forth, no consent was necessary; they were "the king's own," and he was not only entitled to have them, but expected to live on them. Other taxes were matters of voluntary grant, and their history is bound up with the gradual growth of the right of the majority to bind the individual. Peter des Roches, in Henry III's reign, successfully claimed immunity from a tax on the ground that he as an individual had not consented to its levy. We have no knowledge of the important process by which this extreme view of the rights of "liberty and property" was surrendered, and the right of an "estate" to bind its individual members by a majority vote was established. The principle had been recognized in Magna Carta, and taxation by "estates" was the regular practice in medieval parliaments. It was but slowly that taxation was nationalized : each estate made its own grant, and no estate could bind any other. But the "estates" which voted taxes were limited in number; the judges did not tax themselves separately, nor did the prelates, who taxed their temporalties with the temporal peers and their spiritualties in convocation. On the other hand, the merchants, who were not an estate in parliament, often arranged their own taxation. Nor did the class-taxes that were voted correspond with this or any other division of estates : the taxes granted by the knights of the shires were, like those granted by the lords temporal and the lords spiritual in parliament, mainly taxes on land; citizens and burgesses for the most part granted taxes on chattels or moveables, while merchants paid on their merchandize. But the original distinction in kind between danegeld, carucage, tallage and so forth was passing away with the change of land from a source of men into a source of wealth, the acquisition by tenants-in-chief of vast flocks of sheep, and the purchase of land by citizens and burgesses. The effect of this confusion was to break down the system of class taxation : each estate would have to grant and pay various kinds of taxes, and while each continued for a time to grant its own,

the development of common action in the commons'
house led to common taxation. The knights join with
the town representatives, and together they succeed in
depriving the merchants of the right of separate taxation. The church consolidated its claim to grant all
its taxes, temporal as well as spiritual, in convocation
and to collect them itself;[1] while the peers, in return
for their legislative share in general finance, acquiesced in
the taxation of their possessions by grants originating in
the commons. Taxation was thus, by the end of the middle
ages, a national act, except in so far as the church was
concerned : its taxes were granted in two provincial convocations; the laity were all taxed together by act of
parliament. The grant for all is made by the commons
with the consent of the lords; but it takes the form of a
statute, and the sanction behind it partakes less and less
of the nature of a gift by the representatives of those who
have to pay, and more and more of the authority of a
sovereign legislature. In taxation, as in other matters, the
" estates " become one, which is called the state, and national
unity takes the place of class diversity.

A similar process affected the growth of legislation. Before
parliaments existed, the granting of charters by the crown
had exhibited the same tendency to expand from individualism and particularism to collectivism. The earliest charters
are to individual persons or boroughs; then come charters
to classes, such as tenants-in-chief and merchants, and
finally the great charter, which at any rate mentions all
classes of the community. The confirmation of the charters
by Edward I marks the culmination of the charter and the
point at which the charter merges into parliamentary legisla-

[1] See my *Reign of Henry VII*, ii. 39–43. The law does not, however,
appear to have been clear on the matter. In 1480 counsel argued that
grant by the commons was valid without the consent of the lords (*Year
Book*, 21 Ed. IV. p. 48; Hallam, *Middle Ages*, ed. 1878, iii. 108 *n*.).
Possibly anti-clericalism assisted their decision, for the validity of the
grant was contested by the church in the interest of some property that
had been left it. So long as lords and commons made separate grants,
the assent of the lords would not be necessary; it was different when
lords and commons were taxed by the same grants and when taxation took
a definite legislative form. See Appendix III (*n*).

tion. Here, too, the individual petition comes first, and gradually merges into petitions which are common, except that the church is reserved. It is not, of course, that all legislation is general or public, but all legislation is backed by the commons. The distinction is clearly marked in the last volume of the "Rolls of Parliaments." About half the petitions are common; the rest are presented by the commons *ex parte*, on behalf of some individual person or corporation.[1] The former become public, the latter private acts; and this familiar differentiation is first adopted in the sixteenth-century statutes, although the principle of discrimination is not that adopted to-day : and grants of taxes to the crown are often, in Henry VII's reign, classed as private acts. Still they are all acts done in a national parliament, and that is the recognized method of making secular law at the end of the middle ages.

This nationalization of politics was fatal to the medieval conception of jurisdiction as something inherent in lordship of the land; and by a process which has never been traced in detail parliaments developed a practice of making their legislation applicable *tam infra quam extra libertates* within as well as outside liberties. Gradually the distinctions between one franchise and another, and between all franchises and the remainder of the realm, were whittled away; and ideas of legal uniformity and of equality before the law begin to find expression in phrases that meant more than the old and empty platitude *omnes homines natura æquales sunt*. The King of England, the Emperor Charles V was told in 1551, had but one law by which to rule all his subjects,[2] and that was law made in parliament. Nothing could be less medieval : a contour map of medieval England indicating the various heights of jurisdictional privilege would have revealed an infinite diversity of inequality; and a vast and patient work of levelling was required before the king's writ ran throughout the land and reduced its people to equality in his courts of law. But the equalization of

[1] E. g. *Rot. Parl.*, vi. 290–2, 294, 298, 331.
[2] *Calendar State Papers*, For., Edward VI, p. 137.

L

liberty by means of parliament must be reserved for separate treatment, and so must the nationalization of the church, the greatest of medieval liberties and the latest of the spheres into which parliament ventured to intrude.

Parliament was, of course, no more than the instrument of comprehensive social, economic, and political forces. It had little to do directly with the nationalization of language and literature, without which there could have been no national state, though it can hardly be doubted that the association of men from all parts of the country in common discussion at Westminster assisted the adoption of a common standard of speech and common habits of thought. Parliament, too, had something to do with the nationalization of defence, whereby that obligation was converted from a burden imposed upon locality and class into a common duty.[1] Resistance to this development was long in dying down. Cornwall, in Henry VII's reign, rebelled rather than acknowledge its liability to taxation for the defence of the Scottish borders; and Hampden's case against Charles I was largely based on evil precedents which distinguished between the obligations of inland and those of maritime counties for naval defence. Similarly, the northern counties were under special liability for the defence of the borders, and were entitled to corresponding privileges. Particularism was of the essence of the middle ages, and it was only broken down by the common spirit developed in parliaments and by the common taxation they provided for national objects.

Every national state has necessarily undergone processes

---

[1] Particularism, however, often found expression even in parliament. In 1339, for instance, the commons disclaimed all obligation for the protection of the Scottish Marches and the keeping of the Narrow Seas (*Rot. Parl.*, ii. 103). If the Wardens required assistance, it should be provided, the commons contended, by the great council, without charging "la commune"; and as for naval defence, it was the business of the barons of the Cinque Ports, who for that purpose possessed "honours" above all commoners of the land, did not contribute to the aids and charges touching the land, and took endless profits arising from the sea. Therefore they should guard the sea as "la commune" did the land, without pay, as other towns and havens which had navies were bound to do (*ibid.*, ii. 105).

of nationalization. In some the process has been sudden and revolutionary, and the fusion has taken the form of an explosion. In others the nationalization has proceeded on purely monarchical lines and has thus produced a despotism. In England the process was slow and parliamentary. Had England developed a system of estates independent of its judicial parliament, had its representative systems and its parliaments been provincial and manifold, as in France, the bond of national unity could only have been forged here, as abroad, by the growth of royal authority. The union would have been personal, not parliamentary : it would have resembled the unions between France and Brittany, or England and Scotland in 1603, and not that between England and Scotland in 1707; and where the bond of union is the person of the sovereign, liberty cannot be safe; because for the sake of unity men will strengthen the bond of union and thus enhance the authority of the crown.

Charles I might have succeeded could he have played off a parliament of the north against another of the south; and a diversity of parliaments would have rendered each one of them weaker against the crown, as well as less national in its outlook. When the estates-general of France had sunk into abeyance, the *parlement* of Paris aspired to play the part of its English namesake. It failed because, save for the name, the two bodies had little in common. The *parlement* of Paris was but one of many French *parlements*, and it had long excluded all representative elements from its closing doors of privilege. In England all the estates had entrenched themselves in the high court of parliament, and had used its judicial machinery of impeachment and attainder with deadly effect against the royalist champions. The English estates were the grand jury of the nation, because they sat in a parliament which was a court of law. There was no national presentment of offenders in France, because the *parlements* excluded the estates, just as lower French courts extruded the jury. The time-honoured maxim that union is strength has nowhere been illustrated in such a variety of aspects as in the history of the English parliament.   It has embodied a national union of law and politics, of class and class, of province and province—a union slowly and painfully achieved in the course of ages, and not under the sudden stress of emergency.   In part the creation and in part the creator of English nationality, the English parliament is the essence of modern England.

CHAPTER VIII

THE GROWTH OF REPRESENTATION

THE fundamental difference between the English and other parliaments lies, we have seen, in the fact that it combines a system of popular representation with a high court of justice. Unlike all other courts of justice, it is therefore representative, and unlike all other representative assemblies, it is a court of justice. Further, the court was also the council, and a parliament was a joint session of executive, judicature, and legislature. This connexion between the governing and representative bodies was indispensable to national democracy. City-states can govern themselves by direct action without representation. National states can be maintained without representation, but without it they cannot govern themselves or determine national policy. Aristotle's maxims about the limited size of a state are sufficiently familiar; but they are all based on the assumption that a state cannot be self-governing unless the citizens govern directly, and themselves fulfil the functions of legislators, judges, generals, and admirals. According to the Athenians, the state required the whole life of its citizens; they were to be ready to undertake any political duty, and every other claim on their time was subordinate. A man who had to earn his living should be precluded from citizenship, because he lacked time and energy for public activity; and the occasional exercise of a vote at the polling booths would have seemed to them a poor qualification for citizenship. This conception in itself was fatal to modern ideas of democracy, because the mass of producers were excluded from political rights and duties; in Athens they were largely slaves, and Athenian democracy was really an aristocracy based upon the most odious of class distinctions. No doubt it rendered a high ideal practicable for the favoured few, who were expected to realize themselves and attain their highest individual development in the service of the state. But even the capacity of virtue was denied to the slave and the mechanic; an impassable gulf was fixed between them and the citizen; most men were slaves by nature, and such they must remain. The non-Greek peoples were called barbarians and excluded from the scope of Greek morality.

The Romans were more cosmopolitan; they disbelieved in this natural inequality of men, and Cicero thought that all men were capable of progress and of virtue. But the absence of any idea of representation prevented the realization of these comparatively liberal views in the expanded Roman state. Rome as a city could be democratic, but not as an empire; and the wider grew Rome's dominion the more autocratic grew its government. The more its sway expanded, the more did its governing class contract. Direct popular participation in politics can never be more than municipal in scope, and the city-democracy that tries to govern an empire fails in its task and incidentally ceases to be a democracy. Athens, Rome, Venice all point to the incompatibility of *imperium et libertas* when either is divorced from the principle of representation.

The evolution of this principle has, therefore, provided an escape from the dilemma upon either horn of which every ancient state was sooner or later impaled, has rendered possible the national democratic state, and has reconciled liberty and empire; and the credit for this discovery has been claimed for political or ecclesiastical theorists of the middle ages. Representation has been regarded as a great democratic principle first elaborated and applied in the organization of the friars and particularly of the Dominican Order in the thirteenth century, and its adoption for parliamentary purposes has been ascribed to the influence which Dominican confessors exerted over the minds of English kings and statesmen.[1] The part played by theorists in the practical development of human affairs is a question upon which theorists are apt to differ from other people; but probably the theorist, especially if he has been fortunate enough to possess a great gift of literary expression, has received more than his share of responsibility for the good and evil in history. Machiavelli is believed to have corrupted the politics of the sixteenth century, Locke to have prepared men's minds for the Revolution of 1688, and Rousseau to have stimulated that of 1789. It is well to remember that Machiavelli's *Prince* was not written until real princes had given the most striking manifestations of his principles, that Locke's *Two Treatises* were published two years after the Revolution of 1688, and that Rousseau's resonant phrases were borrowed from ancient Roman law. It was the aptness of these doctrines to the conditions of the time that gave them their vogue, but they did not create the conditions, and in other circumstances would have fallen on stony ground. The soil is not less important for the harvest than the seed, and in the case of political ideas the seed is in the air, blown by the wind, and not sown by the hands of individual men.

Representation is, moreover, an ambiguous word which needs to be defined before we can deal with its development. It does not necessarily imply election. When Emerson wrote his *Representative Men* he said nothing about a popular vote; nor was Hobbes thinking about the franchise when he described the sovereign as the representative of all the citizens. Charles I on the scaffold claimed to be the true representative of his people; and the house of lords has not infrequently made the same claim against the house of commons. In Germany after 1815, when the constitution of various German states was under discussion, it was contended that the peasantry needed no special representation because they were adequately represented by their landlords; but there was no suggestion that landlords should be elected by their tenants. Nor does election necessarily

---

[1] Cf. E. Barker, *The Dominican Order and Convocation*, 1913.

mean popular election : the Calvinist commonly talks about
the elect, but they are not chosen by ballot.   Election does
not, in the middle ages, reveal the person of the elector, and
means no more than selection by the persons authorized to
select.   It is a matter of common knowledge that knights
of the shire were selected in the county court, but by whom
they were really chosen is merely a matter of surmise.

It is idle to seek the origin of representation in its vaguer
sense; for the representation of states by their governments and ambassadors is almost co-eval with the state
itself, and when Hobbes writes of the sovereign representative he is expanding the Roman juristic maxim *quod principi
placuit legis habet vigorem . . . utpote . . . populus ei et in eum
omne suum imperium et potestatem conferat.*   Cæsar was omnicompetent because Cæsar was the repository of every citizen's
powers; he was the universal agent, the representative of all.
It was in this sense that the feudal lord represented his
tenants and that the priest and four "best" men represented
the village community in the hundred and shire-moots; and
it is only in this sense that parliaments were representative
during the earlier periods of their existence.   Modern ideas
of representation assume that the representative is bound
by the will of the represented, but the will of the people is
a modern fact which largely partakes of fiction.   There
seems in the middle ages to have been a total absence
of specific instructions from constituencies to their
members.   Election promises were unknown, and they appear
in their earliest form in sixteenth-century undertakings on
the part of candidates to serve without exacting the wages
their constituents were legally bound to pay.   They were
elected to bind their constituents, and not to be bound by
them; they were to come empowered to execute the proposals of the crown, and not to impose upon the crown the
proposals of their constituents.   The growth of the popular
will is the most important, obscure, and neglected content
of English domestic history.   It takes place behind and
under the forms of representative government; but the form
of government no more reveals its controlling power than

the structure of a ship tells us whether it is run by the captain or the crew, and our representative parliament has been the instrument in turn of king, lords, and commons. It is easy, therefore, to exaggerate the importance of representative forms in the middle ages. On the other hand, it should not be ignored; the development of the machinery of the constitution was important before the people had learnt to drive it, and no democracy has ever constructed a workable constitution until it has been taught the elements of politics.

The earliest forms of English representation appealed to the interests of the government and the selfishness of the majority rather than to popular ambition. The " best " men, who were required by royal ordinance to attend the local courts, were certainly not elected; they may have been a sort of local hereditary aristocracy, like the twelve lawmen of Chester and Lincoln, of whom we read in Domesday. Under the Norman and Angevin kings they were probably the holders of the " best " tenements, and the obligation to do suit at the county court was attached as a condition to certain holdings. Representation was, in fact, an unpleasant incident of feudal service.[1] This is the popular attitude in the middle ages towards parliament, as towards the shire court; it is not a question of who is anxious to serve, but of who is obliged to attend.

The business to be done is also that of the crown; it is the king's writs by which the suitors are summoned, and it is mainly the " pleas of the crown " that are heard in the county court. No doubt humble folk are interested in having justice done, but it is the crown which discovers that *justitia magnum emolumentum.* Justice is done for the sake of its proceeds, and representation is used by the crown for purposes of justice and finance. The county court consists of jurors, who represent the county; *ponere se super patriam* is to go throw oneself on a jury, and the verdict of the jury is the county's act. It is also upon the county that taxation is later imposed, and its re-partition among the

[1] See above, p. 109.

smaller communities is left to the county court or to the sheriff. But attendance is all a matter of service determined by tenure. By a statute of 1294 it is enacted that no one with less than forty shillings a year in land can be empanelled on a jury in the county court.[1] The boon consists in the exemption of the poor; but the burden becomes in time a franchise. These jurors elect the knights of the shire in the court to which they are summoned for jury-service, and in Edward I's statute we have the origin of the forty-shilling freehold vote. In 1430 the vote has become a privilege, and a famous statute prohibits its exercise by those whom Edward I had freed from jury-service. The important point is that every voter is first a juror : he is only a voter because he is a juror; he can only enjoy the franchise because he discharges an obligation. The vote is not a matter of individual right, but of duty to the community.

The idea that any one had a right to a vote would have been unintelligible in the fourteenth century, and its discussion would have seemed as irrational as the question whether a man has a right to serve on a jury to-day. He may have, but the point does not arise, because no one thinks of claiming the right. Men are more concerned with their liability to be summoned; and it was his liability to attendance at the shire court and to election as member of parliament that troubled our medieval ancestor. Whether he was a baron liable to individual summons or a knight or a burgess liable to election, he was anxious to escape the liability; and the constituencies were of like mind. Sometimes a recorder was bound by the terms of his appointment to serve the borough in parliament and thus relieve the burgesses. The two knights for Oxfordshire who fled the country on their election to parliament exemplified a common frame of mind among the elected, and Torrington, which secured a charter giving it perpetual exemption from

---

[1] *Rot. Parl.*, i. 116. Forty shillings had previously been made the limit of suits over which the county court had jurisdiction (Pollock and Maitland, ii. 540–1).

representation in parliament,[1] typified the attitude of the electors. The shires could not expect such favours, and their representation remained constant throughout; but the 166 cities and boroughs from which Edward I had summoned representatives to parliament had sunk to less than a hundred in the reign of Henry VI. The number of members was smaller than these figures would indicate, for sometimes, to save expense, Cornish and Devonshire constituencies returned identical members.[2] Local parsimony prevailed over national interest. Not only did the borough which evaded representation escape the liability for members' wages, but it got off with lighter taxation. Boroughs which were represented only by the knights of the shire were taxed with the shires, and paid a fifteenth, while boroughs with representation of their own had their own taxation and paid a tenth (o). Parliamentary ambition was a feeble incentive when representation meant extra taxation, and when attendance at Westminster involved responsibility without power or profit. Parliament was not then a career, and it opened no paths to promotion. Members were men of business reluctantly diverted from their private affairs for occasional public service; and the few who aspired to political eminence had to choose the church or the service of the king or of a baronial magnate.

Representation, in fact, was nowise regarded as a means of expressing individual right or forwarding individual interests. It was communities, not individuals, who were represented, just as it was communities and not individuals who were taxed in parliaments. The poll-tax, when it appeared in 1380, was resented because it was a departure from the old tenths and fifteenths which were levied on boroughs and

[1] *Rot. Parl.*, ii. 459*b*; Maitland, *Const. Hist.*, p. 174; the exemption was secured in 1366 and confirmed in 1368 (*Cal. Patent Rolls*, 1364-7, p. 246, 1367-70, p. 115). Edward III, in granting the petition of the men of Torrington, remarked that " vos ea occasione laboribus et expensis multipliciter gravati fuisti, ad vestrum damnum non modicum et depressionem manifestam."

[2] See J. J. Alexander in *Trans. Devon. Assoc.*, 1910, xlii. 260. In 1362 one John Hill was returned for six Devonshire constituencies, and John Wonard for two Devonshire and two Cornish seats.

shires and were not imposed *viritim*. The re-allotment of the burden of taxation, like the determination of the borough franchise, was a matter for local option and arrangement; and there was the greatest variety in both spheres. The statute of 1430 regulated the county vote on a national uniform principle; but until 1832 no attempt was successful to introduce uniformity into the borough franchise. In some boroughs the parliamentary franchise was limited to members of the governing body, in some to the " freemen "; in others it was extended to all who held burgage tenements, or even to all who paid scot and lot. This local diversity adds to the difficulty of the discussion whether women possessed a vote in the middle ages. That women could sit in parliament is certainly unproved, and the fact that the husband of a woman who held an entire barony was liable to a special writ of summons implies that she was exempt. The instances of women appearing in parliament, upon which reliance has been placed, relate to its judicial functions, and women still frequently appear in courts of law. The vote, it must be remembered, was grounded in jury-service, and unless it can be shown that women were personally liable for that and other forms of service, there is no reason to suppose that they exercised a parliamentary vote.

Nevertheless women did occasionally return, or assist in returning members to parliament, not because women's right to vote was admitted, but because it was the land rather than men that parliament represented, and occasionally women held the land upon which the burden of representation had been fixed. Feudal service was always regarded as due from the land rather than from the individual tenant, and so long as the crown obtained its service it cared little who performed it. The liability was first the lord's, who generally passed it on to his tenants; but if tenants were lacking, the obligation reverted to the lord. Thus by the sixteenth century the borough of Gatton had lost all its burgesses, but retained its parliamentary obligation of service. The return was, therefore, made by means of indenture between the sheriff and lord of the manor; and once, at any rate, during the minority of her son, it was made by Dame Alice Copley. In dealing with medieval representation we have always to think in terms of feudal service rather than in those of democratic principle. The boroughs are represented because they are collective tenants-in-chief on the king's demesne; and the shires, too, are in a sense tenants-in-chief, in that they "farm" the royal rights of jurisdiction. Parliament was the king's head court,[1] and it was composed of those who owed service to the crown.

But the feudal form was filling with the breath of national life and popular consciousness, the outcome of the fourteenth century and the sign of the passing of medieval things. The growth of a national literature illustrated by Chaucer and still more by Langland, and of a desire for national expression in religious thought exemplified by Wycliffe's works; the substitution of a national weapon, the longbow, for the mailed knight and the feudal castle; the development of industry and commerce at the expense of the agricultural monopoly of wealth; the triumph of national feeling over local particularism during the Hundred Years' war; the effect of the mobility of labour in breaking down manorial isolation, all made themselves felt in the parliamentary sphere. Classes that had been ignored were forcing their way into politics, and the beginnings of popular education were fostering a wider-spread national intelligence. The foundation of great schools and colleges and the growth of universities are familiar illustrations of this spirit. Not less significant was the fact that villeins, although they might be fined by their lords for so doing, were beginning to send their children to school.[2] Thus Langland found an audience, and the English people discovered itself. Prosperous villeins who sent their

[1] This phrase was used by James I (Prothero, *Select Statutes*, etc., 1898, p. 400), but not, as implied by Dr. Prothero, of the English Parliament. It occurs in his *Trew Law of Free Monarchies*, which dates from 1598, five years before James became King of England (see McIlwain, *Political Works of James I*, Harvard Univ. Press, pp. xxv, 62).

[2] In 1372 a customary tenant was fined heavily by his lord (who was a bishop) for putting his son to school without the lord's leave (Maitland, *Collected Papers*, ii. 399).

sons to school attended the county court themselves, and contributed to the tumultuary elections which led to the restricting statute of 1430. Similar irruptions into the oligarchical circles of municipal government led to corresponding restrictions of the municipal franchise.[1] These restrictions were less important and less permanent than the movement by which they were provoked, and their significance lies in the indirect evidence they provide for the growth of a political consciousness among the mass of the population. It may have been a sign of grace when the commons complained in 1436 that sheriffs often returned members who had not been elected.[2]

Probably here we have also the explanation of the curious fact that about then the ebbing tide of parliamentary representation begins to turn, and the number of boroughs returning members to increase. The lowest limit was reached in 1435, when only ninety-four made returns; Henry VI added eight and Edward IV five. Henry VII apparently made no change,[3] but under the later Tudors the increase was rapid and steady. Later on we shall see that the attribution of this increase to Tudor designs upon parliamentary independence is not a tenable theory; and even if it were, their attempt would illustrate their appreciation of the importance of parliamentary support. It is more probable that the creation of new boroughs, and restoration of parliamentary representation to others which had lost it, was due to a deeper national impulse. We have at least one protest from a Tudor secretary of state that there were too many members already, a refusal to listen to Newark's petition for representation, and a hint that the government in 1579

---

[1] See my *Reign of Henry VII*, ii. 181–5, for restrictions on the borough franchise at Leicester and Northampton.

[2] *Rot. Parl.*, iv. 507.

[3] The difficulty of tracing accurately the growth of parliamentary representation is increased by the defectiveness of the lists of members printed in the *Official Return*. Apart from one for 1491 in *Harleian MS.* 2252, f. 28, there are no lists between 1477 and 1529, although research among borough archives and elsewhere may help to supply the deficiency (*p*). Something may also emerge from the neglected records of the Crown Office recently transferred from Westminster to the Record Office.

contemplated the abolition of rotten boroughs.[1] The demand
for representation now came from below, from prospective
electors themselves or from neighbouring magnates seeking
an easy seat in the house of commons. Boroughs were
bought up in the sixteenth century; the eldest sons of peers
became candidates for election; the proceedings of the
house were considered worth recording in *Journals ;* candidates offered to serve without their wages; and even bribed
the electors, not to escape, but to secure, election. Men no
longer fled the country when elected, or transferred their
liabilities to their tenants. A member of parliament had
become an important person, a seat in the house an object
of ambition, and the house itself a place of political power.
The seats of the mighty were filling with popular candidates.
Elections were contested, and electors were canvassed;
boroughs refused to accept neighbouring magnates' nominees,
and riots were not infrequent. The burden of representation had become a privilege, because people had grasped the
fact that through it they could impose their will on the crown,
instead of the crown through it imposing its will upon them.
The forms of the partnership remained, but the predominance was changing hands.

National spirit had fused local prejudices. Members are
regarded as serving their country and not merely their shires
or boroughs; and residence ceases to be an indispensable
qualification. The legal requirement stood, and the matter
was often debated in the house; but the national view
prevailed over the letter of the law, and parliament was
saved from the dead hand of medieval parochialism. Other
influences, no doubt, contributed to this result; insistence
upon residence would have defeated aristocratic designs on
the commons, and have excluded many privy councillors

[1] T. Wilson to the Earl of Rutland, June 17, 1579 (*Rutland MSS.*,
Hist. MSS. Comm. i. 117) : " I have moved the Queen for the town of
Newark, and have obtained her consent that the book shall be engrossed
by Mr. Attorney, and all the articles allowed, save the nomination of
two burgesses. It is thought that there are over many already, and
there will be a device hereafter to lessen the number for divers decayed
towns." Newark did not obtain parliamentary representation until 1673
(*Official Return*, i. 526).

of the crown. But the substitution of landed gentry for timorous townsmen stiffened the back of the commons, and is definitely assigned by a Venetian ambassador as the cause of the recalcitrance of one of Mary's parliaments; [1] and even the election of privy councillors testified to the growth of popular influence. In Edward I's reign a councillor was summoned *ex officio* to parliaments, and a parliament was a meeting between council and estates. Now, instead of sitting *ex officio*, the privy councillor sought popular election, and in Thomas Cromwell and William Cecil we have the first striking examples of the " old parliamentary hand "; both sat continuously in the commons until they were raised to the peerage, and both were there in the interests of the nation and not in those of their constituencies. The *communitates* have become the *communitas*, England is one whole instead of many parts, and in politics and history the whole is greater than the sum of all the parts. Out of the fusion arises the national patriotism of Elizabethan England.

The sixteenth century is indeed the great period of the consolidation of the house of commons, and without that consolidation the house would have been incapable of the work it achieved in the seventeenth. Under the Tudors it becomes a compact and corporate unit, and acquires a weight which makes it the centre of parliamentary gravity. Its transference, in Edward VI's reign, from the chapter house to St. Stephen's chapel [2] brings it under the same roof as the parliament chamber, and provides ocular demonstration of its position as an integral part of parliament. The commons no longer *comparent in parliamento* by traversing the street between the abbey and parliament with the Speaker at their head; they are already " in parliament " when they meet by themselves, and their domestic discussions become parliamentary instead of extra-parliamentary proceedings. Each representative is now a limb, a " member " of parliament, a phrase which appears in the fifteenth

[1] *Venetian Calendar*, vi. 251.
[2] See below, p. 333.

century,[1] was used by Henry VIII when vindicating the privileges of the commons, and gradually secured a popular vogue; and a prominent member is described in Elizabeth's reign as "the great parliament man." The house is a national representative : every Englishman is "intended," in Sir Thomas Smith's phrase, to be present either in person or by proxy; and the house derives its authority from the fact that it embodies the will of the English people. The laxity which in the middle ages put up with the absence of a majority of elected members, and assumed that absence, like silence, gave consent, was no longer tolerated. The clerk kept a book of attendance : no member was allowed to go home without leave, and those who did so were prosecuted before the king's bench. Down to 1558 the leave had to be obtained from the crown; in Elizabeth's reign it begins to be granted by the house itself.[2]

Slowly, too, the house developed a corporate consciousness bred of prolonged and intimate association. The medieval parliament was an affair of weeks; it seldom had more than one session, and members rarely sought re-election. Every house was, therefore, a body of strangers, speaking perhaps incomprehensible dialects, distrustful of one another, here to-day and gone to-morrow, never, in most cases, to meet again, and utterly unable, on account of their transitory existence, to acquire confidence in one another or to develop leadership and parliamentary skill. On rare occasions before 1509 a parliament was called back for a second session; but it is during the reign of Henry VIII that the modern practice begins, and it begins with the parliament that wrought the Reformation. Summoned to meet on November 3, 1529, its existence was continued until April 4, 1536, and during that period it held eight sessions extending over more months than the days of the average

---

[1] *Rot. Parl.*, v. 240, vi. 191; cf. Smith, *De Republica Anglorum*, ed. Alston, p. 63.

[2] A bill to control the unlicensed absence of members passed the commons, but not the lords, in January 1554-5, and three similar attempts were unsuccessfully made in the following session (*Political History of England*, vi. 147-8), and yet another on November 9, 1558.

M

medieval parliament.   By the end of that period members of the house of commons must have acquired a familiarity among themselves, a knowledge of parliamentary procedure, and an acquaintance with national politics such as no house of commons had ever possessed before.   The experiment was unique in the sixteenth century, but a later parliament of Henry VIII had four sessions, and the first of Edward VI had three.   Mary saw fit to change her parliaments with greater frequency, and five were elected during the five years of her reign, only one of which met for a second session. Elizabeth had not her father's faith in parliament; but most of her parliaments sat for more than one session, one session lasted over three months, and one parliament was undissolved for nearly nine years.   The leading members, moreover, both of the government and of the opposition, are constantly re-elected; the ordinary *personnel* of the house grew more stable; and if Cecils and Bacons placed parliamentary experience at the service of the crown, Nortons and Wentworths used it on behalf of the liberties of the commons.

Internal consolidation was accompanied by expansion, and the number of members increased during the Tudor period by more than fifty per cent.   There were fewer than three hundred when Henry VII ascended the throne; there were more than four hundred and fifty when Elizabeth died. Henry VIII added eight members to the representation of Lancashire, two each to London and Middlesex, Cornwall, Norfolk, Suffolk, and Buckinghamshire, and one to Shropshire; he "shired" Wales and Monmouth and introduced twenty-four Welsh members to parliament; he also incorporated Cheshire, and even extended the parliamentary system to Calais, leaving the county palatine of Durham alone outside the national organization.[1]   Edward VI added fourteen members to Cornwall, four to Northamptonshire, and two each to Hampshire, Yorkshire, Lincolnshire,

---

[1] A bill "to have two knights from Durham into the parliament" was introduced in the house of commons on January 18, 1562–3, but apparently got no farther.   The above figures are only approximate.

"QUEEN ELIZABETH IN PARLIAMENT

A. *L: Chancellor.* B. *Marquises, Earles &c.* C. *Barons.* D. *Bishops.* E. *Iudges.* F. *Masters of Chancery.* G. *Clerks.* H. *Speaker of ye Comons.*
I. *Black Rod.* K. *Sergeant at Armes.* L. *Members of the Comons house.* M. *Sr Francis Walsingham Secretary of State.*

PARLIAMENT IN THE 17TH CENTURY.

Cheshire, Staffordshire, and Wales. Mary increased the representation of Yorkshire by ten members, that of Oxfordshire by three, of Kent, Northumberland, Norfolk, Hertfordshire, Buckinghamshire, and Worcestershire by two each, and of Northamptonshire and Berkshire by one apiece. Elizabeth's additions amounted to fifty-nine against forty-five made by Henry VIII, thirty by Edward VI, and twenty-seven by Mary; sixteen new members went to Hampshire, twelve to Cornwall, six to Suffolk, four each to Kent, Yorkshire and Lancashire, two each to Devon, Notts, Gloucestershire, Shropshire, Staffordshire, and Surrey, and one to Wales. It was reserved for James I to grant special representation to the universities of Oxford and Cambridge, which gratefully elected his nominees; but by 1603 the house of commons was more completely representative than it had ever been before, and in spite of the acts restricting the franchise it is probable that the electorate was also growing wider. The amount of free socage was increasing in the counties, and the bar of serfdom was steadily being removed; at the disputed Norfolk election of 1586 three thousand voters are stated to have been present,[1] though in the boroughs the widening of the franchise had to await the period of the Long parliament and the Commonwealth.[2] The facile explanation of all this expansion on the theory that it was due to the efforts of the crown to pack parliaments will not bear examination. The Cornish boroughs, which are usually chosen to substantiate this hypothesis, were in reality notorious for the independent and even fractious spirit exhibited by their representatives and for the paucity of privy councillors among their ranks.[3]

---

[1] D'Ewes, *Journals*, p. 396.   [2] See below, p. 324.

[3] At least four pronounced protestants sat for Cornish constituencies in the first parliament of Mary's reign; Peter and Paul Wentworth and James Dalton were elected by Cornish constituencies in Elizabeth's reign; and under James I and Charles I nearly all the leaders of the parliamentary opposition found seats at one time or other in Cornwall, including Sir John Eliot, Hampden, Coke, Sir E. Sandys, Holles, Hakewill, Sir R. Phelips, Sir Henry Marten, and John Rolle. Hallam's theory (*Const. Hist.*, i. 45) that these Cornish constituencies were created to foster the influence of the court over the commons is not corroborated by the evidence.

It is more reasonable to suppose that the house of commons was reflecting the general growth of national sentiment and of the popular desire for a voice in its own affairs. People who repudiated absolute authority in the church would not remain submissive to political autocracy.

There were, of course, defects enough in the sixteenth-century representative system from the modern point of view. The lower classes had small means of asserting what little political will they possessed; and the greater the influence which the house of commons acquired, the greater the eagerness of landlords and aspiring lawyers to manipulate its elections. The social status of burgesses rose with the prestige of the house, aristocrats canvassed for seats which medieval craftsmen had sought to avoid, and in the eighteenth century both houses of parliament were appanages of the highest class of society. But the electorate was never reduced to the same uniformity : the representative system consisted of sections or samples; but the sections were vertical, not horizontal, and the samples came from various social strata. The county voters had to be freeholders, and the restriction was arbitrary enough, but it included in the franchise many who were poor and excluded many who were rich. The forty shillings, which had been a serious property disqualification in the reign of Edward I, was a trifling sum in that of George III, and many of the forty-shilling freeholders must have been very poor men. Again, the franchise in many boroughs was democratic, more democratic before than after 1832; and while the great reform bill mitigated many abuses and swept away some anomalies, it disfranchised numbers of poor electors, and created a grievance which fostered the Chartist movement.

Feudal traditions, however, long clung to our franchise law, and with them the theory that it was the land, and not men which should be represented in parliament. The "stake in the country," which was used in the eighteenth century to defend the monopoly of political power by the landed aristocracy against the claims of mere wealth derived from banking or commerce, was employed in the nineteenth against the claims of intelligent poverty; and some contended that the number of a man's votes should be proportionate to his possessions.[1] Even now mere wealth does not entitle a man to a vote at all unless that wealth is converted into terms of the tenure or occupancy of land and what stands thereon. Mere intelligence does not count at all in our franchise laws except in so far as it accounts for university representation. Vast inroads have, however, been made on feudal theory by ideas of universal suffrage, and the real issue with regard to representation is whether the individual or the family is the unit to be represented. Modern socialism tends to make the state the sole form of society and to weaken every other bond of association; and parliament, instead of representing communities or families, is coming to represent nothing but individuals.

[1] These views were almost entirely abandoned in the debates on the Franchise Act of 1917.

CHAPTER IX

PARLIAMENT AND LIBERTY

It has been remarked by a skilled American observer of English politics that " private property in England is, on the whole, less secure from attack on the part of the Government to-day than it was at the time of the Stuarts." [1] A similar substratum of truth would underlie the statement that there was greater liberty before the beginning of parliaments than there has been since or is likely to be again; and the days when a wealthy magnate like Peter des Roches could evade a tax by voting against it must seem to many a golden age of liberty and property, from which England has been steadily falling away ever since parliaments were invented to rob the individual of his liberty by means of other men's votes. There is, however, no end to the paradoxes for which liberty has been the excuse or the justification. The crimes perpetrated in its name have been as multifarious as the sins committed on behalf of religion or the battles fought for the sake of peace.

It is the penalty of general and inspiring conceptions that they mean so many different things and inspire different minds in so many different ways. " When I mention religion," said the frank but reverend Mr. Thwackum, " I mean the Christian religion; and not only the Christian religion, but the Protestant religion; and not only the Protestant religion, but the Church of England." [2] Orthodoxy is my 'doxy; heterodoxy is other people's. True liberty is my liberty; other people's is their presumption. Servants take liberties, but are not often, in the minds of

[1] A. Laurence Lowell, *Essays on Government*, pp. 81, 82.
[2] Fielding, " Tom Jones " in *Works*, ed. 1859, p. 26.

their masters or their mistresses, entitled to what they take. " Like every other struggle for liberty," writes Bishop Stubbs of the Great Civil War, "it ended in being a struggle for supremacy." [1] Charles I fought for liberty no less than did the parliament or the army, the English, the Irish, or the Scots. Both north and south fought for liberty in the American civil war, the north for the liberty of the negroes in the south, the south for liberty to manage its own affairs. Masters and men are fighting all over the world for liberty, masters for liberty to employ their capital as they think fit, men for liberty to choose their own conditions of labour. Like charity, liberty covers a multitude of sins.

Nothing has proved more elusive than liberty, and its endless pursuit has filled the pages of English history. Men thought, and still think, it was achieved by Magna Carta; but it had to be fought for again in the fourteenth century, in the Great Civil War, and at the Revolution of 1688. Glorious as it seemed to the Whigs, even that vindication of liberty failed to satisfy men for long; reform bills in the nineteenth century were one after another hailed as heralds of a newer freedom; and even after the parliament act of 1911 liberty seems to some of us farther off than ever. Nor are we singular in our discontents. The thirteen American colonies fought a war of independence to achieve their liberty; they won, but three-quarters of a century later they were still fighting a sterner civil war for liberty; and the latest generation of freeborn Americans carried into office and power in 1912 a president whose banner bore the strange device "the new freedom." Man, said Rousseau, is born free, and everywhere he is in chains; man, it would rather seem, is born a slave and ever he is seeking to burst his bonds.

The fallacy lies in " man "; it also lies in " liberty." To say that man has achieved liberty is an inaccurate way of stating that some men have achieved some liberty. The problem of liberty, like that of property, is one of distribution, and cannot be divorced from that of equality. There was sense and logic in the union of the trinity of the French Revolution :

[1] *Constitutional History*, iii. 637.

there can be no liberty without some equality.   But the third
of the trio, fraternity, supplies—at least to an American
student—the best illustration of the difficulty we have to
face in tracing the growth of liberty.   Every American
undergraduate knows what a fraternity is; to an English
undergraduate it looks like an embryo college.   It is a
voluntary association of students for social—some think for
anti-social—purposes.   Like every association, its value
consists quite as much in the many undesirable persons it
excludes as in the select few it comprehends.   Fraternities are,
indeed, too select for ultra-democratic feeling in the United
States, and in more than one legislature bills have been introduced to abolish them as contraventions of democratic
principle.   Now, if a measure were passed by congress
guaranteeing to all fraternities in perpetuity their privileges
and their property, it is easily conceivable that such a measure
might come to be called the great charter of fraternities.
But it is not less easy to understand that the excluded
majority might fail to discern any connexion between such
a measure and the democratic ideal of fraternity.

   That is the position of Magna Carta.   It is the great
charter of liberties, but not of liberty, and few habits are
more fatal to historical understanding than that of assuming
that the same word has the same meaning at different
periods.   We have no constants in history.   It is far safer to
assume discrepancy than identity, and it is an elementary precaution to warn beginners in history that medieval Germany
might include Austria but not Prussia, Cambrai but not
Breslau.   These changes in the territorial meaning of familiar
terms are comparatively simple and obvious; the vicissitudes
in the terminology of ideas are more subtle, and even eminent
archivists have provided striking illustrations of the dangers
of ignoring them.   Sir T. Duffus Hardy assumed that
religio in the thirteenth century meant religion, and was
astonished at John's modernism when he discovered a royal
licence *condere novam religionem*, although John was guilty
of nothing worse than granting a baron leave to found a
religious house by alienating certain lands into mortmain.

Yet the difference between *religio* and religion was not greater than that between *libertas* and liberty; and John was as medievally-minded when he granted Magna Carta as when he licensed a baron to found an abbey.

The medieval *libertas* and *religio* have this in common to distinguish them from their modern synonyms. Both were concrete and material; both are now abstract and ideal. The transformation from the one to the other has been the common characteristic of linguistic development. The expansion of a nation's mind is seen, like that of a child's, in the expansion of the meaning attached to the terms it uses. One child has been known to think that Eleanor of Aquitaine was corpulent because she was described in a textbook as " one of Henry II's stoutest adherents "; and another imbibed the same idea of God from being told of His omnipresence. Liberty and religion are very local to primitive minds : local gods become tribal deities, and then the national gods of chosen peoples. But even Israel revolted against a God which had to be worshipped in Judah, as England murmured against a pope in Avignon, and nations had to advance far on the path of civilization before they relinquished their conviction that their God spoke in their vernacular and gave them special protection in battle.

Their liberties were as their deities, peculiar to themselves, circumscribed in their operation, bound to the soil, tangible, visible, and concrete. The *genius loci* was at the bottom of both; and famous shrines had their counterpart in great liberties. The general idea was lost in the local manifestation; and our Lady of Walsingham belongs to the same class of phenomena as the "liberties of the Fleet." Liberties were always attached to particular persons or places; there was nothing general or national about them. They were definite concrete privileges, which some people enjoyed, but most did not. The first clause of Magna Carta—*quod ecclesia anglicana libera sit*—seems to be general enough; but the explanation that follows shows that all it meant was that cathedral chapters should be free to elect their bishops, and presumably that the king should not be free to refuse them their temporalities.[1] Possibly the explanation was a royalist gloss, and the demand for ecclesiastical freedom meant, in the minds of those who made it, that the restrictions imposed on the liberties of the church by the Constitutions of Clarendon should be ignored : as a matter of practice they were ignored in the later middle ages, and this was assuredly a more general liberty than any conceded in the charter. For the rest, the liberties of the *ecclesia* were simply the sum of the particular liberties of each ecclesiastic. They were rights of patronage and jurisdiction; and contention over these " liberties " of the church is quite as rife in the middle ages among churchmen themselves as between church and state. In both spheres alike liberty was an adjunct, almost a form, of property; and it was prized for its material and financial attributes.

It was almost always a local monopoly. The liberty of a town consisted largely in its right to rate its inhabitants and to levy tolls on all who frequented its markets. The liberty of a baron consisted in his authority over others, in the court he owned, and in the perquisites of his jurisdiction. To deprive him of this jurisdiction over his villeins was an infringement of his liberty expressly prohibited by the thirty-fourth clause of the charter. Another infringement of liberty forbidden by the charter was the reduction of the number of villeins on the estates of a ward of the crown. That was a " waste of men " which impaired the value of the lands, and the emancipation of his villeins infringed the liberty of the lord. Just as one man's food is another man's poison, one man's liberty was another's servitude. The liberties which the barons hoped to secure at Runnymede were largely composed of the services of their villeins. A liberty was in no sense a common right or a popular conception. It has been defined as a portion of sovereign authority

---

[1] There is nothing in Magna Carta to compel the king to invest an elected bishop with his temporalities, and the impossibility of binding the king in this way rendered the concession almost nugatory from the first.

in the hands of a subject; and the popularity of liberty entirely depends upon the extent of the portions and of their distribution. Medieval liberties were large, but their recipients were few. They were the exceptions to the rule; it was because they were rare privileges and not common rights that the framers of Magna Carta set so much store upon liberties. When the house of commons began to deal with the subject in Edward III's reign, it had a different tale to tell; it begged the king, in 1348, to grant no more liberties in the future. Every franchise or liberty was so much land and so many people cut off from the common law, excluded from the beneficent operation of king's writs and royal justice, and subjected to the arbitrary will of the owner of the liberty.

To redistribute and equalize liberty has been one of the principal functions of parliament; and the petition of 1348 is the earliest indication of its grasp of the problem. But one of the greatest obstacles to reform is commonly the reformers' frame of mind; and the keenest opponents of other men's privileges are often the stoutest defenders of their own. Parliamentary concentration on the task of reducing liberties was impeded by the addiction of members to their own; and so long as constituencies were evading parliamentary representation in order to lessen their share in taxation and save the expense of members' wages, the house of commons could not be a very efficient instrument of reform. The local interest ever outweighed the common advantage during the middle ages; and parliaments, while they gave vent to complaints, failed to enforce a remedy. The Good parliament of 1376 was followed by a worthless successor, and the commons by themselves were hardly able to compel the adoption of a single reform throughout the middle ages. It was not they who checked Edward I, removed Edward II or Richard II, or disposed of Henry VI or Richard III. Changes of government were sometimes legalized in parliament, but they were made outside, by unparliamentary methods and forces; and these same forces which made and unmade kings were themselves the repositories of the "liberties" of which the

commons complained. Indeed, the more they made free with
the royal prerogative and took liberties with the crown,
the greater grew their own. " Get you lordship," wrote one
of the Paston correspondents in 1450, " *quia ibi pendet tota
lex et prophetæ.*" [1] Lordship and liberty were much the
same thing, and the over-mighty subject grasped an ever-
increasing share of sovereign power. As late as Elizabeth's
reign it was said that the men of Northumberland would
have no other prince than a Percy, and in Yorkshire the
sheriff had little power against the bailiffs and stewards
of the northern earls. The so-called constitutional experiment of the Lancastrians consisted in little more than giving
rein to the local liberties of the magnates, who in the Wars
of the Roses took the bit between their teeth.

The extent of the liberties claimed by these magnates
is difficult to realize, but without some appreciation of it
we cannot explain the Tudor autocracy or understand how
that despotism coincided with a vast movement of national
liberation. It was not merely that the over-mighty subject
excluded royal writs from his franchise and defied the crown
from his feudal castle. We now regard the armed forces
of the nation as the armed forces of the crown, but then the
crown controlled but a fraction of the military strength of
England. Each magnate had his council of state, his council
learned in the law, and his bands of armed retainers, with
which he could do more or less as he liked. In a state trial
of 1554 it was urged in defence of the Duke of Suffolk that
there was nothing treasonable in a peer levying his forces
and making proclamation that foreigners should quit the
realm. [2] Technically the contention was sound, but the
picture of peers raising forces and making proclamations
on their own account in the middle of the Tudor period
indicates the largeness of their liberties. In Elizabeth's
reign even members of her council considered it not incompatible with their loyalty to carry on diplomatic correspondence of their own with foreign powers and to invoke foreign
assistance in their struggles with their colleagues. The law

[1] *Paston Letters*, i. 156.   [2] *Chron. Queen Jane*, Camden Soc., p. 60.

of treason, too, protected them as well as the crown; if an offence against the latter might be high treason, an offence against the former might be petty treason; and an act of Henry VII speaks of a man's master as being his sovereign.[1] The idea of a single all-embracing national sovereign was still in the making, and lords still regarded themselves as princes [2] enjoying sovereign liberties.

The destruction of these liberties was the great service rendered by the Tudors to the cause of English liberty. Parliament in the middle ages had failed to nationalize liberty; with the help of the crown that nationalization was achieved in the sixteenth century. Liberty was made more common by redistribution; the great liberties of the few were diminished, the meagre liberties of the mass increased; and dukes and serfs make a simultaneous disappearance from the England of William Shakespeare.[3] The liberation was achieved, like most acts of emancipation, by despotic means. Even the act emancipating British slaves was passed in 1834 by a parliament in which the slaveholders were not represented and over which they had no control; emancipation was imposed by the north on the south of the United States at the point of the bayonet; and it was an autocrat of all the Russias who emancipated the Russian serf. So it was the Tudor despots who emancipated England from its medieval " liberties." Henry VII restrained the liberty of maintenance and deprived the nobles of their hosts of armed retainers; [4] and by means of the Star chamber he checked their liberty of packing, bribing, and intimidating juries. Henry VIII, by an act of parlia-

---

[1] See below, p. 228.

[2] The modern restriction of *princeps* or prince to members of royal families is an illustration of the centralization of sovereignty. Cf. Shakespeare's *King John,* "Now these her princes are come home again."

[3] With the execution of Northumberland in 1553 and Suffolk in 1554, Norfolk became the only duke in England, and he was attainted in 1572; for more than half a century England was destitute of dukes. Similarly the marquisates were reduced to one—Winchester. With regard to serfs, Sir Thomas Smith declares that they were practically non-existent in his time, though some instances of manumission are found earlier in the century.

[4] See my *Reign of Henry VII,* ii. 65–77.

ment,[1] took many medieval "liberties" into his hands; he improved upon the petition presented by the commons in 1348, and not only refrained from granting liberties, to the hindrance of the common law and oppression of the common people, but revoked the grants that had been made. The Tudor prerogative courts, the councils of the North, of Wales, and so forth, gathered into their hands the liberties of the marcher lords, and reduced the realm to a common order.

Nor was it only lords whose liberties were restricted in the interests of national freedom. The franchises of corporations might be as fatal to general liberty as the privileges of peers. Bacon described gilds as "fraternities in evil," Sir John Mason thought corporations more hurtful to the realm than anything else; and in 1682 the citizens of London were declared liable to fine and imprisonment for "presuming to act as a corporation."[2] They, too, were possessed of portions of sovereign authority which they used to the common detriment. London tried to impoverish other English cities by forbidding its merchants to frequent their markets, and England presented a welter of conflicting and restricting municipal jurisdictions. The "freedom" which cities now confer on eminent politicians is a survival from times and conditions in which every Englishman was a foreigner outside his native town, with no liberties in any city but his own. Nor did he possess much liberty even there. Municipal independence was no guarantee of individual freedom; and in many a medieval city renowned for its fight against despots the individual's liberty was confined by a minute and meticulous regulation unknown to oriental tyranny. His every act was regulated for him from the

[1] 27 Henry VIII, c. 24; cf. 32 Henry VIII, c. 20. There are still survivals. The city of London is exempt from justices of assize. The Marquis of Exeter, as lord paramount, appoints all magistrates in the soke of Peterborough (*Vict. Hist. of Northamptonshire*, ii. 423–4, 427). Halifax had its own "gibbet-law," and there are still quaint "liberties" in Kent (McIlwain, p. 360).
[2] Leadam, *Star Chamber*, Selden Soc., vol. i. p. cli; Tytler, *Edward VI*, i. 362; *Foreign Calendar*, 1547–53, p. 90; Maitland, *Collected Papers*, iii. 311.

cradle to the grave. He could not leave the parish in which he was born or the trade to which he was bred, or carry on business except in accordance with cast-iron rules. The necessities of self-defence in a limited space compelled the closest formation, and individual liberty was a luxury which municipal independence could not afford. National strength and protection relieved the need for congestion. City walls and castle-keeps could disappear with civil war and feudal anarchy, and civic liberty could spread to the bounds of the sea behind the shield of a nation's navy. It was not mere chance that the dynasty which created England's fleet destroyed its civic independence and subjected municipal legislation to national control.[1] By centralizing power the Tudors expanded English liberties and converted local privileges into a common national right.

They did it by means of parliament, and could not have done it without. For one thing, only the common feeling produced by the co-operation of local representatives at Westminster could have prepared the way for the requisite surrender of local prejudice and the merging of local in national liberty. For another, nothing less than an act of the crown in parliament could have constrained these local and personal liberties. It was sufficiently revolutionary that even an act of parliament should override a medieval liberty; for the notion of fundamental law was deeply ingrained in the medieval mind, and the possessors of liberties based their possession on a divine or natural law that was beyond and above the power of kings or parliaments. Magna Carta was long regarded as fundamental law, and repeated protests were made that all things done in contravention thereof, judicial or legislative, within or without parliament, should be regarded as null and void. The growth of positive law at the expense of divine and natural law, and of the idea that human will and mundane counsels could amend the foundations of society, is the beginning of the sovereignty of parliament. But without that overriding

---

[1] 19 Henry VII, c. 7; cf. Leadam, *Star Chamber*, vol. i. p. cli; and my *Reign of Henry VII*, vol. i. p. xliv, vol. ii. 198–9.

sovereignty to limit and abolish them, English medieval liberties would have petrified society on a mould of local and class particularism, and have produced that kind of ossification which stereotyped oriental communities and even reduced France to the necessity of bursting its social shell for the sake of expansion.[1]

As it was, the crown in parliament secured a free hand through the tacit or actual surrender of the claim to indefeasible liberty on the part of individuals and associations. The attachment of the medieval mind to this autonomy was pronounced, and it has been said that the indestructibility of the individual will was the strongest characteristic of the middle ages.[2]   Even in the administration of justice the accused could refuse to submit to the verdict of his country; he could " stand mute," *i. e.* decline to plead.   It is true that the one form of torture countenanced by English law, the *peine forte et dure*, could be applied to overcome this resistance; but if he died under its pressure, the court had to go without its verdict.   He died an innocent man and his property could not be touched.   When Henry VIII was attacking the monasteries infinite pains were taken to secure " surrenders " in preference, or at least as a preliminary, to parliamentary confiscation.   In every sphere the particularist manifestation was strong compared with the national, and parliaments only succeeded in overriding the individual because every Englishman was " intended " to be present in parliament, and an act of parliament was understood to be by representation the act of every individual.   Its sovereignty was the sum total of the will of every member of the community.   It monopolized power and prepared the way for the Austinian dogma that law is the command of the state.   Liberty therefore came to depend, not upon an immutable divine or natural law, but upon the will of the community as expressed in acts of parliament which

---

[1] Cf. the French declaration of 18 August, 1792 : " A state that is truly free ought not to suffer within its bosom any corporation, not even such as, being dedicated to public instruction, have merited well of the country " (Maitland, *Coll. Papers*, iii. 311).

[2] Gierke, *Political Theories of the Middle Age*, ed. Maitland, pp. 81–2.

could extend, restrict, or redistribute the various liberties possessed by different classes.

The effect of this development of parliamentary power was to make it possible to moderate the inequalities of medieval liberty; and, while the overmighty subject suffered crushing blows in Tudor times, the age was for the mass of English people one of liberation. Liberty became a national matter rather than the privilege of a class or a locality. Curious relics of local liberties still remain; but for the most part these anomalies were, during the sixteenth century, merged in common and equal rights guaranteed by acts of parliament and enforced by royal or national law courts. It was the destruction of these barriers and the fusion of classes that produced the intense national and patriotic feeling of Elizabeth's reign. The trinity of estates fades into the unity of the state.

The state, however, and its organized expression in parliament were of composite character; and each of its elements struggled for supremacy. England had been unified under the ægis of the high court of parliament; there were to be no local sovereignties, no provincial parliaments, no autonomous church, and that " parliament cannot err " became a doctrine recognized even by royalist judges.[1] But within the precincts of this court, crown, lords, judges, and commons contended for the mastery, and asserted their " liberties " in a medieval spirit. James I and Charles I were just as intent upon " liberty " as the house of commons or chief justice Coke; and to each element in the constitution liberty meant its liberty, that is to say, its independence and irresponsibility. James had engraven in his heart a " law of free monarchy "[2] and he tried also to impress it on his people. By this freedom he meant independence alike of pope and parliament, and dependence only on God. Nor was James peculiar in this view; his most illustrious victim agreed. The prince, quotes Raleigh with approval, *non*

---

[1] *Letters and Papers of Henry VIII*, vol. xxi. pt. ii. p. 345; Gardiner, *Select Documents*, ed. 1889, p. 54.

[2] See *Political Works of James I*, Harvard Univ. Press, pp. 52 *sqq.*

N

subjicitur nisi sua voluntate libera, mero motu, et scientia certa ; and any constraint absolved him from his bond.[1] Charles also contended that in defending the liberties of kings he was making common cause with his people. Government was nothing pertaining to them; it was his " liberty " : theirs consisted in living under such laws as protected their lives and property, and not in controlling the government. He claimed that the free choice of advisers was a liberty possessed by every man, and that parliament, in attempting to make his ministers responsible to it, was robbing him of a liberty enjoyed by all his subjects.[2] Like true medievalists, the Stuarts based their claim upon a divine, immutable right; but they added a Reformation doctrine that this right was immune from papal arbitrament, and a further contention that it was based on primogeniture. That was the one kind of predestination which commended itself to James I; and his divine hereditary right of kings was a cross between scholastic politics and Calvinistic theology. With it parliaments had nothing to do : no positive law made by human hands could amend an ordinance of God.

Parliament's conception of liberty was hardly less self-centred. Liberty was its liberties. Whence they had been derived was of little concern to members, and their historical scholarship was worse than that of the Stuarts. But convictions that have no historical basis are often political assets. Parliament was convinced that its liberties were immemorial, that they were irrevocable rights independent of the grace or favour of the crown. Parliament was, it told James I in 1604, above the law;[3] it regarded itself as responsible neither to the crown nor to the people, and its privileges as being the expression of its own autocracy. Coke, on the other hand, was concerned with the liberties of the judges; according to him they were independent and irresponsible. They were the supreme interpreters of the

---

[1] Prothero, *Select Documents*, p. 409.
[2] Gardiner, *Select Documents*, pp. 157, 285–6.
[3] Prothero, *Select Documents*, p. 290.

common law, and the common law was to him what divine
right was to the Stuarts and parliamentary privilege to the
house of commons, something above the reach of amendment either by crown or by parliaments.[1] He looked upon it
as perfect and fundamental, and upon the judges as the
arbiters of the constitution, in much the same way as
federalists regard their supreme courts. His view was a
reversion to the thirteenth century, when Magna Carta was
the constitution and *judicia* were the only form of legislative
amendment. " Magna Carta," he said, " is such a fellow
that he will have no sovereign ";[2] and he, as chief justice
of common pleas, was its high priest. To him the autocracy
of the bench was the highest kind of liberty. Nor did
Cromwell differ radically from these conceptions, though he
gave them a different turn. The army's title to rule was
a divine right, proved by victories vouchsafed by the
God of battles; and the supreme magistrate must have
liberty to establish that form of religion in which he believes;
otherwise he is denied his freedom of conscience.[3]

The constitutional struggle of the seventeenth century
was an effort to deprive kings of their liberties, and it was
consummated in the Revolution of 1688, which robbed the
crown of liberty of conscience and imposed upon it a whole
decalogue of prohibitions. Liberty was transferred from
king to parliament, and parliament could authorize the king
to commit every one of the acts which it declared illegal
without its consent. While bounds were set on every side
to the freedom of the crown, none were imposed on that of
parliament; and for three-quarters of a century after the
Revolution the house of commons asserted an independence
and irresponsibility as great as that which the Stuarts had
claimed for themselves. It interpreted its liberties as including powers to deny the right of petition to the crown, to

[1] The lawyers in parliament held similar views, and in 1604 the Speaker
described the common law as a compound of the law of God, the law
of reason, and the law of nature, and therefore as being immutable
(*Commons' Journals*, i. 254*a*; McIlwain, p. 63 *n*.).
[2] *Ibid.*, p. 83.
[3] Carlyle, *Cromwell*, ed. Lomas, ii. 382.

refuse as a matter of privilege the right of electors to vote, to exclude members whom they had elected, and to admit candidates they had rejected. To report speeches delivered and to publish division lists taken in parliament was denounced as countenancing the mischievous idea that members were responsible to an authority outside the walls of the two houses; and their parliamentary liberties were even invoked to give an extra-legal protection to members' fishponds and rabbits.[1] Parliamentary privilege was, in fact, the last of medieval liberties to be reduced by common law. Nor is the medieval conception of liberty yet extinct; it survives in the independence sometimes rashly claimed for the house of lords. For independence is like liberty, a vague but stimulating word, and its value depends upon the sort of immunity it implies. Independence of the house of commons is at least a plausible claim to make for the house of lords. But one of its boldest members has contended that even though a measure were approved at a dozen general elections, the house of lords would be entitled to reject it. This is frankly independence of public opinion; it is the liberty of Magna Carta and the Stuarts, a liberty to the hindrance of the common law and oppression of the common people.

What then did the Whigs mean by that " civil and religious liberty " which they were never tired of toasting and thought they had won by the glorious revolution? Clearly it did not imply to them a universal franchise, a share of every man in the control of government. Not one Englishman in fifty possessed a vote in the eighteenth century; even the agitators of Cromwell's time scouted the notion that servingmen should vote, and for a hundred years and more after the revolution the Whigs as a whole opposed any extension of the franchise. Electors must be " free and independent," independent, that is to say, of masters and employers. The Whig conception of liberty was not very different from that of Charles I; government was not a matter pertaining to the people; for the vast majority liberty should consist in

[1] McIlwain, p. 376; this was only an extension of the privilege which protected members' servants from arrest.

freedom from molestation, the kind of liberty which every benevolent despot of the eighteenth century tried to bestow on his subjects. Liberty of conscience they conceded, and some liberty of speech and worship; but the Test acts still remained upon the statute-book, freedom of the press was still restricted, and that kind of liberty which implies a right to vote was ignored. It was not until 1917 admitted as an indispensable element of freedom; for the whole population was supposed to be free, while only one sex wielded the vote. Parliament in 1688 thought that liberty was achieved when the houses controlled the crown. Their liberties were no doubt secured; but the Whigs failed to realize that unless the nation secured control of parliament, parliamentary liberties might become as dangerous to the community as the baronial liberties of 1215 or the royal liberties of the Stuarts.

This failure was largely responsible for the American war of independence; but the authors of that revolution no more succeeded in solving the problem of liberty than did the Whigs in 1688. Indeed, they provided perhaps the most striking example in history of the facility with which men can be blind to any liberties but their own; and there are few more ironic spectacles than that of a community consisting largely of slave-owners proclaiming in fervid tones their devotion to the rights of man. When they spoke of man they meant white, and not yellow, red, or black men; and their gospel of universal liberty was only intended for application to themselves. But, even apart from the races more highly coloured than the colonists themselves, the assertions of liberty in which American constitutions abound have left a good deal to be desired by the descendants of those who framed them; and latter-day citizens of the United States have discovered that the mere assertion of the principle of liberty is a poor substitute for its definition. No one, runs the most famous of the commonplaces of American constitutions, shall be deprived of his liberty without due process of law; and the interpretation thereof has been left to the supreme courts of the various states. A few samples will suffice for illustration. A state legislature passed a measure prohibiting employers from paying wages in kind instead of coin; its supreme court declared the law invalid because it infringed the employer's liberty without due process of law.   Similar measures to compel the provision of washhouses for miners and to prevent the use of the stars and stripes for commercial advertisement have been pronounced invalid in the sacred cause of liberty.   That a man may do what he likes with his own was for long one of the cardinal principles of American sociology, even when " his own " included his human chattels.   Liberty was linked with property and became the liberty of property, the servitude of men.

From these judicial extravagances England has been saved by the historical fact that parliament is the highest court in the land.   Every act of parliament is due process of law, and no inferior court can declare it invalid, while in the United States no legislature is a court, no legislative act is due process of law, and a supreme court can often frustrate the legislature of the state.   But the problem of liberty remains unsolved.   At the revolution of 1688 men imagined that all was gained with the achievement of civil and religious liberty; in the nineteenth century they pinned their faith to political liberty and looked for the advent of the millennium with the vote.   In the twentieth we are still seeking for a new freedom, for a fresh liberty, which some would call moral and some economic.   What is liberty without a living? " We know," declared the Levellers more than two and a half centuries ago, " that England cannot be a free commonwealth unless all the poor commons have a free use and benefit of the land." [1]   " So you stand upon natural right," Ireton had retorted to Rainsborough in one of the great army debates of 1647, " then show me the difference between the right to a vote and the right to subsistence." [2]   Ireton's purpose had been to explode the right to a vote; but the justice of political liberty once conceded, it is hard to defend the justice of economic dependence

---

[1] G. M. Trevelyan, *England under the Stuarts*, p. 283 *n.*
[2] Morley, *Cromwell*, p. 231.

The ceaseless struggle for liberty has therefore taken at last an economic turn. The liberties of Magna Carta implied the servitude of villeins; the enfranchisement of villeins portends the "servile state." For the liberties of masters we have the liberties of men, and for the subordination of the many the restriction of the few. The rise of democracy, like every other struggle for liberty, ended by becoming a struggle for supremacy. But it did not solve the problem of liberty. Even the democrats feel that freedom is not identical with the rule of the majority; and syndicalism is a reversion to medieval liberty, in that it is an attempt to substitute group-control for state-control, a sort of democratic feudalism, a compromise with anarchy, and a counterpart of the capitalistic feudalism of the trusts. But the restoration of particularism would mean anarchy, and anarchy is more fatal to common liberty than any form of polity, because it leaves the common man at the mercy of his unscrupulous or over-mighty neighbour. Sovereignty is the only bulwark against civil war, the only arbiter of rival claims, and the only guarantee of peaceful liberty; and sovereignty can only be the national will expressed in parliament. Parliament alone can expand and redistribute economic liberty, as it has expanded and converted the private liberties of the middle ages into the common rights of modern times. Its arbitrament is indispensable, for otherwise struggles for liberty will be chronic, barbarous, and inconclusive. The individual cannot be isolated in the state; his liberty is always a matter of relationship to others; and the greater the liberty of any particular man, the less is the liberty of his fellows. Struggles for liberty always end in struggles for supremacy, because liberty depends upon control. My liberty consists in the restraint imposed upon the actions of other men; it is worth nothing if they are free to do what they like, and theirs is a phantom if mine is absolute. Liberty uncontrolled is the licence of tyranny, and the alpha and omega of common liberty is the common restraint of the individual.

There is only one solution of the problem of liberty, and

it lies in equality. Without some equality there can be no common liberty; and the equalization of liberty has been one of the greatest achievements of parliament. There are, indeed, endless kinds of equality, some of them idle dreams, some pernicious, others desirable, and some accomplished. Abstract or mathematical equality has no value amid the infinite and inevitable inequalities of human conditions; and the most fervent apostles of human equalities do not hope to go further in the promotion of equality in physique than giving every child an equal chance of healthy development. But more has been done than that with regard to the results or implications of physical inequality. Men vary in physical strength; but so far as their social relations go that inequality has been abolished. The weak are as safe as the strong in civilized communities, and the strong are effectually prevented from using their strength to the detriment of their weaker neighbours. Yet there must have been a period in social evolution when this refusal to permit the strong man to do what he liked with his own physical strength seemed, at least to the strong, an outrageous interference with personal liberty. Of what use was his strength unless he could use it as his taste or conscience suggested? There is, in fact, no more reason why a man should be allowed to use his wealth or his brain than his physical strength as he likes; and the principle which controls the one should also control the other. No one hopes to equalize physical strength; no sane person expects to equalize wealth or mental equipment. But liberty in the employment of each should be restrained by the same social considerations. The liberty of the weak depends upon the restraint of the strong, that of the poor upon the restraint of the rich, and that of the simpler-minded upon the restraint of the sharper. Every man should have this liberty and no more, to do unto others as he would that they should do unto him; upon that common foundation rest liberty, equality, and morality.

That is the golden rule for the liberties of the subject. Others, it is true, must possess more extended powers. A police constable and a prime minister must have wider liberties than the private citizen; but these are matters, not of right, but of obligation, service, and responsibility. Their liberties are their duties, imposed upon them by the community; and the greater the liberty, the more exacting the obligation. Freedom is grounded in service : as of old in England a man was a voter because he served on a jury, so to-day a man wields power because he is a minister. We have princes and governors galore, but their ministers are their masters, because they are responsible. It has been the supreme good fortune of England that her constitutional history and her liberties started from service and duty, and not from the rights of man. These were the natural product of an impious generation which ignored man's obligations, and looked upon him as an anarchist to be judged by the liberties he seized and not by the services he rendered. " They made and recorded," said Burke, " a sort of institute and digest of anarchy called the ' Rights of Man.' " [1]

Absolute rights are, indeed, fatal to society, and it would be easy to strangle a community with liberty and property. One of the causes, said Hobbes, which tend to the dissolution of a commonwealth, is the idea that the subject possesses such a right of property as excludes the sovereign. No taxation could be raised if the individual had an absolute right to all his property, and no railway could have been constructed without acts of parliament overriding the liberty of landlords to do what they liked with their own. But if property has its liabilities and its limitations for the sake of the common good, so too has labour. If, for instance, the interest of the consumer is a valid objection to a protective tariff, it can also be pleaded against a minimum wage. If the interest of the community is the supreme consideration, it must be superior to the liberty of any section ; and any differentiation must be based, not on the absolute

---

[1] Speech on Army Estimates, 1790, in *Works*, ed. 1834, i. 378; Boston ed. 1865–7, iii. 221. Burke referred to the French, and not to the American " Rights of Man."

right of any class, but on the value which concessions to a particular class may have for the community as a whole.

The only criterion of such issues is the common sense and conscience of the community expressed by means of parliament. On that all liberty must depend. It is thought by many that such decisions, which are fundamentally questions of morals, should rest with the church, and not with the state. But churches are many, and they do not always agree. Judgement by churches would be judgement by groups, with no final arbiter in case of divergence; and divergence without a supreme tribunal involves an ultimate appeal to the barbarous arbitrament of social, political, or economic warfare. To some institution representing the whole community we must therefore have recourse; and in its service we must seek our liberty. Medieval liberty was a monopoly, an irresponsible trust; modern liberty should be a trust for the community; and given that equal condition, there need be no equality in the powers entrusted. Much is required from him to whom much is confided. There need be no servitude in that service and no servility in that state. Obedience to a tyrant is slavery, but the service of mankind is liberty. The proudest of the titles of the pope is *servus servorum Dei*, and the highest ambition of an Englishman is to be prime minister, the chief servant of the people. The nearer we get to a perfect master, the nearer does our service approach to perfect freedom.

CHAPTER X

THE progressive interference of parliament with medieval liberties inevitably involved a conflict with the church, for the Church in England was the greatest and most august embodiment of medieval liberties, and the first clause of Magna Carta guaranteed that the *ecclesia anglicana* should be free. To that clause the great charter owes not a little of the admiration it excites in modern times. It is a clause which appeals with equal force to the catholic and to the free churchman; and no principle commands more general acceptation than that which is read by different schools of thought into the opening words of John's surrender. It is, however, a singular fact that the liberty thus guaranteed to the church, and explained in the following clause to be freedom of election, is a liberty of which the church was effectually deprived four centuries ago. It is true that under the Reformation settlement the crown issues a *congé d'élire* whenever an episcopal vacancy has to be filled, and that the chapter concerned meets and elects its head. But the *congé d'élire* is speedily followed by *letters missive* in which the crown designates the person to be elected; failure to comply involves liability to the penalties of *præmunire*, that is, total forfeiture of goods and imprisonment for life; and the fact that no chapter has ever braved these penalties by neglecting to elect the crown's nominee must be accepted as proof that the church has been, and is, content to forgo the liberty granted by Magna Carta. These matters were settled by statute in the sixteenth century, and the instrumentality of parliament in the suppression of ecclesiastical freedom harmonizes with its general attitude towards medieval liberties. But before discussing the relations between parliament and the church, it is well to attempt some definition of our terms.

The church has many meanings; indeed, it might almost be said that the long story of theological controversy turns mainly on its interpretation. Apart from the church invisible, the church visible may mean the whole church of God or any particular branch thereof to which the speaker belongs; every churchman, free or other, will limit the church by his definition of the faith; and the more numerous the articles of his faith the smaller will be the number of the faithful. The medieval catholic was less perplexed about his frontiers; there was but one church and one great schism. The Greek and the Roman communities belonged to one catholic church, though each regarded the other as schismatic. But, while more comprehensive in this respect, the medieval church was more circumscribed in another. No layman could be a churchman; the *ecclesia* was composed of ecclesiastics. The distinction survives in popular parlance, and "to enter the church" is the vernacular for taking holy orders and becoming an ecclesiastic. Modern confusions, no doubt, have crept in; "churchman" is used with a somewhat offensive implication to distinguish Anglican laity and clergy alike from nonconformists and from Roman catholics, and on theological grounds it is held that one "enters the church" at baptism. But this is not the language of medieval times. When parliament or the council speak, as they often do, of *tous estats de sainte église*, they do not include a single layman; and even as late as the seventeenth century, when Bacon describes Henry VII's countenance as being "reverend and a little like that of a churchman," he is not contrasting it with that of a nonconformist or that of an unbaptized infant.[1]

The point is of some importance, because no understanding is possible of the relations between church and state without clear conceptions upon it, and the confusion between modern

[1] Bacon, *Henry VII*, ed. 1870, p. 402.

and medieval ideas is widespread and persistent. It has, for instance, been recently remarked, in an attack upon Maitland's views of canon law, that the statutes of provisors and præmunire were passed " by representative bodies of Anglican churchmen." [1] But " churchmen " could only be translated into medieval Latin as *viri ecclesiastici;* and the only ecclesiastics present in parliament protested unanimously and vigorously against the passing of these acts. There was the clearest and sharpest antithesis between lay and clerical authority, between courts that were royal and those that were christian, between *regnum* and *sacerdotium*. *Regnum terrenum*, declared a medieval publicist, *est malum et diabolicum et opponitur regno cœlesti*.[2] There was nothing in common, wrote Queen Mary to Cardinal Pole, between the body politic and the body ecclesiastical.[3] The famous altar-piece at Mansfield, which produced so profound an impression on the youthful Luther, represented the church as a ship in which alone lay salvation from the waters of destruction; no layman was in the ship, no churchman in the water. The state appeared, at least at times, to Hildebrand and his pontifical successors as the work if not the sphere of the devil.

This, no doubt, was the extreme papalist view, in which few English prelates concurred. For after all the state, in England at least, was largely the work of their hands and the sphere of their activities. They sat in parliament, almost monopolized chancery, and were often predominant in the king's council. The wordy warfare, in which papalists and imperialists developed a whole literature of analogies and abuse, appealed to metaphysical Germans and perfervid Italians rather than to stolid Englishmen, who had not the same personal or patriotic concern in the struggle

---

[1] Ogle, *Canon Law*, 1912, p. 106, although Mr. Ogle himself has just (p. 103) distinguished between the medieval meaning of " churchmen " and the " fuller modern sense which includes the laity." On p. 60 he also identifies the " prelatz et autres gentz de seinte eglise " with the royal and baronial patrons (*Rot. Parl.*, ii. 233). Churchmen are defined in the *Rot. Parl.* for 1376 (ii. 336) as prelates and "hommes de Sainte Église, c'est assavoir, chanons, prebenders, et persons."
[2] Maitland's *Gierke*, p. 110.   [3] *Poli Epistolæ*, pt. iv. p. 119.

between a German *regnum* and an Italian *sacerdotium*.   The investiture controversy was feebly reflected in England, where, except for occasional outbursts from Beckets and Winchelseys, churchmen and laymen worked well together under a common and temporal sovereign; and the comparative feebleness of the roots which the papacy struck in English soil helps to explain the ease and completeness with which they were torn up by the Tudors.   It was seldom that an English prelate went so far as archbishop Winchelsey when he asserted that English ecclesiastics owed a twofold allegiance to the pope and the king, and that their allegiance to the pope took precedence of their allegiance to the king. The medieval contest in England was not so much a foreign war between English monarchy and the papacy as a domestic struggle between lay and ecclesiastical jurisdictions.   Sometimes a powerful pope took over the lead of the clerical forces, but more often it was an insular combat of barons and bishops, royal prohibitions and episcopal injunctions, and papal intervention was not always welcome to those on whose side the papacy intervened.

The papal yoke lay light upon the conscience of the average English prelate, perhaps because it bore so heavily on his pocket; and the oaths of fealty exacted by the Roman pontiff were probably taken with mental reservations over and above the express reservation contained in the oath he swore to the king.   He was ever a baron as well as a bishop, and his barony was a bond with the crown not easily ignored.   Moreover, a bishop had frequently from his youth up been nurtured in the service of the crown.   Rome was a distant place to the medieval Englishman; only one attained the papal chair,[1] and he had been a stranger to England from his youth.   English cardinals were few and far between.   The papacy was in every sense a foreign government, for which there was little, if any, enthusiasm among the ranks even of English churchmen.   Maitland's jest about Anglo-Catholics, who believe that the English church was protestant before the Reformation and has been

[1] Nicholas Breakspear, who was Pope as Adrian IV from 1154 to 1159.

catholic ever since, was perhaps deserved; but it is quite probable that there have been more sincere adherents of the papacy in England since the breach with Rome than there were before it. The dogma of papal supremacy was academic and disputable in orthodox circles till the close of the middle ages. Œcumenical councils deposed popes one after another; and the Pilgrims of Grace had little to say for the pontiff. He was not an integral part of the catholic faith, and there were other supports than the papacy for the catholicism of medieval England. But after the breach, and still more after the Edwardine Reformation, the papacy seemed the only bulwark of the catholic church; catholicism became bound up with Rome, and most catholics dedicated to the pope their loyalty to the faith. There was a new and a stronger bond between Rome and English catholics than had existed in the middle ages.

But this old English indifference to the papacy did not imply the independence of the English church. During the later middle ages English churchmen were devoted to a catholicism which they did not identify with the papacy, but they feared and detested the approaches of nationalism. The arguments for English ecclesiastical independence generally fall very wide of the mark. Nothing, for instance, could be more misleading than the contention that Henry VIII did no more than William I had done when he claimed to determine which pope should be recognized in his dominions. Henry eradicated the jurisdiction altogether : William merely asserted a voice in the determination who should wield it. He no more thought of abolishing papal jurisdiction than the Whigs thought of establishing a republic when they substituted William III for James II. Nor would the argument, if sound, establish the independence of the English church; it would merely establish her dependence on the English monarchy.

A more serious source of error is confusion of chronology. It will not do to build fourteenth-century independence on arguments from the Anglo-Saxon period. The middle ages were, like other times, a period of change; and what is true of one century is false of another. Provincial independence was obviously greater before the catholic church had been organized by Hildebrand and his successors. Cranmer selected the pontificate of Nicholas II (1058–61) as the epoch at which the church became corrupt, or, in other words, the epoch at which archbishop Stigand was condemned by papal legates and provincial independence was submerged in catholic organization. It might be safer to put the matter in Stubbs's fashion, and say that in England the time had come for Lanfranc and Anselm as well as for William of Normandy and Henry of Anjou. The point is that Lanfranc and Anselm were not English; they represented the ecclesiastical aspect of the Norman Conquest and the submergence of English insularity beneath the waves of continental culture. From that time for two centuries there was even less English independence in the church than in the state. The law and the language, the ritual and the organization of the church, all came from abroad; the episcopate was almost closed to natives; and there was nothing national in the inspiration of the monks and friars. To the end of the thirteenth century England was catholic to the core. Our concern here is with the two and a half succeeding centuries, during which England emerged from these catholic conditions and parliaments assisted in developing the nationalism which involved a gradual differentiation and then independence of type. The history of the constitutional relations between parliament and the church turns mainly on the friction between a secular body, growing more and more national, and an ecclesiastical body clinging more and more closely to the international system on which it was based and from which it derived its support.

The antagonism was fundamental, although it only developed with the growth of the English national state; for in England the church was Latin, but the state Teutonic. In Latin communities the conflict was less pronounced and the Reformation made little way, for there both state and church were based upon identical Roman principles; empire and papacy, said Zwingli, both came from Rome. Both claimed a divine and not a popular sanction.[1] In Teutonic states, on the other hand, the ruler's commission came from below, not from above; and the form at least of popular election survived the attempts of the church to base secular monarchy also on a divine right conveyed and interpreted by herself. For a time, indeed, during the halcyon days of the papacy, the Latin ecclesiastical view obscured the secular and Teutonic, and in France it achieved a lasting victory. But in England the growth of representation, which enveloped the central government, withdrew it further and further from the domain of Latin ideas. A divergence set in which led to conflicts of jurisdiction and finally ended with the submission of the clergy to Henry VIII.

This divergence permeated both organisms. The papacy, that ghost of the empire sitting enthroned in the midst of the ruins thereof, inherited the spirit and carried on the traditions of Cæsar. Its law was the law of Rome; its principle was unlimited monarchy; its divisions were Roman provinces, carefully drawn to divide and undermine national sentiment. It trusted to revelation and not to representation. Its legislation consisted of papal bulls and not of the acts of an assembly; its courts required no juries, for a system claiming infallibility could hardly invoke the aid of common intelligence. Its taxes were not voted, but imposed. The clergy in England granted their aids, their tenths, and their subsidies to the king; they granted none to the pope, because he took them without their leave. First-fruits and tenths were not voted in convocations; they were levied by papal command; and the " taxatio " under which the clergy groaned was named after the pope or the papal collectors.[2] The pope was God's vicegerent; he had no need of consent. Harmony, no doubt, was always desired between the Vicar of Christ and his flock, but harmony must

---

[1] Both emperor and pope were, indeed, elected, but one by seven princes and the other by cardinals.

[2] *E. g.* the " taxatio Norvicensis " of Walter Suffield, Bishop of Norwich and papal collector in 1253, and the " taxatio " of Pope Nicholas IV in 1291. Cf. Wilkins, *Concilia*, iii. 646, " Alexander VI papa . . . imposuit clero Anglicano subsidium unius integrae decimae."

O

be secured through the obedience of the sheep and not through the shepherd's concessions. A theocracy could not parley with popular pretensions.

The Teutonic state was more a matter of compromise. Royal elections involved electoral promises, and Norman kings themselves began their reigns with charters to their people. Even before parliaments were created, royal acts of legislation were constitutions rather than institutes, measures set up by agreement and consultation, and not imposed by sole authority. Kings levied, indeed, their rents or feudal services, but other aids and scutages had to be given them by their subjects; and Edward I's maxim, *quod omnes tangit ab omnibus approbetur*, was the antithesis of the principle of papal sovereignty. With the growth of parliament the necessity for consent grew ever more insistent, and with it widened the breach between the foundations of church and state. Edward I attempted a union by summoning churchmen and laymen alike to the high court of parliament; but the reigns of his son and his grandson witnessed the failure of the experiment, and in course of time the side which rejected the union for the sake of independence fell into a state of subjection.

The conflict of ideals developed a practical conflict of jurisdictions. It was not a simple matter of warfare between two organisms, each with its own code of laws; for both were subject to both jurisdictions. Churchmen were under the law of the land as well as under that of the church; laymen were subject to canon as well as to civil law. It was strife between two kinds of allegiance, in which every man was divided against himself; he had two sovereign lords, the pope and the king, and while the clergy inclined to the pope, the laymen preferred the king. Each, however, made his choice at no little risk to himself; and the dilemma, in which the soldier may find himself placed to-day, between the risk of court martial if he refuses when ordered to fire upon a mob, and the risk of trial for murder if he obeys, is a rare inconvenience compared with the distraction of the medieval Englishman between the courts christian and the courts of his king. He might be outlawed if he obeyed the church and excommunicated if he obeyed the king. He might be treated as a bastard by royal judges and as legitimate by the authorities of the church; for the famous refusal of the barons in 1236 to assimilate the laws of England to those of the church and to recognize legitimation by the subsequent marriage of parents, had no effect upon ecclesiastical jurisdiction, and down to the Reformation the ecclesiastical courts administered one law of legitimacy and the secular courts another.[1] He might be granted probate by one court and be refused possession by another; for in the fourteenth century the church was encouraging villeins and women to make wills, which the commons complained in parliament was contrary to reason.[2]

Friction between the two jurisdictions was incessant, because their frontiers were disputed, and there was no supreme court to settle the issue; the two supreme authorities were the parties to the suit. Henry II attempted a settlement by the Constitutions of Clarendon, and Edward I another by his writ of *circumspecte agatis*. There were few acres in the whole field of secular jurisdiction which might not be invaded by clerical courts. Everything to do with marriage, the making and administration of wills, and the faith was left as a matter of course to the clergy, though an attempt to include debt among matters of faith provoked a clause in the Constitutions of Clarendon. If a debt was confirmed by an oath, it brought the debtor within the sphere of ecclesiastical jurisdiction; for the oath was *interposita fides*, it established a direct relation between God and the debtor, and of those relations the church was the only arbiter.[3] These were questions which drew the laity into the clerical courts; still greater efforts were made to keep the clergy out of the clutches of the secular law, and

---

[1] Maitland, *Canon Law*, pp. 53–4; Makower, *Const. Hist.*, pp. 422–3; *Rot. Parl.*, ii. 153, 171; *Letters and Papers of Henry VIII*, vii. 1385.
[2] *Rot. Parl.*, ii. 148–51.
[3] The attempts to draw debts and other secular contracts into the courts christian were the subject of perpetual complaint in parliament; cf. Maitland, *Memoranda*, p. 305; *Rot. Parl.*, i. 219, 293, ii. 142.

the most resounding blows in the conflict between the two jurisdictions were struck over the *corpus vile* of the criminous clerk.   Maitland has illumined the legal intention of Henry II's proposals without attempting an estimate of their results. But it seems clear that victory rested with the church : judgement, indeed, appears to have gone to the secular court, but execution remained in the tender hands of ecclesiastical authority which was precluded from shedding blood.   In 1351, in answer to a petition of the clergy, Edward III maintained his jurisdiction over churchmen so far as high treason was concerned, but admitted benefit of clergy for murder and other crimes on condition that the church inflicted perpetual penance and prison—a condition that was kept with exceeding laxity.[1]   Benefit of clergy continued to shield the clerical criminal to the end of the middle ages, and the chief liberty of the church, exclaimed a puritan in Elizabeth's parliament, had been a liberty to sin.[2]

This conflict of jurisdictions was fatal to a parliamentary union between church and state; for parliament was a court of law, but only a court of secular law, and a supreme court from which spiritual jurisdiction was withheld had little attraction for churchmen.   Laymen had been drawn to Westminster because parliament was held three times a year to redress grievances and settle disputes about which the judges were in doubt.   The clergy, indeed, participated in so far as they were subject to secular law, and clerical proctors presented clerical petitions in parliaments as late as the reign of Edward III.[3]   But parliaments provided no remedy for abuses in the clerical courts; no writs of error could right a spiritual wrong in parliament, and for redress

[1] *Rot. Parl.*, ii. 244.   The control of the courts christian over the criminous clerk ceased of course when the clerk ceased to be a churchman; but only the church could degrade him into a layman.

[2] D'Ewes, *Journals*, p. 167.

[3] Triers of clerical petitions in parliament were appointed in 1347–8 (*Rot. Parl.*, ii. 164).   In 1366 there were petitions from the four mendicant orders and the universities of Oxford and Cambridge, which were not represented in parliament (*ibid.*, ii. 290); and in the Good parliament of 1376 petitions were presented from the clergy of the province of Canterbury, though it does not appear that those clergy were represented (*ibid.*, ii. 357).

against their official superiors the clergy must look elsewhere; appeal from them lay not to the king at Westminster, but to the pope at Rome.[1] The laity also suffered from this disability, but it went more to the heart of the church. Parliament was not the final resort for matters in which the affections of churchmen were mainly involved. The original motive which led to lay demands for regular parliaments did not exist for the church; and its absence reinforced the other inducements which counselled the clergy to abstain from participation in parliamentary business. The judicial system which linked the representatives of the laity to parliament did not bind the church to a temporal court; trial by their peers in parliament was repudiated by the prelates, and churchmen contended " that no clerk would be arraigned before the king's judges on any criminal charge, since for such cause no soul could judge them save the pope." [2]

Nor would they submit to the taxation of their spiritualties in parliament. The essence of frankalmoign, or spiritual tenure, was its immunity from temporal jurisdiction, and freedom from parliamentary taxation seemed a natural corollary of freedom from parliamentary jurisdiction. The claim appears in time to have been extended to all the property of the church, and clerical taxes were voted in convocations and collected by clerics appointed by the prelates.[3] The clergy, indeed, were a body of men set apart from the community, and the indelible character of priesthood sanctified their liberty. There is some justification for the protest against regarding church and state as two independent and rival communities, and for the contention that the "respublica christiana" was a single community governed by two sets of officers, the spiritual and the temporal magis-

---

[1] Cf. *Memoranda de Parl.*, pp. 34, 82, 111–12.
[2] *Rot. Parl.*, ii. 151–3.
[3] See my *Reign of Henry VII*, ii. 39–43. The voting of clerical taxes in convocation instead of in parliament dates back at least to 1339, when the Archbishop of York was adjured in parliament to urge his clergy to make liberal grants in their forthcoming convocation at York (*Rot. Parl.*, ii. 105–6).

trates.[1]   But we cannot explain the issue of their strife by leaving out of account the army they strove to command. Constitutionally the *ecclesia* was a body of ecclesiastics, a corps of officers without any private soldiers.   The privates at least were entitled to no benefit of clergy; they took no part in electing clerical proctors, and were not represented in the councils of the church.   Clerical representatives represented no one but the clergy, and the house of commons would have resembled convocation if it had been elected by temporal magistrates.   The circumstance that the bulk of the English people was represented in parliament, but not in convocation, has been the decisive factor in the constitutional conflict between the *regnum* and *sacerdotium*.   The contest had not been unequal so long as parliaments consisted solely of councillors; but Edward I began to enlist the services of the English people in parliament, and thus decided beforehand the issue which was brought to a head by Henry VIII.

There were causes enough for the aloofness and aversion from parliaments shown by the church in the middle ages. Some were common to it and to other orders, and we have seen how the numbers of attendant barons and burgesses dwindled during the fourteenth and fifteenth centuries. The service was irksome, and the clergy disclaimed their liability.   With them it was not a question of dwindling by special grace, but of total exemption by right.   The bishops, of course, and the abbots, who held baronies of the crown, were summoned, or were liable to be summoned, as barons; and their only escape was to disown their baronial tenure.   But the crown had a feeble claim to the suit and service of clerical proctors in the high court of parliament : they were not individually tenants-in-chief, and they did

---

[1] Figgis, " Respublica Christiana " in *Trans. Royal Hist. Soc.*, 3rd Ser., v. 63–88.   Curiously enough Dr. Figgis' view is that of Marsiglio of Padua, who insists on the sovereignty of the *universitas fidelium*, as represented by the Prince.   But Marsiglio was a prophet of the Reformation rather than an exponent of the medieval church.   There are worse theories of the origin of the Reformation than that which ascribes it to the growth of Dr. Figgis' idea of the medieval church

not, like the knights of the shire and burgesses, represent collective tenants-in-chief. The clergy of a diocese were not a *communitas* which farmed its own shire, or belonged, like a borough, to the royal demesne. Edward I, as a matter of fact, had never summoned the clergy by writ to parliament; he summoned the bishops *quâ* barons, but merely admonished them to bring their clergy with them. The writs that the priors, archdeacons, and proctors obeyed were not royal, but episcopal, and the clergy were really attending upon their bishops and not upon the king.

For a brief period down to 1332, and possibly later, their attendance was twofold, upon the bishops in parliament and upon the bishops in convocation. But insistence upon this double duty was quietly resisted by the clergy and tacitly abandoned by the crown; nothing less than a royal writ could secure lasting attendance in parliament, and even that failed to constrain most of the abbots to come. When, after the opening of each parliament, the various estates were told to withdraw and consider apart the business of the session, the clergy had not, like the knights and the burgesses, to devise a new *domus communis;* they already possessed in convocation a domestic organization, to which they naturally had recourse, and there they debated their grants and other responses to the demands of the crown. So far they were acting like other estates : the precise difference in procedure was that, instead of returning and announcing their decisions in parliament through the mouth of the Speaker, they communicated them through the prolocutor of convocation or through the prelates. As late as 1332 clerical proctors put in an appearance in parliament; but they deliberated apart, and in time their appearance in parliament ceased altogether. It was considered sufficient that convocation should meet simultaneously, and transact apart the business which would otherwise have required attendance in parliament. Occasionally the view was expressed that the assent of the clergy in parliament was essential to the validity of its proceedings, and in 1397 Sir Thomas Percy, steward of the royal household, was appointed a clerical proctor for this purpose.[1] But this was a unique occasion, which prefigured Thomas Cromwell's vice-gerency; and the unanimous protest of the prelates in parliament was considered no bar to the statutes of provisors and præmunire.

This clerical retreat to their convocations, however costly it may in the end have proved to the national influence of the church, evaded some difficulties and coincided with ecclesiastical traditions.   There were two convocations, not one, and when the clerical proctors ceased attendance in parliament, those for the northern province escaped the toilsome journey to London.   Their convocation met at York, and its gathering there gratified the provincial feeling which tended to separate England north from England south of the Humber.   It also avoided the scandalous scenes, of which there was always a risk, when the two archbishops met in the same assembly.   Each prelate was jealous of his primacy, and neither would suffer the other to bear his cross before him.   The archbishop of Canterbury had no jurisdiction over the clergy of York, and York had none over those of Canterbury.   They were entirely independent one of the other; the only links between them were their common subordination to the papacy and to the crown.   The latter kept them in order in the king's council and parliament, but the only presence that could secure unity in an ecclesiastical assembly in medieval England was that of a papal legate *a latere*.[2]   Peace could be kept in a parliament where the archbishops sat as tenants-in-chief of the crown; it

---

[1] *Rot. Parl.*, iii. 348, 356; Cotton, *Records*, p. 368. Percy's was a singular appearance, as he was said to have full power and authority committed to him by the prelates and clergy of the realm, not of one province alone, and was a layman to boot. In this capacity he joined in the condemnation of Archbishop Arundel, and took the oath " pur et en nom del dit clergie " to observe all the resolutions adopted by Richard II's Shrewsbury parliament.

[2] The so-called " national " councils of the English church only met when the presence of a special papal legate gave them " national " unity by imposing a superior papal authority on the two provincial archbishops. The links between Canterbury and York were never both national and ecclesiastical : when they were national they were secular, and when they were ecclesiastical they were papal.

could not be guaranteed where clerical proctors sat under
rival archbishops. Either, however, could reign supreme
in his own provincial synod.

Of greater consequence was the fact that this provincial
organization fell into line with the whole governmental
tradition of the church. The papacy inherited from the
empire its provincial system, and Constantine perpetuated
the work of Diocletian. Nationalism was the antithesis of
the Roman church and of the Roman empire, and no nation
was made a province in either sphere; each was divided
into two or more provinces, and the papacy never borrowed
from the empire with greater success than when it adopted
the imperial maxim *divide et impera*. Had not the English
state, through the instrumentality of the crown in parliament, developed a stronger sense of nationality than the
church, there could have been no national reformation
and therefore no national church. The " establishment "
of the English church consists in the secular framework of
unity which the national state imposed upon two provinces of
the Roman church; it could only be achieved by a complete
repudiation of the Roman imperial and papal tradition.

Every manifestation of nationalism opened, in fact, a
fresh breach with the catholic church. The growth of
English language and literature led to demands for the use
of the vernacular in the services of the church, while churchmen clung to their catholic Latin as an expression of
unchanging unity in the church and a symbol of their segre-
gation from the people. The cry for the bible in English,
satisfied at first by translations from the Vulgate, produced
at length translations from the originals, and undermined
the authority of the catholic standard. The growth of
national legislation in parliament, accompanied by the
inroads of positive man-made law upon the old cosmopolitan
laws of reason and of nature, produced English law out of
the international legal systems of medieval Europe; and
the more English our secular law became in the hands of
English parliaments, the more certain and incessant would
be its conflict with the canon law of the church, which,

if it changed at all, grew ever stranger to England. Church
and state in England could agree fairly well so long as neither
was national; they could not agree when one became more
and more English and the other more and more Roman,
nor even while one was becoming national at a much greater
pace than the other. An insular commons and a catholic
clergy could not be combined in an English parliament.

We must not, however, imagine that the barons, or even
kings, were much more national than the clergy; and to
regard their interested protests against papal interference
as evidence of national resentment, is hardly more rational
than to regard the same protests as proof of the independence of the church of England. There was too much particularism in England in the fourteenth century to permit of
a really national movement against the papacy, and the
petition of the barons in 1307 and the statutes of provisors
and præmunire were instinct with medieval notions of
liberty. They were designed to protect the peculiar rights
and property of the king and his barons against ecclesiastical encroachment, and the animus is as much against the
clerical courts in England as against the *curia* at Rome.
The barons in 1307 contend that *seinte église . . . soit fundé
par le roi et par ses ancestres et par les ditz contes, barons, et
leurs ancestres*, and that, inasmuch as they had founded the
church, they were entitled to its advowsons untrammelled
by the claims of the ecclesiastical courts to all the goods
of intestates and to all lands not specifically mentioned in
testators' wills. They complain of the efforts of the pope and
his clerks to secure cognizance of all debts, and to draw into
the church courts all suits relating to the temporalties as
well as to the spiritualties of churchmen; and they conclude
with a rhetorical anticipation of ruin " unless God arises
and His enemies are scattered " by the temporal prince
and his council, with the assent of the nobles and magnates.[1]

[1] *Rot. Parl.*, i. 219; cf. *ibid.*, ii. 144–5. The description of the act
of 1351 as " the first statute of provisors " (Stubbs, ii. 430) is somewhat
misleading. The statute of Carlisle in 1307 had sought to protect the
advowsons of lay patrons, and in 1343 parliament endeavoured to secure
its better execution, but no answer to its petition is recorded on the " Roll."
The statute of 1351, while reciting the statute of Carlisle, goes on to
protect the English ecclesiastical patrons.

This sounds like a first blast from the trumpet of Henry VIII, but the note is very baronial; the church is "founded" on property, and the liberty proclaimed is the right of secular property to determine spiritual preferment. The same is the purport of the statutes of provisors. No one is thinking of the national liberties of the English church; the freedom of election promised in Magna Carta has already disappeared, and the issue is between papal and royal or baronial nomination. It is royal and baronial rights of presentation that are to be protected against the Vicar of Christ and his appointments; and so far as national sentiment was involved, it was only concerned with the probability that English barons would prefer more English clerks than would a French or Italian pope. Already Englishmen's catholicism was breaking down before their prejudice against alien bishops; but the baronial objection to papal provision was the same, whether it was exercised on behalf of an English or a foreign clerk. The animus of the statute of præmunire was somewhat less sectional, but more comprehensively anti-ecclesiastical; it was aimed against all infringements of royal jurisdiction, whether by the papal *curia* or by any subordinate ecclesiastical court in England. No distinction was made between them, and English prelates supported the papacy with their protests in parliament.

Nothing, indeed, could be a greater travesty of the truth than the representation of these statutes as protests of English churchmen against the pretensions of Rome. After the days of Grosseteste there were few clerical protests against the papacy. Ecclesiastical chroniclers continued to grumble for a time at papal taxation; but they were soon more concerned with the encroachments of parliament on their immunities, and began to feel that the liberty of the church depended on papal protection. The pope was the supreme governor of the church,[1] and English churchmen made common cause with him against all forms of temporal jurisdiction. The endless petitions in parliament against the papacy are all petitions of the commons, against which the prelates protest, sometimes with and sometimes without

[1] *Rot. Parl.*, ii. 172.

success. The only point upon which the prelates concurred with the commons in disputing papal claims was in resistance to the payment of Peter's pence.[1] It was the laity, not the church, which attacked papal provisions, reservations, and even firstfruits.[2] There were many clerical petitions presented by the prelates in parliament, but not one was antipapal. Their purport is very different : they complain bitterly that the king's courts imprison clerks against the law and liberties of the church, that lay ministers enter upon ecclesiastical fiefs in retaliation for the fines and dues levied by the clergy, that aids are exacted from churchmen who are exempt from parliamentary service and had not consented to their imposition, that people are forbidden to pay their tithes to God and holy church until the king is satisfied of his taxes. They contend that the king's judges have no jurisdiction over clerks, nor even over the laity in such matters as bigamy, matrimony, bastardy, and licences for mortmain; and they demand that prohibitions issuing out of the royal courts of justice, royal commissions of inquiry into the working of ecclesiastical courts, and summonses to the clergy to answer in chancery suits about tithes should cease, and that churchmen should be exempt from all tolls, purveyance, and so forth.[3] These were the coveted liberties of the English church; they constituted freedom from the English state, not independence of the papacy.

That freedom from Rome is fictitious. The crown might, and did, indeed, by means of its temporal jurisdiction protect to some extent English churchmen from the pope; the ecclesiastical courts provided no protection whatever. The

---

[1] *Rot. Parl.*, ii. 290; cf. ii. 336-9. The assent to these anti-papal statutes is always limited to "les contes, barons, et autres sages lais gentz du conseil" (*ibid.*, ii. 161), and often the dissent of the prelates is recorded (*ibid.*, ii. 284-5, iii. 264, 340-1).

[2] The Commons' petition in 1373 and 1377 against the payment of firstfruits (*Rot. Parl.* ii. 320, iii. 18) is an interesting anticipation of sixteenth-century legislation, and still more so are the proposals made in parliament in 1387 and 1413 that they should be paid to the king and not to the pope (*ibid.*, iii. 214), and that, owing to the papal schism, bishops elect should be confirmed by the metropolitan acting upon king's writs without further excuse or delay (*ibid.*, iv. 71).

[3] *Rot. Parl.*, i. 392, ii. 129, 151-3, 357-9, iii. 25-7.

famous statutes of præmunire set no limit to the pope's control over English ecclesiastical courts; their object was to defend the king's temporal jurisdiction from papal aggression working through the courts of the church. In 1348 a claimant to a living pursued his appeal to Rome; on his return to England he was sued and imprisoned, not because he was appealing from an English ecclesiastical court to the papal *curia*, but because he was bringing before the pope a suit belonging to royal cognizance; and his defence was that the living was held in spiritualty.[1] To appeals from English spiritual jurisdiction to the pope the English crown had not the least objection in the middle ages; such appeals were often facilitated by the crown, which discountenanced their reception in parliament.[2] It was its own temporal jurisdiction that the crown was concerned to protect; and it insisted upon that protection against both the lower courts christian in England and the highest court christian at Rome.

The strife was ever between English secular courts and catholic spiritual courts, and the evidence all points to the natural conclusion that English churchmen took their stand by the catholic church. Any other attitude has only been made to appear plausible by reading back into the middle ages the conditions of later times, when the hold of nationalism over Englishmen's minds had immensely strengthened, and the hold of catholicism had correspondingly weakened; and the unhistorical creation of a national church in the middle ages is the offspring of a desire to give the authority of antiquity to a conception which seeks to make the best of both ages, and to combine in the Anglican church of to-day the medieval advantage of freedom from the state with the modern advantage of freedom from Rome. That twofold liberty is by no means an impossible or an unworthy ideal, and the historian's only objection is to the claim of such an achievement to be a conservative or reactionary reproduction of medieval conditions. Similar arguments

---

[1] *Rot. Parl.*, ii. 178b.
[2] E.g. *Ibid.*, i. 3, 40b, 41–2, 375b, ii. 151–3, 161; Maitland, *Memoranda*, pp. 34, 82, 111–12.

from an imaginary past have been used to advance the causes of liberty, socialism, and nationalism, and most reformers have decked out their principles of progress with prehistoric plumage.

To the medieval churchman his duty in the conflict of laws was clear. By all that he held most sacred he was bound to cleave to the pope; every churchman took the oath of canonical obedience, while an oath of allegiance to the king was only taken by tenants-in-chief and officials. Those who took both, such as bishops, took first their oath to the pope, and were required to give it precedence. If they committed treason, it was for the pope, and not for the king or for the peers in parliament to condemn them. The king, indeed, maintained the contrary; but when Henry IV enforced this view at the expense of archbishop Scrope, his deed was regarded with horror and held to be the cause of the king's subsequent troubles. Churchmen stood by the laws and the liberties of their church; and the louder grew the claims of nationalism, the closer they clung to their privileges and to the protection of the pope. Some prelates, at least, preferred papal provision to the chances of election;[1] and the statute of provisors, it was contended in 1415, stopped the preferment of university students, starved the church of learned clergy, and thus promoted the growth of heresy and schism. The commons also on one occasion petitioned the crown for a remedy against the evil effects of that royal and baronial legislation;[2] but it was to papal protection that churchmen looked more and more for the safeguard of their faith and for the security of their liberties against the encroachments of parliament and of the royal courts.

In the face of these disruptive forces the wonder is not that parliament and the church should have fallen apart, but that churchmen should have retained so long the position they did. Church and state, however, had this much in common: both, in the higher ranks at least, had been permeated with feudal influence; and while the clerical proctors

---

[1] *Rot. Parl.*, ii. 154.

[2] *Ibid.*, iv. 81; cf. Nicolas, *Proceedings of the Privy Council*, i. 282, ii. 113.

disappeared from the houses of parliament, bishops and abbots remained. The crown might excuse the attendance of others, or allow them to be represented; but it successfully insisted upon the liability of its greater tenants-in-chief to a summons, and imposed fines ranging from forty to a hundred pounds on those who failed to obey. The force of passive resistance prevailed to some extent even among the greater tenants-in-chief; by Edward III's reign [1] twenty-eight abbots had already secured definite exemption from the customary summons, and while the number of barons sank from a hundred to less than fifty, the number of abbots declined from seventy-two under Edward I to a regular twenty-seven under Edward III's successors. Of the twenty-seven who were summoned few attended, and in 1513 it was declared by the judges that the presence of abbots was not essential to parliament.[2] When the philosophical historian comes to describe the decline and fall of the house of lords in modern times, he will probably attach no little importance to the habitual absence of most of the peers from their parliamentary duties; and similarly it may be pointed out that, had not some forty-five abbots evaded their summons to parliament, it would not have been possible for Henry VIII to obtain a majority for the dissolution of the monasteries. The church had done its best to abandon parliament before parliament surrendered it to the king.

In both cases the abandonment was merely the outward sign of a growing distaste and lack of sympathy. Churchmen would have continued to throng the high court of parliament had they continued to feel at home in its portals. But their heart was elsewhere; and while an encroaching nationalism increased the alienation, it weakened the feudalism which bound bishops and abbots and barons to the crown and to one another. Hildebrand had dreaded the corruption of the church by feudalism; but feudalism had at least saved the church from an isolation in which it could only stand secure so long as it retained its incorruption. The bond between the church and parliament was weakened, not

---

[1] Pike, *Const. Hist. of the House of Lords*, p. 349; cf. *Rot. Parl.*, ii. 119.
[2] *Letters and Papers of Henry VIII*, ii. 1131, 1313; Pike, p. 327.

because abbots and proctors feared corruption, but because they evaded their duties and feared the loss of their liberties. Taxation of themselves by themselves, self-made legislation, and independence of everything save of Rome, were their cherished desires; they chose isolation, and they fell from lack of support.

There was nothing strange in this isolation. The association of individuals in classes and the dissociation of class from class were characteristic of the middle ages; and in preferring to concentrate in convocation, instead of dividing their attention between it and parliament, the clergy were adopting the same policy as the commons themselves. Indeed the consolidation of estates in the house of commons imposed upon churchmen the alternative of absorption or separation. The definite parting of the ways is commonly placed in the reign of Edward II; but clerical proctors attended at least at the opening of the parliament of March 1332, when the prelates, remarking that some of the business propounded by Geoffrey le Scope on behalf of the crown was not within the competence of the clergy, suggested that they and the clerical proctors should separate from the laity for the discussion of their own affairs; the clergy, too, were dismissed with the knights, citizens, and burgesses after the six days' session, while the prelates, earls, barons, and councillors were ordered to remain.[1] Similar arrangements were made in the following December; but it had already become the practice to hold convocations simultaneously with a parliament, and thither the clergy resorted when they retired from the parliament chamber to discuss their parliamentary business. The clerical committee or estate of parliament was absorbed in the lower house of convocation, and it became impossible to distinguish between the *personnel* or the action of the clerical proctors summoned to parliament and of those summoned to a provincial synod.[2]

[1] *Rot. Parl.*, ii. 64b, 65b, 67.
[2] Makower, *Const. Hist. of the Church*, p. 355. Nor is there a clear distinction in medieval terminology, though now it is usual to reserve the word "convocation" for the provincial assembles of Canterbury and York summoned by royal writs, with the *præmunientes* clause, as a

In 1339 it is clearly in convocation that the clerical proctors voted their grants to the crown.[1] The dissociation from parliament involved also a dissociation of the proctors of York from those of Canterbury; for if the two convocations ever sat together (except when a papal legate *a latere* held a "national" council) the practice was soon discontinued, and at the close of the middle ages the convocation of York did not commonly meet at the same date as that of Canterbury or as parliament. Indeed, it was clearly impossible for the archbishop of York and his suffragans to be simultaneously in their places in parliament at Westminster and in convocation at York.

Abstention from attendance in parliaments on the part of the lower clergy did not, however, mean an absence of clerical petitions; and at first the clergy seemed to lose nothing by their retirement. In 1340 their petitions were read after those of the commons by the king's order, and statutes were made to give them effect with the assent of all the estates.[2] A hardly less pleasing harmony was exhibited as late as 1376, when the commons of York presented a petition against the excessive fees extorted by the archbishop from his clergy.[3] But by that time harmony was exceptional, and a rift had developed between the commons and clergy. The petitions of the clergy continued, throughout the fourteenth century, to be presented and read in parliaments, and the practice was for the judges to be required to assemble in the presence of some of the prelates and provide a remedy.[4] To this habit the commons offered an increasing resistance, and in 1377 they asked that no ordinance should be made in parliament without their leave on a clerical petition, and that the commons should not be bound by constitutions adopted in convocation; "for," they declared, "they do not wish to be bound by any statute

---

part of the parliamentary system, and to describe the other provincial and diocesan assemblies, summoned merely by the archbishops and bishops, as "synods." Synods might be summoned at any time, convocations only with parliament.

[1] *Rot. Parl.*, ii. 106.   [2] *Ibid.*, ii. 113, 244.
[3] *Ibid.*, ii. 352.   [4] *Ibid.*, ii. 358.

P

or ordinance without their assent." [1]   In 1382 they secured
the repeal of a statute against heretic preachers, on the ground
that it had been enacted without their consent, and they
declared their determination not to bind themselves or their
successors more to the prelates than their ancestors had been
in times past.[2]

This rising temper proved fatal to clerical legislation in
parliament. Petitions from individual prelates, clerks, and
clerical corporations continued to be occasionally presented
in the Lancastrian period; but the collective petitions
of the clergy disappear from the proceedings in parliament,
and the church had to content itself with its limited powers
of legislation in diocesan and provincial synods. This
retreat was not without its compensations. The sphere
of legislation was, indeed, limited to the affairs of the church,
but those affairs extended far beyond the persons and the
property of the clergy to the marriages, wills, faith and
ecclesiastical dues and duties of the laity; and no royal
or other lay assent was needed. This autonomy was, of
course, restricted by papal jurisdiction, but whatever feeling
had existed in the days of Langton and of Grosseteste against
the Roman *curia* had weakened before the nearer enmity
of the commons assembled in parliament. In 1389 the prelates, alike of Canterbury and of York, solemnly protested
in parliament on behalf of themselves and all their clergy
that they repudiated then, as they had always repudiated
in the past, every statute tending to restrict the power of
the pope or the liberty of the church, and required their
protest to be enrolled as a permanent witness to their deed.[3]
For them the liberty of the church had come to depend upon
the jurisdiction of Rome. Such was the inevitable result
of growing aloofness from a parliament which was becoming
more and more the focus of national unity and the organ
of national independence.

This general alienation made the exception to it, the
retention of the bishops in parliament, a matter of enormous

[1] *Rot. Parl.*, ii. 368.   [2] *Ibid.*, iii. 141; Stubbs, ii. 628.
[3] *Ibid.*, iii. 264.

consequence. They formed the link between church and
state, being themselves both barons and bishops; and they
were the pivot upon which the whole government of medieval
England turned. In the twelfth and thirteenth centuries
we have, indeed, prelates of the uncompromising stamp
of Becket and Winchelsey, who were churchmen first and
last, and viewed the state with the eyes of an Innocent III
or a Boniface VIII. But from the fourteenth century we
get, as a rule, prelates of the type of Wykeham and Morton,
less single-minded as churchmen, but more patriotic as statesmen. Rightly they held it their function, not to press to
extremes the claim of their order, but to mediate between
the opposing forces. They tempered clerical zeal in convocation and secular anger in parliament. Theirs was not a
popular attitude; but perhaps it was well for both church
and state that bishops owed their appointment, not to election,
but to bargaining between the king and the pope, and that to
the holiness of their orders they usually added the qualification of long years in the service of the king. Assuredly it was
this connexion, their regular obedience to writs of summons
to parliaments, which helped to delay the final conflict of
church and state, and moderated its fury when it broke out.
Had there been less compromise before the reformation,
there would also have been less after it, and bishops would
have gone the way they went in really protestant countries.

They could not, however, indefinitely stop the secular
inroad by parleying at the gate, charmed they never so
wisely; and the last of the ecclesiastical statesmen hastened
the final assault by overdoing the part. Ecclesiastical
liberties and jurisdiction might be tolerable so long as they
were scattered in various hands; but when concentrated
in Wolsey's to an unprecedented extent, they evoked an
unprecedented resentment. His extraordinary legatine
powers made him supreme over both the provinces, and
constituted a national papacy;[1] and the union of this

[1] The authority of a *legatus a latere* overrode that of a *legatus natus* just
as a special envoy supersedes *ad hoc* a resident ambassador. The two
archbishops were always *legati nati*, but Wolsey secured a permanent
position as *legatus a latere*, and his exceptional powers enabled him to give

authority with his control of the state was a precedent for the combination under Henry VIII. If there was to be national autonomy in church as well as in state, and if the two corps of ecclesiastical and secular officers were to be united under a single command, the crown was a more natural head than a cardinal; for nationalism was inherent in the state, but exotic in the church, and a legate of the pope could only play at independence of the papacy.

Wolsey himself clearly foresaw and foretold that with him would fall the liberties of the church. Like other medieval liberties, they passed by the grace of parliament into the hands of the crown. It was a comprehensive but incomplete process of nationalization, in which the act of supremacy and the act for the submission of the clergy were merely details. These were but trifles compared with the revolution which made it possible to call the laity churchmen, and then to term them "religious" [1]—a revolution brought to its consummation when men began to expect the appeals which move their souls to fall, not from the lips of official clergy, but from those of the poet, the playwright, the philosopher, and even the politician. Fundamentally the movement was one to equalize churchmen and laymen by reducing the liberties of the church; and extremists would have whittled away to nothing the difference between the two, pronouncing every man a priest and abolishing the "Aaronic" vestments, benefit of clergy, and ecclesiastical jurisdiction. The clerical estate was to be merged in the national state, and its affiliations with the international papacy to disappear. In its political and constitutional aspects the reformation was no more than a stage in the progress of nationalism, and medieval petitions in parliament provided precedents for most of Henry's acts. The payment of annates and the

---

to the convocations of the two provinces the appearance of a national council of the Church. Overriding Archbishop Warham's summons of the Canterbury convocation to St. Paul's, he summoned both it and the York convocation to meet before him at Westminster in June 1523 (*Letters and Papers*, iii. Nos. 3024, 3239).

[1] The "religious" in the middle ages were the members of the religious orders; no parish priest could be religious, and the change of "religion" in Henry VIII's reign was primarily the dissolution of the monasteries.

pursuit of appeals to Rome had been attacked in the four-teenth century, as well as the papal appointment of prelates; and even an archbishop had asserted the right of the crown to prevent the translations and defy the excommunications of the pope.[1] Nationalism was, in short, invading the church on its march to its modern omnipotence; and in the latest of days we have seen international bonds, whether in the form of socialism or finance, pacifism or catholicism, shrivel like wisps of straw in the consuming fire of national passion and prejudice.

The loss of the church's liberties increased those of the crown and threatened those of the people. It is not, indeed, that the rôle, ascribed by Lord Acton to the catholic church, of protecting the liberties of the individual against the tyranny of the state has been filled with much success. Countries in which the catholic church retained its liberties between the Reformation and the Revolution were not conspicuous for the freedom enjoyed by the individual or by the nation; and liberty was not more at home in France, Italy, and Spain during the seventeenth and eighteenth centuries than it was in England, Holland, and America. For it was not with other people's liberties, or with liberty in general that the church was concerned, but with its own; it interfered, not to save victims from the state, but to claim them for itself, not to enforce freedom, but to establish jurisdiction. Its ideal was medieval independence, and not modern liberty. Nevertheless, the concentration of medieval liberties in the crown, which created modern sovereignty, was a menace to liberty from which England, Holland, and America were saved, not by the reformation, but by revolt against their monarchs. The great rebellion of 1642 sprang in a sense from the Tudor acts of supremacy.

For those acts of 1534 and 1559 united two incompatible forms of sovereignty—the absolute jurisdiction of the pope, instinct with Roman tradition, and the limited jurisdiction of the king, with its Teutonic and feudal restrictions. Care had, indeed, been taken in drafting the acts to meet the

[1] *Rot. Parl.*, iii. 304.

consequent danger; and the crown, as supreme head or governor of the church, was only authorized to exercise such jurisdiction as properly belonged to the ecclesiastical courts; otherwise, said the lord chancellor, Audley, in a significant conversation with Bishop Gardiner, " you prelates would enter in and order the laity as you listed." [1]   Coke fought a long battle in defence of Audley's interpretation; but only the great rebellion brought success to his cause. For the acts of supremacy had made the crown the keeper of its own conscience, the judge of its own liberties, the controller of its own powers.   In the middle ages the courts christian had been restrained by those of the crown, and those of the crown by those of the church.   But was the crown to restrain itself? were prohibitions of the king's bench to impede the high commission? was præmunire to limit the royal supremacy? [2]   The crown could be trusted in the middle ages to see that the courts christian did not overstep the mark; but would it be equally jealous of their liberties when they exerted a royal jurisdiction and proclaimed the divine right of kings?   The court of high commission answered the question, and Charles I and Archbishop Laud paid with their heads the penalty.

The civil war of the seventeenth century was thus prepared by the least constitutional measures of Henry VIII, for the act of supremacy was really a revolution.   That there was something fundamentally unconstitutional in Henry's government has been widely felt, but wrongly expressed in the constitutional terms of a later age.   Parliament became so closely identified with the constitution that nothing done by parliament was regarded as unconstitutional, and every unconstitutional course was interpreted as an infringement of parliamentary liberties.   So men were led to express their conviction of Henry's tyranny by attempt-

---

[1] Gardiner to Somerset, October 14, 1547, Foxe, *Acts and Monuments*, vi. 43.

[2] " How," asked James I, " can a king grant a *præmunire* against himself?" (*Political Works*, ed. McIlwain, 1918, p. 334).   Bishop Gardiner, in the letter quoted above, expressed a similar disbelief in the possibility of restraining by *præmunire* a minister of the king.

ing to prove his designs upon parliamentary independence. But the least constitutional acts of Henry's reign were acts of parliament, and he strained the constitution by expanding, and not by restricting, the sphere of its activity. He did not minimize, but magnified parliament. Under his rule its privileges were consolidated, its *personnel* was improved, its constituency enlarged, its political weight enhanced in foreign eyes, its authority increased, its sessions made more frequent and prolonged. He did not invade parliamentary liberties; he led a parliamentary invasion of the liberties of the church and of feudal franchise.

Under his impulse parliament was called upon to deal with clerical privileges, papal jurisdiction, and even with matters of faith; and the chief constitutional demands of the Pilgrimage of Grace were that the church of England might enjoy the liberties granted by Magna Carta and " used until six or seven years past," and that spiritual matters should be dealt with by convocation. These were liberties denied by parliament, and not to parliament; and this parliamentary invasion was unconstitutional in the sense that it was based on a novel theory of an omnicompetent " crown in parliament," and on a repudiation of a jurisdiction, the independence of which had been acknowledged and enjoyed for centuries. The English clergy, indeed, made their submission in both their provincial convocations; but the abandonment of the catholic position by two provinces was not, and could hardly be, regarded as constitutional by the rest of the catholic church. The revolution only became constitutional through the process by which triumphant treason ceases to be treason, that is, by success, and by the recognition of the supremacy of the crown in parliament over all competing jurisdictions. The constitutional aspect of the Anglican Reformation can only be summed up in the dubious maxim *quod fieri non debuit, factum valet;* and nations have ever since paid toll for a national sovereignty which is based on the sixteenth-century claim of parts of mankind to independence of the rest.

CHAPTER XI

THE GROWTH OF SOVEREIGNTY IN PARLIAMENT

IT has been said that the supreme achievement of the Reformation is the modern state.[1] The truth that lies in an epigram often bears restatement in a reversal of its parts, and it might be as true to say that the Reformation was the supreme achievement of the modern state. Certainly in England it was largely the work of the Tudor monarchy, which was rather a cause than a result of the Reformation. There is, however, a fundamental truth in this connexion between the Reformation and the modern state, and it concerns the nature of sovereignty. Without the Reformation there could have been no such thing as modern sovereignty; for the sovereignty of every medieval monarch in western Christendom was limited by the recognized claim of the pope to hold kings responsible for certain of their acts and to inflict pains and penalties for the infraction of certain rules of conduct. They were not exempt from citation to Rome, and they could not afford to assert that divine right of irresponsibility with which protestantism endowed their successors.

It would, however, be a mistake to regard this achievement of sovereignty as an act of creation. The crown in parliament is legally omnicompetent, because it was never created, because there never was made that social contract to which philosophers in the pre-scientific ages of history were wont to ascribe the origin of the state. The act of creation involves the relation between creature and creator, and the purpose of the theories of contract was to impose the limitations

[1] Figgis in *Cambridge Modern History*, iii. 736.

involved in that relation, and to bind sovereignty down to
the terms and conditions that pleased its imaginary creator.
Wherever a constitution has been made, and power has
been conferred by a definite act, limitations have been
imposed by its makers. But no one made the English
crown or the English parliament, and no powers have been
conferred upon them; for that reason they are unlimited.
No one has had the right to confer, and therefore no one has
had the right to limit their sovereignty. It grew, and
things that grow have a power divine beyond that of things
that are made with hands.

The slow evolution of sovereignty in England precludes
any theory of its special creation at any particular period;
and the process reaches back beyond the middle ages and
spans the whole course of English history. If it is an error
to regard sovereignty as the creation of the age of Luther
and Machiavelli, it is a greater error to regard the English
constitution as complete in the reign of Edward I. In spite of
the growth of parliament during the fourteenth century and
of the Lancastrian experiment, it is the imperfection rather
than the perfection of government that strikes the observer
at the close of the middle ages. The burden of Fortescue's
complaint is the lack of governance in England, and
Machiavelli attributed the political ills of his time to lack of
will. He was thinking, not of the individual will which
superabounded in the over-mighty subject, but of will in the
state. The " Rolls of Parliaments " are full of lamentations
over the king's failure to execute justice; and a profounder
study than these plaintiffs gave to the subject suggests that
it was the king's power rather than his will which was at
fault. Nor was the lack of governance a novel grievance :
under the " greatest of the Plantagenets " complaints are
made in parliament of livery and maintenance, champerty
and riots ; and petitioners allege that no truth can be obtained
of juries, so corrupted are they by rich men's bribes.[1] The
captains and ringleaders of anarchy were, no doubt, greater
men in the reign of Henry VI than in that of Edward I, but

[1] *Rot. Parl.*, i. 96, 183, 201; Maitland, *Memoranda*, pp. 109, 286-7, 305.

the concentration of the forces of disorder in fewer hands
did not necessarily increase the extent of the evil, and weakness of government was endemic throughout the middle
ages.

Nothing, indeed, could be wider of the mark than the
popular identification of feudal times with royal despotism
or of the progress of constitutional liberty with the whittling
away of sovereignty.   Freedom without sovereignty is the
idle dream of anarchists; and sovereignty without freedom
is the aim of bureaucratic despots.   Neither is safe without
the other, and it was the absence of national sovereignty that
left medieval England a prey to feudal disorder.   The
government, as Maitland has remarked, was occupied less
in governing than in struggling for existence; and the impediments that hampered its action were not merely material
forces, but the ideas of liberty and law which were
ingrained in medieval man.   Some were due to intellectual
immaturity.   When the law confessed its inability to discriminate between murder and homicide, proclaimed that
" the thought of man shall not be tried, for the devil himself
knoweth not the thought of man," [1] and only distinguished
crimes of violence according to the accidents of the time and
place of their committal, there was little hope of justice, and
inadequate security for execution so long as the individual
was entitled to defeat the law by " standing mute." [2]   To
this deep-seated distrust of human capacity or rectitude
was due the resort to judicial methods like trial by fire or
water, by which the hope of justice was frankly abandoned
to the miraculous interposition of superhuman powers, an
attitude of mind which still survives in the belief that
victory in battle is a judgement of God.

This disbelief in human achievement, natural enough in
the early stages of political evolution, explains the medieval
conception of law.   Nowadays law is regarded as something
which man has made; then man could not make law at all.

---

[1] Maitland, *Collected Papers*, i. 304, 315, 453.
[2] Not abolished until 1772. Cf. L. Vernon Harcourt, *His Grace the Steward
and Trial by Peers*, p. 228.

It had been made for him, directly by God in the form of divine law, or indirectly by God in the forms of the law of nature or the law of universal reason. Really this law was custom sanctified by the church; but whether regarded as custom in heathen communities or as the direct or indirect expression of the divine will in Christian states, no king or parliament could make, repeal, or amend it. They might proclaim or apply it, but they could not create it; it was immutable and eternal, and all alike, prince and people, were subject to its dictates. These laws, however, required an interpreter, especially since they often conflicted. Few schools of political thought have failed to find justification in the laws of nature, or of reason, or of God—from the absolutist to the tyrannicide, from the individualist to the communist; and the conflict of laws demanded a supreme arbiter in the interests of peace. Sovereignty, therefore, appears in a judicial guise and sits in a court of law; and the king in his council in parliaments interprets the law before he pretends to make it. Our earliest laws—apart from customs which are not conscious creations—are judicial decisions. Indeed, most formal acts in the early middle ages were regarded as the judgements of a court: even a declaration of war was a *judicium super eum ire*,[1] and from it descends the right of the high court of parliament to consultation on such issues. Treaties of peace are recorded on the rolls of that court as late as 1420.

A decision in court, however, makes law, and legislation begins under judicial forms. But the ordinances of Edward I, for instance, should be regarded rather as general instructions to judges and others in their administration of existing law than as deliberate and conscious efforts to alter the law. Magna Carta was a treaty rather than an act of legislation, and with its corollaries, the *Confirmatio Cartarum*, and the *Articuli super Cartas*, continued to be regarded as fundamental law, infractions of which, even by parliament itself, were *ipso facto* invalid.[2] But constitutional and social

[1] *I.e.* on a vassal; see above, p. 92 *n.*
[2] *Rot. Parl.*, i. 285.

development was outgrowing rigid conceptions, and the law
which satisfied past generations had to be supplemented:
even the constitution of the United States has required
amendment. The medieval supplements to the constitution
of the world took the form of positive law, that is, of law
imposed by human authority. But this law, made by man,
was inferior to the older laws of God and nature: those
were, so to speak, the constitution, these the provisional
regulations made under its authority. The prince was
above the laws he made, but subject to those of God
and nature; [1] an offence against the latter was *malum in se*,
an offence against the former was only a *malum prohibitum*.[2]

It was from these immutable laws that medieval liberties
were derived: they were absolute rights, not the concessions
of human authority. Kings and parliaments had not given
them, kings and parliaments could not take them away.
Louis XIV declared that even he, with his plenitude of royal
power, could not deprive his grandson of his hereditary right
to the Spanish throne.[3] Hereditary right was divine, and
the monarchical character was indelible: not all the water
in the rough, rude sea could wash the balm off an anointed
king. So thought Richard II, Mary Stuart, and Charles I. As
with the *regnum*, so with the *sacerdotium;* and not until 1870
did the English parliament admit that a clerk in Anglican
orders could divest himself of the indelible character of
priesthood.[4] The peerage was not to be outdone by priests
or kings; in the course of time it established for itself an
indefeasible privilege which kings and priests have lost,
and in 1894 three eldest sons of peers attempted in vain to
evade the impending doom of a nobility inseparably blended
with blue blood.[5] Thus is man's liberty impeded by the
barriers he has sought to raise in its defence.

[1] " Positiva lex est infra principantem sicut lex naturalis est supra "
(Aegidius Romanus, quoted in Maitland's *Gierke*, p. 176).
[2] Prothero, *Select Documents*, 1898, p. 402; Coke placed the common
law almost on a level with the older fundamental laws.
[3] Torcy, *Mémoires*, ed. 1850, pp. 710–11.
[4] 33 and 34 Vict. c. 91; Anson, *Law and Custom of the Constitution*,
1908, II. ii. 326–7.
[5] See below, pp. 274, 306.

These were the liberties of the great, but those of the humble were based on the same foundation of imprescriptible right. Private property was by some medieval thinkers placed outside the sphere of public power,[1] not indeed on the ground that it is inherited, but because it originates in the labour of the individual, and was thus a right independent of the community. Citizens were regarded as shareholders who could not be deprived of their shares by a vote of the majority or by any other means than their own voluntary concession.[2] Medieval history, says Stubbs, is the history of rights and wrongs, to be followed by a modern history of powers, forces, dynasties.[3] In theory every one's right was indestructible; society was, in fact, static and not dynamic. There was no power to reform a right, and the only way to dispose of it was to prove that it was " usurped "— like the supremacy of Rome. In practice, of course, the absence of means of legal redress led to violent measures on the part of those who felt themselves wronged or incommoded by the rights of others. The legal employment of torture was probably due to the same process of thought; even the criminal must consent to plead or confess, and without his individual surrender there could be no legal verdict. The weakness of the state was the parent of its cruelty. It was hemmed in by iron laws and indestructible rights; it could not create or modify the conditions of its existence, and the " Rolls " of medieval English parliaments are records of their conscious infirmity.

The greatest of all these limitations imposed on the state were those imposed by the church. Indeed, from Hildebrand onwards papalists had contended that the state had no rights or powers at all except in so far as they were derived from, and controlled and guided by, the church : *papa ipse verus imperator*, declared the canonists of the twelfth century, and the prince only wielded the sword as the officer of the pope. The pope was the judge, the king the executioner.

---

[1] John of Paris, quoted in Maitland's *Gierke*, p. 180.
[2] *Ibid.*, p. 167; cf. *Collected Papers*, ii. 318–19.
[3] *Lectures on Medieval and Modern History*, ed. 1887, p. 239.

He was a dreamer of dreams.   The lawyers and statesmen of his time were hard pressed to secure a foothold or two in Marsiglio's promised land; and the boldest of legal fictions and the hardiest of assumptions had to be made by the *principans* to extend that field of positive law of which he was master, at the expense of that field of natural law to which he was subject.   The secular prince borrowed most of his maxims from the law of the church, a sphere in which the pope's claims to divine authority had enabled him to exalt his *lex positiva* above the *lex naturalis ;* for the pope was, so to speak, the *legatus a latere* of God, while nature and reason were merely *legati nati* whose authority was over-ridden by special commission.   From the canon law was taken the phrase *ex certa scientia*, whereby the statute or ordinance disposed of the defect arising in natural law from the absence of " just cause " for the invasion of private rights; from it, too, came the *lege non obstante* clauses, which calmly assumed the plenitude of the sovereign's power over all other laws.[1]   Richard II, however, borrowed whole-sale; he not only claimed to be " entire emperor " in England, but appropriated the contention of Boniface VIII that he had *omnia jura in scrinio pectoris sui ;* [2] and in many other respects he attempted to anticipate the new monarchy. But the time was not ripe, and Richard himself was not the man to wield the sceptre of a saviour of society.   The Lancastrian experiment and the Wars of the Roses were still required to convince the English people that sovereignty was a necessary supplement to liberty, and the Reception, the Renaissance, and the Reformation were needed to complete the rout of feudalism and fortify the monarchy.

The reception of the Roman law by almost all the kingdoms of western Europe was one of the great movements which marked the close of the middle ages.   It completed

---

[1] Maitland's *Gierke*, p. 185.   For an early use of *non obstante* in England see *Rot. Parl.*, ii. 167.

[2] Maitland's *Gierke*, p. 176; cf. *Letters and Papers of Henry VIII*, iv. p. 1839; *Rot. Parl.*, iii. 343.   Richard was accused of having said " quod leges suæ erant in ore suo et aliquotiens in pectore suo; et quod ipse solus posset mutare et condere leges regni sui " (*ibid.*, iii. 419).

the *translatio imperii* from the moribund Holy Roman
emperor to the lusty national king, who appropriated the
legal effects of the deceased world-sovereign. Technically
the Roman law was never "received" in England, and
the resistance of homespun English law is a momentous
chapter of English legal history.[1] But English law was only
successful in its resistance because in the earlier stages of
its existence it had been inoculated by Henry II and the
curia regis, as well as through the canon law, with some of
the principles of the rival system, and was therefore the
better prepared to withstand the legal epidemic of the
sixteenth century. Even so the struggle was long and
arduous, and did not end till the revolution of 1688 expelled
the Stuarts and gave the victory over the civilians to the
common lawyers. In the interval between the premature
efforts of Richard II and the fall of his followers, the Stuarts,
maxims of Roman civil law played a great part in English
history, a part which, though dangerous to self-government,
was essential to the establishment of the sovereignty of the
state. "If we should do nothing but as the common law
will," wrote the president of the Council of Wales with respect
to Welsh disorders, "these things so far out of order will
never be redressed"; [2] and the prerogative courts and councils
of the Tudors found in the Roman law indispensable aids
to the suppression of local anarchy. Tudor officials were
nearly all trained in the civil laws, and while the study of
canon law was forbidden by Henry VIII, attempts were
made to found a college of civil law at Cambridge, and
chairs of civil law were endowed at both universities. Civil
law was an apt weapon against both the canon and common
law, and "imperial" became one of the favourite adjectives
of the crown.

While the invasion of Roman law released sovereignty
from the trammels of common law, the Renaissance tended
to relax the restraints of morality; and Machiavelli, the

---

[1] See Maitland, *English Law and the Renaissance*, 1901.
[2] Rowland Lee to Cromwell, July 18, 1538; the letter is abbreviated
in *Letters and Papers*, XIII. i. 1411; cf. Skeel, *Council of Wales*, p. 68.

political philosopher of the Renaissance, has been acclaimed as one of the fathers of the modern state. His offence was not so much that he invented political immorality, as that he laid bare the secrets of princes, and treated politics as a science and an art with its own principles and technique which were, like those of surgery or navigation, independent of morals. The state was the only available instrument for the work of political reformation, and it could only achieve that work by being liberated from the conventions of medieval thought which had left society bankrupt at the close of the fifteenth century. Machiavelli's contribution to political sovereignty was his assertion of freedom of will for the state.

Luther's was his assertion of its freedom from the papacy,[1] and the Reformation broke one of the bonds which fettered the sovereignty of kings; it rendered them irresponsible except to God. While Machiavelli, like Hobbes, contemplated the possibility of a sovereign republic, Luther tied his cause to the chariot wheels of German territorial princes, and his political theory evoked many echoes in the England of the Tudors. The jurisdiction of the pope was abolished as " usurped," and canon law was subjected to royal veto. The king was thus *lege solutus* so far as the greater portion of medieval law was concerned; and of the law that remained he was the final arbiter. From Roman civilians he learnt that *quod principi placuit legis habet vigorem;* and even the common law of England could now be made and unmade by the crown in parliament, and interpreted by the king's own courts. The crown in parliament was emancipated from the control of fundamental law and from the medieval liberties which were derived therefrom. The conflict of independent legal systems was at an end; they were all fused in national law and subjected to a common sovereignty. There was only one divine right, and that was the right of kings; all the rest were " usurped." The king was the supreme head of one body.

The medieval distinctions between churchmen and laymen were swept away or reduced to insignificance, and laymen

[1] He may also have helped by his denial of free will to the individual.

in time were even called churchmen. Ecclesiastics were required or encouraged to assimilate the habits and customs of their flocks, to discard their clerical vestments and assume the bonds of matrimony. The concentration camps of monasticism were broken up, and their inmates dispersed among the civil population. Every form of loyalty except allegiance to the national king was discouraged; and the characteristic hostility of the Roman law to every association that weakened the direct connexion between the state and the individual was reflected in the attitude of Tudor statesmen to corporations.[1] Ecclesiastical colleges and chantries felt the brunt of this animosity, but secular guilds and municipal corporations found their liberties restrained by acts of parliament, and their freedom of internecine legislation controlled by chancery. Medieval rights gave way to modern law, and all municipal authority was regarded as a concession from a sovereign parliament and not as a derivation from imprescriptible right. The passion for national independence left little room for the independence of church, class, or corporation; the many estates were fused in the single state, and their liberties were confiscated in the interests of national sovereignty. The revolts of the Tudor period are nearly all local, sectional, or ecclesiastical protests against this national consolidation. The Cornishmen in 1497 resent taxes levied for the defence of the Scottish borders: the Pilgrims of Grace complain of the neglect of the house of lords to begin each day's proceedings with the time-honoured recital of the first clause of Magna Carta, and of the transgression by statute of the liberties of the church;[2] and the northern earls in 1569 were fighting a last fight for feudal freedom from the state.

This monopoly of sovereignty was something new in English and in other history. There was little of it in the middle ages, but only suzerainty of many sorts. Every lord

---

[1] See above, pp. 174-6.
[2] *Letters and Papers of Henry VIII*, xi. 1182 (2), xii. pt. i. 401; Dodds, *Pilgrimage of Grace*, i. 360.

was " sovereign " to his man, and every master to his servant. Even an archbishop was "sovereign" to his suffragans, and a husband to his wife.[1]   To kill one's lord was treason, petty it is true, but none the less a worse offence than murder. What real sovereignty there was had been discovered by the pope when he stepped into the shoes of the Roman Imperator, and he alone was sovereign in the modern Austinian sense. For the barbarians had not only shattered Roman empire, but dissipated sovereignty, and it easily slid down the slippery slopes of the feudal pyramid.   Much of it passed, for instance, from the king of the French to the Norman duke, from the duke to the Angevin count, and from him to the count of Maine, before it sank into the minds of the people of Le Mans; and a sovereignty which had to satisfy so many mouths was a diluted form of political authority.   The medieval *prerogativa regis* was a purely feudal conception;[2] the king was regarded as simply paramount landlord, and his prerogative only affected his subjects *quâ* tenants.

But the royal prerogative of the Tudors affected their relations with every subject irrespective of his tenure; the "sovereignty" of masters over men, and with it petty treason, almost disappeared in one conception of sovereignty and a single notion of high treason.   Even the sovereignty of the pope had had its rivals; that of the Tudors had none.   The subject's relation to the crown became his political all in all. All the liberties and jurisdictions which had intervened between the subject and the national sovereign were abolished, and Englishmen were brought into direct and constant contact with the state.   The relationship, therefore, assumed an overwhelming importance, and created a problem of absorbing magnitude.   Sovereignty might be tolerable while

<hr/>

[1] 12 Henry VII, c. 7: " their master or their immediate sovereign "; *Rot. Parl.*, ii. 244–5 : " et le dit evesque . . . eit receu mandement de . . . son soveregn erchevesque "; *Paston Letters*, i. 78 : " to my soveregn, John Paston "; *Rot. Parl.*, 4 Henry VIII, prefixed to *Lords' Journals*, vol. i. p. xxix: " that every lord espiritual and temporal and every sovereign of monastery . . . that every such lord, sovereign, master, mistress, or other householder;" *Taming of the Shrew*, Act v. Sc. ii. 147: " Thy husband is . . . thy sovereign."

[2] On the so-called statute *Prærogativa Regis*, see Maitland, *Collected Papers*, ii. 182–9.

it was distributed in many hands; it took on a forbidding aspect when gathered into one. Contact often means conflict, and popular hostility is only aroused by the jurisdiction with which people are brought into touch. Hence the popular risings and resentments of the middle ages were directed against ecclesiastical and feudal jurisdictions, because those were the authorities under which most men suffered. There were no really popular rebellions against the crown; the movements against the crown were baronial or ecclesiastical, because it was the crown which threatened the liberties of the magnates and the church.

But now the crown has absorbed and wields these juris-dictions; the buffers are removed, and a king who demands the undivided loyalty of his subjects runs the risk of their undivided disaffection. The crown has enveloped church and state alike in the ample shield of its supremacy, and that shield must bear the brunt of every attack on the powers the crown has absorbed. Every movement for liberty becomes an attack on the crown : the strife is no longer between barons or bishops and the king, but between the king and his parliament or his people. The crown had become the universal agent and everybody's proxy; and its monopoly of powers involved a monopoly of responsibility. Medieval sovereignty, dispersed in local franchises and in the privileges of orders and estates, and bound down by fundamental laws, might be irresponsible; but modern sovereignty, triumphant over canon and over common law, and over all excluding liberties, must be made responsible or must be dismembered. It was well that Leviathan should have a giant's strength; it was ill that he should use it in a giant's spirit. The problem of the seventeenth and eighteenth centuries was whether to dismember or harness Leviathan, and how to effect the process. The Americans preferred dismemberment of sovereignty and the separation of powers. England decided for unity of powers combined with responsibility for their exercise; it hitched a democratic wagon to *le roi soleil*.

The explanation of this choice is found in the history of

the English parliament. It inherited, but did not divide the sovereignty of the crown; or rather, there was no demise of powers at all, but a rearrangement of predominance in the partnership. The crown had never been sovereign by itself, for before the days of parliament there was no real sovereignty at all: sovereignty was only achieved by the energy of the crown in parliament, and the fruits of conquest were enjoyed in common. It was a happy thing that no English king ever delegated powers to an English parliament, but preserved them entire, so that in due time the people should enjoy them. For delegation would have meant division, and division would have meant subtraction. But since there was no delegation from the crown, there was no circumscription of the powers of parliament. It was summoned to do whatever might be proposed.

No doubt, in reality, and also in men's ideas of what was right, the competence of the crown in parliament was severely restricted; and possibly the obvious narrowness of those limitations dispensed with the need of definition. For we only limit powers which may conceivably be used or abused; it is but lately that men have begun to talk of sovereignty or property in the air, and we are not yet reduced to dealing by statute with property in sunshine or in rain. If Edward I had had James I's notions of sovereignty, he would have been more chary of summoning parliaments to share it with him; and if barons and churchmen had dreamt of the lengths to which the crown in parliament would go under the Tudors in dealing with their liberties, they would early have insisted on a written and rigid constitution. They did, in fact, try to stereotype Magna Carta, fortunately without success. But, on the whole, the poverty of parliamentary force enabled it to avoid definitions of its authority until the Tudors had discovered in parliament the aptest instrument for their designs. It was then too late for the threatened liberties to protest, for the crown in parliament was the interpreter of the extent of the powers it exercised; it was judge, jury, and criminal all combined, so far as its offences against fundamental law and medieval liberties were concerned, and the political efficiency of combining a supreme court with a legislature has seldom been illustrated with more striking effect.

Nor was there ever a more signal proof of political genius or more fortunate coincidence of interests than that which led to the co-operation of crown and parliament under Henry VIII. The two were knit together in terms of the closest alliance in their conflict with rival jurisdictions, and each found its advantage in exalting, instead of in fighting, the other. The way in which parliament magnified Henry VIII is written in the statutes of the latter half of his reign; and the king repaid the compliment. " We," he declared to the commons, " be informed by our judges that we at no time stand so highly in our estate royal as in the time of parliament, wherein we as head and you as members are conjoined and knit together in one body politic, so as whatsoever offence or injury during that time is offered to the meanest member of the house is to be judged as done against our person and the whole court of parliament." [1] It was in his reign that the Speaker's claim for personal freedom of speech was expanded into a claim on behalf of every member,[2] and there is no instance in which Henry himself violated those privileges, respect for which he enforced upon others. Parliamentary sanction was sought to an unprecedented extent for the acts of the crown.

It was not the debasement, but the exaltation of parliament that impressed the witnesses of the process; and malcontents sneered at that " thirteenth article of our creed, added of late," that parliament cannot err,[3] a doctrine which even royalist judges admitted under Charles I.[4] Parliament, says Sir Thomas Smith, " representeth and hath the power of the whole realm . . . and the

---

[1] *Letters and Papers of Henry VIII*, vol. xvii. pp. iv, 107; Holinshed, *Chronicles*, iii. 956.
[2] *Lords' Journals*, i. 167; Hakewill, *Modus Tenendi Parl.*, p. 213; Manning, *Speakers*, p. 192.
[3] *Letters and Papers of Henry VIII*, vol. xx. part ii. p. 345.
[4] Justice Berkeley on ship-money, Gardiner, *Select Documents*, ed. 1889, p. 54.

consent of parliament is taken to be every man's consent." [1]
L'État, c'est moi was the boast which Voltaire put into the
mouth of Louis XIV : in England the state was not the
crown, but a fusion of all the estates, and every free Englishman could share in the glory reserved in France for the king.
Sovereignty was vested, not in a single person, but in a composite and representative body, which expressed the national
will and mind, and not merely that of a monarch. It was
this national will that gave the Tudors their strength; it
was a new will to be free from the old restraints, and it sprang
from a disappearance of the medieval distrust in human
rectitude and capacity, and from a growth in conscious
control over national destinies. He knew not, Burghley
was wont to say, what an act of parliament could not
do in England; [2] and the long list which Sir Thomas Smith
gives of the things which parliament could do and did,
trespasses far and wide on the old forbidden domains of
immutable law, and sets no bounds to the sphere of national
legislation.

Not that the old landmarks of thought were suddenly
swept away or submerged in one or two generations. They
still survive in conservative affections, and iconoclasts themselves use the arms of the past to break with the past.
Richard of York claimed in 1460 that hereditary right
was part of the law of nature. [3]   Henry VIII alleged the
will of God and the law of nature as the two foundations
of royal authority; and chief justice Coke tried to place
man-made common law on a pedestal above the reach
of king or parliament. That there was a law of nature,
a law of nations, and a law of reason outside the scope of
statute was a conception which lingered long in the judicial
mind. Lord Mansfield laid it down that " the act of parliament 7 Anne c. 12 did not intend to alter, nor can alter, the
law of nations."   In the seventeenth and eighteenth centuries
the courts often declared statutes null if against reason or

---

[1] *De Republica Anglorum*, ed. Alston, p. 49.
[2] McIlwain, *Political Works of James I*, p. 329.
[3] Fortescue, p. 207.

fundamental law;[1] and to-day, after all the labours of Austin, the church declines to recognize the ecclesiastical jurisdiction of the judicial committee of the privy council, which is based on parliamentary statute. It holds that the law of the church, which is thereby overridden, rests on a higher authority than any positive law of the state. This ground was common to all parties to the constitutional struggles of the seventeenth century—to crown and commons, peers and judges. All claimed to hold what they held by right. But they also held this in common, that they could override the rights of others by statute. The commons disposed of endless rights by statute and ordinance during the Long parliament; and crown, church, and lords employed statutes for similar ends at the Restoration. Parliament, which is not regarded by high churchmen as a sufficient authority for the jurisdiction of the privy council, was good enough for a Test act and a Clarendon code Indefeasible right is, in fact, the right of oneself; and fundamental law is the law one invokes to restrain legislation by other people. As a minority dwindles, its attachment to fundamentals develops; but the more completely parliament represents the nation, and government grows responsible, the less does the nation demand restrictions on sovereign power. Fundamental laws and written constitutions are, in the main, expressions of the distrust which a people feels of its government or a government feels of its people.

So sovereignty has grown with popular representation and popular education.[2] The revolution of 1688 weakened the king, but strengthened the crown. The reform acts of the nineteenth and twentieth centuries enfranchised masses who used their votes to demand more and more governmental activity; and a cabinet has at its disposal to-day a wealth of resource and a profusion of powers beyond

---

[1] McIlwain, *The High Court of Parliament*, pp. 271, 281–3, 329.
[2] So modern is our " sovereignty " that it is not even mentioned in Cowell's *Law Dictionary*, and so different is its modern from its medieval meaning that we had early in the nineteenth century to adopt a variation of the word and use " suzerainty " to express what medieval writers meant by " sovereignty."

the wildest dreams of a Tudor or Stuart despot. The royal prerogative, so long feared and disliked, grows by leaps and bounds, for the advice of ministers has become the act of the crown, and ministers themselves the agents of the people. "The progress of constitutional liberty in this country," it was remarked long ago, "is shown not so much by the actual restraints that have been imposed upon the powers of the crown, as by the efforts which have been made to render the king's advisers responsible to parliament." [1]

Thus did England deal with the problem created by the monopoly of sovereignty and the decay of medieval restraints. Three alternatives were conceivable as means for preventing a monstrous tyranny. Sovereignty might be limited, it might be divided, or it might be kept intact but entrusted to ministers responsible to the nation for every detail of its exercise. Each of these expedients was tried in turn by England during the seventeenth century: experience taught it to prefer the third. Influenced perhaps by the short-lived experiments of the Commonwealth and Protectorate, but more by the exigencies of their own situation, and misled by the superficial appearance of the British constitution and by deductions therefrom by French philosophers, the Americans chose the second, and constructed a constitution on the basis of a divided sovereignty and on the dogma of the separation of powers. They believed that undivided sovereignty meant unbridled tyranny; and their descendants still maintain that the sovereignty of parliament is a doctrine inapplicable to the United States, and therefore to any free imperial community. The fiction that there is, or ever was a separation of powers in the English constitution, and the assumption that in that separation lies the sole guarantee for effective liberty, are based upon historical and other arguments which require further investigation.

[1] Nicolas, *Proc. of Privy Council*, vol. vi. Introd. p. cxl.

CHAPTER XII

THE SEPARATION OF POWERS

HOWEVER closely and completely an institution or a constitution may be studied by those familiar in practice with its working, there is always something further to be learnt by regarding it from a distant and external point of view, by examining the efforts made at imitation, and even by investigating intelligent misconceptions of its spirit and its working. No commentary on the British parliament is more illuminating than the constitution of the United States of America, and nothing helps to understand the sovereignty of parliament so clearly as the doctrine of the separation of powers. That doctrine was deduced by Montesquieu from his study of the English constitution in the first half of the eighteenth century; it was accepted as valid by Blackstone a generation later; and it was preached with unquestioning fervour and conviction by the authors of the American federal constitution and of the State constitutions in which that Union abounds. The division of the functions of government into legislative, executive, and judicial is indeed as old as Athens and Aristotle. But Montesquieu " was the first to demonstrate that the separation of governmental powers is indispensable to civil liberty "; [1] and the American constitution—" the greatest government God ever made," as it has been rashly called by an ex-president of the United States—was the first to be constructed on that principle. A few quotations will explain the meaning of the doctrine and the fundamental importance that has been attached to it.

[1] W. Bondy, *The Separation of Governmental Powers* (Columbia University), 1896, p. 13.

" When the legislative and executive powers are united in the same person or body," says Montesquieu, " there can be no liberty "; and again, " there is no liberty if the judicial power be not separated from the legislative and executive." [1]   " Wherever," declares Blackstone, " the right of making and enforcing the law is vested in the same man, or in one and the same body of men, there can be no public liberty." [2]   " I agree," echoed Alexander Hamilton, " that there is no liberty if the power of judging be not separated from the legislative and executive powers."   Washington, in his farewell address, carried the argument a step further : [3] " the spirit of encroachment," he declared, " tends to consolidate the powers of all departments in one, and thus to create, whatever the form of government, a real despotism "; and the first constitution of Massachusetts, adopted in 1780, attempted to guard in perpetuity against the danger.   " In the government of this commonwealth," it provides, " the legislative department shall never exercise the executive and judicial powers, or either of them; the executive shall never exercise the legislative and judicial powers, or either of them; the judiciary shall never exercise the legislative and executive powers, or either of them; to the end that it may be a government of laws and not of men." [4]

This is a far cry from Fleta's *rex enim habet curiam suam in concilic suo in parliamentis suis;* and an Englishman who is not overwhelmed by this weight of testimony, who is not convinced that this drastic separation of powers has ever existed, or exists in England to-day, and yet is persuaded that his country is not quite a stranger to civil, religious, and political liberty, is tempted to put one or two preliminary questions.   Firstly, if this separation of powers existed, as Montesquieu and Blackstone believed that it did exist, in England and her colonies in the first half of the eighteenth century, and if this separation of powers is so unique a guarantee of liberty and so sovereign a remedy

[1] *Esprit des Lois*, xi. c. 6.   [2] *Commentaries*, 5th ed., i. 146.
[3] Bondy, p. 17.   [4] *Ibid.*, p. 19.

against despotism, why was it necessary for the American people to issue a declaration of independence and resort to war in defence of their liberties and the rights of man? Secondly, why, after that demonstration of the inadequacy of the separation of powers to secure liberty, did the fathers of the American constitution adopt it as their palladium and enshrine it in the heart of their constitutional affections? Thirdly, why, after the unanimous acceptance and careful elaboration of the principle, was it necessary seventy-five years later to wage another and a still more terrible war to define and ensure that liberty so amply guarded by the constitution? And fourthly, what, after a century and more of " a government of laws and not of men," and after a double and triple assurance of liberty, is the exact point of a presidential campaign with " The New Freedom " as its war-cry? [1]

It is no part of my purpose to attempt an answer to any one of these questions. They are suggested merely in criticism of the confident assertion that liberty cannot exist without a separation of governmental powers, and of the optimistic assumption that with that separation liberty is secure; and they may perhaps help to reassure some of us in our belief in English liberty, of which we should otherwise be bereft. For assuredly there is no separation of powers in the British constitution, and Montesquieu was at fault alike in his observation and in the deductions he made therefrom. It was easy, indeed, to be misled on the point, and as a matter of fact he was only assuming as accomplished an ideal at which the house of commons deliberately aimed in the early part of the eighteenth century. It was the age of place bills; distrust of the crown was rampant since the days of the later Stuarts; and all connexion between the court and the commons was considered corrupting. Many attempts were therefore made to preserve the independence and purity of the legislature by excluding from it all servants of the crown,[2] and thus establishing a

[1] This was President Wilson's battle-cry in the election of 1912.
[2] The demand was put forward as early as 1536 in the Pilgrimage of Grace (*Letters and Papers of Henry VIII*, xi. 1143, 1244).

complete separation between the legislative and executive powers. Montesquieu's mistake lay in his failure to realize that the growth of the cabinet, the pivot of the modern British constitution, was already destroying that separation. It is more singular that Blackstone and the American lawyers should have adopted the misconception, though there was some excuse for failure to discern the responsibility of the executive to the legislature in George III's cabinets between 1763 and 1782.

The fundamental unity of governmental powers in England is apparent from the briefest survey of the constitution. It is not a mere form that all powers, executive, legislative, and judicial, are vested in the crown. Every item of legislation throughout the British empire is enacted by the king, in person or by deputy; "every single act of administration, from the arrest of a suspected criminal to the declaration of a war, is in express terms his act. The formula is carried out logically and minutely; his image and superscription appear on every coin, his monogram on every mailcart . . . he is every day plaintiff in a thousand suits and president of a hundred courts." [1] The capacities of the lord chancellor are almost as varied as those of the crown : he is the head of the judicature, he presides over one branch of the legislature, and he is an important member of the supreme executive. We have two supreme courts of appeal, the house of lords and the judicial committee; one of them is a branch of the legislature, the other a committee of the executive council. So far from there being a rigid separation between the legislature and the executive, there is the closest possible connexion. Textbooks say that the legislature controls the executive; publicists complain that the executive controls the legislature. The cabinet is part and parcel of the legislature; and but for the presence of ministers in the houses of lords and commons, parliament would be unable to discharge its constitutional functions.

The judicature stands more apart, but there is no separation of powers or even of persons. Judges are lords of

[1] *The British Empire*, ed. A. F. Pollard, 1909, pp. 169–70.

parliament, they are appointed by the executive, and they can be removed on an address from both houses of parliament. Parliament itself is a court, and discharges judicial functions. In private bill legislation, a committee of either house can hear counsel on both sides and summon and cross-examine witnesses. Each house has its bar, to which petitioners and offenders may be called. Parliament can pass acts supplementary to, or overriding the verdicts of lower courts. It has passed hundreds of acts granting divorce which could not be obtained from the courts; and by acts of attainder and impeachments has brought many a head to the scaffold. Such methods may not recommend the fusion of powers to transatlantic critics; but at the worst they bear comparison with the presidential assassinations and lynching of negroes which have darkened the abodes of purer democracy. More important are the facts that parliament defines and determines the law and the justice which the courts administer, and that no judge can dispute the legality of an act of parliament. Nor had parliament to wait on the bench before it could levy an income-tax, legalize trade unions, or abolish trusts.

This absence of delimitation is the natural characteristic of a constitution that has grown, and not been manufactured. The separation of powers in politics corresponds to the fixity of species in natural science; and both ignore evolution. But the history of parliament is mainly concerned with the evolution of institutions from a common protoplasm and with their mutual struggles for recognition and predominance. The influence of common origin pervades every branch of English government, and behind all its specific functions there lies a fundamental unity symbolized by the crown. But there has been specialization and differentiation, for every organism which fails to specialize becomes inefficient; and we have firstly to trace the differentiation which gave colour to Montesquieu's fancied separation; secondly, to indicate the limits which made his interpretation fiction and not fact; and thirdly, to inquire how far these limitations involved the disastrous results which seemed so patent to the founders of the American constitution.

We revert to Fleta's description of parliaments, and find that his conception of a composite body consisting of court, council, and parliament is amply borne out by the records. Doubtless the executive was the earliest and the most prominent of the composite functions of government; war begat the king, and his first duty was execution. There was little scope for " judgement " in primitive law, and less for legislation under the rule of primitive custom. What judgement and legislation there was, was passed by the king, and it was only by a slow process of differentiation that he partially divested himself of the personal exercise of these functions. The Norman and Angevin rulers judged and legislated as well as administered, and even under Edward I there was no clear discrimination. When the king holds his court in his council in parliaments, he can clearly do anything; but it is also clear that the king in council can legislate without the assistance of parliament. Most of Edward's legislation was promulgated before the days of his Model Parliament. Even such separation of powers as may be implied in the requirement of the assent of lords and commons to legislation has never been completely effected, and in 1872 the crown, in abolishing by an order in council the purchase of army commissions, carried a measure which had failed to pass the legislature.

The consent of a council to legislation was, no doubt, secured in practice at an early date, and probably Edward I's council assented to all his enactments. But, in the first place, the power of the council to veto legislation has never been formally admitted; its constitutional function was merely to advise, and it is no part of the law of the constitution that the crown must take the advice of its council. The secrecy which has always enveloped the deliberations of the executive in England precludes any accurate knowledge of the extent to which English kings have overruled, or been overruled by, their councils; and down to the reign of George III it is often impossible to determine how far the policy of the executive was that of the king or his ministers. Secondly, a council is primarily part of the executive, and proof of its fullest control over legislation would not establish any separation of powers.

The presence of the king's council in parliament, and the extent of its identity with the lords of parliament, render it well-nigh impossible to distinguish in the middle ages between the assent of the council to legislation and the assent of a second chamber; and for indications of any clear distinction between executive and legislative functions we have rather to look to the relations between the crown and the commons, who were no part of the council. The matter is complicated by taxation. Apart from the regular feudal aids and tallages, which were regarded as rent rather than taxes, and therefore required no consent for their exaction, there was never any idea that the crown could tax its subjects without their consent; and taxes were considered as voluntary grants made to the king by the estates in parliament. Not until towards the close of the middle ages did taxation take even the form of legislation; [1] and the grant of taxation is only germane to the separation of powers in so far as the control of supplies enabled the commons to assert an influence over legislation.

The claim of the commons to a voice in legislation is supposed to have been finally established by the statute of York in 1322. [2] It is probably nearer the truth to say that the claim was then first advanced; and before we can accept even this modified version, various qualifications have to be made. Firstly, if the claim extended to all legislation, centuries elapsed before it was completely admitted, and there is at least plausibility in the contention that it was only understood to apply to what would be called to-day constitutional changes or alterations of fundamental law, leaving the king in council still free to legislate in ordinary

---

[1] The earlier grants were made in the form of an indenture; and even when we come to " acts for a tenth," etc., they often contain indentures.
[2] *Statutes of the Realm*, i. 189; *Report on the Dignity of a Peer*, i. 282–3; Hallam, *Middle Ages*, ed. 1878, iii. 233; Stubbs, *Const. Hist.*, ed. 1887, ii. 369, 628.

R

matters by means of ordinances.[1] Magna Carta, the *Confirmatio Cartarum*, and the *Articuli super Cartas*, were undoubtedly regarded as fundamental law; and the commons, in asserting a voice in legislation, would naturally begin with the more obvious, moderate, and conservative claim, instead of with a sweeping radical pretension. But, further, it must be remembered that "the commonalty of the realm," on whose behalf the claim is made, is a phrase of very vague meaning. It may or may not include the city and borough representatives; it may or may not exclude the clerical proctors, but it cannot safely be identified with the still undeveloped house of commons.[2] It is quite possible, moreover, that the real emphasis of the statute is not upon "commonalty" at all, but upon the phrase "in parliaments"; and on this interpretation the statute was better observed than on any other. Its meaning would then be that matters of state were to be determined in parliaments, and not in great councils, albeit great councils sometimes contained representatives of cities and boroughs as well as prelates, earls, barons, and knights, and continued to be summoned throughout the middle ages. There was certainly a well-recognized distinction between the functions of parliaments and great councils, though the subject has received comparatively little attention.[3] Finally the mere silence of a public meeting, such as the assembly of estates was before the organization of the house of commons, would be taken as giving consent. No real consent, and therefore no approach to a distinct share in legislation, can be claimed for the commons until it is expressed in documentary forms.

Ten years later, however, we have in the records of the parliament of March 1332, the definite statement that certain measures "ordained" by the earls, barons, and

---

[1] G. T. Lapsley in *Engl. Hist. Rev.* xxviii. 118–24; Tout, *Reign of Edward II*, pp. 150–1; Conway Davies, *Baronial Opposition to Ed. II*, 1918.

[2] " Whenever you meet that word ' commonalty ' in ancient proceedings, you must translate it a community not the commons " (Palgrave in *Rep. on Public Petitions*, 1833, xii. 21).

[3] See below, Chap. xiv.

other magnates were read before them, the king, the knights of the shires, and the *gentz du commun*, were found pleasing to them all, and were fully agreed to.[1] Further progress is marked in 1340, when twelve knights of the shire and six borough members were added to a committee of prelates, earls, and barons to try and examine certain petitions *et de les mettre en estatut*.[2] In 1343 there is fuller evidence of the activity of the commons : not only is their advice asked, and articles drafted by the lords submitted for their consent, but they add provisions of their own, and the ensuing statutes are said to have been " ordained " by *la commune* as well as by the king and the peers.[3] These proceedings imply the existence of that machinery for deliberation and the expression of opinion without which consent was the merest form; but they do not imply any recognition of the claim that the assent of the commons was indispensable to legislation, and in spite of the repeal of the 1382 statute against heretic preachers,[4] there remained a sphere of ecclesiastical legislation which the commons did not dispute.

The distinction between statute and ordinance continued obscure till the sixteenth century;[5] and the province of proclamations was contested into the seventeenth. Sir Thomas Smith, no despiser of parliaments, tells us that " the prince useth to dispense with laws made "; and even the Whigs, at the revolution of 1688, while abolishing the suspending power, only abolished the power of dispensation " as it hath been exercised of late." There were famous orders in council during the Napoleonic wars; and if it had not been possible in 1906–7 to legislate by similar means, the Transvaal and Orange River colonies might not have received responsible government yet. Over vast areas within the British empire the crown can legislate without the sanction of parliament; nowhere can parliament legislate without the sanction of the crown; no important measure

[1] *Rot. Parl.*, ii. 65.   [2] *Ibid.*, ii. 113.
[3] *Ibid.*, ii. 135–9.   [4] See above, p. 210.
[5] Cf. *Rot. Parl.*, ii. 12; Nicolas, *Proc. of Privy Council*, vol. iii. pp. vi, 22; Stubbs, ii. 426–7.

can pass without the goodwill of the executive cabinet; and legislation by means of departmental regulation tends to increase. From the top to the bottom of our constitution, from the privy council down to county councils, borough councils, district councils, and parish councils, every administrative body possesses, within limits laid down by the law, legislative powers as well. The notion that the executive "should never exercise the legislative and judicial powers or either of them" is one which could only commend itself to an unsophisticated community with the simple conceptions of the first constitution of Massachusetts. So far from the separation of powers being a constitutional dogma in the British empire, it is regarded as almost unconstitutional—and in the Australian Commonwealth it is positively illegal—for an executive minister to be long without a seat in one or other branch of the legislature. The crown has dissociated itself from no powers and no functions of government whatsoever: it has associated with itself in the exercise of those powers an ever-widening circle of popular representation, and every extension of that circle has added to the strength and unity of the will expressed by the crown.

Imperfect and superficial as has been the separation between the executive and legislative powers, the divorce between the executive and the judicature has hardly been more complete. Between council and *curia* a distinction is barely discoverable in the reign of Edward I. The judges are all members of the council; the supreme arbiter of differences between the lower courts is a common session in council in parliament; and it is to the council that petitions in parliament against judicial abuses are referred. It is true that from the days of Henry II certain members of the council are assigned for specific judicial purposes, and that their specialized functions crystallize into the three courts of common law, king's bench, exchequer, and common pleas; but it was long before the idea of "once a judge, always a judge" obtained. Judges of the common law courts were often employed in executive functions, and the temporary " assignment " of commissions of knights and others for judicial purposes was of constant occurrence; even to-day there is no fixed line between judicial and other functions, and laymen are often employed in judicial inquiries. We are told, indeed, that about 1345 the judges of the three courts cease to be sworn of the council.[1] But in Richard II's reign they are still assessors or advisers of the council for legal purposes, and parliament insists on their presence in the council on these occasions. Late in the reign of Henry VI they are still in attendance, though they protest that they are of the council for matters of law and not of politics.[2] In Tudor times the two chief justices were commonly members of the privy council, and down to the present day all law lords and lords justices of appeal are sworn privy councillors, while a committee of the council exercises the functions of a supreme court of appeal for vast areas of jurisdiction. If one of our two supreme courts of appeal is a branch of the legislature, the other is a committee of the executive council.

Moreover, the abandonment of the council by the common law judges did not in the least involve a separation between the judicial and executive functions of the council. It simply emphasized the abandonment to the council of all jurisdiction which could not be brought within the narrowing and hardening frontiers of the common law, a process to which the need for Tudor despotism has ingeniously been attributed.[3] For it left enormous and growing fields of jurisdiction unprovided with any judge except the council and its offshoots. Equity was thus left to the executive; chancery was the king's council in chancery,[4] the star chamber was its sessions for dealing with over-mighty subjects, the court of requests its sessions for hearing poor men's complaints, and the councils of the North and of Wales were its provincial delegacies. Nor was it only in

---

[1] Baldwin, *King's Council in the Middle Ages*, p. 76.
[2] *Ibid.*, pp. 205; cf. Nicolas, *Proc. of Privy Council*, i. 76, ii. 304, iii. 112, 132, 151, 313; the council still remained a *curia*.
[3] Cf. Nicolas, i. 297–8.
[4] Baldwin, pp. 241–2; Nicolas, iii. 36.

the sphere of central government that administrative and judicial functions were combined. The union is still more marked in the activities of the justices of the peace. They administered the statutes of labourers and apprentices, the vagrancy acts and the poor law; and they acted also in petty and quarter sessions in a judicial capacity. In spite of a multiplicity of local government acts, this combination continues to this day, and to enforce a separation of powers we should have to send to the scrap-heap our whole system of magistracy. We should also have to break up our courts-martial, our consular courts, and our ecclesiastical courts, in all of which executive officers act judicial parts. The affairs of the British empire cannot be managed on the lines of the original constitution of Massachusetts; and the doctrine of the separation of powers was an ingenuous attempt to reduce the infinite complexity of human government to the sublime simplicity of a constitutional rule of three.

So far we have been dealing with the retention by the executive of legislative and judicial functions. A similar refusal to obey the rules of abstract political science is seen in the retention by the legislature of its hold over the executive and judicial powers, and in the retention by the judicature of no slight power of making law. In the days of Edward I and his immediate successors, when parliaments met three times a year, a good deal of administrative work was discussed and done in parliaments, and the " Rolls " contain pages of details which read exactly like the later " Acts of the Privy Council." But the expansion and popularization of parliament, and its development into estates and houses, made it less and less suitable for the transaction of administrative business. This was withdrawn more and more from the cognizance of the king's council in parliament to that of the king's council out of parliament, and the council itself became less a *magnum consilium* and more a *consilium privatum, secretum,* or *continuum.* But the council remained an integral part of the legislature; the lord chancellor presided in the parliament chamber, whether he was a peer or not, and secretaries of state were given by statute in 1539 official seats on the woolsacks. The presence of privy councillors in parliament was not a Tudor novelty introduced to influence its decisions, but a practice handed down from the reign of Edward I; the novelty consisted in their presence in the house of commons rather than in the parliament chamber, and illustrates the growing importance of the commons rather than the servility of the electors. They were then, as they are now, the means through which the wishes of the legislature were impressed, if not imposed, upon the crown.

This link between the executive and legislature was never, in spite of place bills, broken; and the more the actual details of administration were withdrawn from parliament, the more it began to insist upon the general responsibility of ministers. Impeachments and acts of attainder kept the principle alive from the reign of Edward III to the Revolution, when more refined and effective methods for achieving that end were devised in the practices of voting supplies and legalizing the maintenance of the army and navy for one year only at a time, and of refusing the means of carrying on government to ministers of whom the commons did not approve. The control of the executive by the legislature is not laid down as a principle in any law of the constitution; it is none the less the essence of the constitution, and it is a contradiction in terms to attribute a separation of governmental powers to a constitution the essence of which consists in the control of one by the other.

The connexion between legislature and judicature has throughout English history remained no less intimate. Parliaments began in a court of law : their original functions, indeed, seem to be hardly distinguishable from those of the later chancery; their forms of proceeding by writs, bills, and petitions were identical, and in many minute details they still preserve evidence of their common origin. To devise new remedies for new wrongs, to hear and determine pleas that had been delayed or about which the judges differed, were the oft-enunciated purposes of parliaments. The core of every parliament was a session of judges in council, and the earliest pictorial representation of the parliament chamber shows that its inmost circle consisted of four woolsacks arranged *vis-à-vis* to facilitate intimate confabulation (*q*). On the upper woolsack sits the chancellor, on the sacks to his right and left the justices of the king's bench and of common pleas, and the master of the rolls, and opposite him the masters in chancery. Behind the judges there sit, in outer rings, the bishops and abbots to the right and the temporal peers to the left; and below the bar, opposite the chancellor, stand the Speaker and the commons; and all these elements represent the legislative accretion on the judicial core. No assembly organized from the beginning as a legislative body would have assumed the configuration of the parliament chamber.

The distinction between judicature and legislation goes back, however, a long way; and its earliest traces may perhaps be found in the distinction made in chancery between judicial and original writs. The former might issue as matters " of course," *de cursu*, but " the granting of specially-worded writs was regarded as an important matter, which required grave counsel and consideration . . . it was no judicial act." [1] In time it was thought that only a parliament could devise new remedies and ordain new forms of procedure, that is to say, that only parliament could legislate. This, however, was a limitation of chancery and not of parliament, and there was no suggestion that delays and abuses arising out of common litigation could not be redressed by bills and petitions in parliament. The gradual loss of judicial business by parliament was due to its political development,[2] to the growing rarity of its sessions compared with the permanence of the council and chancery, and to the development of " common " petitions as a means of dealing with grievances which were most

---

[1] Maitland, *Collected Papers*, ii. 122–3; Pike, *Const. Hist. of House of Lords*, p. 296. See above, p. 39 and Appendix III, note (*f*).
[2] See above, pp. 128–31.

widely felt and enlisted the greatest support. But even
when individual petitions come to be habitually referred to
the council and chancery, the answers are given *per auctoritatem parliamenti,* and continue for a while to be entered on
the " Rolls." [1]   It is an instance of delegation of functions,
not of separation of powers.   The legislature long retained
in its hands the power of punishing state offenders by means
of impeachment and acts of attainder, or, in other words,
of dealing judicially with persons whose influence might
render them immune from lower courts or whose offences
could not easily be brought within the four corners of the
common law.   It also retains judicial authority over its
own precincts, members, and servants.   Even the claim of
the commons to hear the evidence against Thomas Seymour
in 1549 and their condemnation of Floyd in 1621 were based
upon precedent,[2] and represent attempts to retain a share
in the common inheritance of parliament, and not a spirit
of radical innovation.   In the same way, the reference of
individual petitions to courts of law did not preclude the
passing of private acts of parliament to grant relief or
impose disabilities where other means might fail : down
to 1857 an act of parliament was the only means of
annulling a valid marriage.   It is to the house of lords
that appeal lies from the civil courts in the British Isles,
and the distinction between the house of lords as a
legislative chamber and the house as a court of appeal
is merely one of practice, and is no part of the law
of the constitution.   Finally, while parliament will rarely,
if ever, intervene nowadays to reverse a judicial decision,
it will and does intervene to reverse the principles upon
which that decision has been based; and by passing acts
of indemnity it can bar judicial action in multitudes of cases
in which the logic of common law would inflict intolerable
injustice.

The withdrawal of the judicature from executive functions

---

[1] Nicolas, *Proc. of Privy Council,* i. 73, ii. 307, 309, v. p. xi; Leadam,
Star Chamber, i. pp. xxiii–xxiv; see above, p. 128.

[2] See below, p. 309, *n.* 2.

has been a more comprehensive, but still a gradual and an incomplete process. The prerogative courts of the Tudor period were councils as well; and the justices of the peace did most of the work of local government till late in the nineteenth century. A lord chief justice sat in the cabinet as late as the same century, and the lord chancellor continues to do so to-day. Lords justices were frequently appointed to govern England during the reigns of William III, and even the first two Georges, when the king was abroad,[1] and lords justices have governed Ireland for considerable periods of its history. Judges have acted as colonial governors in all parts of the British empire, and some of the greatest founders of New England, like Bradford and Winthrop, combined in their persons the supreme judicial and executive functions, without presumably entailing upon those colonies the deplorable consequences deduced from the combination by the framers of the constitution of Massachusetts. It was, however, to the government of men that those logicians seem to have had the greatest objection.

Their boldest effort was to deprive the judicature of all control over legislation. In England, as we have seen, the judges practically made the laws in the middle ages, and a chief justice alleged the fact in court to support his understanding of a statute. Baronial jealousy, however, which insisted that judges were mere ministers of the crown and could not be peers, succeeded by Richard II's reign in reducing their status in the high court of parliament to that of mere advisers without a vote; and in 1586, when they fell foul of the privilege claimed by the commons over the Norfolk election case, that house, too, resolved that " though the lord chancellor and judges were competent judges in their proper courts, yet they were not in parliament." [2] It is not unlikely that this limitation applied originally only to that function of the judicature about which the barons were most sensitive, namely, the trial of peers.

[1] See Prof. E. R. Turner in *Engl. Hist. Rev.*, xxix. 5453–76.
[2] Prothero, *Select Documents*, p. 130.

But the statute of 1539 clearly states that no one under the degree of a baron, although he were lord chancellor, lord treasurer, lord privy seal, lord president of the king's council or chief secretary, and sat in the parliament chamber in virtue of his office, " could have any interest to give any assent or dissent in the said house." [1] The anomaly of having a lord chancellor to preside over a house in which he " had no interest to give any assent or dissent " was gradually removed by the practice of creating the lord chancellor a peer, though the rule did not become invariable until after the reign of Queen Anne. The cause of the anomaly by which judges sat in a house in which they had no votes was the removal of the business for which their presence was primarily required, to another sphere. " In proportion as this channel enlarged, *i. e.* direct access of petitioners to the council, chancery, etc., instead of *via* parliament, the number of parliamentary petitions decreased. Equity continued to gain rapidly upon parliament, and about the time of Edward IV, when equity was fully established, the remedial jurisdiction of parliament wholly ceased, and it does not appear to have been revived to any extent until the time of James I." [2] The lords recovered their jurisdiction after the fall of the prerogative system under the Stuarts; and the anomaly of judges sitting in a house which dealt with no judicial business was subsequently eclipsed by the anomaly of an assembly of hereditary peers exercising a supreme appellate jurisdiction independently, or even in defiance of, their judicial advisers.[3]

But the denial of votes to the judges in the house of lords did not dispose of their influence over legislation. It has been claimed by a lawyer that in the fifteenth century " the class legislation of parliament was defeated by the national

[1] 31 Henry VIII, c. 10.
[2] Palgrave, *Report on Public Petitions* (Parl. Papers), 1833, xii. 19; McIlwain, p. 133; Maitland, *Memoranda*, p. xxxiii. Palgrave's statement probably requires a good deal of qualification; it may be due to the fact that parliamentary petitions for the period are not in the Record Office, but at Westminster.
[3] The decision of the house of lords on the right of the crown to create life peers was taken in opposition to the advice of the judges.

legislation of the judges "; [1] and Coke points out that the judicial decision in Taltarum or Talcarne's case effected a reform which had been often rejected in parliament. The year books of Henry VII contain ample evidence that before legislation was introduced into either house its principles were discussed and settled by the judges in common session. Thus they laid down the principle of Poynings' law nine years before it was enacted; they defined the law of attainder before bills were introduced to give it effect; and they decided that an act was not valid unless passed by the house of commons. [2] Statutes, indeed, were still regarded as measures to give effect to the law as interpreted by the judges. Bacon's encomium on the practice of frequent consultation between the crown and the judges was suggested by his historical reading; and James I's predilection for it was no constitutional innovation. It can only be regarded as unconstitutional in the light of *ex post facto* generalizations from later constitutional practice. The practice admired by Bacon was no doubt objectionable from the democratic point of view, because it made the judges the final arbiters of the liberties and laws of the English people so long as parliament could be muzzled or suppressed. But the remedy did not lie in increasing the separation of powers. Judges make a great deal of law to-day : they do so even in the United States, in spite of the paper guarantees of " a government of laws and not of men."

The truth is, that human affairs cannot be cut up into mathematical portions and confined in logical categories. The separation of powers is a will o' the wisp, and the rigid restriction on paper of the United States judicature to strictly judicial functions has, in point of fact, enabled it to determine all sorts of political, executive, and legislative questions. A legislative veto is a legislative power, and the veto of the supreme court on American legislation has

[1] Mr. (now Justice) Scrutton, *The Land in Fetters*, p. 76.
[2] My *Reign of Henry VII*, ii. 10–11, 19, iii. 292–4; Vinogradoff, " Constitutional History and the Year-Books " in *Law Quarterly Review*, xxix. 1–12; McIlwain, p. 325.

been as effective as ever was the royal veto in England. Without the leave of the judicature no trade could be defined by the legislature as a dangerous occupation, no limit could be set to hours of labour, no restraint imposed on the conditions of employment, no measure taken to further social reform, because such measures always involve some restraint on somebody's liberty or property, and according to the constitution no such restraint could be imposed " without due process of law," by which is meant, not due legislation, but judicial procedure. In the United States the solution of the problems of social reform depends more upon the judicature than upon the legislature. By declaring an income-tax unconstitutional the supreme court compelled the legislature to devise other forms of taxation until the constitution was amended; and it thus controlled taxation as well as legislation; for a particular course of action can always be dictated by the authority which can veto all alternatives.

Nor does the separation of powers prevent that arbitrary exercise of them, which the framers of the American constitution dreaded so intensely. It is rather thereby facilitated, for within its sphere each authority is irresponsible and unchecked; and each department is, under the constitution, the final and exclusive judge of its own competence. Each of the powers of government in the United States has greater opportunities for arbitrary action than in England. Every legislative body is, for instance, the arbiter of the validity of its own elections, a system that produced many scandals in England until it was abolished by reference to the judges. Within the executive sphere the president can do what he likes for his prescribed four years; no popular agitation, no vote of censure by the legislature can drive him from office, and the only practical means of removal is assassination. He can, indeed, be impeached, but only for crime and not for his policy. Nothing, too, can dissolve the legislature before its term is finished, and neither legislature nor executive can correct an interpretation of the law by the supreme court, however violent or opposed to the public conscience it may be. There is a total absence of that mutual responsibility and control which has proved a far better safeguard of liberty in England than has the separation of powers in the United States.

Here, the legislature can turn out the executive or the executive dissolve the legislature at almost any moment in response to a national outcry. Either can force an appeal to the people, on this condition, that it is willing itself to submit to the same arbitrament. There is nothing sacrosanct or fixed about the cabinet's tenure of office or the duration of parliament; a parliament may be dissolved at a premier's nod, and a cabinet will not last a month unless it possesses the confidence of the legislature. Its conduct of affairs is reviewed in the legislature day by day by means of questions and answers, and, if necessary, by motions for adjournment or of want of confidence. Even the judicature is not exempt from responsibility; it is true that judges are seldom removed by the formal means of an address of both houses of parliament, but informal hints that such might be necessary are not so rare, and are as a rule effective. A more salutary check on judicial extravagance is the knowledge that decisions like some of those pronounced by supreme courts in America would precipitate acts of parliament preventing their repetition.

This system of mutual responsibility is at once the effect and the cause of confidence, which is the basis of the constitution of the British empire. The keynote of the American constitution was, on the other hand, distrust—distrust of the government and also distrust of the people. The fundamental assumption was that every man is by nature not free, but a tyrant. " It is," declared John Adams, " by balancing each of these three powers against the other two that the efforts in human nature toward tyranny can alone be checked and restrained, and any degree of freedom preserved." [1] They were not to co-operate for the production of good, but to counterwork one another for the prevention of evil. It was assumed that each would do wrong unless

[1] Quoted in Bondy, p. 17.

it was checked; and the people could not be trusted to check them. Congress cannot force an appeal to the people against an obstinate president, nor the president against an obstructive congress. The president's term was fixed, and re-election discouraged, lest he should by long tenure of office so corrupt the electorate, or create by means of the system of spoils so powerful a party machine that he would become dictator and the electors helpless. He was to be prevented from governing badly, and not encouraged by governing well to look forward to a renewal of the nation's confidence. Indeed, the people were not to elect him at all, but a college of prudent men better fitted to choose a ruler for the people than the people themselves. The idea of a people finding its ablest men and trusting them so long as they are able and willing to serve it, still seems foreign to the United States, and the framers of the constitution did their best to hamper the process and harness the popular will. Theirs was the age of paternal despots, but rarely has paternal despotism laid its dead hand on the future with greater effect than in the rigid conditions of government which the United States constitution imposed on four generations of freemen.

This fundamental distrust,[1] expressed in the separation of powers, explains the reason why American efficiency, so marked in private concerns, has been so fettered in government. The constitution was framed under the dominance of the old popular prejudice that there must always be a fundamental antagonism between the interests and instincts of the government and those of the governed. No one could really be trusted with the exercise of sovereign power. It was therefore put under the lock and key of a rigid and written constitution, and such powers as were permitted exercise were divided. Thus the American legislator attempts to legislate without the co-operation and advice of the expert in administration, and the administration is isolated from the wholesome influence derived from daily contact with a popularly elected congress. The expert,

[1] " Free government is founded in jealousy, not in confidence " (Jefferson in 1798).

indeed, is reserved for private adventures and not for the public service; and conditions which no American would tolerate in his private business are regarded with equanimity in the affairs of the nation. The civil servants of the state are treated as no individual would treat those on whose service he relies. Ambassadors are relegated to private life at every change of government; they are paid on such a beggarly scale that wealth, and not capacity is the first requisite for a diplomatist; and even a secretary of state has been driven to eke out subsistence by lecturing tours. The public conscience is indifferent to these details, because the public believes in private enterprise, but does not realize the claims of efficient national government. The separation of powers is an expression of this distrust and indifference, and helps to explain why American politics are unattractive to so many American minds.

There were good reasons for the adoption of that principle in the eighteenth century, but those reasons are passing away. Distrust of sovereignty was the natural product of centuries during which it had been exercised in the interests of the sovereign and not in those of the people; and confidence grows slowly in a people with few communications. The previous independence of one another enjoyed by the thirteen colonies, and the vast extent over which their scattered and heterogeneous population was spread, engendered distrust of a common sovereignty. Subsequent extensions of territory and the mighty influx of alien immigrants with no ideas in common delayed the consolidation to be expected from the development of communications, the filling up of vacant territory, and the pressure of external forces. The alien immigrant still provides the " boss " with the raw material for his machine-made politics, and feeds the public distrust of a government subject to such manipulation. When the " hyphenated " American disappears, the " hyphenated " system of government by separation of powers will go with it; and an American nation will trust a national government with the full powers of sovereignty.

The separation of powers will then be reduced to its true proportions as a specialization of functions. That has been the limit of differentiation in English government. Executive, legislature, and judicature have been evolved from a common origin, and have adapted themselves to specific purposes, because without that specialization of functions English government would have remained rudimentary and inefficient. But there has been no division of sovereignty and no separation of powers. The head cannot do the work of the heart, nor the hand that of the foot; but that is no reason for disconnecting them one from the other, and endowing each with a will of its own. Above all we need a brain and a conscience to move every limb at will and without the abnormal exertion of recourse to the cumbrous machinery of reconstitution. We need not dissolve our unity of will in a trinity of powers; and that unity of will is expressed by the crown in parliament.

S

CHAPTER XIII

THE CROWN IN PARLIAMENT

THE establishment of sovereignty in parliament secured unity of power, but did not determine its distribution among the various elements which made up that composite body; and the forms of the constitution were equally compatible with monarchy, aristocracy, or democracy. Whichever element prevailed would have national sovereignty at its disposal, but there was no clear indication which that element would be. Each of the factors in parliament, crown, lords, and commons, has claimed at different times a predominant share in the partnership; and from the end of the Tudor harmony to the passing of the parliament act in 1911 the struggles between them have filled many pages of constitutional history. The crown was clearly the effective factor in parliament under Edward I, and with considerable fluctuations it retained its predominance until the Stuart period. That predominance was, however, disputed by the lords, whose constitutional influence was exerted in the middle ages by means of the council in parliament, and in modern times by means of the peers in parliament. The reform bill of 1832 initiated the predominance of the commons in parliament which was completed by the parliament act of 1911. Nevertheless, the fundamental difference between the evolutionary growth of the British constitution and the revolutionary creation of other systems consists largely in the fact that the crown was never expelled from parliament, and remains an essential factor in its organization. Parliament may hold the crown in solution, but the crown is not dissolved.

The conception of crown and parliament as two distinct entities confuses the interpretation of much of our constitutional history. It arose in the Civil War, and was perpetuated by the eighteenth-century dogma of the separation of powers which was stereotyped in American constitutions. But it was always a fundamental misconception of the English constitution; it tends to falsify history and to render unintelligible the actual working of the constitution of the empire. The problem for the constitutional historian is not to discriminate between the powers of the crown and those of parliament, but between the things the crown could do in council and the things which it could only do in parliament. The powers of the " crown in parliament " have never been defined, and they have no constitutional limits. The " crown in parliament " wields a sovereignty which legally and constitutionally is absolute; and the separation of crown and parliament is a dichotomy which divides the indivisible, and promotes the cause of anarchy.

There had, indeed, been a real separation of powers in the middle ages between *regnum* and *sacerdotium*, and none save a few extremists denied that each had an independent jurisdiction. Edward I often in parliament refused to trench upon the sphere of the ecclesiastical courts,[1] and he gave that sphere an elastic interpretation in his writ *circumspecte agatis*. On the eve of the Reformation the king's judges denied that an act of parliament could make the king an ecclesiastical person,[2] and parliament itself, in the reign of Henry VII, was chary in restricting the enormous liberties of clerical criminals. It was this well-nigh universal recognition of a supreme ecclesiastical jurisdiction that was repudiated by the act of supremacy against the will of the catholic church and without the consent of nine-tenths of its provinces. The revolution was, however, successful, and its effect was to establish the absolutism of the " crown in parliament," which is a very different thing from the supremacy of the crown over parliament.

The problem, therefore, is not to define the unlimited and

[1] Cf. *Rot. Parl.*, i. 3, 42, 46.
[2] McIlwain, pp. 277-9. If he was a semi-ecclesiastical person, he was made so by the ecclesiastical unction he received at coronation and not by any Act of Parliament.

undivided authority of the " crown in parliament," but to trace, firstly, the limitations of the " crown in council," and, secondly, the shifting weight of the various elements in that composite entity the " crown in council in parliament." The restriction of the powers of the " crown in council " was effected by parliamentary legislation; and it was possible to limit the " crown in council " by that method, because from the time of Edward I onwards the " crown in council in parliament " had admittedly enjoyed fuller powers than the " crown in council." It had long been possible to appeal from the king in person to the king in sober council, by writ of error from *coram rege* to the king in parliament; and in repeated great councils it had been held that only in parliament could questions of peace or war be decided.[1] The delimitation of the powers of the various elements in the " crown in council in parliament " could not, on the other hand, be easily achieved by parliamentary legislation, because crown, lords, and commons each possessed, since the fifteenth century, an absolute veto over the resolutions of the others. Hence the great changes in this sphere were accomplished by open force in the Civil War and at the revolution of 1688, and by veiled coercion in 1832 and 1911. Similarly it was not by legislation, but through decay of power that the crown lost its veto, and the lords their hold on finance and administration.

The problem of the crown in council does not fall within the scope of this essay except in so far as concerns its relations with parliament. Its domestic history has been treated in a number of admirable monographs, whose main defect is that they leave on one side the position of the council in parliament and its relations with the council out of parliament.[2] It is with the former that we shall have to deal; but

[1] Nicolas, *Proc. of Privy Council*, vol. i. pp. xxxviii, 144. It was a stipulation of the treaty of Étaples in 1492, following the precedent of Troyes in 1420, that it should be confirmed by the three estates of the two realms (2 Henry VII, c. 65). Cf. *Cottoni Posthuma*, pp. 13–39, and Vernon-Harcourt, *His Grace the Steward*, p. 248. For detailed proceedings on writs of error in parliament cf. *Rot. Parl.*, iv. 18, 411–13.

[2] See Baldwin, *The King's Council*, 1914. Cf. Nicolas, iv. 185–6, and *Rot. Parl.* iv. 424b, for references to " the king's great council in parliament " and the king's " council out of parliament."

inasmuch as the council—whether in parliament or not—was subordinate to the crown, it will be convenient to discuss first the position of the crown in parliament.

The throne, which the lords have sought to exclude from their house, is more than a bare symbol; for the crown in parliament is a real presence, which did not cease to be real when it ceased to be corporal.   Down to the middle of the seventeenth century no one visualized, and no artist depicted parliament without the king enthroned in the midst thereof. In the reflex light of later history Henry VIII's presence in parliament has been regarded as exceptional intervention with a view to interference with its liberties.   But time had been when the royal presence was the rule and not the exception; in the sixteenth century the throne in the parliament chamber was not intended to be empty; and its vacancy to-day does not indicate that the king has no right to be present, but that the lords have reduced that right to an empty form.[1]   The crown is, indeed, the core out of which the rest of parliament has grown; for the crown expanded into the " crown in council," and then into the " crown in council in parliament."   Constitutional theory thus represents historical fact.   Historians a generation ago were wont to trace in Anglo-Saxon localism the original liberties of the English constitution, and liked to dwell upon its analogies with the equally local and primitive liberties of Uri and Schwyz.   It is significant that the same historians admired federal government, and saw in the constitution of the United States a true reflection of English constitutional principles.   That there were germs in common is obvious; but the differences are fundamental.   The English constitution has always been unitary; those of Switzerland and the

---

[1] The minority of Edward VI, followed by the reign of two queens, contributed as much towards the sovereign's absence from parliament as the reign of Queen Anne, followed by those of two Germans, did to a similar absence from the privy council.   The parliament chamber, of course, must not be confused with the house of commons.   The commons protested in 1523 against Wolsey's presence as infringing their liberties; and, while the commons often visited Henry VIII—and, indeed, insisted upon their right of access—it is doubtful whether Henry VIII ever visited the house of commons.

United States are federal, and in neither is there anything corresponding to the crown in parliament. Their constitutions start from the lowest forms of political association, which only delegate to the higher, remaining themselves the residuary legatees of sovereignty. The English constitution starts with the crown and works downwards; in England local legislatures only receive the powers the nation grants; in truly federal states the nation only receives those which the local assemblies bestow. The forms of federal government are more flattering than our own to popular susceptibility, but place greater impediments in the way of effective national action.

Parliament is thus an emanation from the crown; it was summoned by royal writs to meet in a royal palace, and the royal business always stood first on its medieval agenda. The crown accorded or rejected its petitions at will, and *le roy le veult* is still the phrase which, pronounced in parliament, makes an act. Throughout the middle-ages the commons remain but suitors, and the lords the counsellors, of the crown in parliament. It is the crown which legislates, on the petition of the commons and the advice of the lords. Legislation in parliament has the highest sanction; but it is not the only method of legislating, and the crown has never been completely debarred from legislating without parliament by means of ordinance, proclamation, and order in council.[1] The financial needs of the crown and the commons' control of the purse made every parliament an exchange and mart, in which the commons bargained for legislation, and the crown for grants of money. But this was the custom and not the law of the constitution. If the crown needed no grants, the commons could extort no legislation; they could always petition, but the right of petition in itself confers no power to initiate legislation.

There was no doubt about the power of the crown to prevent legislation by lords and commons; there was more ambiguity about the power of the lords and commons to

[1] As recently as December 1919 the attorney-general argued in court that by proclamation the crown could prohibit every kind of import.

prevent legislation by the crown, and this legislation might be
effected either in parliament or outside.   Within the parliament chamber it might seem that legislation by the crown
would be controlled by lords and commons.   But effective
machinery for this purpose was conspicuous by its absence
at the close of the middle ages.   The indispensable forms
were few; a bill must be read in the parliament chamber,
and the king must give his assent.   But Henry VII thought
he could pass an act of attainder in parliament without
consulting the commons.[1]   The judges decided against him,
and he accepted their opinion.   But the assent of the commons was often little more than a form.   " Howbeit," writes
a parliamentary correspondent of the said act of attainder,
" ther was many gentlemen agaynst it, but it wold not be,
for yt was the king's pleasure." [2]   The lack of commons'
Journals before 1547 makes it impossible to speak with
confidence, but Bishop Stubbs's assumption that the account
given by Sir Thomas Smith of Elizabeth's parliaments holds
good for the fifteenth century is somewhat rash.[3]   Of any
three readings in either the lords or the commons there is
no evidence before 1495, and any legal requirement of assent
by the commons was fully met by the word, or even perhaps
by the silence, of the Speaker at the bar of the parliament
chamber.   Bills, first read in the lords, were sometimes
" transportatæ " across to the commons in the chapter
house for their consideration; and their petitions were
" baillées aux seigneurs."   But many an act in the fifteenth
century begins with none of the modern formulæ, but with
such phraseology as " the king calling to remembrance," or
" the king remembring " such and such circumstances,
ordains, enacts, or establishes such and such a remedy,
generally with, but often without mention of the assent of
the lords spiritual and temporal and of the commons.   There

[1] See my *Reign of Henry VII*, ii. 19; *Year Book*, 4 Henry VII, p. 18.
[2] *Ibid.*, i. 32.
[3] Stubbs, *Const. Hist.*, iii. 483.   For reasons which I have given in
Trans. Royal Hist. Soc., 3rd Ser., viii. 26–7, the absence of commons'
Journals before 1547 seems to me clearly due, not to loss of the MS., but
to the fact that no *Journals* were compiled.

is sometimes a curious blend of the autocratic formulæ of Roman and papal law with parliamentary language which illustrates the menace of the " reception " to the English constitution. Edward IV, for instance, " of his most blessed disposition, mere motion, and certain science, by the advice and assent of the lords spiritual and temporal, and of the commons of this realm in this his present parliament assembled, and by authority of the same, ordaineth, enacteth, and establisheth that all and every acts and act made in any of the parliaments holden since the first day of his reign, or in this present parliament made or to be made, be not in any wise prejudicial " to the dean and canons of St. Mary's, Leicester.[1]

There was abundance of royal legislation in parliament in the reign of Henry VII. On the thirty-first day of parliament, in the twelfth year of his reign, the king " with his own hand delivered in a bill of trade then read " ; [2] and legislation thus royally introduced was not necessarily, and perhaps not at all, cast in the form of parliamentary petitions ; it may have been Henry VIII or Thomas Cromwell who first selected this humble garb for the royal proposals. Nor was there yet any rule that all acts of parliament required the commons' consent. No doubt the " communes petitiones " represented the wish of the commons ; but that house had as yet established no right to debar the individual petitioner from access to the crown in parliament ; and the petition of the city of Gloucester to Edward IV in the parliament of 1473 is granted by the king by the advice of the lords, and is enrolled as an act of parliament, without any intervention by the commons.[3] The legislative power of the house of commons rests upon the denial of the right of the crown to legislate upon the petition of the individual. Individuals and groups of individuals can petition the crown, but no such petition can now become law unless it is adopted as a common petition of the house of commons. The right of the subject to secure legislation by individual petition to the crown in

[1] *Rot. Parl.*, vi. 48*b*.　　　[2] *Cottoni Posthuma*, 1672, p. 54.
　　　　　[3] *Rot. Parl.*, vi. 49; cf. *ibid.*, v. 68.

parliament was one of the medieval liberties destroyed by the growth of the house of commons. The commons could only limit the legislative discretion of the crown by controlling the approach of the individual petitioner, and the house adopted the practice of presenting petitions *ex parte* in order to block petitions not backed by themselves. Most of the individual petitions, which are becoming " private acts " in the fifteenth century, are presented in this way to the crown and lords in parliament; but the access of individuals to the crown in parliament was not yet completely barred, and the king could make acts in parliament on the petition of other bodies than the house of commons.

The commons themselves connived at a wide legislative discretion on the part of the crown outside parliament. In 1504 parliament, acquiescing in Henry VII's declared intention of not calling another together for a " long time," and recognizing the hardship thus inflicted on applicants for the repeal of their attainders, empowered the king to repeal several acts by letters patent.[1] By legalizing a benevolence in 1495, it countenanced royal taxation without parliamentary grant,[2] feeling perhaps that the individual's liberty was not more seriously violated by the gift he made to the king than by a tax imposed by parliament. Legislation concerning foreigners, if not regarded as being outside the scope of parliament, was held to be at least equally a matter for council; and in 1515 the lords determined that a certain bill *possit tam per concilium quam per actum parliamenti provideri, cum non concernat subditos domini regis, sed extraneos.*[3] Foreign trade came within this discretion, and in 1534 Henry VIII was authorized by act of parliament to repeal or revive all statutes since 1529 touch-

---

[1] 19 Henry VII, c. 28; *Rot. Parl.*, vi. 526; *Statutes of the Realm*, ii. 669. Edward IV exercised this power (Baldwin, p. 427) merely on the advice of his council. Parliament in 1523 gave it to Henry VIII for life (*Lords' Journals*, vol. i. p. cxxi.).

[2] 11 Henry VII, c. 10; *Statutes of the Realm*, ii. 576.

[3] *Lords' Journals*, i. 56. Cf. *ibid.*, i. 17: " Et dictum et decretum est per dominum cancellarium et episcopum Wynton., quoad provisiones pro mercatoribus de Hanse, quod provisio pro ipsis per regem signata sufficiet eis absque assensu dominorum aut domus communis "; also *ibid.*, i. 41.

ing exports or imports.[1] It seemed a greater extension of
the royal prerogative when he was authorized to leave the
crown by will, though he was never empowered to leave it
away from his one child whose legitimacy was beyond
dispute.[2] But the highwater mark of royal legislation was
reached by the statute of proclamations, which gave them
the force of law.[3]

This *lex regia* has excited so much attention, and gives
rise to such apparent contradictions, that it deserves careful
consideration. The point that most forcibly strikes the
student of history, as distinct from the student of law, is
the extent to which this act remained a dead letter. It
may be that it was Cromwell's rather than Henry VIII's
proposal; Bishop Gardiner relates a conversation between
Henry VIII, Cromwell, and himself, in which Cromwell advo-
cated the policy of making the king's will the law, and
Gardiner replied by advising the king to make the law his will.[4]
Cromwell fell in 1540, the year after the statute of proclamations was passed; Gardiner became the most influential of
Henry's advisers, and the act was almost ignored. A
hundred and twenty proclamations are known to have been
issued between the passing of that statute and Henry's
death,[5] and not one of these seems to depend for its validity
on the statute. The great majority of them relate to
matters arising out of the state of war between England
and France in 1543, matters which down to this day are
regulated by royal proclamation; and the rest were mostly
the mere proclamation or publication of statutes passed
by parliament. Either Henry VIII did not interpret the
statute as conferring new powers of legislation on the
crown, or else he refrained from using them. It is no
less certain that he did not regard the statute as enabling
him to dispense with the assistance of parliament in
legislation. Sessions were as frequent after the statute

---

[1] 26 Henry VIII, c. 10.
[2] 28 Henry VIII, c. 7; 35 Henry VIII, c. 1.
[3] 31 Henry VIII, c. 8.
[4] Foxe, *Acts and Monuments*, vi. 45–6.
[5] Steele, *Tudor and Stuart Proclamations*, i. 20–31.

as before it, and the numerous bills that were introduced and passed give little support to the supposition that Henry could have achieved the same objects by proclamation. It never seems to have occurred to any one that the king might, for instance, have confiscated chantries by proclamation, although the bill for that purpose was hotly debated and narrowly escaped defeat.[1] Some bills were actually rejected, but no steps were taken to repair their loss by means of the powers which the statute of proclamations is supposed to have placed in Henry's hands.

The act would appear, then, to have been a piece of gratuitous dogma, more in keeping with Stuart pretensions than with Tudor practice, unless some other interpretation of it is possible. It may be, however, that Tudor lawyers were more literal than modern historians, and that when parliament passed " an act that proclamations made by the king shall be obeyed," it never dreamt of extending the sphere of proclamations or restricting that of parliamentary statutes. It simply meant that within their proper and recognized sphere proclamations were to have the binding force of law—and unless they have, they are useless even to-day. That sphere was, indeed, defined by the act itself, which provided that none of the king's lieges should " have any of his or their inheritances, lawful possessions, offices, liberties, privileges, franchises, goods or chattels taken from them or any of them, nor by virtue of the said act suffer any pains of death other than shall be hereafter in this act declared." It was not to be used to repeal any existing laws, "nor yet any lawful or laudable customs," and the people really affected by the act were "such persons which shall offend any proclamation to be made by the king's highness, his heirs or successors, for and concerning any kind of heresies against Christian religion." The act of proclamations was in effect an act to put into practice the theory of the act of supremacy. That act had been merely declaratory, and had contained no pains and penalties; the treason act of 1535 had, indeed, penalized

[1] See below, p. 336.

the denial of the royal supremacy, but it was the act of proclamations in 1539 which first gave the new supreme head something of the power of independent legislation which had belonged to the pope.[1] The supreme head of the church was not to be subject to parliamentary conditions in the exercise of his supremacy; and the ecclesiastical sovereign was to be the crown in council and not the crown in parliament. If there had ever been a crown in convocation other than the pope's, Henry VIII would assuredly have been tempted to retain and enhance the position, and to make the crown, rather than the crown in parliament, the link between church and state. As it was, the dichotomy of the provinces discouraged the presence of the crown, and the vicegerent was not at home in an ecclesiastical assembly. Cromwell had no successor in that capacity, and convocations were left to the prelates and proctors. The act of proclamations itself did not prevent the six articles from being an act of parliament and not a royal proclamation; and in 1547 the legislative independence of the supreme head was destroyed by Somerset's repeal of the act of proclamations.[2] The crown in parliament would not tolerate an English pope in council.

Cromwell, however, represented the crown elsewhere than in convocation,[3] and the real importance of his position

---

[1] Offenders were to be tried by the council (34 & 35 Henry VIII, c. 8), which was thus to exercise a jurisdiction similar to that exercised by the later high commission; although during the debate on the bill, promises were given that nothing should be done under it contrary to an act of parliament or common law (Gardiner to Somerset in Foxe, *Acts and Monuments*, vi. 43). This, however, was the ecclesiastical aspect of the statute of proclamations. Its general purpose was to revive the waning respect for royal proclamations. Such importance had in recent years come to be attached to parliamentary statute that the impression had been produced that other forms of legislation were very inferior in authority, if they were law at all. This was a far cry from the time when Edward I could enact all his legislation in council. Henry VIII did not attempt to recover Edward's comprehensive sphere, but the statute of proclamations gave him, within the shrunken limits of his legislative power, the same authority as parliament possessed in its more extended sphere.

[2] The repeal was effected by a single sentence in 1 Ed. VI, c. 12.

[3] It is notable that as vicegerent of the supreme head Cromwell was by 31 Henry VIII, c. 10, given a place in the house of lords on the right, or ecclesiastical side of the throne, and above the archbishop of Canterbury.

in parliament was due to the fact that, while the crown had a recognized place in the parliament chamber, it had none in the house of commons. Its absence accounts for some of the irresponsibility and factiousness of the commons during the fourteenth and fifteenth centuries; and when Henry VIII began to look for a lever in parliament against the prelates, both in their convocations and in the parliament chamber, he felt the need of some agency in the house of commons. This was the part designed for Cromwell from his first entry into Henry's service in 1529. Wolsey's intervention in 1523 had merely brought the Speaker, but not the commons to their knees, and subtler methods than intimidation were required to maintain harmony between ambitious monarchy and a rising house of commons. The separation had never been complete, for, while the commons withdrew from the parliament chamber to the chapter house, they were often accompanied by lords of the council and of parliament, deputed to give them the benefit of their wisdom and advice; often, too, the commons were directed to deliberate in some chamber in the palace, in order that they might be near the lords for consultation. But stronger bonds were needed than deputations; and harmony between crown and country could best be secured by identifying the agents of the crown with the representatives of the constituencies. The process, however, by which councillors became largely identified with elected members of parliament belongs rather to the position of the council than to that of the crown in parliament.[1]

The distinction was clearer in the sixteenth century than it is to-day, because the crown was then little more than the king, while the council was only a body of advisers whose advice need not be taken. The crown did not, so to speak, consist of the cabinet, and the crown in parliament was manifest in the very personal action of the Tudors. The practice of royal commission was in its infancy; and, although the expedient was adopted to save Henry VIII

[1] See below, pp. 295-7.

from the pain of giving a personal attendance at the attaint-
ing of his queens, the parliamentary action of Tudor
sovereigns was, as a rule, immediate and direct. Not that
the sovereign ever pronounced with his or her own mouth
the decisive phrase *le roy le veult, le roy s'avisera,* or *soit
fait comme il est desiré ;* [1] and the notion that he signed
or signs acts of parliament is a popular superstition.[2]
The giving or withholding the royal assent was not quite
so blunt a process; and the king would have had reason to
complain had he been expected to make up his mind on
the merits of a long list of bills awaiting his enactment
during the brief interval which elapsed between the reading
out of their titles by the clerk of the crown and the pronouncement of the royal decision by the mouth of the clerk
of the parliaments. The king, like the commons and
other " estates " of parliament, needed time and privacy
for deliberation, which was impossible *in pleno parliamento,*
where decisions were announced, but were not taken; and
just as the commons had withdrawn from the parliament
chamber to the commons' house, so the king decided upon
his action, not in the parliament chamber, but in an adjoin-
ing council-room.[3] No doubt he had had earlier opportunities of acquainting himself with the contents of such
bills as he had not personally inspired; but his final determination on the bills, as they emerged from the two
houses, was reached in secret conclave on the last day
of the session; and was announced by the clerk after the
king, commons, and other " estates " had assembled *in
pleno parliamento* for the crowning work of the session.[4]

[1] The third of these phrases was used when the bill was what we should
now call a private bill (Hakewill, *Passing of Bills,* 1641, p. 78) ; other phrases
were used for the royal acceptance of money grants.

[2] Palgrave went so far as to assert that " signatures are never found
in ancient documents " (*Rep. on Petitions,* 1833, p. 21). When the king
signed bills, he signed them before introduction; but these were only
bills affecting the property of the crown, which cannot, even to-day, be
introduced without the royal consent. A bill for the restitution of an
attainted felon or traitor had to be signed in this way before introduction, because its passing would mean the crown's loss of the forfeited
goods. Cf. Hunne's case in *Engl. Hist. Rev.,* July 1915, p. 482.

[3] Now called " the robing room " (May, *Parl. Practice,* ed. 1883, p. 593).

[4] " In the open parliament " is Hall's version in 1529 (*Chronicles,*
p. 763).

It was not merely on this last day of the session or by the exercise of the veto that the crown partook of the business of parliamentary legislation. We have seen Henry VII introducing a bill with his own hand, seeking to pass another without consulting the commons, and drafting most of the acts of his parliaments in the language of royal edicts. The commons were a far less negligible quantity under Henry VIII, at any rate after 1529, and the autocratic form, at least, disappears from the phraseology of the statute book. The co-operation of lords and commons is always expressed in the language of an act, and parliament is always alleged as its authority. The king's " remembrances " and " considerations " are veiled behind the less personal terminology of parliament. It was Henry VIII's policy to envelop himself in parliament, and he did it with such success that the crown was never thenceforth able to divest itself of its parliamentary robes. He wove parliament like a garment round his royal carcase for protection; and the king-spun constitution of the realm was all the closer in texture because parliament had ever been an outcome of the crown. Henry VIII was not a mere member of parliament, but its very head; and when the head condescended to debate the six articles it confounded all the members by its learning.[1] Parliament met in the king's palace; its rooms were allotted by the king's chamberlain, and its members were sworn before the king's steward or his deputies;[2] it betrayed in all its trappings its origin as a feudal court. It was summoned, prorogued, adjourned, dissolved by the king or his ministers at his pleasure. Its clerks were the king's clerks, and even the serjeant-at-arms, who attended the Speaker of the house of commons, was a king's serjeant, appointed by him and removable at his pleasure. The king's attorney and solicitor-general, and his serjeants-at-law attended the house of lords, not as the servants of an autonomous house, but as the servants of the king, doing his service in

[1] *Letters and Papers*, xiv. i. 1040; Pocock (*Burnet*, vi. 233) prints " God's learning " for " his learning."
[2] D'Ewes, *Journals*, pp. 39–40.

his great council chamber.[1] The Speaker was nominated and paid by the crown,[2] though the nomination was veiled more decently than that of bishops after the second act of appeals; and the subsequent election by the commons only grew more real than the election of a bishop by his chapter with the contest over Onslow's election in 1566 and the success of the commons in Lenthall's case at the opening of the Long parliament. The lords, as befitted a royal council, never secured even the pretence of a power to elect a presiding officer, who could only preside in the absence of the king; and to this day the lord chancellor is appointed by the crown, and need not be a peer, except as a matter of deference to the historical fictions on which the lords have sought to build their house. The whole machinery of parliament was part of the permanent machinery of the crown temporarily applied to the purpose of holding the king's high court.

Gradually the two houses secured control of this machinery, but this control has been less perfectly won by the lords than by the commons, who could never be overridden by a threat to double their numbers by royal creation. Neither lords nor commons could, it is true, come to parliament without a royal summons; but while the crown summoned a peer by name, its summons to the commons was addressed to communities, who could choose what members they pleased. No doubt a good deal of pressure was brought to bear at different times upon constituencies to elect representatives acceptable to the crown; but this pressure was of little avail in the shires, and even in the boroughs it was not so formidable an obstacle to freedom of election as the influence of the county magnates. The crown could also create new boroughs by charter; but

[1] When Onslow was elected Speaker in 1566, it was contended, though unsuccessfully, that his duty as a serjeant-at-law in the upper house overrode the commons' claim on him as their Speaker (D'Ewes, pp. 98, 121; cf. Elsynge, p. 82).
[2] Tytler, *Edward VI*, ii. 163; Campbell's *Materials,* ii. 217. His fee in 1485 was £100; but in 1563 Speaker Williams writes that the allowance the queen was pleased to make was never certain, but more or less according to the length of the parliament (*Cal. S. P.* Dom., Addenda, 1547–65, p. 535).

as early as the reign of Elizabeth the motive for new creations
was rather the political ambition of the constituency than
the desire of the crown for " king's friends " in the house
of commons; and secretary Wilson, replying to a petition
for parliamentary representation from Newark in 1579,
remarked that the government thought too many parliamentary seats had been created already, and was considering the question of reducing the number of rotten
boroughs.[1]   James I created university constituencies,[2] but
Charles II's letters patent to Newark seem to have been the
last occasion upon which the crown increased the house
of commons by charter instead of by act of parliament.

With the lords it was different.   An attempt was made
in 1719 by the peerage bill to limit the power of creation
by the crown.[3]   It failed, and was not repeated; and while
the power of the crown to modify the size of the house of
commons has been abolished, its power to create peerages
is unlimited.   The bishops, too, have ever been in practice,
though not in theory, royal nominees; and from the
Reformation to the Revolution the royal supremacy over
the church gave it great control of the house of lords.
But its control over temporal peers diminished.   During
the Tudor period the crown could compel a peer's attendance; if for good reasons he were allowed to stay away,
he had to seek royal licence to appoint his proxies, and
over his choice the crown could exercise a veto.[4]   The crown
could also prevent an unwelcome attendance.   There was
no law requiring the crown to summon any one; alien
peers were not summoned by Henry VII,[5] nor, apparently,

---

[1] See p. 159 *n*.
[2] Both universities received writs for James' first parliament, but
apparently Cambridge made no return.   James conferred a similar
privilege upon Trinity College, Dublin, in 1613.
[3] Lecky, i. 230–1.
[4] Lodge, *Illustrations*, i. 252–3; cf. *Cottoni Posthuma*, pp. 264, 267;
Elsynge, pp. 32, 119–20.
[5] For instance, Philibert de Chandé, the leader of Henry VII's Breton
contingent in 1485, who was created earl of Bath, was never summoned
to parliament; nor were Louis de Bruges and John de Bruges, who
were successively earls of Winchester (see my *Henry VII*, iii. 320).
The latter " resigned " his earldom in 1500 (Doyle, *Official Baronage*,
ii. 700).

T

alien bishops by Henry VIII;[1] and some temporal peers who were not aliens seem to have been ignored.[2] But custom was hardening towards the creation of hereditary right, and in the reign of Charles I the lords laid down the doctrine, which Charles disputed, that the crown had lost the power of preventing, by neglect to summon or by countermanding the summons, a peer from attending the house of lords. The houses in the seventeenth century succeeded in reducing the crown's control of their *personnel* to the creation of peers.

They also succeeded in reducing almost to nothing the legislative powers of the crown both in and out of parliament. Under the Tudors the crown had legislated out of parliament by means of proclamations, and in parliament, not only by the negative method of the veto, but by the positive methods of introducing and amending bills. Henry VII added provisos to bills when giving the royal assent, and the provisos thus incorporated in the act became law without any consideration of them by lords or commons.[3] Queen Elizabeth exercised similar powers of amendment on one occasion at least,[4] but she seems to have been the last sovereign who did so. Parliament retorted on the crown the limitation of speech which Elizabeth is generally, though erroneously,[5] supposed to have imposed on the house of commons by the mouth of lord-keeper Puckering. "Your liberty of speech," he is misrepresented as saying, "consisteth in yea or nay." The liberty of the crown in legislation was reduced to a like dilemma, from which the

---

[1] *E. g.* Campeggio, bishop of Salisbury (1525–34), and John de Giglis, Silvester de Giglis, Julius de Medici, and Jerome de Ghinucci, bishops of Worcester between 1497 and 1534.

[2] *E. g.* Robert, lord Ogle, was not summoned between 1529 and 1544 (Round, *Studies in Peerage*, pp. 330 *sqq.*); and according to Chapuys Darcy and three bishops were forbidden to attend in 1534 (*Letters and Papers*, vii. 121). Chapuys is very unreliable in these matters, but Elsynge, clerk of the parliaments, writing as late as 1625, says: "Now of late they which are in the king's displeasure have had their summons, but with a letter from the lord chancellor or lord keeper not to come, but to send a proxy" (*Parliaments*, ed. 1768, p. 59).

[3] *Rot. Parl.*, vi. 182, 186–7, 460, 496.

[4] D'Ewes, *Journals*, p. 341*b*.

[5] See J. E. Neale in *Engl. Hist. Rev.*, xxxi. 128–37.

alternative was soon removed. Since the reign of Queen Anne the crown has lost all discretion in the matter of accepting or rejecting bills that have passed the two houses.

The disuse of the royal veto was not so serious a loss as the denial of the right of the crown to suspend and dispense with the law when made. For clearly it would not matter what laws were made if the crown could not be forced to carry them out; and this compulsion was the hardest of all the tasks for a legislature to impose on an executive. In the sixteenth century there was no idea of any such parliamentary coercion of the crown. Parliament alone could make laws, but the crown alone could carry them out, and it rested entirely with the crown to determine when, where, how, and to what extent the laws should be enforced. Parliament passed the act of six articles in 1539; it was no infraction of the constitution, as then understood, when the crown abstained for a year from enforcing its doctrine.[1] No penalties would have been incurred by any one had the crown and the church in Mary's reign refrained from burning a single heretic, notwithstanding the *de hæretico comburendo* statutes which parliament had re-enacted. In 1559 the act of supremacy enabled the crown to impose the oath of supremacy; it was considered prudence when Elizabeth refrained from exacting that oath from the judges and from Englishmen north of the Trent. Parliament, indeed, had hitherto limited its action to two objects: it had restrained the crown from moving in directions of which it disapproved; it had empowered the crown to move in directions of which it approved; but it had not compelled the crown to move at all.

A legislature cannot, however, ensure the administration of its own laws unless it controls the executive which admin-

---

[1] There are no penalties in the act of six articles; it is simply declaratory, like Henry VIII's act of supremacy. But common law and statute law already provided penalties enough for heresy; and the " bloodiness " of the "six articles" merely consisted in the doctrinal direction they gave to general powers of persecution with which Protestants themselves were loth to dispense.

isters them; and judgement is futile without execution. If the executive is to judge when and whether there shall be execution, the legislature has little part in government unless it controls the executive. There can be no real separation of powers in a self-governing community, and the Long parliament, early in its career, realized the futility of mere legislation. The fundamental issue was raised when parliament, in the Grand Remonstrance, demanded control of the king's choice of ministers and asserted their responsibility to it, while Charles retorted that government was nothing pertaining to subjects.[1] Occasions upon which it might be necessary to suspend or dispense with particular laws will never be lacking in any community, however perfect its laws or peaceful its people; but the judge of these occasions must be the maker of the laws. In other words, the maker of the laws must be the maker of the government.

In the sixteenth century the crown in council was the government, and the crown in parliament was the maker of the laws. Harmony was effected by the predominance of the crown in both. The subjection of parliament to Henry VII was much more patent than its subjection to his son; but the relative positions of crown and parliament under Henry VIII have often been regarded as the most striking illustrations of the unconstitutional character of Tudor rule. Yet the real gravamen of the charge of unconstitutional government against Henry VIII is not that he went about to break parliaments, but that he broke the bonds of Rome. It is difficult to discover anything unconstitutional in his relations with his parliaments; no king had for a century relied upon parliament to the extent that he did after 1529, and none did so again until the Revolution. There was nothing unconstitutional or unprecedented in his frequent presence in its midst, in its releasing him from his debts, enabling him to decide between rival claimants to the succession, or to legislate within his proper sphere by means of proclamations. But it was uncon-

[1] Gardiner, *Select Documents*, ed. 1889, pp. 129, 157, 171, 285.

PARLIAMENT IN 1742.

stitutional for parliament to deprive the pope of his spiritual jurisdiction, to dissolve royal marriages, and pass the act of six articles; or rather, these things were only constitutional in the light of a theory of parliamentary omnicompetence which had not been recognized before, and was repudiated by older jurisdictions. It was Henry's extension, and not his restraint, of parliament that makes his rule unprecedented. The claims of parliament to deal with the church were as much a usurpation as any papal pretension; and it was only the success of the revolution that made its principles constitutional.

Those principles were, however, established, and the crown in parliament became an undisputed sovereign with an unrestricted sovereignty. The emphasis was on the crown, but the crown sank beneath its weight. One child and two women, despite Elizabeth's vigour, could not countervail the emphasis of parliament; and before 1603 distraction was obvious in the partnership. The maker of the laws was no longer at one with their executor. A century of struggle under the Stuarts resulted in the victory of the legislature. The prize was the control of the administration, and the crown in parliament became to all intents and purposes the council in parliament, a council consisting of members of parliament, owing to parliament their position in council, and responsible to parliament for their conduct of affairs.

CHAPTER XIV

THE COUNCIL IN PARLIAMENT

THE king's council in parliament has, since the reign of Edward I, been the pivot of the English constitution, and to-day it is a distinguishing feature of British systems of government that the executive should be part and parcel of the legislature. The novelty of the cabinet does not consist in the link which it forms between the crown and parliament, but in the fact that by its means parliament controls the crown. The king's council had always formed a similar link, but by its means the crown controlled the parliaments. It is, however, modern phraseology, misapplied to most of our constitutional history, to speak of links between parliament and the crown. We might as well speak of links between man's mind and man; man is not man without a mind, and parliament was no parliament without the crown. Metaphors, however, and especially the metaphors of mechanics, fail to express the meaning of human associations. It is well to remember that councils and parliaments consist of men, and that when a man is a member of a council and of a parliament he is much more than a link between the two assemblies. Identity cannot be constituted by any amount of connexion, and much of the difficulty of understanding medieval history arises from the habit, to which the constitutional historian is prone, of regarding the different activities of the same men as distinct and definite institutions. A council is merely a body of men doing certain things "in council"; a parliament is often little more than the same men doing somewhat different things "in parliament"; and the difference between a council and a parliament lies for the

278

most part in the different things they do and their different modes of action. A parliament is at first no more than the counsellors of the king sitting in a particular kind of session called a parliament.[1]

A like anachronism of differentiation led Coke to multiply Edward I's council by four, and to crystallize its different functions into so many different bodies. But while it seems clear that Edward I had only one council, Edward II had two,[2] one which was chosen by him and was called his secret or privy council, and one which was forced upon him by his baronage and was called the *magnum concilium*. The two forms of council represented two rival parties, and their place in the constitution rose and fell with the varying fortunes of the king and the lords ordainers. No doubt both parties were working on the common foundation of a council without an adjective; but the barons were seeking to make it *magnum* and the king to keep it *secretum*, and there was little that was common to their finished products. One party produced the peerage, the other the privy council. The council has been the cockpit of contending factions and constitutional principles. Which was to be its master, the king or the barons, or, last of all, the commons? Upon that issue it would depend whether the council became a privy council, a *magnum concilium*, or a modern cabinet, and England an autocracy, an oligarchy, or a democracy.

The contest is fought in the open under Edward II and sometimes on the field of battle. But Edward III was strong enough to prevent open schism in the government, and the strife was conducted behind closed doors. Its

---

[1] Maitland calls it a " parliament of the council " (*Memoranda*, p. lxxx).

[2] Prof. Baldwin rather minimizes the distinction between the *magnum concilium* and the privy council, and contends that one was merely a full, and the other a secret, session of the same body. But it seems difficult on this theory to account for the definite article in the term *le grand conseil* which we find in Edward II's reign, or for the description of Wykeham as *capitalis secreti consilii et magni consilii gubernator* in 1377 (*Rot. Parl.*, iii. 388a); although the fact that he held these two offices and was also at the same time keeper of the privy seal indicates the common element in these councils. It is perhaps significant of the growing importance of the privy seal that Wykeham should be its keeper, after having been chancellor ten years before.

history is therefore obscure, and we can say little more than that the struggle was not one for the control of a definite institution, but one to define a vague claim on the part of the barons to give counsel to the crown and on the part of the crown to select its own advisers. Nor was it even so simple as that; for the actions of the crown were multifarious, and a right to advise it in some matters did not involve the right to advise it in all. The issue cannot be understood without reference to the gradual differentiation of the functions of government. It seems clear that the magnates established their claim to be the council of the crown for all matters, legislative or judicial, involving an alteration or interpretation of the law of tenure, at least of freehold tenure; and such petitions were regularly dealt with by legislation in parliaments containing a *magnum concilium*, or were referred for judicial decision *coram magno concilio* out of parliament.[1] With regard to matters of policy and administration the magnates were less successful. They did, indeed, succeed in reducing the status of the judges in the council, both in and out of parliament, to that of advisers without a vote; and the principle was ultimately accepted, and even asserted, by the judges themselves that they were " of council to the king " only for legal and not for political business.[2] The magnates also made efforts to exclude the clerical element from the council;[3] but they were naturally unsuccessful in their attempts to make the secret, continual, or privy council of the king a great council of magnates, just as their predecessors had failed in the reign of Henry II to prevent the conversion of the *curia regis* from an occasional assembly of turbulent barons into a regular body of expert justices. They might be *consiliarii nati* of the crown, but it remained with the crown to say when it wanted their counsel; and the *magna concilia* of the fifteenth century were always

---

[1] Cf. Baldwin, pp. 279-80, 325, 334. Possibly the " law of the land " meant the " landlaw."

[2] Nicolas, *Proc. of Privy Council*, i. 76, iii. 151, v. 76-9, 268-9; Baldwin, pp. 76-8, 205.

[3] Baldwin, p. 83.

specialiter congregata, while the secret council was *continuum*, and needed no special summons.[1]

This secret or continual council took more or less definite form in the reign of Richard II. Nicolas's *Proceedings* begin in 1386,[2] and a *Journal* of the council has lately been found for 1392-3.[3] This council had a clerk of its own, charged to keep its minutes,[4] and Richard II relied on it to control his unruly uncles and enable him to develop a preliminary sketch of the " new " monarchy. His failure produced a reaction towards a *magnum concilium*, and *grands conseils* become frequent with the accession of Henry IV.[5] It is possible to regard the council as a single institution, of which the *grand conseil* was an occasional expansion, and the privy council a more continuous contraction;[6] but it is obvious that these expanded and contracted sessions were tending to form distinct institutions. In 1377 Wykeham was described as *capitalis secreti et magni consilii gubernator;* a room, in Westminster Palace was called *camera magni consilii*, and we find the definite article in *le grand conseil* and the *seigneurs du grand conseil du roy*.[7] We can no more regard the great and privy councils as a single institution merely because the greater contained the less, than we can identify parliament with the council because a session of the council was the core of every parliament; and we must not deny a distinction because it is hard to draw.

Discrimination is not, indeed, easy as regards size, *per-*

[1] Nicolas, *Proc. of Privy Council*, iii. 322, iv. 262.
[2] These *Proceedings* do not represent a register or regular series of any kind; and Nicolas's volumes are for the most part made up of scattered notes collected from many sources. He prints, however, a " council-book " extending from 1421 to 1435, and a collection of original minutes to 1460. Between 1435 and 1540 there is another gap in the council-books, which are, however, fairly continuous from 1540 onwards.
[3] Baldwin, pp. 389-90.
[4] There are " clerici " of the council in Edward III's reign, but they are probably " clerics," rather than clerks, of the council, in contrast with the " lords " and " bachelors " of the council.
[5] Nicolas, i. 102, 107, 144, 156, 180.
[6] There seems to be little evidence of a privy council before Henry VIII's reign; the phrase *en prive conseil* which occurs in 1381 (Baldwin, p. 125) means " in private conclave," and not " in the privy council."
[7] Baldwin, p. 369; *Rot. Parl.*, iii. 388a; Nicolas, i. 180, iii. 223.

sonnel, or functions. We have record of a *grand conseil* consisting of ninety-two members;[1] but another contained but thirty-three,[2] while a council which is not called great numbered as many as thirty-two.[3] The same variety of " estates "—dukes, bishops, abbots, earls, barons, bannerets, bachelors, knights, esquires—might be represented in the great and in the privy council;[4] both were summoned under the privy seal, they had the same clerk, and such records as were kept were on indiscriminate files.[5] Nor were their functions more clearly distinct. That of a *grand conseil* was probouleutic, and in the fifteenth century it seems generally to have been called to consider whether a parliament was necessary or not. In 1389 a larger council than usual advised the summons of parliament.[6] In February 1400 a great council taxed itself in order to avoid a parliament and taxing the common people.[7] A few months later another great council considered whether it was possible to declare war without consulting parliament, and diverse views were expressed.[8] In 1430 a great council agreed that a parliament should be held, and in 1432 a great council, sitting in the parliament chamber at Westminster, presented a petition relating to taxation, tallages, and the war with France.[9] In 1433 a great council sat in the green chamber at Westminster (where another council sat in 1437 without being great), and we find a distinction drawn between the king's great council in parliament and the king's great council out of parliament.[10] Bedford in 1434 speaks of his

[1] Nicolas, vi. 290–1.
[2] *Ibid.*, 1. 102; the *conseil* mentioned (*ibid.*, i. 144) seems to have been *grand*, although it had only twenty-three members.
[3] *Ibid.*, ii. 7.
[4] Baldwin, p. 121; Nicolas, i. 18, 59, 100, 102, 144, 156, 237, ii. 85–9, 98–9, 156, iv. pp. xxxv–vi, lx, lxvi, 262, v. 64–5, vi. 214–16, 290–1, 298, 333–4, 339–41.
[5] Council records were " filed," chancery records enrolled; one of the objections to the council was that its records were not enrolled, and could not, therefore, be " counter-rolled," or controlled, " comptroller " being the English for " contrarotulator."
[6] Nicolas, i. 17; cf. *Rot. Parl.*, ii. 146.
[7] Nicolas, i. 102, 107.   [8] *Ibid.*, i. 144.
[9] *Ibid.*, iv., Chron. Cat., pp. x–xi, xxxvi.
[10] *Ibid.*, iv. 105, 185–6, v. 153.

services " as well in your said parliament as in your great council," and in 1430 his letters, directed " al consilio privato regis," distinguish between it and " magno concilio speci-aliter congregato." [1] In 1435 a great council at Sheen,[2] consisting apparently of only twenty-two members, nearly all peers, discussed the Council of Basle, relations with France, and other matters. In October 1454 fourteen bishops, two dukes, eight earls, and seventeen barons were sum-moned to a great council (thirteen more were summoned later) which drew up ordinances to regulate the king's household.[3] To another great council next year there were summoned eighteen bishops, twenty-four abbots and priors, five dukes, nine earls, the prior of St. John of Jerusalem, and thirty-five barons.[4] This list well-nigh exhausted the peerage, and few parliaments contained as many as the ninety-two who were summoned to this great council. Early in Henry VI's minority it was asserted that the government appertained to the lords spiritual and tem-poral assembled in parliament, in the great council, or in the continual council; [5] and on the eve of the Wars of the Roses the great council was little more than the " house " of lords out of parliament.[6] The knights and esquires, who figured largely in the great councils of early Lancas-trian years, had disappeared.[7] The great council had grown at once both greater and less comprehensive, and the omission of commoners was outweighed by including nearly the whole of " the peerage." The wheel had come full circle, and had brought the great council back to the point at which it stood in 1258 and 1311. It was the old alternative, baronage or the crown, a great or a privy council.

Thirty years of civil war disposed of the claims of the great council to govern England, and then the Tudors

[1] Nicolas, iii. 322, iv. 225. [2] *Ibid.*, v. 64–5.
[3] *Ibid.*, vi. 216–23. [4] *Ibid.*, vi. 290–1. [5] *Ibid.*, iii. 233.
[6] This assimilation was helped by the narrowing of the " peerage." There was a broad distinction between " the great council " and the " peers of the land " in 1352 (*Rot. Parl.*, ii. 245).
[7] In 1455, however, one or two knights or esquires were summoned from each county to attend a council (*ibid.*, vi. 339–41).

created a real and lasting privy council. This was the work of Henry VIII and not of his father. Henry VII's council is an enigma; once or twice at least he called a great council, in which appointments were made and war was discussed with France. Of a privy council no mention has been found, and it might seem that his council was simply a number of men whom the king consulted as individuals if and when and how he pleased. Yet there were " council-times "; and a president of the council, whose office is commonly dated from 1530, existed in 1499 in the person of FitzJames, Bishop of London, and in 1506 in that of the notorious Edmund Dudley.[1] It may be that Henry VII felt his monarchy to be too new to risk giving it a master in the shape of an organized council; he needed advice, but he did not want control, and he preferred the private advice of a minister to that of a council meeting. At any rate, the organization of the privy council seems to date from 1526. Henry VIII had, indeed, a council from his accession, but it appears to have been a loose and unwieldy affair until Wolsey superseded it for most practical purposes. In 1526, however, the king selected twenty of its members to attend his royal person; and of these twenty ten were to " give continual attendance in the causes of his said council, unto what place soever his highness shall resort." [2] This was only an outline, which was not filled in until after Wolsey's fall, and the inner ring of ten does not correspond with the later organization of the council. But twenty remained the average number of privy councillors under the Tudors, who were clearly marked off from the " ordinary " council.[3]

[1] *Cal. Patent Rolls*, Henry VII, ii. 471. The obscurity surrounding the council is illustrated by the fact that this detail in Dudley's biography remained unknown until the publication of this volume of the Patent Rolls in 1916. See *Engl. Hist. Rev.*, July and Oct. 1922 and Jan. 1923.

[2] Nicolas, vii. pp. v–vi.

[3] Councillors not sworn of the privy council are said to have been members of the *concilium ordinarium*, a phrase unknown apparently in the Middle Ages (Baldwin, p. 112), and perhaps invented by Sir E. Coke. Cf. Sir R. Wingfield's remarks : " It is above twenty-four years since I was first sworn of the king's council, and after of his private council, being his vice-chamberlain," and " I have been sworn of his council above twenty years and of his privy council above fourteen years " (*Letters and Papers of Henry VIII*, vii. 1525, viii. 225). The " king's

The *grand conseil* sank beneath the weight of England's *grand monarque*.

When it was averred in 1427 that the government of England (during a royal minority) appertained to the lords spiritual and temporal, in parliament, great council, or continual council assembled, the varying form of the assemblies was clearly regarded as a mere matter of detail, compared with the essential identity of their constituency; and the sole advantage of a great over the privy council consisted in the weight and wisdom of a multitude. The matters discussed in great councils were also discussed, and could be decided, in privy councils. When the great council advised the summons of parliament, it was not the great but the privy council which instructed the privy seal to move the lord chancellor to issue the writs; and it could have done so without a great council at all. There is no principle of discrimination between the councils of Henry VI. The abeyance of monarchy undermined the foundations of privy councils, just as its revival under the Tudors proved fatal to great councils. " Great " and " privy " are, in fact, simply expressions of aristocracy and monarchy in terms of the council. The distinction is only marked while the struggle is even, as it was under Henry III and Edward II. The predominance of over-mighty subjects in the fifteenth century disintegrates the privy council, and the triumph of a Tudor king reduces the great council to a nullity. The council under Henry VI grew so great and so diffuse that it lost all specific gravity, and the lack of central governance led naturally to local anarchy and civil war. It was the failure of conciliar government in the fifteenth century that made straight the path for personal monarchy in the national state as well as in the catholic church.

---

counsel learned in the law " never formed a council; they were simply the legal members of the council. The *commune concilium* is still more elusive; in Magna Carta it probably means " common advice," but Thomas Kent is said to be described as " clericus communis consilii domini regis " on the *Coram Rege* roll, 30 Henry VI, m. 8 (Vernon Harcourt, *His Grace the Steward*, p. 385 *n.*).

Some discussion of the king's council was a necessary prelude to any examination of the position of the king's council in parliament. The question is obscure, because the position is involved : *habet enim rex curiam suam in consilio suo in parliamentis suis.* But there is no doubt about the immanence of the council in parliament, and the history of the conflict between executive and legislative is more precisely the process of determining what the council can do by itself and what it can only do in parliament. It may help us if we remember that when we speak of parliament doing anything at all, we are employing what is perhaps the most convenient fiction in the constitution. It is a figure of speech like that employed by Americans when they say that " congress " does this, that, or the other, or by Wesleyans when they speak of " conference " settling the affairs of their community. Really, it is certain people in parliament, in congress, in conference, who do these things; and the association of parliament with the active voice is a modern development. In the middle ages parliament is always passive : the king holds a parliament, summons a parliament, and does many things in and to a parliament. Others besides the king may also do things in parliament, but parliament itself does nothing; it does not even grant taxes. The " estates " tax themselves in parliament, but parliament does not tax them.[1] Justice is done and law is made in parliament; but it is the king in council who judges and ordains. In course of time the reality becomes a form, the petition of the commons determines the act of the king in parliament, and inertia is transmuted into energy. Parliament, however, remained a convenient ambiguity

[1] It is a fundamental though gradual change when, during the fifteenth and sixteenth centuries, taxes, instead of being several grants severally made by different estates in parliament, take a legislative form, and derive their sanction, not from the good-will of the givers, but from the sovereignty of the legislature; and there is no better illustration of (*a*) the amalgamation of the estates into the state, and (*b*) the consequent growth of the sovereignty of parliament. Taxation became a part of positive law, and it was against this " imposition " that the American colonists, reverting to medieval ideas, rebelled. Prof. McIlwain's criticism of the sovereignty of parliament is based on the same idea (see *History*, iii. 162–4).

for the crown in parliament, the lords in parliament, the commons in parliament, as well as for any combination of the three; and it is more decent to say that the parliament act of 1911 was passed by parliament than that it was dictated by a majority in the house of commons.

Parliament in the middle ages was, therefore, a set of conditions under which men acted rather than itself the agent. The atmosphere was that of a royal and feudal court, held in the "hall" of a king's palace with its precincts marked by the "verge" of the king's lord steward. The presence of the king's council was essential to the *curia*. There were endless councils without a parliament; there could be no parliament without a council. The council was the first of the constituent elements in parliament; and it is very difficult to say at what point any other element becomes essential. The earliest "Rolls of Parliaments" are not concerned with the doings of an elected or a representative assembly, and the acts of councils continue to be entered on the "Rolls of Parliaments" down at least to 1371, and for two generations later, so far as the council was determining matters referred to it by parliament.[1] Indeed, one of the reasons why council records do not begin until the reign of Richard II is that councils and parliaments had not been clearly enough differentiated to require different kinds of records. The whole of Edward I's original work as a legislator was done in council before he summoned his model parliament of 1295; and his successors continued for more than a century to enter on the parliament rolls, which always remained in the custody of the council,[2]

---

[1] Baldwin, pp. 107, 386; cf. *Rot. Parl.*, ii. 304, iv. 334, 506. The council also used the rolls of chancery and of the exchequer for recording its proceedings. It had no roll of its own, and used the rolls of its three chief organs, the council in chancery, the council in the exchequer, and the council in parliament. Like parliament, the council depended upon the agency of the executive departments which had developed before either of the deliberative organs of the constitution.

[2] Maitland asked (*Memoranda*, p. lxxxiii) when the parliament roll passed out of the custody of the council into that of the house of lords. The answer appears to be "never." The rolls of parliament have always been chancery records (since they were lost by the exchequer). The *Journals*, of course, have, on the other hand, always been in the custody of the houses.

judicial decisions adopted out of parliament. There was apparently down to 1322 no parliamentary function, save that of taxation, which could not be discharged by the council alone; and even the saving clause needs qualification. Merchants often taxed themselves in unparliamentary meetings, and as late as 1400 the " estates " in a *grand conseil* taxed themselves to avoid recourse to parliament.[1] In 1371 a great council had even varied a subsidy previously granted in parliament.[2] We trace a distinction, which seems clear enough in modern times, back to a period in which the line is blurred and wavering, and then farther to where it disappears altogether; in history, as in the simpler biological studies, absolute origins are beyond our ken.[3]

The council in parliament is thus a session or series of sessions of the council expanded in ways and for purposes which by degrees become more and more definite. The first purpose was certainly to provide the freest access for petitioners to the council. It has been said that parliament sought, by appointing receivers and triers of petitions, to deprive the council of its jurisdiction, as it also sought to deprive it of legislation.[4] But this view attributes to parliament a conscious activity the centre of which is difficult to locate. Things done in parliament are sometimes done by one estate or other, but more often by the council or the crown. It is true that the commons grew more and more insistent that their petitions should be turned by the council in parliament into statutes, but that is not quite the same thing as depriving the council of legislation, and the council had invited petitions in parliament long before

[1] Nicolas, i. 107. It was possible to speak of the " estate " of councillor, which ranked next to an earl's (Baldwin, p. 402), and also of the " estates " of the council, as well as of the estates of parliament and of the estates of the church (Nicolas, v. 88); but in no case was the number limited to three.
[2] *Rot. Parl.*, ii. 304; cf. *ibid.* iv. 301. See below, p. 330.
[3] There are two technical distinctions between parliaments and councils. Parliaments are always summoned under the great seal, councils under the privy seal. Secondly, the warrant to the chancellor to summon a parliament mentioned no names, while they were always specified in the warrants to the lord privy seal to summon a council. Cf. Elsynge, pp. 63-4.
[4] Baldwin, p. 324.

the commons developed a will of their own or devised the means of expressing it. The receivers and triers were, moreover, appointed by the council, and probably before parliament met. Their names were certainly announced in 1341 some days before the attendance was sufficient for the business of parliament to begin.[1] The appointment in parliament of a bishop, two earls, and two barons to hear and determine all complaints against the king's ministers for infractions of the ordinances of 1311,[2] seems to have been an abnormal demand on the part of the lords ordainers; and the more usual practice was for the council to appoint triers of petitions to determine such as they could and merely refer the rest to parliament. It was the council which arranged that petitions presented in parliament should be free of charge, while writs sued out of lower courts required fees; kept procedure in parliament free from the petrifying formalities of common law; and provided in parliament a means for reviewing and correcting the whole administration of justice. It is a late development of self-consciousness when the creature comes to regard itself as its own creator.

The second purpose for which the council held expanded sessions in parliament was to provide for the grant of taxation under the guidance of those who required the taxes and would spend them; and the somewhat monotonous series of addresses with which parliaments were opened in the middle ages played no small part in the slow education of the commons in the sense of political responsibility. Grants might have been extorted locally; but, granted in scores and hundreds of local gatherings, they would have been voted without that realization of national necessity which is the foundation of all responsible government; and it might have been thought that the inevitable place in which these explanations should have been made, and these taxes voted, was the court to which all the king's lieges owed suit and service, were it not for the fact that outside England the king's highest court

---

[1] *Rot. Parl.*, ii. 126. [2] *Ibid.*, i. 286.

U

and the estates-general were divorced, and taxes were not granted where justice might be done in return. Fortunately in England the council remained embedded in parliament, while parliament came to imply an ever fuller representation of all sorts and estates of men.

This continuance of the council in parliament is a feature of the English constitution which parliament itself in the seventeenth and early eighteenth centuries endeavoured in vain to efface and destroy. At the end of the middle ages the parliament chamber is alternatively called the great council chamber. In 1539 we have a detailed statute regulating the place of councillors in the upper house, whether they are peers or not; and in 1541 we read that "on 21 March the council sat not, for that they sat both forenoon and afternoon at the parliament."[1] It was not until after the Revolution that attempts were made by means of place bills to exclude the council from the house of commons. They failed of their purpose, and they never applied to the house of lords. Historical development and the spirit of the constitution proved too strong for the doctrinaire philosophy and prejudices of the revolutionary Whigs.

More complicated than the retention of the council in parliament was the definition of the council to be retained therein. We have seen that "council" might be protean in its variety. It might be a large council of magnates or a minute council of ministers; it might represent a baronial opposition or a monarchical administration. Which was to be its predominant characteristic when it sat in the midst of the estates in parliament assembled? Would the council preserve the shadowy unity which its growing diversities had not quite destroyed in the middle ages, or would it become so fixed in its diverse aspects that all sense and all appearance of identity would be lost? This seems, in fact, to have been the fate of the council. The diverse trend towards a great and a privy council got beyond control, and the two aspects of the council became

[1] Nicolas, vii. 329, 330.

two different things. In other words, the expanded session
of the council in parliament set up for itself as a house of
lords, while the privy council was preserved as the administrative organ of the crown.[1] Both, however, continued inherent in parliament, though the schism between great
and privy councils led to the emphasis of the connexion
between the great council and parliament, and weakened
that between parliament and the privy council; and to this
discrimination is due the differentiation between the legislature and executive. The great council dissociated itself, or
emancipated itself, more and more from the crown, and
became less and less a council, although its members continued their claim to be *consiliarii nati* of the king. The
privy council, on the other hand, came to be more and
more regarded as an executive body, whose claims to
legislate were viewed with increasing distrust.

The process by which the great council emancipated
itself from the crown and became a house of parliament
was the evolution of the theory of a peerage. Its earlier
stages have already been indicated.[2] The possession of
certain rights of jurisdiction, or the possession of certain
lands, called a barony, to which these rights were attached,
came to be regarded as constituting a peerage of the realm
and as entitling the possessor to a special writ of summons
whenever a great council or a parliament was held. It
was originally a liability, rather than a right, which was
attached to tenure *per baroniam*, and in the fourteenth
century kings were moved to impose or threaten heavy
penalties for disobedience to the summons. The peers,
indeed, were more anxious to deny to others the rights of

---

[1] The distinction was less clear when the council sat in the Star
chamber and came to be called a " court "; it was sometimes even called
a " senate " (" coram dominis in regio senatu secus nuncupato the Sterre
Chamber," *Lords' Journals*, i. 72), and barons claimed as barons, but
unsuccessfully, a right to be summoned to it as they were to the house
of lords. Their failure to establish their claim was possibly due to the
fact that cases involving a peer's loss of freehold were dealt with, not
in the Star chamber, but by the peers in parliament; and their land
was ever the main concern of the " pieres de la terre." Other matters
might be left to the crown and council.

[2] In chapter v.

peerage than to fulfil their own duties themselves; and at the very time that measures were being taken to punish their neglect of parliament, they were insisting that other members of the council were no more than assistants or attendants without a right to vote. This reduction of the status of the judges and law officers of the crown affected both the council in parliament and the council out of parliament. From the middle of the fourteenth century they ceased, it is said, to be sworn of the council [1] and became merely legal assessors. As such they continued to sit in parliament, but even under Henry VIII, who was no respecter of peers, it was admitted that the king's lord chancellor himself had no right or interest entitling him to a vote in parliament unless he were a peer. The same measure was meted out to other councillors of the crown : the attorney- and solicitor-general and the king's serjeants-at-law continued to receive the councillor's special writ of summons to parliament, and the former do to this day, though they never obey the summons, and the abeyance of the order of the coif put an end to another rusty link between council and parliament. But constant though their presence was in Tudor parliaments, and active as their service— and that of their colleagues, the masters in chancery [2]— was in the upper house, these legal dignitaries had no vote on the legislation which they prepared. So, too, the other official members of the council were reduced to the position of advisers to the peers. The great officers of state were given a place by statute in the house of lords whether they were peers or not; [3] but if they were not peers they

[1] Baldwin, p. 76. This statement is subject to considerable reservations; it can only mean that the judges ceased to be political advisers of the king. They remained his legal councillors, and the two chief justices were, as a matter of fact, sworn of the privy council in the sixteenth century. The lord chancellor, moreover, has never been deprived of his place in council.

[2] In 1536 the northern rebels complained at Pontefract that " those of the chancery " were growing neglectful of their " office amongst the lords " in not providing them with copies of bills before they were introduced in the commons (Dodds, *Pilgrimage of Grace*, i. 360; *Engl. Hist. Rev.*, v. 568; *Letters and Papers*, xii. i. 410).

[3] 31 Henry VIII, c. 10.

sat lower than if they were, on their respective benches, while the secretaries were banished to the upper woolsack beside the chancellor.[1] Apart from the legal members no such discrimination between peers and other councillors was suffered to disturb the council out of parliament; and commoners like Thomas Cromwell and Sir Francis Walsingham were just as much "lords of the council" as their noble colleagues. Indeed, the success of the peers in parliament was counterbalanced by their failure in the council out of parliament. There the council became effectively royal and privy; the *magnum* dropped off from *concilium*, and the magnates under the Tudors almost disappeared from the privy council. Such peers as survived were almost all of the newest creation. Cromwell and Cecil were not of the council because they were peers; they were made peers because they had long served in the council, while others, such as Walsingham, were nearly as influential without attaining to peerage at all.

Nor did the reduction of councillors to the position of assistants in the house of lords render their assistance a negligible quantity. Tudor law was judge-made law, not so much by interpretation in the courts, as by discussion in council; and the year-books and law reports are replete with judicial decisions on constitutional principles.[2] The judges did, in fact, in Tudor times fulfil to some extent the function of the supreme court under the constitution of the United States, and Bacon's encomium of the consultation of judges by the crown was a deduction from his historical study of Henry VII's reign. It was the judges who decided that Henry could not pass an act of attainder without the consent of the commons, and Henry accepted

[1] See above, p. 251. Behind the lower woolsack sat or knelt the clerks of parliament. Barons of the exchequer had apparently no regular place in parliament. They were summoned in 1305 (Maitland, *Memoranda*, pp. cvii–viii), but not apparently in Edward III's reign (cf. *Cal. Close Rolls* 1374–77, 1377–81, *passim*). Glover, however, in his *Pompa Parliamentaris* gives them as present in 1585, while D'Ewes' picture represents them as absent; see Appendix.

[2] Apparently the judges sat for this purpose (among others) in the exchequer chamber, and discussed principles without necessarily waiting for a case to be brought before them by a writ of error.

their verdict as final. It was the judges who, in the first
two months of his reign, discussed what should be done
in parliament with the problem of a king *de facto* who was
de jure an attainted traitor, and a Speaker who was in an
equally parlous case.[1] It was the judges, too, who laid
down the principle of Poynings' law years before its enactment, and they also determined the procedure by writ of
error in parliament, declared that there were things which
parliament could not do by statute, decided what bills
should be promoted by the government, and defined the
limits of ecclesiastical franchise. The precise relation of this
judicial action to parliament has not been explained; but
whether the advice was tendered in or out of parliament,
and whether it was regarded as advice or decision, it is
clear that both crown and parliament acted upon it.

The legal members of the council were equally active in
sessions that were undoubtedly parliamentary. It has been
thought that they were really responsible for the provisos
which the king frequently added to bills when giving the
royal assent, and that they exercised the chief influence in
that meeting in the robing chamber of the palace which
decided whether the royal assent should be given at all.
Under Henry VI it had been referred to the two chief
justices to determine which of the acts passed in parliament
should be considered statutes and proclaimed, and which
should be merely handed over to the clerk of the council;[2]
and it may be that the judges were responsible for no slight
alterations in bills between their passage in parliament and
their final appearance on the statute rolls. In parliament
itself the lawyers of the council had much to do with legislation; and in the first years of Henry VIII's reign, at least,
a bill was rarely committed to any one else.[3] At every stage,
indeed, their influence was felt—in the preliminary discussion

[1] *Year-Books*, Henry VII, ed. 1679, p. 4; cf. my *Henry VII*, ii. 10–11.
[2] Nicolas, iii. 22.
[3] *Lords' Journals*, i. 1–57 *passim ;* the judges, the attorney- and solicitor-
general, the serjeants-at-law, and masters in chancery were the usual
committees for bills; on one occasion (*ibid.*, p. 56) a bill was committed
by the lords to the attorney-general " to be reformed " after it had
reached an eighth reading.

of principles before the bills were framed, in their actual drafting, in their amendment during passage, in the royal provisos, and in their final form on the statute-book. The laws of England would have been singular things had it been left to peers and popular representatives to make them; and the king's council in parliament played no small part in English constitutional history.

Notwithstanding these eminent services to parliamentary legislation, the position of the council in parliament grew more precarious. Henry's act of 1539, indeed, gave some councillors a statutory right to attend the house of lords, independent of a peerage; but unless they were peers they could not vote, and the act did nothing for those councillors who held no great office of state. It was anomalous that a lord chancellor like Sir Thomas More should preside over, and day by day adjourn, the council [1] in parliament without even a casting vote in its proceedings; and the anomaly was only removed by the growing practice of creating the chancellor a peer, which incidentally ruled out from the chancellorship any ecclesiastic who was not a bishop. By the same intrusion of peerage into the council in parliament other great offices of state were restricted to peers; and those who were not peers were deprived of their traditional place in parliament, which they had occupied since its origin, when the core of every parliament was a session of the council.

From the menace of this exclusion from parliament the council was saved by the house of commons, and the constituencies welcomed those whom the peers had rejected. The multitude of privy councillors in the house of commons during the Tudor period has often been used as a proof of the packing of parliament; but the contention ignores the fact that so long as parliaments had existed councillors had received their special writs of summons. It is a strange inversion of parliamentary history, and the real novelty of Tudor times was not that councillors sat in parliament, but

---

[1] The entry of an adjournment of the house of lords in its *Journals* during the session of 1533 is frequently "hodierno *consilio* soluto."

that they sat as elected representatives instead of as crown nominees, just as the attorney- and solicitor-general to-day prefer—unless indeed they have no option—the risks of contested election to obedience to a certain royal summons. The change was twofold : councillors sat in the house of commons instead of in the house of lords, and they sought election. It was natural that they should think they had some claim upon the constituencies, and that the electors were not making any great concession in choosing those who had, in any case, a legal right to sit in parliament. Probably to-day, if peers of the United Kingdom could sit in the house of commons, it would not be considered an arbitrary proceeding to offer themselves for election. Under the circumstances the amount of pressure actually brought to bear upon constituencies to elect privy councillors as their members seems to have been slight; probably they were as glad then to get privy councillors to represent them as they are to-day to get cabinet ministers as candidates.

The change, by which privy councillors submitted to popular election and sat in the house of commons, is important as a recognition of the growing weight of the house of commons and of the popular element in the constitution. It points in the same direction as the election of the eldest sons of peers, the purchase of boroughs, the bribery of electors, the ambition of aspiring politicians to become members, the abeyance of residence as a qualification, and the capture of country seats by London lawyers. Possibly the transference of councillors from the upper to the lower house was by way of preference rather than compulsion, and they vacated their place in the house of lords because they found greater respect and an ampler scope in the house of commons. In the upper house they had become assistants, if not servants; in the lower they were more than equal to their colleagues. They formed the link between the government and the commons, and did their best to produce harmony between the two. Both Cromwell and Cecil owed their influence largely to their position in the commons, and they regularly reported to their sovereigns the feeling of the house,[1] and to the house the wishes of the government. The privy councillors always formed part of the deputations sent by the house to impress its views on Queen Elizabeth with regard to such matters as her marriage, the succession to the throne, the execution of Mary Stuart, and abuses like monopolies; and when supply was under discussion the amount was always referred to a committee which consisted of the privy councillors in the house and an equal number of private members.[2] Their position was that of genuine mediators; they performed a duty to the house as well as to the crown, and they did not always agree with one another in what they said in debate. It was the divorce between the Stuarts and their people which rendered their position untenable, and raised the issue whether they were servants of the house or ministers of the crown.

It would hardly be an exaggeration to say that this identification of privy councillors with popular representatives was as important a stage in the development of responsible government as the growth of representation itself; for responsible government was not established by summoning representatives to Westminster, but by embodying those representatives in the government or the government in those representatives. If parliament was to remain something more than an irresponsible opposition, there must be unity between it and the government; and responsible government involves the responsibility of the executive as well as that of the legislature. The executive must be responsible to the legislature, but in an equal measure the legislature must be responsible for the government. In the middle ages a connexion, if not unity, had been maintained by the presence of the council in parlia-

---

[1] Cf. Cromwell's letter to Henry VIII in 1534 (*Letters and Papers*, vii. 51). In Elizabeth's reign the house grew sometimes restive over these reports, and still more so under the Stuarts; but to make them has continued to be a regular duty of the leader of the house.

[2] D'Ewes, *Journals*, p. 124; *Commons' Journals*, i. 53, 74, 83, 104, 116, 119.

ment, and by the advice that was constantly given by
councillors and magnates to the commons in their domestic
sessions in the chapter house. The tendency to exclude
councillors as such from parliament threatened a complete
separation of powers; and the danger was only averted
by making some councillors peers and securing for others
seats in the house of commons. The council in parliament
was thus preserved from extinction; and it was the council
in its most royal and " privy " form that was saved, not
merely the council in that " great " and attenuated form
in which it assumed the guise of the house of lords.

CHAPTER XV

THE PEERS IN PARLIAMENT

THE house of lords has long been regarded as the most stable and conservative element in the British constitution, and among the claims that have been made on its behalf to the political gratitude of the English people is the assertion that seven hundred years ago it extorted Magna Carta from King John. In reality, few elements in the constitution have been based upon a more ambiguous foundation or have suffered more radical changes. The lords themselves are still in doubt about their origin; and while they agree on the palpable fiction that Edward I created, and intended to create, a number of hereditary peerages, they differ as to the date of the creation, and within recent years they have decided that a summons to the parliaments of 1283 and 1290 both did and did not create hereditary peerages. Some peers sit in the house of lords by a title which the house of lords itself has declared invalid in the case of other claimants. At one time the title was tenure by barony, at another writs of summons, and at a third creation by letters patent. Most peers sit in the right of their fathers, but others have sat in the right of their mothers, and a few in the right of their wives or of their sons. There are many peers who cannot sit in the house of lords, and some of the lords who do sit are not peers. Some sit because they are elected by their fellow-peers, some because they are elected by episcopal chapters on the nomination of the crown. Some are elected for life, some until they resign, and some for a single parliament. Some have been born peers, some have achieved peerage by various means, including purchase,[1] and others

---

[1] James I instituted a regular tariff: £10,000 for a barony, £15,000 for a viscountcy, £20,000 for an earldom (Pike, p. 355).

have had it thrust upon them. Almost every principle upon which the house was founded has been inverted during its construction; and, whatever may be its defects, neither its history nor its composition is lacking in variety.

In an earlier chapter an attempt has been made to trace the evolution of peerage and the process by which the peers sought to monopolize power in the king's council, to convert it into a council of magnates and, when it sat in parliament, into a house of peers. The process has been as prolonged as the growth of the constitution; it was not finished at the close of the middle ages, and the latest steps towards completing the hereditary character of the house of lords were not taken until the nineteenth century. It is a house of lords, but the lords are not all hereditary, and it is not yet a house of nothing but peers who are. Fortunately or unfortunately, its case is one of arrested development; and the changes that threaten in the future are likely to be in the direction of reversion to its original type, at any rate to the extent of reducing or eliminating the principle of peerage which was superimposed upon the council in the later middle ages. For that, if for no other reason, the history of the peers in parliament is of immediate interest.

The fundamental change in the house of lords has been its conversion from the king's great council, sitting in parliament in virtue of royal writs, into a body of legislators basing their right to legislate and their independence of the crown upon the principle of primogeniture. As early as 1346 a distinction had been drawn between the councillors and the magnates in the great council in parliament.[1] Judges, for instance, were summoned to treat with the king and others of his council; other councillors, who eventually come to be known as peers, are summoned to treat with the king, *prelatis, proceribus, et magnatibus.* The distinction was not reflected in the designation of those who sat *in camera magni consilii vocata le parlement chambre;* they were all called "seigneurs" or "lords," and the term included the coun-

[1] Elsynge, pp. 25–7; Hale, *Jurisdiction of the Lords*, ed. Hargrave, 1796, p. 25; Baldwin, p. 76; Pike, p. 247.

cillors as well as the prelates and magnates. A knight
might well be a lord of parliament.[1] But the differentiation grew with the increasing stress on " peerage," although
peers and peerage are not words found in parliamentary
records of the early Tudor period. Nowhere, indeed, in
the sixteenth century do we find any clear statement of
peerage theory, and Cowell, in his *Interpreter* (1607),
vaguely defines the peers as those whom the king summons
by special writ to parliament. The anarchy of the Wars
of the Roses and the authority of Henry VII militated
against the enunciation of a constitutional doctrine;
both conditions rendered a right to sit in parliament of little
practical value. It was not until parliamentary struggles
superseded the arbitrament of war and the autocracy of the
crown that a seat in the house of lords became an object
of desire and a means of political power.

Henry VII was thus left to do much as he liked in the
parliament chamber. Opposition which had not been settled
at Bosworth had recourse to conspiracy and rebellion; and
the futility of parliamentary opposition freed Henry from any
temptation to interfere with traditional methods of summons.
Lords who might have resisted in council had already
committed themselves to treason and been disposed of by
more drastic methods than the refusal of writs. The same
conditions obtained in the early years of Henry VIII; and
it was not until a momentous revolution in domestic politics
was broached that fundamental divergence of view led the
crown to consider its constitutional ways and means of
success. The first indication of the coming crisis was
connected with that famous controversy between the church
and the laity which arose over Richard Hunne's case in
1515;[2] and in that year the judges, acting as interpreters
of the constitution, declared that the presence of the spiritual
lords was not essential to parliament.[3]

---

[1] Cf. *Lords' Journals*, vol. i. p. xxvi. : " every other knight, not being lord
of the parliament."
[2] See Miss Jeffries Davis in *Engl. Hist. Rev.*, xxx. 477.
[3] Pike, p. 327; *Letters and Papers of Henry VIII*, vol. ii. pt. i. Nos.
1313–14.

Meanwhile practice had crystallized, and Henry VIII
was too prudent to attempt to enforce the constitutional
doctrine of his advisers in this respect.   Nor did he interfere
with the routine of chancery in issuing special writs of
summons; the fact that chancery continues to issue such
writs to the law officers of the crown, which have not been
obeyed for centuries, suggests that Henry was wise to leave
its practice alone.   Occasionally he seems to have sent a
private intimation to a lord that he would do well to refrain
from coming to parliament; and when they wanted to
abstain they had, of course, to seek his permission.   But the
regular writs were issued as though the crown had no option
in the matter, and the only method Henry took to modify
the *personnel* of the house of lords was the creation of
peers.   The dissolution of the monasteries materially altered
the composition of the house, but that was not the object
of their suppression.   The Italian and absentee bishops of
Salisbury and Worcester were deprived by statute,[1] there
being no means by which the church in England could rid
itself of the incubus; but the bill was not passed for the
purpose of catching votes.   It is doubtful, too, whether that
was the motive of Henry's few creations in 1529.[2]   The
Boleyns would in any case have been ennobled, whether
their votes were needed or not; and the real question was
not how to obtain a majority of lay over clerical votes, but
whether any lay majority could legally bind the church in
spiritual matters against the votes of its representatives.
The critical resolutions were carried, not by a created
majority, but by a conference between the two houses, in
which the spiritual and temporal peers were equally represented, and the commons voted with the latter.   The small
number of twenty-eight temporal peers summoned in 1523
was quite abnormal; and even in 1534, when Henry had

---

[1] *Lords' Journals*, i. 80.
[2] Round, *Studies in Peerage History*, pp. 330, etc.   Lord Ogle was not
summoned between 1529 and 1544, Darcy was kept away in 1535-6, and
possibly Tunstall in 1532; but these instances are too few to justify any
generalization, except that the crown's control over its own summons
was not quite extinct.

raised the number to fifty-four, they were fewer than the temporal peers summoned in 1454.

The dissolution of the monasteries reduced the number of spiritual peers from forty-seven to twenty-one; and while Henry VIII increased the number of bishops from twenty-one to twenty-seven, the abolition of the papal jurisdiction and of all but the form of capitular election gave the crown substantial control of these votes. At the end of his reign the majority of the existing peers had been created by Henry VIII; but Mary relieved the church in England of its subjection to the crown by subjecting it to the papacy, and the Elizabethan settlement of religion owed nothing of its triumph to royal control over episcopal votes in the house of lords. Her success, however, placed twenty-six spiritual peerages at her disposal, and these, with half a dozen temporal creations, made the house of lords as safe in her keeping as a pocket borough. At her death the temporal peers numbered sixty, and the house of lords contained eighty-six members, which was slightly less than its average size since 1350; only during Henry VII's reign and the early years of Henry VIII had the number sunk below eighty, and the difference lay in the reduction of the spiritual peers from more than half to less than a third of the whole house.

It was the Stuarts who, in seeking to control the house by creations, rendered it uncontrollable. No doubt it was inconvenient for James I to inherit a house of lords consisting of eighty-six members, none of whom he had created. The bishoprics, of course, gradually fell into his hands, and by creating fifty-four peers he nearly doubled the temporal peerage, but failed to make it amenable.[1] On the eve of the Scottish Union the temporal peers numbered a hundred and seventy-six; that act added sixteen, the Tories created twelve to pass the treaty of Utrecht, and these, with the bishops, endowed the House of Hanover at its accession with an upper house of two hundred and thirty. Nevertheless the younger Pitt was the only begetter of the Victorian

[1] See *Deputy-Keeper of the Records* 47th *Report;* Pike, pp. 357 *sqq.*

house of lords. Owing partly to the Irish union, but more to Pitt's desire to enlist support among the *nouveaux riches* of the war and the industrial revolution, the peerage had grown over fifty per cent. at the time of his death.[1] The house of lords itself numbered three hundred and fifty-one members in 1806. The policy of control by creation had clearly reached its limit, and the house of lords was independent at last. For the first time in its history it contained, in the nineteenth century, an overwhelming majority of members who had been born, and not created, peers. During the middle ages the spiritual peers, who were not hereditary, always outnumbered their temporal colleagues. The bishops, new creations, and their friends among the old enabled Elizabeth, the Stuarts, and even Pitt, to counterbalance hereditary independence; and the sons of Pitt's house of lords were the first generation of peers by primogeniture to be undisputed masters of their own house. It was not a mere coincidence that that generation brought the country to the verge of revolution in 1832. The hereditary principle is not the rock upon which the house of lords was founded, but the rock on which it foundered.

The multiplication of the size of a council six- or sevenfold involved a radical change in its functions and composition; and the house of lords became less and less a council, less and less judicial, less and less a body to get things done, and more and more an opposition. A body of six hundred men can hardly be more than a public meeting, and both houses of parliament are now, in fact, public meetings which do most of their useful discussion by way of private conversation. The difference is that while the house of commons is a public meeting of plenipotentiaries, the house of lords is a public meeting of private persons with very unequal qualifications for the discharge of their

---

[1] It has been more than doubled again since 1806, and 433 new peerages were created between 1880 and 1920. The total membership of the house of lords was 741 in 1923; and the original proportions of ecclesiastical, and representative Scottish and Irish, peers to those of the United Kingdom, have entirely disappeared; see Appendix III, note (r).

public duty. The best apology for the house of lords as a political authority is the fact that for five-sixths of its business it consists of less than one-sixth of its members; but it is a precarious title, which depends upon the non-user of rights by the great majority of their proprietors, and the house of lords is a serious drawback to the advantages of allowing a constitution to grow, instead of constructing it on a plan. It does not represent any conscious design, and it would never have entered into the mind of man to construct a second chamber on the principles which it is presumed to embody.

The original obligation out of which it grew was the liability of tenants who held land from the crown to render suit and service at the king's court. The service was of value because it was largely military, and great holders of land were in a better position than others to provide armed forces. But the advice that was also expected would be expert, because in the middle ages the management of England was a problem akin to that of the management of the domains which the tenants-in-chief possessed. A peer like Thomas of Lancaster, who held five earldoms, might be presumed to enjoy the practical experience which would make his advice of value to the crown. But the crown also possessed the right of selecting, by special writ of summons, the tenants-in-chief whose advice it valued and desired; and it was not from among them exclusively that kings formed their council. Others were included for legal skill not possessed by the barons, and later on there were added men of commercial experience and political wisdom, as English policy grew more complex and embraced multifarious interests. The holders of land were, however, entrenched in the council, and gradually the breach was widened between baronial councillors, whose point of view was local and territorial, and those new men who depended on the crown, and viewed politics from the centre as royal or national business. This divergence differentiated the great from the privy council, and left the former in parliament as the embodiment of the landed interest; it was on

x

questions relating to the tenure of land that the *magnum concilium* claimed and secured the decisive voice, and it was the policy of strict entails, designed to preserve the integrity of great estates, that led to the recognition of primogeniture as the main title to a seat in the house of lords. This development was but slowly affected by the growth of industry and commerce, because the wealth derived therefrom was so largely invested in land that the interests of the two classes always tended to coincide, and wealth in land continued to be the basis of the house of lords; indeed, one of the motives of the dissolution of the monasteries was to provide new lands for the *nouveaux riches*, and many of our ducal houses were founded on the spoliation of the church.

Wealth in land and wisdom in council are not, however, synonymous terms, and the conciliar character of the house of lords was obscured by the peerage. While the house asserted with growing emphasis its claims as a strictly hereditary peerage, it clung tenaciously to powers it had possessed as a council; and its history for some two centuries has consisted mainly of struggles to retain rights of jurisdiction and legislation which were growing more and more anomalous. Most of the privileges of the house came to it in its capacity as a royal council; and as recently as the Act of 1876 appeals to the house of lords were described as being heard " before her Majesty the Queen in her Court of Parliament." [1] But the sovereign had gradually been deprived of all discretion in determining the composition of his court and council in parliament. In the Bristol and Arundel cases, in the reign of Charles I, the lords declared that a writ of summons could not be refused to a peer, and that the king could not prevent him from obeying it.[2] At

---

[1] Pike, pp. 268, 306.

[2] Gardiner, *History of England*, vi. 91–115; Hallam, i. 379–80; *Lords' Journals*, iii. 544; Elsynge, pp. 59–60, 192–242. As recently as 1601 Elizabeth had afforded a precedent for Charles I by directing Rutland, Bedford, Cromwell, Sandys, and Montague not to appear in parliament although writs of summons had been sent them (*Acts P.C.* 1601–4, pp. 218–19, 221).

the Restoration they re-affirmed the inalienable right of peers to their seats, while they repudiated all the medieval principles from which those rights were deduced. They abolished all feudal services, of which attendance at the king's court was one;[1] they decided that the possession of a barony, the original ground for the exercise of jurisdiction, constituted no right to a peerage;[2] and they denied their obligation to obey the royal summons to parliament, while claiming the right to come if they chose.[3] All conception of duty was merged in privilege; and, taking a leaf out of the Stuart note-book, the lords grounded their privilege on indefeasible hereditary right. Peerage became indelible save by attainder; no misdemeanours and no incapacity could deprive a peer of his dignity; and the Revolution of 1688 left the peerage in possession of rights which it denied to the crown. The peer might, indeed, be excluded from parliament for his faith or misconduct, but he did not thereby cease to be a peer.

The claim of a body of landlords to be the highest court of appeal over the whole complicated sphere of civil jurisdiction was the most singular of the anomalies arising from the simultaneous retention by the lords of the powers of a council and their repudiation of the principles on which it was constituted. Edward I's " parliaments of the council " had been held to determine the law's delays and the judges' doubts, matters which were commonly settled after the barons and elected commons had departed; and the sentence of the high court of parliament was that of the king in council. As late as the reign of Henry VII the judges are the exclusive arbiters of this jurisdiction; but

[1] Pike, pp. 356–7.

[2] In the Fitzwalter case (1669), reaffirmed in the Berkeley case (1861). The principal ground for this decision was the reasonable argument that a " barony " was devisable by will, and that if peerage attached to a barony, and a seat in the house of lords to a peerage, the holder might dispose of political power by sale or by bequest. The objection did not lie against the medieval tenure by barony, because the tenant could not then dispose of lands which belonged to the crown.

[3] Disobedience to the royal writs of summons became common form with the peers as time went on, and no king since the Restoration was in a position to impose the penalties for dereliction of duty which had been regular in the middle ages.

by the middle of the nineteenth century the peers had
turned the council so topsy-turvy that not only had they
arrogated to themselves, a non-judicial body, the supreme
decision on points of law, but they had reduced the real
lawyers to assistants and advisers. The history of this
blue-blooded revolution requires a little attention.

No doubt a claim to jurisdiction seemed natural to a
baron; for a barony in the middle ages consisted largely in
the jurisdiction and profits therefrom which it implied. But
a barony was valued by its medieval possessor, not for the
opportunity which its courts afforded him of displaying
legal wisdom, but for the emoluments which accrued from
the dispensation of justice; it was the lord's steward who
judged, while his master received the proceeds of judgement.
Moreover, the king, as lord paramount of the land, occupied
in the high court of parliament the same position of privilege
that the baron held in his baronial franchise; and the only
right the barons possessed in the king's court was to be tried
by their peers, not to try other people. When Edward I
made parliament the common receptacle for his subjects'
petitions, it was to himself and his judges in council, and
not to a public meeting of peers, that he provided access.
The commons, however, having sifted the petitions and
made the important ones common, took to the practice of
referring the rest to the council and departing without a
reply. Presently direct access to the council, and through
the council to chancery, by means of bill or petition, was
accorded by statute; the stage of reception and reference
by parliament to the council was omitted, and from the
reign of Henry IV original jurisdiction in parliament rapidly
decreased.[1] The petitions which had flowed in thousands
to parliament were diverted to chancery, the courts of
star chamber and requests, and other departments of the
council. This was a characteristic feature of the Tudor
period, and during the first seventeen years of James I's

---

[1] Hale, *Jurisdiction of the Lords*, ed. Hargrave, 1796, p. vi; Palgrave,
Report on Public Petitions (Parl. Papers, 1833, xii. 19); McIlwain, p. 133;
Nicolas, *Proc. of Privy Council*, i. 73, v. p. xi; Leadam, *Star Chamber*
(Selden Soc.), i. pp. xxiii–iv, lix–lx; Baldwin, pp. 243–9.

reign there is said to have been only one writ of error brought before parliament.[1]

Dissatisfaction, however, with the uses to which the Stuarts put the jurisdiction of their prerogative courts led to a demand for its revival in parliament; and the popularity of the impeachment of Stuart ministers afforded the lords an easy re-entry. But in the interval the lords had converted the king's council in parliament into a house of peers, and under the guise of restoration a supreme appellate jurisdiction was vested in men the like of whom had never possessed it before. The commons, indeed, were not quite content with this restoration; they wanted a place in the sun of parliamentary jurisdiction, and a grand contest of legal wits was waged over the question whether or not the commons were judges in parliament.[2] Their distrust of the Stuart judges distorted their history and precluded a real restoration; and they had in the end to be satisfied with the part of the grand inquest of the nation, presenting offenders against the state for the judgement of the peers. From this jurisdiction, which was of first instance with the commons as prosecution, the lords proceeded, in the reign of Charles II, to claim an appellate jurisdiction without any intervention of the commons. The abolition by the Long parliament of the prerogative courts, to which the council had delegated much of its jurisdiction, had left a void in that sphere which the common law courts could not fill; and the peers stepped into the breach. Their

[1] Elizabeth had provided in 1585 for the hearing of writs of error from the queen's bench in the exchequer chamber when parliament was not sitting.

[2] Floyd's case in 1621, in which the Commons inflicted severe penalties on one who was not a member of their house, is well known (Gardiner, iv. 119–21; Hallam, i. 360–2), and is supposed to have been unprecedented. But in 1529 Henry VIII writes to Lady Worsley forbidding her to molest any further a clerk accused of attempting to poison her husband, " as the House of Commons has decided that he is not culpable " (*Letters and Papers*, iv. 5293, v. 117; his case had apparently been brought up from king's bench to parliament on a writ of error); and the house, before passing the bill of attainder against Thomas Seymour in 1549, resolved that it would hear the evidence "orderly as it was before the Lords" (*Commons' Journals*, i. 9), though the answer was that it was not necessary in that "court." Each part of the high court of parliament was claiming to be a whole.

assumption was not unchallenged, but the commons were engaged upon a similar assumption in the sphere of finance; and when the peers asked for records establishing the monopoly of supply claimed by the commons, the lower house retorted with a similar demand for the evidence upon which the lords based their assumption of appellate jurisdiction. Both houses were, in fact, appropriating the effects of a languishing monarchy, and they agreed to divide the spoil. The divergence of parliament into two houses prevented the common enjoyment of the fruits of parliamentary triumphs; and the lords acquiesced in the commons' control of taxation, while the commons accepted the claims of the lords to the sole exercise of appellate jurisdiction.

The subservience of the judges to the Stuarts relieved the peers of any sense of obligation to share with them their newly-won powers; and the position of the judges in the high court of parliament grew steadily worse. Having been limited to judicial functions, they were reduced even there to giving advice; then their advice was rejected, and at length, in 1856, the peers refused to consult them.[1] The revolution had reached its limit when the supreme court of appeal refused to consult the judges, whose presence alone gave a shred of historical and moral support to the claims of the peers; and the judges soon had their revenge. The mere pressure of public opinion drove the peers from the position they occupied, and no peer who neither holds nor has held high judicial office under the crown now ventures to sit when the house of lords is acting as a supreme court of appeal. The efficiency of the house of lords in its judicial capacity depends upon the rigorous abstention from its proceedings of every peer who owes his position to primogeniture; and so far as jurisdiction is concerned, the peers have abandoned the hereditary foundation of their house.

This abdication was not without awkward logical consequences, and the question arose why primogeniture should qualify peers to make the laws which it did not qualify them

[1] Pike, p. 377.

to interpret. The question was emphasized by the increasing stress laid by the peers upon peerage as the sole qualification for membership of their house. The judges were not the only victims of this exclusive principle; one by one the non-hereditary and conciliar elements were excluded even from the subordinate position of advisers to the house. The serjeants-at-law have been abolished; the law officers of the crown and the masters in chancery have ceased to attend, and privy councillors are reduced to standing on the steps of the throne, where they may be seen, but may not be heard. The lord chancellor and other great officers of state have only been retained by the practice of forcing upon them the livery of the peerage; and the bishops alone remain to testify that a reputation for wisdom was once considered a necessary qualification for membership of the king's great council in parliament. Even they have suffered. They have been denied the status of peerage, notwithstanding their assertion in parliament in 1352 that they were peers for precisely the same reason as earls and barons;[1] and the grounds for this astonishing denial are worthy of it. Bishops do not inherit their bishoprics, but attain them by merit; and if they commit treason or felony, they are not tried by the peers.[2] The house seems to have based itself on the reason for which Palmerston approved of nomination for the civil service: "there was no damned merit about it." The bishops survived this attack on their dignity, but not without loss. Their number had been reduced to comparative insignificance by the enormous creations of temporal peers, and they formed but a twentieth part of the house in the nineteenth century. But the possibility of increasing this exiguous figure alarmed the temporal peers or their nonconformist supporters; and in 1847[3] it was enacted that, however much bishops might multiply, their seats in

---

[1] See above, p. 65. This principle had been laid down in the Constitutions of Clarendon: "archiepiscopi, episcopi . . . habent possessiones suas de domino rege sicut baroniam, et inde. . . . sicut barones ceteri, debent interesse curiæ domini regis cum baronibus" (c. xi).

[2] The reason, of course, was that in the middle ages the prelates had claimed the higher privilege of being tried by spiritual men in the ecclesiastical courts.

[3] 10 & 11 Vict., c. 108; Makower, pp. 211–12.

the lords should never exceed twenty-six. The two archbishops and the bishops of London, Durham, and Winchester [1] are always members of the house, but the rest have to wait until the chances of seniority entitle them to rank with those whose wisdom comes by birth.

Logic is not perhaps an important ingredient in political institutions, but defiance of logic has been carried to extremes in the house of lords. It claims to be founded on right, but it has made havoc of that right by its own resolutions. Episcopacy entitles some, but not other bishops to sit; peerage entitles a peer in England to sit, but not one in Scotland or Ireland, unless he is also elected. The crown could create as many peers in perpetuity as it pleased, but it could not, until 1887, create a single peer for life.[2] It could "ennoble" a man's blood and limit its flow to eldest sons; but it could not exert discretion in the sending out writs of summons which no one else could issue. Inasmuch as no mention was, naturally, made of heirs in the writs of summons by which peers were first begotten, the house of lords has presumed that descent was intended to heirs-general, whereas when descent is first suggested in the creation of peers by letters patent, it is only to heirs male; so that the heirs of a man who was never intended to have a hereditary peerage are better provided than those of one who was. The house of lords is not, in fact, founded on any principle; its basis is a patchwork of legal fictions, inconsistent rights, illogical decisions, and palpable absurdities. It represents an attempt to reduce the variant ideas and conditions of different ages within the compass of a legal formula, and to erect that formula into an absolute right defined and definable by its possessors alone.

That autonomy claimed by the peers has fortunately never become the law of the land; and their attempts to

---

[1] These three bishoprics are given precedence over the others by 31 Henry VIII, c. 10.

[2] The Appellate Jurisdiction Act of 1876 gave the crown power to create two lords of appeal in ordinary, and to summon them to sit and vote in the house of lords so long as they fulfilled their judicial functions; in 1887 this period was extended to the term of their lives.

limit by statute the crown's power of creation have always been defeated. The crown cannot, it is true, create more than a limited number of Irish peers; and it cannot create any Scottish or English peers (as distinct from peers of the United Kingdom) at all. Nor can it add to the number of bishops in parliament. But these restrictions on the peerage have little reference to the composition of the house of lords. No creation of Scottish or Irish peers would add to the number entitled, by the respective acts of union, to election as representative peers; and there are obvious limits to the erection of episcopal sees. More serious was the peerage bill, which was passed by the lords in 1719, and only thrown out by the commons on a division after a masterly speech by Walpole. By one of the ironies of history the Tories had, in 1712, provided the only precedent for the creation of peers with the express purpose of carrying a bill in the house of lords; and the Whigs in 1719 attempted to make its repetition impossible by providing that the crown should never create more than six new peers at a time. It has been thought that the success of the peerage bill would have prevented reform; it would certainly have promoted revolution, from which the country was only saved in 1832 by the power of the crown to create in the last resort sufficient peers to override the opposition of the house of lords. The crisis recurred in 1911 in the same form; and the same arguments and even the same phraseology were used as in 1832.

The problem of the house of lords has been complicated by the fact that peerage has from first to last been a social, rather than a political question, and its intrusion into parliament was as much an anomaly as the attempted intrusion of an estate of merchants in the fourteenth century. From the sixteenth century onwards no statesman gained politically by translation from the house of commons to the house of lords; and from Walpole's time a seat in the house of lords has been regarded as a positive drawback to political ambition. Front-rank politicians only accept promotion to it as a sacrifice in the interests of their party, as an easy stage on the road to retirement, or as social gilt for a vice-royalty or dominion governorship. It is for its social, rather than for its political attractions that a peerage is sought, and it is sought most keenly by those who feel the need of social status.   The few instances in which it has been used as a reward for distinguished service, as a means of providing for the conduct of the business of liberal governments in the house of lords, or as an expedient to secure a place in parliament for wisdom which shrinks from the turmoil of popular election, are only exceptions to the general rule.   The political responsibilities which once attached to peerage are commonly evaded; the work of the house of lords is done by a tenth of its members; and the abstention of the rest is as much a political portent as was the avoidance of parliament by the great majority of abbots during the later middle ages.   Whatever form the reconstruction of the house of lords may take, it would be well to guard against a political trust being treated as a means of social gratification.

Meanwhile the house lingers on under sentence of death. The preamble to the parliament act of 1911 held out a promise of reconstitution of which more urgent affairs have postponed the fulfilment; and the party truce following on the war precluded discussion of even the principles of reconstruction.   One or two points are, however, almost beyond the stage of debate.   It has been pretended that the principle of primogeniture could not logically be excluded from the house of lords and retained in the monarchy; and it is true that, if the political claims of the crown and the house of lords were identical, the principles which determine their position could not be divorced.   But the Stuarts were ejected from the throne because they clung so tenaciously to what they regarded as their hereditary rights, and the crown has remained hereditary only because it has abandoned its veto on legislation.   Had the house of lords practised a similar self-restraint, its hereditary basis would have been equally secure.

Such inactivity would have been the negation of what the

house of lords considers its proper function as a second chamber. The difficulty is that political powers, even those of a second chamber, cannot be divorced from responsibility, and hereditary right is incompatible with responsible rule. That is why James II fled to France in 1688 and the peers were compelled to pass the parliament act in 1911. No second chamber which claims a right of veto can nowadays be based on anything but popular election. But a second chamber may be very useful without merely obstructing the work of the first; and there is ample scope in modern legislation for revision, suggestion, and amendment without the right of rejection. Such work might well be done by a non-elective body of experts, whose advice would be welcomed so long as it was not given by way of dictation. Nor is it indispensable that the two chambers of parliament should both cover the same and entire field of activity. One of the old distinctions between council and parliament was that the council could regulate foreign relations, while parliament controlled domestic affairs.[1] The house of commons is little adapted for the work of diplomacy; and foreign policy is, as a matter of fact, settled by agreement between a few politicians on the two front benches. The committee of imperial defence is a more formal expression of the same political necessity; and there seems no adequate reason why these two functions should not be associated with a small and efficient second chamber. It is not essential to the maintenance of the party system that party lines should overrun the whole field of domestic, imperial, and foreign politics; and some discrimination is inevitable if the common sentiment, which pervades the British realms and transcends their party divisions, is ever to find an organized expression in a common imperial government. Congenital disqualifications have impaired the health of the second limb of the body politic, and it might well be made the subject of an imperial operation.

[1] *Lords' Journals*, i. 56.

CHAPTER XVI

THE COMMONS IN PARLIAMENT

In the middle ages the commons only appeared "in parliament" with the Speaker at their head, and save for his orations they were dumb. To-day when men talk of parliament, in nine cases out of ten they are thinking of the house of commons; and to say that the house of commons wields nine-tenths of the sovereignty of parliament is an under- rather than an over-statement of the truth. This predominance is almost entirely the result of growth during the last four centuries; for, in spite of the idealistic pictures drawn of the constitutional progress of the commons during the fourteenth century, their position at the end of the fifteenth was precarious, and there seemed no obvious reason why they should not fall into the same condition of impotence or abeyance as third estates in France and Germany, the Netherlands and Spain. Not only did parliaments grow less frequent,[1] but the number of members showed an alarming tendency to shrink, and whereas Edward I summoned 322 representatives of cities and boroughs, Henry VI in 1445 summoned but 198.

The deductions which have been drawn from the writs of summons and the returns thereto [2] may, however, be wrong in this respect, as they certainly are with regard to the size of a medieval house of commons. Just as there was many a slip between judgement and execution, so there was a considerable hiatus between a member's return in the sheriff's writ and his bodily presence in parliament; and an

---

[1] See above, p. 131.
[2] *Official Return of Members of Parliament* (1878), pt. i.

examination of other records suggests that the members elected were regarded merely as a panel from which a far smaller attendance was actually secured. These other records are the writs *de expensis*,[1] which members who did attend sued out to recover their wages and their expenses from their constituencies. They are careful documents, giving the exact number of days during which members served on their journeys and at Westminster, and the sums vary with the distance from London of the different constituencies. A comparison of the details they provide with the official return of elections reveals a startling discrepancy. The number of members " returned " to fourteenth-century parliaments was sometimes nearly three hundred; the number of those who actually attended, according to the writs *de expensis*, was seldom a hundred, and never more than a hundred and fifty. To these the shires contributed their regular seventy-four—two knights for each of the thirty-seven shires; but the cities and boroughs whose names occur during the fourteenth century vary in number from three to thirty-eight.

It might be thought that these writs, as entered on the close rolls, are defective, that many burgesses were too proud and independent to claim their wages, and that their numbers may have been far larger than these writs indicate. But there are few voids in the writs obtained by knights of the shire, and if these landed gentry were not too proud to claim their wages, the business-like burgesses can hardly be credited with contempt for such considerations. London and York, it is true, made their own arrangements for feeing their members without recourse to these writs, York paying its members double the usual rate;[2] and a similar arrangement may account for the absence of Bristol, Winchester,

---

[1] These are entered on the Close Rolls, which have now been calendared for nearly the whole of the fourteenth century.

[2] Davies, *York Records*, p. 15; on p. 138 the York members are described as " citizens and knights of the parliament for this honourable city and shire." On June 6, 1483, Richard III ordered four members to be returned for York, and four were elected, contrary, says Mr. Davies, to all precedent; but cf. Sir T. Smith, *De Republica*, ed. 1906, p. 42, line 6.

Salisbury, Southampton, Norwich, and Yarmouth from the writs *de expensis*. The Cinque Ports also do not figure in them; but although summoned from 1322 they apparently made no return until 1366, and a return to the writ is no proof of actual presence at Westminster. When we find Oxford, Canterbury, Newcastle, Hull, Cambridge, Northampton, Nottingham, Portsmouth, Lincoln, Leicester, Gloucester, Derby, Bedford, Rochester, Southwark, Warwick, Worcester, Exeter, Ipswich, Shrewsbury, Stafford, and Carlisle among the cities and boroughs to which writs *de expensis* were addressed, it is difficult to discover more than half a dozen constituencies to put with London, York, and the Cinque Ports, as making their own arrangements and thus adding largely to the numbers given in the writs. Save for these exceptions those writs may be taken as a fairly accurate indication of the size of the house of commons.

On their showing the fullest house, after 1335, in the fourteenth century was in the famous Good parliament of 1376. But even then only twenty-two cities and boroughs appear on the writs *de expensis;* and the addition of London, York, and half a dozen others would bring up the total attendance to 134 members, sixty from the cities and boroughs, seventy-four from the shires. Earlier in the century twenty-six boroughs have writs enrolled for the February parliament of 1328, thirty-eight for that of the following April, thirty-four for that of March 1334, and twenty-six for the parliament held at York in May 1335.[1] But on no later occasion during the century did the number exceed twenty. There were eighteen in the parliament of February 1371, sixteen in that of 1362, fifteen in 1351 and 1358, and thirteen in 1352 and 1357. In other years the figure descends to eleven, nine, eight, six, and five, six being the most frequent number. After the Good parliament there is some improvement in numbers and a great increase in regularity; and in the six succeeding parliaments[2] the boroughs receiving writs *de expensis* were never fewer than

[1] See Appendix II.
[2] 1377 (two parliaments), 1378, 1379, 1380 (two parliaments).

eleven nor more than thirteen. But these cities and
boroughs are not by any means the same. Thirty-eight
boroughs in all appear in the writs for one or more of these
six parliaments; but Oxford alone is represented in all.
No other borough appears in more than four of these
parliaments; nineteen of them send representatives only
to one, and ten only to two, though the attendance from
cities and boroughs, which made their own bargain with
members, was probably far more regular.

These figures explain some familiar facts and suggest some
novel reflections. They help to account for the predominance
of the knights of the shire in the medieval house of commons,
and for the fact that the house of commons—*domus communitatum*—really means house of the shires. When
seventy-four knights were regularly present, and the number
of burgesses varied from sixty to twenty-six, numbers and
regularity of attendance combined with social superiority
to give the knights control of the house. They also explain
how the house found room for its sessions in the chapter
house of Westminster abbey. But more important is the
light they throw on the position of medieval parliaments.
Reluctance to attend was not an isolated phenomenon, but
a general and successful attitude. Constituencies accepted
taxation to which their absence gave consent, rather than
send and pay members to protest; and only in imagination
can medieval parliaments be regarded as representative of
a nation. They were mere representative specimens, and
aloofness from national affairs, rather than participation in
them, was the characteristic of the age. We have thus to
alter the perspective in our views of constitutional development. The activity of parliaments from the middle of the
fourteenth to the middle of the fifteenth centuries was
transitory and unsubstantial; it was due to the weakness
of the monarchy and the factions of the peerage, and
was not based upon any broad national ambition for self-
government or sense of political responsibility. Political
consciousness was active among the landed gentry of the
fourteenth century, and the petitions of the Good parliament

express their ideas as Magna Carta does those of the greater barons. But middle-class politics could not develop until far more than a score of cities and boroughs would trouble to send their spokesmen year in and year out to Westminster; and the Lancastrian Fortescue who wrote at the end of the period has nothing to say of the constitutional importance of the house of commons.

It was a slow growth, and its birth must be connected with that general stirring of national impulse in English bones of which Wycliffe, Langland, and Chaucer were some of the exponents. A desire for self-expression in English language and literature was followed by a desire for self-expression in English politics; and the generation which saw the founding of schools like Winchester and Eton, and a dozen colleges at Oxford and Cambridge, also witnessed the beginnings of a political efflorescence.[1] It was not a renaissance, for there is no evidence that the lower classes in England had ever desired expression before; their legal designation was " cattle," and it is probable that that was a truer description than our romanticists would have us believe. It is assumed rather than proved that the mass of these " chattels " were baptized in the early middle ages or regarded as having souls of their own. The peasants' revolt of 1381 is their first expression in politics, and it did not stand alone. The Lancastrian statutes limiting the country franchise to forty-shilling freeholders are only intelligible on the assumption that villeins had begun to undertake an attendance at county courts which their betters had thought a burden. Municipal and even national records were beginning to be kept in a language they understood, and their economic emancipation was followed by their intrusion into politics.

Only, of course, a minority of villeins rose to reinforce the freeholders and stimulate the middle class; but it is at one of the lowest ebbs in English politics, the middle of Henry VI's reign, that we can trace the beginning of the flow of popular interest in politics. The writs of summons to parliaments issued by Edward I had been

[1] See above, p. 157.

admonitions from above; and the inertia of the mass to which they were addressed caused a steady decline in their number. But about 1445 the tide begins to turn. Hitherto the desire had been to escape the burden of representation, but now new boroughs begin to send members to parliament, and within a generation the number of burgesses returned rose from 198 to 224. The number of new boroughs created in Wiltshire suggests a connexion with the growth of clothing towns in that county. More marked was the growth in actual attendance; and within a century the miserable two or three score of borough members who had feebly supported the knights of the shire had swollen to some two hundred or more.[1] In 1533 a borough member was for the first time elected Speaker of the house of commons,[2] and from the reign of Henry VIII there is no discernible distinction in dignity or influence between a knight of the shire and a borough member. Thomas Cromwell sat for Taunton and William Cecil for Stamford, though doubtless the eminence of these borough representatives was due to the weakness of feudal, and strength of monarchical, influence in the boroughs as well as to the growing political weight of the middle classes.

The house of commons had become a place of importance. In 1455 the Duchess of Norfolk had written of the need of securing the election of members who belonged to her husband and were his " menial servants."[3] But it was Henry VIII who thrust the house of commons into political prominence. Before 1529 there is hardly a reference to its proceedings in the dispatches of any foreign diplomatist or

---

[1] The figures given by contemporary writers are always grossly exaggerated. In 1549 the privy council itself speaks of nearly four hundred members being present in the house of commons (*Acts of Privy Council*, ii. 260); but the recorded divisions in the house seldom reach three hundred votes in the sixteenth century. On 19 April, 1554, however, 321 members took part in a division, and in 1555 the bill to restore firstfruits and tenths was carried by 193 to 126 votes; in 1593 the commons agreed with Bacon's views on the financial relations between the two houses by 217 to 128 votes, and this would appear to have been the biggest division in Tudor times.

[2] Humphrey Wingfield, M.P. for Yarmouth. T. Williams, Speaker in 1562–3, was M.P. for Exeter.

[3] *Paston Letters*, i. 337.

Y

observer; from that time onwards the correspondence of French, Venetian, and Spanish ambassadors becomes one of the main sources of parliamentary history, and papal nuncios and imperial envoys vie with one another in trying to influence its decisions. With nearly half the peers, and at least four-fifths of the clergy against him, Henry had need of the house of commons, and he cultivated it with sedulous care. The commons had always been the main source of petitions to the crown, and it was an obvious tactical advantage if Henry's desires could come before the lords of the council in parliament in the guise of petitions or bills from the commons. It would appear from Lord Darcy's complaint in 1536 [1] that the lords had developed the practice of securing from the masters in chancery copies of bills and petitions before they were read in the commons, and even of pronouncing on their admissibility. This practice was now discouraged, and henceforth Tudor and Stuart sovereigns used the Speaker, and not the lords of the council in parliament, as the medium for expressing their views on the propriety of bills which members sought to introduce. It was to the interest of the crown to shift the balance of legislative power from the lords to the commons; and in 1536 the Speaker is first recorded to have asked for access on behalf of himself and of his colleagues to the king in person. [2]

The result was an enormous increase in the prestige of the lower house. Its domestic proceedings had never appeared on the rolls of parliaments, but in or soon after 1547 [3] it began to keep *Journals* of its own. The eldest sons of peers thought it becoming to seek election; [4] magnates

---

[1] *Letters and Papers of Henry VIII*, xii. pt. i. 410; Dodds, *The Pilgrimage of Grace*, 1915, i. 360.

[2] *Lords' Journals*, i. 86, 167; Elsynge, p. 176.

[3] The extant *Journals* begin with 1547, but probably the record was not compiled until later in Edward VI's reign.

[4] Two of the earliest instances were Francis Russell, eldest son of the first Earl of Bedford, who was M.P. for Buckinghamshire 1544–52 (*Commons' Journals*, i. 15), and Francis, eldest son of the second earl, who was M.P. for Northumberland in 1572. Cf. Sir R. Bagnal's request for a seat to the Earl of Rutland on the ground that he wanted "for his learning's sake to be made a parliament man" (*Rutland MSS.*, i. 207).

bought up boroughs to provide themselves or their friends with seats, and were besieged with applications for their influence. Candidates began to pay, instead of being paid for election.[1] Boroughs which had let their representation fall into abeyance sought for its restoration, and those which had never had writs began to seek them.[2] Lawyers and other aspiring politicians went about looking for seats, and the obligation of residence was ignored in spite of the rejection by the house of commons of a bill to relax it in 1571.[3] Parliament was providing a career, and in Elizabeth's reign we hear for the first time of some one being a " great parliament man "[4] who was not a member of the privy council. A score of members in Elizabeth's reign made names for themselves throughout England by what they said and did in the house of commons.

The growth of the house of commons was reflected in the expansion of its numbers, the increase of popular interest in elections and in the proceedings of the house, and in the development of its privileges and powers. Wales, Cheshire, Berwick, and Calais were brought within the sphere of parliamentary representation, and the creation of new boroughs was slightly, if at all, due to the crown's desire to pack the house. Under Henry VII and Henry VIII forty-five new members were added, under Edward VI thirty, under Mary twenty-seven, and under Elizabeth fifty-

[1] The first known case of bribing electors occurred in 1571, when Thomas Long, " being a very simple man," gave the mayor and another citizen of Westbury £4 to secure his election (Commons' Journals, i. 88; D'Ewes, p. 182). Returns for this parliament are among the De Tabley MSS. The mayor and his colleague in corruption were condemned to restore the £4 to Long and pay £20 to the Queen. Long himself was simultaneously put in the pillory, not for this affair, but for reporting the Queen's death (Hooker's " Journal of the House of Commons " in Trans. Devon. Assoc., xi. 483). In the same session the house was troubled by reports of the bribery of its members (ibid., p. 488; Commons' Journals, i. 93). For an attempt to bribe a member in Edward IV's reign see Trans. Devon. Assoc., xlvi. 481.

[2] State Papers, Dom. Eliz., xxvii. 23–4; Commons' Journals, i. 83; D'Ewes, pp. 156–7, 159. It was owing to the learning and activity of William Hakewill (see D.N.B.) that several boroughs recovered their representation.

[3] Commons' Journals, i. 84–5; D'Ewes, pp. 160, 168–71; the debate as reported in D'Ewes is of exceptional interest.

[4] Rutland MSS., i. 130.

nine. From 297 members at the accession of Henry VIII the house had grown to 458 by the death of Elizabeth.[1] There is evidence, too, that the number of electors who participated in the choice of their members largely increased, though this is more marked in the county than in the borough elections. In the boroughs the franchise was generally at the beginning of the Tudor period, and it remained to the end, confined to members of the borough council;[2] and it was not until the days of the Long parliament that we find instances, like that of Reading, where the number of electors leapt up from a dozen to over a thousand.[3] At the county elections there were large and tumultuous gatherings,[4] sometimes ending in riots, in proceedings before the privy council, and in disputes between chancery and the commons over the decision of election petitions.[5]

These contests were, perhaps, as much the embers of local faction as the dawn of national politics; and although in Henry VIII's reign members were told to discuss with their constituents what they had seen and heard at Westminster, any instructions given by constituencies to their representatives seem to have been of purely local interest.[6] The idea of deciding questions of national policy by reference to the electors can hardly be traced before 1640; and the parliamentary debates on monopolies at the end of

---

[1] See above, pp. 162-3.

[2] See my *Reign of Henry VII*, ii. 181-9; Davis, *York Records*, p. 138; W. J. Harte in *Trans. Devon. Assoc.*, xliv. 206, xlv. 409-10.

[3] *Reading MSS.*, Hist. MSS. Comm., 11th Rep. App., vii. 187, 189, 192-4; cf. Guilding, *Reading Records*, iii. 488-9, 507, iv. 167-8, 171-2, 298-9.

[4] *Letters and Papers*, x. 1063; Townshend, *Collections*, pp. 22, 286, 295, 298-9, 329-30. A realistic account of "the tumult and tempest" of a poll in 1623 is given in the *Stiffkey Papers* (Camden Soc.), p. 41, where a candidate "sounded his troupes againe . . . and caused all his forces to charge," and secured election by very literally "routing" his opponents.

[5] See the Maidstone and Norfolk election disputes, fully reported in D'Ewes, pp. 393-7.

[6] *Letters and Papers*, v. 171. An excellent example of a sixteenth-century "mandate" from a constituency to its members is given by Prof. W. J. Harte in *Trans. Devon. Assoc.*, xliv. 213: "A remembrance of certeyn articles for Mr. Thomas Williams and Mr. Geffray Tothill, burgesses for the Citie [of Exeter] at the parlyament in January, 1562." Williams was elected Speaker in that parliament, and was given £20 by the corporation for his services "in preferring the suits and business of the City" (*ibid.*, xlv. 409).

Elizabeth's reign were apparently the earliest occasion on which proceedings in the house of commons evoked any popular agitation. Cecil then heard cries in the street : "God prosper those that further the overthrow of these monopolies; God send the prerogative touch not our liberty"; and he remarked in the house that some "would be glad that all sovereignty were converted into popularity." It is ever the economic problem that drives democracy to think of politics, and even then the thought is mainly a matter of feeling; but it was with a novel sensation of horror that Cecil exclaimed in the house in 1601, "Why, parliament-matters are ordinarily talked of in the streets." [1]

Hitherto the commons in parliament had had to fight their constitutional battles without much support from outside, and the popular naval heroes of Elizabeth's time were, when they sat in parliament, always on the side of the royal prerogative.[2] But the corporate feeling which members developed during the long sessions of the Reformation and other sixteenth-century parliaments gave them a novel confidence. The medieval sessions of two or three weeks had given little opportunity to members, who for the most part never attended another parliament, to know one another and develop a common sense. But the seven years' parliament of 1529–36, with each of its sessions extending over months, produced a body of common experience, the effect of which was never lost ; and the *Journals*, commencing in 1547, began to record its results and to provide a firm hold of precedents which gave solidity to the claims of the house. It assumed, step by step, control of itself and its members; and privileges, which had been referred in the fifteenth century to the lords and the judges to determine, were now asserted on its own authority.[3] The right of the Speaker and of the house to license the absence of members was recognized by

---

[1] Townshend, p. 251; D'Ewes, p. 653.
[2] *E. g.* Sir Humphrey Gilbert, Sir Richard Grenville, Drake, and Raleigh.
[3] In 1553 it was a committee of the house which decided that Alexander Nowell, having a seat in convocation, could not have one in the commons. For the growth of capacity and outlook in the commons cf. the debate on Goodwin's case in 1604, *Commons' Journals*, i. 159–60, 939–40.

statute in 1515.[1] In 1553 the house insisted on inspecting the charter to Maidstone, to see if it justified the novel appearance of burgesses from that town; pending its decision they were ordered to absent themselves, and Maidstone had to wait until 1563 to secure its representation.[2] In 1581 the house succeeded in establishing its control of the issue of writs for bye-elections;[3] and it began to compete with the crown's powers of creation by initiating bills to increase parliamentary representation.[4] Liberty of speech, which had been claimed for the Speaker when he appeared at the head of his colleagues in the parliament chamber, was now[5] claimed for the individual member in the house of commons. The commons, who had been a mere part of the high court of parliament, now claimed to be an independent court of record themselves,[6] with complete jurisdiction over their own members, their own proceedings, and their own organization. From being petitioners themselves, they assumed the position of arbiters of the petitions of others.

This is one of the obscure but important aspects of the development of the house of commons; and both its obscurity and its importance require some recapitulation in an effort to elucidate the growth of the legislative functions of the house. Difficulty arises not merely from the absence of *Commons' Journals* before 1547, but from the impossibility of tracing definite stages in the growth of customs, conventions, and institutions which were not made and did not proceed by definite steps. We have

---

[1] 7 Hen. VIII, c. 16.
[2] *Commons' Journals*, i. 25, 63; *Official Return of Members of Parliament*, i. 379–404.
[3] D'Ewes, pp. 281–3, 308.
[4] On January 18, 1563, a bill was introduced into the commons "for levying fines in the County Palatine of Durham, and to have two knights from thence into the parliament"; but it reached the statute-book shorn, at some unknown stage, of the latter provision.
[5] The first recorded claim is that made by Speaker Moyle in 1542 (*Lords' Journals*, i. 167; Elsynge, p. 176).
[6] "This is a court of record. . . . We have a clerk and a register. . . . It is now come to this question, whether the chancery or parliament ought to have authority" (*Commons' Journals*, i. 159–60). As early as 1549 the clerk of the house of commons referred to it as "this court" (*ib.* i. 14).

also to disabuse our minds of preconceptions due to an inevitable tendency to generalize from our evidence in order to simplify our conclusions. The evidence itself is often accessible only in a form which fosters false assimilation; and the uniformity of the printed " Rolls of Parliaments " obscures the diversity of their contents. Legislation may arise from many different sources and take many different forms. Nearly all of it in Edward I's reign is legislation by the crown either on its own motion or on petition from some other body or individual; but no one except the villeins is precluded from access to the freest place in England, and freemen may petition as individuals or as any kind of class or group. The crown has just as much authority to grant redress to one group without consulting the others as it has to do justice to one individual without the leave of his fellows; it is equally entitled to legislate without any petition at all. Edward I, however, developed the habit of doing these things in parliament, and the growth of the house of commons depended largely on its gradual establishment of a monopoly of access to the crown and of control over the crown's responses.

The house could not begin the process until it had acquired solidarity and a claim to be the commonalty of the realm. But this claim was secured during the fourteenth century, and the commons proceeded tentatively to assert an influence, firstly over all petitions presented in parliament, and then over the initiative of the crown. They managed to exclude the merchants as a separate estate from parliament, thus debarring their direct access to the crown in parliament. Next they successfully demurred to the crown legislating on a clerical petition in parliament without their concurrence; and in 1420 they petitioned against the validity of bills endorsed *per auctoritatem parliamenti* without their assent or request.[1] Thus we find clerical petitions in parliament reduced in 1429 to the vanishing point of a single petition that the clergy in convocation may enjoy the like privileges as the laity in parliament,[2] and the clergy

---

[1] *Rot. Parl.*, iv. 127.   [2] *Ibid.*, iv. 347.

themselves to relying on the commons to back and present their petitions in parliament.[1] Individuals, however high and mighty, condescend to the same assistance—an archbishop of Canterbury, dukes, princes, queens, and even kings accept the common fate with royal compensations; and *ex mandato regis* [2] bills of resumption and attainder and provisions for the royal household and royal family assume the guise of petitions of the commons.

No doubt these dignities stooped to conquer, and their submission was somewhat feigned. It was pure assumption on the commons' part to assert a veto on royal legislation, and there was nothing in their writs or in the law to justify the claim. The petition of 1420 was refused, and *per auctoritatem parliamenti* long continued to appear on orders taken in parliament to which the commons had not agreed.[3] The clergy, too, continued to legislate in convocation, and in 1444 " a certain act was made in parliament by the king with the advice and assent of the lords spiritual and temporal " without any reference to the commons.[4] There was no monopoly for the commons yet, but on the other hand, they had their independence of other estates, and no consent save that of the king was needed to give effect to their petitions and their grants. The *Modus* declares that king and commons are sufficient for a parliament, and in 1480 counsel held that a grant by the commons was valid without the consent of the lords.[5] Nor, when we first get records of the various readings of bills and petitions by the lords, do we find that the *communes petitiones* are subject to that process

---

[1] *Rot. Parl.*, iv. 393.

[2] Cf. *Ibid.*, v. 8 *et passim*.

[3] The specific reference by parliament of business, with which it had not had time to deal, to the determination of the council (e. g. *Rot. Parl.*, iv. 334, 506) justified the application of the phrase to such measures taken when parliament was not sitting. A similar use or abuse of the authority of convocation in connection with the Forty-Two Articles has been much criticized without reference to precedents (cf. Gairdner, *Lollardy and the Reformation*, iii. 374–9).

[4] *Rot Parl.*, v. 68; cf. *ibid.*, vi. 49, for a similar instance.

[5] *Year Book*, ed. Maynard, 21 Edward IV, p. 48; Hallam, *Middle Ages*, iii. 108 *n*. See above, p. 144, and Appendix III, note (*n*).

of examination; only the royal assent is expressed, and that is apparently enough.[1]

There are thus at least half a dozen different kinds of parliamentary legislation in the middle ages, and confusion results from treating them all as one and attempting to compress their history into a single line of development. There was legislation by the crown in parliament (i) on its own motion; (ii) on petition of the council; (iii) on petition of the clergy; (iv) on petition by the commons; and the fourth category itself falls into three divisions: (*a*) *communes petitiones* ; (*b*) petitions of individuals adopted *ex parte* by the commons, and (*c*) financial grants. But side by side with the amalgamation of estates there went a simplification of legislative practice. The crown ceased in time to legislate in parliament on its own motion, preferring the forms of popular action; the petitions of the council became either government bills or bills introduced by the house of lords; and clerical petitions disappeared into convocation. There were left the commons' bills, of which the *communes petitiones* became public, and the *ex parte petitiones* private, acts, while the grants of money were given a special legislative form.

Singularly enough it is in connexion with the private *ex parte* petitions that we get the earliest evidence of the now familiar practice of three readings. The form of acts into which the *communes petitiones* were cast apparently discouraged their amendment in the parliament chamber, and there is nothing about three readings of them in the " Rolls "; in the absence of *Commons' Journals* we know nothing of the practice in that house, where the custom may well have been originated. We know little more of the rules adopted by the house in debating finance, though Hall's amusing story of the grants in 1523 shows that the " commons " and knights of the shire retained separate action with regard to their respective tenths and fifteenths, goods and lands.[2] These grants emerged from the house during

---

[1] These *communes petitiones* are kept separate from other petitions on the Rolls until Henry VII's reign.   [2] *Chronicle*, ed. 1809, p. 657.

the fifteenth century in the form of an indenture which was not always observed; and in 1426 the crown and the lords, after mature consideration of the judges in parliament, determined to ignore the conditions imposed by the commons on the grant of a subsidy in the previous parliament.[1]

As a rule, however, supply was accepted as it came from the house of commons, and details of procedure in the lords' house are first recorded in connexion with its more appropriate judicial business arising upon petitions presented by individuals with or without the endorsement of the commons. From the beginning of Henry V's reign, if not earlier, the clerk notes of such bills or petitions that they have been *lectæ, auditæ, et intellectæ coram domino nostro rege ac dominis spiritualibus et temporalibus in prædicto parliamento existentibus.*[2] In 1492 we first hear of their having been read more than once, *sæpe, sæpius,* or *persæpe,* and in 1495 we light upon readings *ter* and *trina vice.*[3] Three readings took some time to become the stereotyped procedure; in 1516 we have reference to a seventh and an eighth reading in the *Lords' Journals,* while the dwindling " Rolls " of Henry VIII's reign drop their mention of three readings and revert to the less specific record of a century before.[4] More important is the fact that these various readings spread to bills of all sorts, except such as were of grace and, being recommended by the crown, needed only one. The contagion of uniformity developed; and the commons, who in earlier days had been content with a single reading, a mere verbal acceptance, or even a tacit acquiescence, began to give three readings to bills which both the crown and the lords now condescended to submit for their approval. The process of assimilation reduced to a single rule of three readings in either house the various methods of medieval parliamentary legislation; but the crown retained its right of legislating out of parliament by

[1] *Rot. Parl.,* iv. 275–6, 301 ; cf. above, p. 288. [2] *Ibid.,* iv. 18 *et passim.*
[3] *Ibid.,* vi. 451–2, 460, 492–3, 512 : *denuo recitatis et intellectis* occurs in 1485 (*ibid.,* vi. 275).
[4] *Lords' Journals,* i. 55–6.

proclamations and orders in council, and the church her right of legislating in convocation, without the crown's participation until 1532, and with it afterwards.

The control of the house of commons, however, over parliamentary petitions steadily increased, and in Henry VII's reign an act was repealed on the petition of the commons on the ground that it had been passed at the suit of a private person in the absence of the members for Lancashire, to which it referred.[1] The direct access accorded to chancery and the council had not debarred, though it had diverted, petitioners from the commons; and, while poorer litigants went as a rule to other courts, powerful suitors resorted more and more to parliament. The commons, by adopting private petitions and presenting them as their own *ex parte* the petitioner,[2] succeeded by steps which have not been traced in establishing the presumption that the crown could not legislate on private petitions in parliament without the commons' consent. The principle was recognized by Henry VII when he sought an act of parliament authorizing him to annul certain attainders in 1504, and this precedent was followed in the early years of Henry VIII; but it was not fully established until the Stuart claims to a dispensing power were repudiated at the Revolution. The authority of the commons over private petitions had been recognized, and perhaps enhanced by a practice, which begins early in the fifteenth century and develops rapidly during its course, of petitioners addressing their petitions to the commons instead of to parliament, the crown, council, or chancery;[3] for when petitions were addressed to the commons they clearly had the option of endorsing them or not.

The rapid development of the prestige of the house of

[1] *Rot. Parl.*, vi. 456–7.

[2] There are innumerable instances of this practice in Henry VII's reign.

[3] Even peers addressed petitions to the commons; cf. the earl of Wiltshire's petition in 1472 " to the full wise and discreet commons of this present parliament" (*Rot. Parl.*, vi. 62). There is abundant evidence from the sixteenth century to justify Prof. McIlwain's doubts about the permanence of the commons' renunciation in Henry IV's reign of any share in judicial power (*High Court of Parliament*, p. 203). In the *Commons' Journals*, i. 45, there is a record of the hearing of evidence, presence of the accused, and confession of the criminal in a murder case (s).

commons during the sixteenth century led to the abandonment by the crown of the coercive measures it had not very
successfully employed to secure attendance, though as late
as Mary's reign members who had gone home without leave
were prosecuted in the queen's bench.[1]   Early in Henry
VIII's reign the clerk of the lower house had been enjoined
by statute to keep a register of the names and attendance of
members of the house ; [2] and from this register may have
come the idea of instituting journals.   But if it was kept,
all trace of it has disappeared, and the *Journals* of the
commons, unlike those of the house of lords, have never
included lists of the names of those present.   In Elizabeth's
reign the house took control of its own attendance, and
frequent resolutions were passed for calling of the roll by
the clerk; but apparently no penalties were inflicted for
absence, and it was left to the constituencies, and afterwards
to the party organization, to control the attendance of
members.   But while the scanty presence of members in
medieval parliaments and the measures adopted to ensure
attendance indicate that the wages paid had become an
inadequate consideration, the abeyance of those measures,
and the full attendance after 1529, show that the political
importance of the house had become a sufficient incentive.
Assuredly during the Tudor period the average presence
in the house was at least double what it had been in the
fourteenth and fifteenth centuries.

Possibly this increase suggested its removal from the
chapter house to St. Stephen's chapel, an important step
in the consolidation of parliament.   We are so accustomed
to associate parliament with magnificent buildings at Westminster, and to think of houses built of brick or stone, that
it requires a mental effort to realize that the house of
commons, like the house of Lancaster or the house of
York, was made of men, and might be anywhere.   Parliament sat in various towns during the middle ages, and its
paraphernalia was easily mobilized.   A few woolsacks and

[1] Coke, *Institutes*, iv. 17; Strype, *Eccl. Mem.*, III. i. 262–4.
[2] 7 Henry VIII, c. 16.

wooden benches, a cloth of estate and a chair for the king, and a wagon-load or so of papers, were all that was required; and even the exchequer was moved about from London to York and elsewhere. But as records grew in bulk and the machinery of government increased in complexity, the mobility of parliament diminished, and it tended to settle at Westminster and there to create a habitation of its own. The king, of course, summoned it to his hall and housed it in his palace, but in time parliament almost expelled the king from his court, and few people think, as they gaze at the houses of parliament, they are contemplating the palace of a king.

The commons, however, had only enjoyed the king's hospitality when they appeared on his business *in pleno parliamento*. Their private confabulations were their own concern, and they found a room outside the palace in the refectory and then in the chapter house of the abbey.[1] There they continued, apparently,[2] to meet till the reign of Edward VI, when they came across to St. Stephen's chapel, within the precincts of the palace. It is singular that this change should have passed almost unnoticed by contemporaries, and should have excited no comment from antiquaries like Stow and Camden. St. Stephen's had been a collegiate church, whose canons gave their name to Canon Row, sometimes called St. Stephen's Alley. It fell to the king by the second chantries act of 1547, and on 22 July, 1550, it was granted to Sir Ralph Vane, with the exception of the upper part above the vault of the chapel which had been assigned *pro domo parliamenti et pro parliamentis nostris ibidem tenendis*.[3] On his attainder it was on 29 April, 1552, given in fee simple to Sir John Gates, the vice-chamberlain, who in his turn was

---

[1] *Rot. Parl.*, ii. 237.

[2] There were exceptions; in 1523, for instance, parliament met at Blackfriars, whither it was also summoned on 3 November, 1529, but adjourned on the 4th to Westminster; and Mary thought of holding parliament at Oxford in 1554.

[3] *Patent Roll* 834 m. 22, 846 m. 28 (per Mr. R. H. Brodie and Miss Winifred Jay); *Literary Remains of Edward VI* (Roxburghe Club), p. 431. The usual story that Henry VIII made this grant is inconsistent with the references to St. Stephen's in the last volume of the *Letters and Papers*.

executed on 22 August, 1553, for his share in Northumberland's conspiracy. Stow remarks [1] that the chapel was thenceforward used as "a parliament house"; but even so, it does not appear to have afforded accommodation for committees, which generally met at the inns of court.[2]

Ostensibly the reunion of the two houses under one roof was a sign of concentration; but the commons came back on very different terms from those on which they had originally departed from the open parliament chamber to seek seclusion in the cloisters of the abbey for their domestic discussions, and the difference did not tend to the unity of parliament. They had gone forth in the middle ages merely as a group anxious for private debate, but carrying with them little of the glamour and authority of the high court of parliament which they left behind them in the seat of power. They came back as one of two houses, claiming an equal share in the dual control of parliament. Henceforth, whatever the commons said or did was said and done in parliament; one roof covered both commons and lords, and one constitutional halo surrounded their actions. The commons returned to parliament to

[1] Stow's *Survey*, ed. Kingsford, ii. 377–9. The reference (*Acts of Privy Council*, 1550–2, p. 172) to an account, dated 2 Dec., 1549, for "works about the parliament house" may concern the alterations to St. Stephen's chapel; for "the parliament house" was coming to be used instead of "the parliament chamber," and to include both houses of parliament (cf. *ibid.* 1547–50, p. 248, 1552–4, p. 20; *Exeter Records*, Hist. MSS. Comm. 1916, p. 51). Foxe, in his recension of his authorities, frequently changes parliament chamber into parliament house. "Domus" is often used of the parliament chamber in the *Lords' Journals* for Henry VIII's reign, and less frequently "domus superior" for it, and "domus inferior" for the commons (*Lords' Journals*, i. 5, 7, 15, 21, 45). In 1536 Cromwell writes of the "nether and upper houses" (Merriman, *Cromwell*, ii. 47). In 1515 (*Lords' Journals*, i. 46) it is suggested that indentures for knights of the shire be brought "into the parliament house" as usual; and in later days each house claimed that this meant its own. In the grant to Vane the house of lords is called "the lords' parliament house," and the house of commons the *domus parliamenti*.

[2] Apparently there was one "committee-chamber of the house" (D'Ewes, p. 253), but the following are some of the places in which committees met during Elizabeth's reign: the Star Chamber, Treasury Chamber, Exchequer Chamber, Inner Temple Hall, Temple Church, Parlour of the Middle Temple, New Hall in the Temple, Lincoln's Inn Hall, Serjeants' Inn, Savoy, Guildhall, Rolls Chapel, Marshalsea, and Court House at Southwark (D'Ewes, pp. 221, 249, 250, 253, 298–9, 300, 363).

dispute its control with the lords, and eventually to oust them from authority. Some, as Sir Robert Cecil remarked in 1601, would convert all sovereignty into popularity; and popularity made less allowance for the peers than it did for the crown.

Cecil's phrase is a significant omen for the constitutional history of the century, in the opening year of which it was uttered. It is also a useful reminder of the strides which the commons had made in the sixteenth century. But for that preparation under the Tudors there could have been no successful struggles under the Stuarts. No parliament in the middle ages had been able to wage a civil war or depose a king; its function had merely been to confirm the work of rival factions and provide titles for successful usurpers, to recognize the *fait accompli*, but not to accomplish it.[1] There had been baronial cliques, but never a parliamentary party, because parliament had possessed no *esprit de corps* and no self-consistency; it was a mere conference in which things were done by kings or by baronial factions. Under the Tudors it became an entity and an authority, active and independent, claiming to speak for a nation in tones to which kings must give ear. The petitions of grace had ended, and petitions of right assumed a political guise.

The commons had, they told James I in his first parliamentary session, yielded much to Elizabeth on account of her age and sex;[2] yet they had spoken in terms of insistence about her marriage, the succession, the execution of Norfolk and Mary Stuart which no medieval parliament would have adopted. It is an obvious criticism of the commons under Edward III and the Lancastrians that they objected to the measures of the crown, but had no policy themselves. They did not, indeed, think policy was their business, and they

---

[1] Little importance can be attached to parliamentary statutes entailing the crown upon successful claimants like Edward IV and Henry VII; for parliament had no option in the matter. Unless the king *de facto* was also king *de jure*, his writs were null and void, and the assembly summoned thereby was no parliament and could make no statutes. Henry IV had taken the precaution of compelling Richard II to issue the writs for the parliament which accepted his abdication.

[2] Gardiner, *Hist. of England*, i. 182.

invariably pleaded incapacity when asked for advice on matters of state. But their tone was different under Elizabeth; they had ideas of religious policy, of economic policy, and of foreign policy which they had not derived from authority and wanted to force on the crown. Even under Henry VIII the commons could be stubborn enough when they liked; attacks on the government were often made by individual members, and the house as a whole refused in 1534 to make spoken words treason, and rejected or amended various bills promoted by the government.[1] The parliament of 1545 has generally been taken as the highwater-mark of Henry's autocratic power; and eminent historians have depicted in sombre hues the servility of the commons.[2] A letter from Secretary Petre, written on the last day of the session,[3] puts its history in a truer and very different light : " the book [*i. e.* bill] of the colleges," he writes, " escaped narrowly, and was driven over to the last hour, and yet then passed only by division of the house. . . . The bill of books, albeit it was at the beginning earnestly set forward, is finally dashed in the common house, as are divers others." More-over, several of those which passed both houses were so distasteful to the king that he vetoed them; and the picture of the king " having his own way in everything " is imaginary. Parliaments and people cannot change their character in a moment; and if Tudor parliaments had been servile, Stuart parliaments would not have achieved their independence.

The Stuarts, however, expected greater subservience from their parliaments than the Tudors had looked for; and their doctrinaire royalism hastened a struggle which could only have been avoided by submission on the part of king

---

[1] *Letters and Papers*, vii. 51 ; *Lords' Journals*, i. 71, 73, 80, 89; Pollard, *Henry VIII*, pp. 288–93.

[2] Cf. Stubbs, *Lectures on Medieval and Modern History*, 1887, pp. 288–9 : " Clearly the independent spirit has nearly evaporated. The ecclesiastical bills pass without a protest. . . . The *Journals* [there are none for the commons] record no opposition or protest; the king has his own way in everything "; and the *Political History*, v. 470, speaks of the king " securing by his repeated presence at the debates a tranquil passage for both measures " (the subsidy act and the chantries or colleges act).

[3] *Letters and Papers*, XX. ii. 1030–1.

or parliament. The commons had developed a will of their own, and the only question was how far that will should encroach. They were firm in their protestantism and in their determination to control supplies; their protestantism provoked an ambition to dictate a protestant domestic and foreign policy, and their determination to control supplies led them to attack the instruments by which the crown sought to enforce non-parliamentary taxation. They were thus brought into collision with the whole administration of the crown, and civil war could alone decide whether king or parliament should dispose of the national forces. The commons appeared to triumph over the lords as well as over the crown in 1649; but the permanent lesson of the struggle was that civil war leads to military dictation, and the common subjection of crown and parliament to the army produced a national resolution to avoid the cure of militarism for the future. James II's attempt to support his government by military force deprived him of any party willing to fight; and without force at its command the crown was at the mercy of parliament.

The Revolution of 1688 did not, however, establish responsible government in England in the sense we attach to the phrase. For in that sense responsible government involves two things : firstly, the responsibility of the executive to the legislature, and secondly, the responsibility of the legislature to the people. The second is the more important of the two, for the American constitution has shown that it is possible to secure popular self-government without making the executive responsible to the legislature. But no popular self-government is possible unless the legislature is responsible to the community; and it was in this respect that the Revolution was defective. The mere exsitence of the house of lords, and its claim to co-ordinate powers with the elected house of commons, hampered the operation of this responsibility. But more important than the irresponsibility of the house of lords in the eighteenth century was the irresponsibility of the house of commons. The commons had in the seventeenth century claimed as autocratic a power

z

as the Stuarts. They asserted for their resolutions the force of law;[1] and by their own authority they had in 1649 abolished two out of the three branches of the legislature. They prolonged their own existence, and excluded their opponents, not merely from the house of commons, but from the rank of electors. It was their " horrid " arbitrariness, as Cromwell called it, which opened the way for the more horrid arbitrariness of military despotism.

The exclusive spirit was still strong in both houses of parliament during the eighteenth century. The reporting of debates and the publication of division lists were denounced as giving colour to the idea that members were responsible to some authority outside the walls of parliament. Expressions of opinion unfavourable to the house of commons, such as the Kentish petition, were voted scandalous, and the house attempted to punish the petitioners as though they had committed a crime. It claimed by resolution to disfranchise electors; it decided disputed elections by party votes in the house; and even went so far as to unseat members who had been duly elected and co-opt candidates who had been duly defeated.[2] Its criterion was its own privilege, and it had little respect for any one else's liberty.

The Revolution had transferred power from the crown to parliament, but not from parliament to the people. The merest fraction possessed votes,[3] and the voters themselves

[1] Prothero, *Select Documents*, 1898, p. 290; Gardiner, *Documents*, 1889, pp. 26–7. In the former, the " Apology " of 1604, the commons assert that the power of parliament is " above the law," and in the latter document Charles I complains that some of them " have not doubted to maintain that the resolutions of that house must bind the judges," and that " their drift was to . . . erect an universal overswaying power to themselves."

[2] On April 13, 1769, the house declared Colonel Luttrell, who had been twice defeated by John Wilkes, to have been duly elected, and falsified the return accordingly.

[3] An important but less familiar struggle was waged in some constituencies over the franchise. Thus, at Reading, on October 22, 1705, the corporation resolved that " for the time to come the mayor, aldermen, and burgesses in their common counsell, in case of members to serve in parliament for this borough, doe first determine and resolve amongst themselves whoe shall be deemed fitt representatives for that purpose "; but on March 4, 1761, it issued a declaration that it never intended to deprive the inhabitants paying scot and lot of their votes at parliamentary elections (*Hist. MSS. Comm.*, 11th Rep., vii. 204, 206).

little power. Elections simply meant a choice of masters, and not a decision of policy. Only twice in the eighteenth century was a general election held to settle a public question, once in 1701 when William III appealed to the country against a Tory house of commons, and secondly in 1784, when the younger Pitt appealed to it against Whig domination. For the rest ministers were changed, policies adopted and discarded, war declared and peace made, without the least reference to the electors. Each election was a local and personal contest, and not a political conflict of principles. A member did what he liked in parliament, subject to the whim of the owner of the borough for which he sat, and the same territorial magnates decided the contests in the shires. The commons in parliament enjoyed the fruits of a victory they had won as representatives of the people, but they did not wish to share them.

George III interrupted this comfortable state of affairs, and turned against parliamentary magnates their own political arts. Their lack of public support facilitated George's operations. He could never have bribed and cajoled a really representative house of commons, but an almost self-constituted body of landlords and their clients could be met with the weapons they used, and it was the success of the " king's friends " which opened the eyes of the Whigs to the need for reform. Unless corruption were checked, George might recover by influence what the Stuarts had failed to retain by force. On the other hand, if corruption were checked and parliament reformed, there would be an end to the Whig system of government. Distracted between fear of corruption by the crown and of reform by popular pressure, the old Whigs and Tories were saved for a time by the French Revolution, which made reform a nightmare; and for another generation the breach between the commons in, and the commons out of, parliament grew wider. Political reform might be stayed by the French Revolution, but industrial changes were not, and the old representative system became inconsistent with every principle of representation.

The reform act of 1832 was, however, essentially a bourgeois achievement; it enfranchised the middle classes, but not the poor, a number of whom actually lost the votes they possessed before. Not until 1867 were the town artisans, nor until 1885 were the agricultural labourers really represented by the commons in parliament. Meanwhile religious and other disabilities were removed, and it became possible for all sorts and conditions of men, Roman Catholics, Nonconformists, Quakers, Jews, Mohammedans, Free-thinkers, to sit and vote in parliament. Within two generations of the reform act the house of commons was converted from a political club, with its membership limited practically to one class, into a microcosm of the nation. It comprehended, not merely one or two estates of the realm, but all; and it monopolized all their powers. It extended its sway, because it abandoned its privilege, and accepted the position of agent to the community. It ceased to claim independence, and so it won legal omnipotence. Once or twice in the later middle ages a clerk with a prophetic soul described the commons' house as the *communitas communitatum ;* the communities have become a community, the estates have become the state; and when we speak of the state we mean the state in parliament.

CHAPTER XVII

THE STATE IN PARLIAMENT

THE State is a word which does not appear in the English language until the close of the middle ages, because the idea it seeks to express had not before dawned on the English mind. It cannot be translated into ancient Greek, because the Greeks could not divorce the idea of the state from the particular form in which it was made manifest to them; and so they had but one word, πολίς, for both city and state. The Latin *respublica* and *civitas* come nearer to our meaning, because the wider experience of the Romans made them familiar with a greater variety of states; but the Romans hesitated to apply either *civitas* or *respublica* to Persia or even to their own *imperium*, while both Persia and the Roman empire are, to our minds, as much states as the cities of Athens or of Rome. It is the modern diversity of political organization that makes both necessary and possible some generic word to express the idea without denoting any particular manifestation. Nevertheless, every member of a state does habitually associate with it in his mind some peculiar characteristic. The German used to conceive of might as the essence of the state, with a soldier as its embodiment and a Hohenzollern at its head. To a Russian the state was largely the tsar, to a Frenchman *l'administration*, and to an American himself.[1] To an Englishman its embodiment is parliament.

This English conception rests on a sound historical basis.

[1] A British judge once addressed an American in court as " one of the subjects of the United States," to which the American objected that he was one of the sovereigns of the United States. But the point of view is changing, and some Americans would say that the States are the state.

The state is a fusion of estates, and the fusion was brought to pass in parliament. The indefinite number of estates which gathered at Westminster in the fourteenth century gradually merged into three, which in the sixteenth century were authoritatively defined as crown, lords, and commons;[1] and the three estates of the realm were melted into the national state by the fervour of sixteenth-century nationalism. Under Henry VIII its complexion was royal, in the eighteenth century aristocratic, and to-day it is popular. But the unity wrought in parliament has never been seriously disturbed since the Civil War and the Revolution; and within England itself, whatever we may say of Scotland, Ireland, or realms beyond the sea, there has been no greater danger of two states than its division, of which Disraeli spoke, into a nation of the rich and a nation of the poor.

Out of this fusion grew the supremacy of parliament. When in the twelfth and thirteenth century the foundations of an English constitution began to emerge, only an estate could tax itself. Thanks to Edward I it could only tax itself in parliament, and the conference in which the taxing was done gradually became the authority for the act. By a somewhat subtle and protracted process, estates which had taxed themselves in parliament assumed, under the garb of parliament, the power to tax, and to bind in various ways, other estates as well; and both the Anglican clergy and the nobility have lost their medieval right to tax themselves, and are taxed by the house of commons, from which they are both by law excluded. The merging of the individual in his " estate " involved the surrender to that estate of his individual liberty; the merging of the " estates " in the state involved the surrender to the state of their medieval autonomy. In England it was a slow and gradual process of parliamentary evolution : and as late as the reign of James I parliament itself

---

[1] Burghley, at a joint committee of lords and commons in February 1585 (D'Ewes, p. 350). Cowell, however, in 1607, gives the modern version (Prothero, p. 410).

speaks of "the state ecclesiastical" as well as of "the whole state of the realm," while the king talks of "the state of monarchy." [1] In France the fusion took the form of sudden combustion known as the French Revolution, the critical stage in which was the agreement of the three estates to sit and vote together as a national assembly, submitting to a majority. The state in parliament has thus become an embodiment of Hobbes's *Leviathan*, and Austin expressed its essence in juridical language when he defined law as the command of the state.

The sovereignty of parliament is, however, only a legal sovereignty; behind it lies the political sovereignty of the electorate and the general will of the people, which parliament is supposed to reflect with more or less fidelity. But the "people" is so indeterminate an expression that its use, let alone its abuse, obscures almost all political discussion. Who are "the people," and to what extent do they really govern? Abraham Lincoln's famous rhetoric at Gettysburg to the effect "that government of the people by the people for the people shall not perish from the earth," has achieved a world-wide vogue, because it expresses a common aspiration without attempting to define it. His words did not state the problem with which he had to deal, nor suggest a solution. Every southerner against whom he fought could subscribe to his principle, and its enunciation no more defined the issue than it provided a basis of reconciliation. The south believed that under this specious phrase Lincoln was asserting a claim to the government of the people of the south by the people of the north for purposes of which the north alone approved; and the remark, which a well-known writer (*t*) directs against the British empire, that "a democracy pretending to sovereignty over other democracies is either a phantom or the most intolerable of oppressions," is not without relevance to the conquest of the southern by the northern States. So far as the south was concerned, Lincoln's recipe was that of Oliver Cromwell—"what's for their

---

[1] Prothero, *Documents*, ed. 1898, pp. 288, 291, 293.

good, not what pleases them—that's the question"; and at Gettysburg he was a unionist rather than a democratic statesman.

His real meaning was that government of the people as a whole, by the people as a whole, for the people as a whole should not perish from the earth; and his essential principle was the right of majorities to coerce minorities. Probably Edward I meant much the same thing with his maxim *quod omnes tangit ab omnibus approbetur ;* and the purport of the principle in application was to exclude such claims of those of Peter des Roches, who asserted immunity from taxation to which he had not consented. The issue of north against south was to determine what was the whole, and what was a part. The south stood to the north in 1861 in a stronger numerical relation than the thirteen colonies did to the mother country in 1776; by what right could those who claimed for the part its independence of the whole in 1776 deny the right of a larger part to assert its independence of the whole in 1861? And if the part is bound to and by the whole, by what right did sections of the catholic church separate from the whole and reform themselves in the sixteenth century? The right to secede has been the political and religious making of the American people, and an indispensable weapon of human progress. We can get no nearer to a principle on Abraham Lincoln's lines than to say that a group of men may, if it can, make and call itself a nation, and may then deny to other groups the rights they themselves claimed to exercise. Ireland illustrates better than any hypothetical case the crucial ambiguities which Abraham Lincoln's wisdom concealed. Government of the people by the people for the people is not in dispute, and all the parties take their stand upon unity, unionists on the unity of the United Kingdom, nationalists on the unity of Ireland, and Ulstermen on the indivisibility of Ulster. The fact that men hold a common principle does not prevent them from waging war to define its application. One faith in parliamentary government will not save us from diversity of parliaments; and so fully has the state been merged in parliament that diversity of parliaments has sometimes meant disruption of an empire.

Nor is the problem a mere numerical difficulty, for the claim that the whole is greater than the part is nothing but a mathematical dogma without significance for human or practical affairs. To the thirteen colonies in 1776, as to the southern states in 1861, the part was greater than the whole; and to many an individual his single soul is more than all the world. It is the essence of all religion that man's relation to God and conscience makes his relation to the state conditional and not absolute; and the absolutism of the state is a form of pagan idolatry. It is only within limits and upon conditions that the whole can dictate to the part, even to so small a part as the individual citizen. To determine those limits and to define those conditions is the function of human progress in politics. To ignore them or to deny their existence, and upon that denial to build a parliament or a state, is to build it upon the sands. Man is a great deal more than a political animal; and the best parts of the best men are those with which parliament has nothing to do. Politics are a second-best business of second-best men, and we do not rank our politicians with our poets and philosophers. Whatever a man may render to Cæsar, he may not surrender his soul. Government of the people by the people only implies control of an indeterminate part of human affairs by indeterminate parts of the human race.

Nor, indeed, is government by the people anything more than a rhetorical phrase; and it is somewhat ironical that the most progressive of Lincoln's admirers have found in government by commission the highest interpretation of government by the people in municipal affairs, and in national affairs a popular dictatorship. Government by the people is government by those whom the people send to Westminster or Whitehall, in either a direct, or a roundabout way, for reasons that may have nothing to do with administration. Questions of war and peace, of foreign

policy, of public health, of education are not determined
by popular election; and the nearer a public body approaches
to direct popular sovereignty, the more circumscribed its
powers will be. A parish council is the authority which
embodies most fully Rousseau's ideal, and its powers are
narrowly limited by act of parliament and carefully
controlled by a non-elective local government board.
Extended powers are only entrusted to bodies elevated high
above the average elector. Even in casting a vote for
those to whom his rulers will be responsible, the voter does
not consciously express an opinion on more than one or two
issues; and the opinion has to take the form of a blunt yes
or no, when the solution will probably be a compromise for
which no one would have spontaneously voted at all.

Government is, in fact, a technical matter with which
only experts are fitted to deal. In the rudest of primitive
societies every individual did a more or less equal amount
of everything, including what government there was; and
some small communities, like ancient Athens, clung to the
idea that office should go by rotation and be determined
by lot. But long before national states were evolved,
functions were highly specialized. Individuals gave up
attempting to do everything equally in order that they
might do some things better. Instead of all fighting pell-
mell by the light of nature, some were made soldiers with
nothing to do except to make themselves expert. Instead
of all keeping watch and ward in turn and pursuing the
hue and cry, a standing police force was created to keep
the community's peace. Instead of all meeting in popular
councils, some were chosen to manage the politics of the
people. From being jacks-of-all-trades men have sought to
be masters of one; for the rest they rely upon representation, and the community only performs its functions by
vicarious skill. Democracy, if it involves a reversion to
the original type of society, in which every man took an
equal share in politics, is a hopeless form of reaction.

But it is only the crudest of doctrinaires who think that
people can govern themselves in the sense of administering

their own complicated affairs. No employer can do all the work of the men he employs; and the best that the public can do is to judge of the work that is done in its service without attempting to do the work of its servants. It is not a bad judge of the effects of legislation and government, because it is the public which feels them; and, as Washington said, people must feel before they can see. They are not, however, good judges of legislative proposals, because to foresee effects requires a natural imagination combined with expert political intelligence. For this reason both initiative and referendum are doubtful expedients. Aristotle's remark that the best judge of a dinner is not the cook, but the diner, is valid in politics; but the diner is not, therefore, a competent cook. The public is a bad legislator, but a competent judge of legislation. A wise public will, therefore, not attempt to legislate itself, but will insist on the responsibility of its legislators, and dismiss them if they fail. Parliament is the skilled legislative agent of the electorate, and there is no reason for its existence unless it is more expert in politics than its employers.

The case for democracy does not, indeed, rest on the wisdom of the electorate; and no one can have any doubt that every extension of the franchise has lowered the average intelligence of the voter(*u*). It is not, however, the brains of the voter, but his interests that justify his claim to a vote. Every class governs in its own interests when it has the chance and is irresponsible; and the only tolerable foundation for the state in parliament is one on which all estates can stand. It was Hobbes's plea for monarchy that the monarch was superior to all class interests; and it is conceivable that an all-powerful bureaucracy might adjust the interests of the various classes with less friction and a finer discrimination than is possible as a result of the rough-and-tumble of British politics. The chief argument for parliamentary government is that results are obtained by discussion between the divergent interests, and are imposed by consent—a method which produces a better average of humanity than the most scientific of despotisms. But it is for parliament to frame those compromises, which we call laws, between clashing interests. Not even the most rabid democracy has proposed to graduate an income-tax by popular referendum; and an actual incident in municipal politics illustrates its humours and its dangers. Six improvements were once submitted to the burgesses of a particular town for approval; all were carried by large majorities. A seventh proposal was to raise a twopenny rate to pay the expense; it was rejected by a majority about as large as that which voted the improvements. It is obvious that the government which carries reforms should be responsible for raising the revenue; there is no sounder rule in the house of commons than that which prevents any one who is not a responsible minister from proposing additional expenditure, and there is nothing more vicious in the United States congress than the practices which arise from neglect of this precaution. There would be little endowment of higher education in England if it depended on the votes of those who do not aspire to profit by it, and little promotion of scientific or other research if it were referred to the masses who cannot judge of its value.

The validity of popular judgement is limited to problems which the public feels, and the bearings of which it can grasp. Practically it is only upon such questions that the mass of voters have any desire to cast a vote. A proposal to close public-houses will in England excite more popular interest than any question of foreign policy; and the technical arguments about free trade and tariff reform have to be reduced in the forum to the vulgar shape of the little loaf, two jobs for one, or taxing the foreigner for England's benefit. The reason for submitting such questions to popular judgement is that the people feel the pinch, and to feel the pinch without the means of relieving the pressure creates a sense of social injustice and friction, which, in its turn, hampers the efficiency and impairs the peace and energy of the community to a greater extent than the lack of trained intelligence Whether wage-earners should be paid in kind, and what is a dangerous trade or a living wage, are questions better left to the political sense of the community than to the highest skill of supreme courts of justice. A court of law is not the place to determine questions of politics, and the fact that the high court of parliament has become more political and less judicial, while retaining the sole control of legislation, is one of the reasons why in England we have no election of judges and no proposals for their " recall " by popular vote.

There is, however, nothing final in politics. The best constitution is that which adapts itself best to the actual state of society. The increase of popular education automatically widens the legitimate sphere of popular judgement; and when the mass of the voters comprehend the conditions of foreign policy there is no reason why they should not claim its control. It is a matter which rests with themselves, and the control will only come when electors feel keenly enough about foreign policy to subordinate to it the petty considerations of personality, local interest, and party feeling, by which most votes are determined at present. But under no conceivable circumstances will the mass of electors become so expert in the increasingly complex problems of politics as to render superfluous the advice and guidance of specially trained intelligence. Government by the people can, under existing circumstances, mean no more than government by agencies which are responsible to the people and regard their authority as a trust to be exercised for the people as a whole, and not in the interest of themselves or of the class to which they belong.

Man is, however, a complex creature, with many needs and feelings for which he requires expression; and it does not follow that any single agency is the best medium for all the requisite forms of expression. For half a century or more there has been a tendency to make the state in parliament the universal and omnicompetent exponent of all that men think or feel. Yet there are all-important exceptions. The German might make the state his religion and the kaiser his great high-priest; but the Englishman has, for the most part, rejected parliament as the proper exponent of his religion, and free church principles appeal to a wider circle than that of the free churches. A sympathetic echo is repeated from opposite quarters, and the syndicalist is one who wants to apply free church principles to his bread-and-butter. He thinks that each group of workers should determine the wage and the hours for which it should work, and the price at which it should sell the product of its labour. A preliminary condition would be the elimination of the capitalist, and the control by the group of the capital as well as of the labour it required; but a more serious difficulty consists in the extent of the bargaining involved with other groups. Before one group could produce anything at all, agreements would be necessary with countless other groups engaged in making the instruments needed by the first, and the regulation of these relations by endless independent sovereignties, instead of by parliament, would seem to involve an amount of friction not far removed from anarchy.

Indeed, the movement has the appearance of a reversion to the medieval system of liberties from which England was redeemed by the growth of parliament. It is a reaction to vocational, and not to local particularism, but it is none the less an effect of restricted consciousness and retarded political education; and it is based on a determination to exalt the group at the expense of the community. It arises from impatience with the slowness of communal action compared with the rapidity of the results secured by strikes and other forms of action by which the group, in moments of parliamentary weakness, can blackmail the community. It is also an imitation of the unprincipled methods by which superior groups of landlords and merchants have "cornered" commodities and taken advantage of national needs to fleece the nation for individual gain. Miners are as much entitled as mine-owners to extort what profit they can from monopoly, and the producer who demands higher wages is on the same moral plane as the trader who raises his prices. The monopoly is the source of the evil; like every other liberty it cannot remain uncontrolled by parliament. It was once said by a statesman of moderate views that the state must control the trade in drink or the trade in drink would control the state. There is a corresponding antithesis between the state and every other form of interest; and the problem again is one which Abraham Lincoln's democratic maxim gives us no help in solving. Both syndicalism and socialism are government by the people; the question is, whether that government is to be by the people in guilds or by the people in parliament.

The fundamental difference between syndicalism and socialism is that one is, and the other is not, fatal to parliament. Syndicalism is disruptive, anarchic, and illogical. It aims at providing a sort of government, not merely by isolating one group from another, but by isolating one aspect of life—the economic—from all the rest, and making the cash-nexus the bond of human society. In the middle ages the guild or group concerned itself with almost all aspects of human activity, not merely with the livelihood of its members, but with their education, their religion, and their amusements. Each guild was a little state and church within itself, with its patron saint, its ritual, its technical education, its rules, which regulated the minutest affairs of each member from the cradle to the grave. The system had its advantages, but it was incompatible both with individual liberty and with national organization; it was a less expanded form of selfishness than patriotism. Presumably its modern imitators do not propose to make education, religion, domestic and foreign policy subject to group control, and therefore dependent on group support. But a group which depends on the community as a whole to supply most of its needs can hardly expect independence in the sphere of its choice. Even economic independence is a chimera; it is impossible to segregate groups of men in a community, and still more so to isolate the different instincts of mankind, and base on one of them a social or political system.

The isolation of the " economic " man is as fatal to syndic-
alists and to Mr. Norman Angell as it was to the classical
economists.   There are things for which men will fight,
however little war may pay, and there are objects for which
they will vote in defiance of all their economic interests.

These *imponderabilia* are the stuff of which politics are
made, and sentiment is the most stubborn of facts with
which the statesman has to deal.   It may be that, while
the economic interpretation of history supplies the key to
the past, the key to the future is in the idealist's hands.
Man is not precluded from aspiration because he sprang
from something like primeval slime, and the state is not
limited to material interests because it grew out of material
necessities.   We are not obliged to fix our vision on the
depths from which we have risen, and the future may lie
in aversion from the past.   The growth of the state in
parliament has been in vain if it is still to be bound to the
conditions from which it has won emancipation.   The
essence of its success has been its constant adaptation to
circumstances, and a fresh orientation of the state in
response to moral development is not less feasible to-day
than it was yesterday and the day before.   It is a childish
mind which only sees in history its superficial repetitions.

The state has, it is true, been made by the selfishness of
men; and it consists of the burdens and obligations which
they have transferred from their shoulders.   Nowadays we
are impressed by the magnitude of the responsibilities the
masses have thrust upon the state since they gained
control of parliament—free education, free food for school
children, free treatment in hospitals, public parks and
museums, and a host of other amenities open to those who
do not pay, as well as to those who do.   But the process is
not new, nor are the masses those who began or have
profited most by the transference.   When William the Conqueror disposed of the land, he merely leased it on terms of
service at his court and in his army; and the whole burden
of national defence lay on the holders of land.   By degrees
these holders were enabled in parliament to fix and limit

this obligation, then to reduce it, and finally to escape it altogether. Each step in their emancipation involved an increased burden on the state, until the whole was transferred from the land to the people. What landlords did in the middle ages merchants achieved by their parliamentary influence in modern times. When new worlds were discovered and the seas made highways of traffic, the merchant adventured at his own risk and expense. It was his enterprise and his concern, and no one else assumed any liabilities if his vessel were robbed by pirates or wrecked on uncharted shores. But gradually the merchants, as they acquired political power, transferred this burden to the state, and it became a matter of national obligation and expense to survey the oceans, build lighthouses, deal with pirates, and render the high seas as safe from human violence as the king's highways on land. Merchant ships need no longer go armed in time of peace, nor sail in convoys; and taxes voted in parliament diminished the risks and increased the traders' profits. It was these two processes which created the English army and navy, and provided the state with its fighting forces.

Other activities of the state have developed in similar ways by parliamentary agency. Instead of a system of blood-feuds by which each family redressed its own wrongs, or of trial by battle, we have a national system of justice. Instead of each man being sworn to arms for the preservation of the peace, we have a national police force. English trade-interests abroad, which were once supervised by the agents of individual guilds and companies, are now in the hands of a national consular service; and the foreign office controls diplomatic relations which were, in the middle ages, largely relations between one corporation and another, and not between national states. One of the difficulties in the early days of diplomacy was the little control which each state exercised over its subjects, and fifteenth- and sixteenth-century treaties have elaborately to lay it down that they are binding on subjects of every degree. Colonies and planta-

A A

tions, which were originally founded at the expense of chartered companies, and ruled by them, have been taken over by the state, and the colonial office is the result. In fact, every department of government represents some obligation or burden which has been transferred by parliament from individuals to the state. The state consists of burdens of which individuals have been relieved; and every subject considers he has a right to innumerable national services. Socialism is not a sudden growth of latter days; it is the product of the parliamentary development of the state.

The English state has thus been created out of the material needs of individuals working by means of parliament; it does not follow that it exists merely for their satisfaction. There is clearly a limit to the process by which every individual seeks to get all he can out of the state; and the costliness of modern socialism is due to the extension of the numbers entitled to vote for parliament. Occasionally general elections have resembled public auctions, at which votes are knocked down to those who promise the greatest amount of parliamentary assistance; and signs have been discovered of ultimate national bankruptcy, unless the rush to draw more and more out of the state can be met by a move to pay more and more in. That is the basis of national service. The state has consisted of the burdens thrust upon it; it should consist of the sacrifices men offer. The historical process must be inverted, and the rights of man subordinated to his duties and responsibilities. The test of future citizenship will be what a man gives, not what he receives; and there is good authority for the belief that to give is the better condition. The function of parliament has been to distribute the burdens imposed on the state by the shirking of individuals; it should be to distribute the benefits accumulated through personal service. The debt should become an endowment, the duty a satisfaction.

There is, however, no virtue in compulsion, and sacrifice ceases to have any value when it ceases to be free. It becomes an imposture by imposition. The strength of a state consists in the extent of the sacrifice its people offer; its weakness in the extent of the sacrifice it extorts. The state, moreover, consists of the sacrifice made; it is not a deity to which the sacrifice is offered. That is idolatry. The state, like parliament, is made of men and women; without them it is nothing. It is not, therefore, an external and mysterious entity. It consists of one's neighbours and oneself, and most of our differences depend upon the emphasis we put upon the egotistic or the altruistic aspect of the state. It is an expression of the mind, or of part of the mind of its members; no quality in which they are deficient can characterize their state, and their predominant attributes will decide its nature. When Treitschke said the state is might, he was merely expressing in other words the German's belief in the duel; and when he repudiated the idea that any international tribunal could bind the national state, he was simply applying to the state that exemption from the rule of law which the duel secures for the individual. Germany's methods of making war merely magnified the characteristics of German personal relations. The state is merely man raised through parliament to the power of the state.

It is doubtful whether the word has not outlived its usefulness. It means too many different things to different people to have much meaning left at all; and in the British Empire, at any rate, we should express our meaning more precisely by speaking of the community than of the state, for confusion is inherent in the use of the same term for the community and for its government. The German had no difficulty in imagining a state whose will and interests were independent of the community, because he felt that he needed a master. British peoples, on the other hand, believe in governing themselves, and to them the state means nothing apart from the community; it is simply the organization of the community on a parliamentary basis. But it is idle to speak of the claims which the community has on the community; and, if the sovereignty of parliament is identical with the absolutism of the state, it is a meaningless term to a self-governing people, unless it means unlimited duty to one's neighbour. There are clearly limits to that duty, and therefore to the claims of the community.

These, indeed, are recognized in practice. Parliament does not impose a common religious service or political opinion; and, though it does impose a common obligation, there are lengths to which that common obligation does not go. The problem is to define the limits of common obligation in terms compatible with individual liberty. It is something to have made the obligation common; it was differential in the days of privilege. Being common, it tends towards equality; for if the basis of the state be obligation, the obligation must be equal. If, on the other hand, the basis of the state is oblation rather than obligation, there is ample scope for aristocracy. No one can ever be compelled to give his best, or will ever give it on compulsion. Compulsion only yields a common mean; and the community is ill-occupied when its activities are devoted to reducing effort to a common level. The trades-union descends to such methods only because its members work for a master; and if the state is regarded as a similar master its service will sink to a similar level. There is no limitation of output when each is a volunteer in a cause that is his own.

The value of the state in parliament is that thus it becomes common property administered by consent. Its obligations, like its taxes, come by way of grant and not of imposition. The grant is a matter of compromise, average, and negotiation; and our efforts to avoid compulsion involve a vast expenditure of energy. We maintain our army by advertisement, and upon appeals to voluntary aid our army relies for its nurses. Upon similar appeals depend our hospitals, our system of higher education, our societies for the prevention of cruelty, and hundreds of other organizations performing functions which might be performed with greater dignity, efficiency, and economy by the state. To achieve the economy, efficiency, and saving of dignity secured by the performance of these functions by the state would, however, involve a conscription of capital; and whatever may happen to lives or labour there must, it seems, be no conscription of wealth. That the claim to men's lives should be thought reasonable and the claim to their capital unjust is perhaps the most striking illustration of the extent to which in a capitalistic state capital takes precedence of human life, and to which, even under a democratic franchise in a parliamentary state, wealth can make its influence prevail over numbers.

But it is only in a parliamentary state that these rival claims of classes and of interests can be adjusted. Syndicalism is no remedy, and direct action in the form of the initiative and referendum is little better. The essential vice of syndicalism is that it is a form of dissociation rather than association, and minimizes, if it does not destroy, the responsibility of each group to others. Power must always be a matter of responsibility, whether it is exercised by an individual, a parliament, or a trade-union. It is a trust, and the idea that its possessor is responsible to and for no one but himself is as pernicious for the voter as for the monarch. No one is really entitled to a vote except in so far as he feels in using that vote that he is exercising a trust for other people. Representation is a means of developing responsibility, and the wider the interests and the group for which the representative is and feels responsible, the broader and the deeper will be his sense of responsibility. Indirectly, too, he educates his constituents in a similar sense. The presence of trade-union leaders in parliament forces upon them a sense of national obligation in addition to their group-responsibility, and in turn the trade-unions which have representatives in parliament will think more nationally than those which have none. The particularism of the American colonies before the war of independence was so pronounced that the mother country had, on occasion, to pay them to defend themselves, and they were quite incapable of concerting a common colonial policy. The reason was that they had no representation in the parliament responsible for their defence, and no common parliament of their own. The problem exists to-day in a modified form, and it underlies the national and imperial politics of the British realms; the narrower the responsibility, the duller the political capacity. It is only by contact with wider issues that the political sense of groups and individuals is quickened, and the greater the emphasis on the particular the feebler the perception of the general. *La petite politique, c'est l'ennemi de la grande.*

Hence the need of an imperial parliament to broaden the outlook of its members, and by their means to communicate that wider sense to their constituents. A member of parliament serves the nation, and not merely his constituency. His constituents do not merely elect a local representative, but cast a vote on national and imperial politics. Local government may bring politics to the cottager's door; a parliamentary vote should raise the cottager to a higher level of political vision. Only in that vision will he see the need of sacrifice and service, bridge the distance which separates and unites his interest and the common weal, and learn the lesson of accommodation. The salt, unplumbed, estranging sea long turned the Englishman's gaze inwards upon his self-sufficient liberties; and a parliament which satisfied his insular aspirations fulfilled his conditions of constitutional perfection. Our kin from afar may train our eyes to scan a wider horizon. It remains to be seen whether the parliament, through which we escaped from the valley of parochial politics into the sphere of national action, can lead to even more extended views. In parliament all the estates of the realm were absorbed and made one for the common weal of England. Can British dominions be absorbed and made one for their common weal in a parliament which shall be no longer a parliament of estates but a parliament of the British realms?

CHAPTER XVIII

THE BRITISH REALMS IN PARLIAMENT [1]

THE design of the foregoing chapters has largely been to indicate the transitional character of every phase of parliamentary development and to emphasize the elastic nature of parliament itself. That elasticity has been somewhat impaired in modern times, and conservatives loved to dwell on the impregnable rocks and rigid foundations of the British constitution, ignoring the fact that rigidity is the death of every living organism. At a period when the elasticity of parliament is of supreme importance to the future of the British realms and of parliamentary institutions themselves, it is well to remember that parliament, which seems to us so definite an institution, was for long nothing more precise than a method of government by debate, and that the sovereignty of parliament is merely an attempt to realize the supremacy of reason. It is well also to remember that when an institution becomes the slave of its own forms and loses the capacity of adaptation and expansion, it courts extinction. The formalism of Anglo-Saxon jurisprudence involved its supersession by the practice of Henry II's judges; and the conservatism of the common-law courts at the close of the middle ages nearly led to their destruction at the hands of Roman lawyers, prerogative courts, and Tudor despots. If parliament undergoes a similar process of petrifaction, it will in time become a fossil. It is not that Anglo-Saxon peoples with parliamentary

[1] This chapter was written in August 1915; a sentence or two relating to the German and Russian constitutions have been changed from the present to the past tense.

marrow in their bones are likely to seek refuge in non-parliamentary methods of government. The question is, whether the high court of parliament, the particular institution in which those methods have been enshrined and developed for national purposes, can adapt itself to wider purposes, or whether new needs will provoke new methods, growing into other institutions. The imperial conference might become an imperial parliament, or the British parliament [1] might absorb the imperial conference. In either case parliamentary institutions would be preserved; but in the former, the existing imperial parliament would sink to a local legislature, and in the latter it would have to undergo a far-reaching transformation. There are, indeed, signs that the traditional English method of settlement by discussion is stronger than the newer omnicompetence of a crystallized house of commons; and, to the discomfort of pseudo-constitutional purists, the decisive discussions over the Insurance Act in 1912 took place outside the house and between representatives who were not its members. In point of fact, this was an unconscious reversion to medieval practice by which the estates had settled details of finance and their attitude towards petitions outside parliament, and had merely reported the result by the mouth of their Speaker to the high court for acceptance or rejection. The precedent of extra-parliamentary debate is likely to be followed on an ever-extending scale; and there seems no reason why it should not, provided that the representatives of the community, who bargain with the parties, are responsible to parliament and that parliament retains the power of ratification or rejection. Legislation is growing too complex for profitable discussion of its details by a body of seven hundred general practitioners of politics; and it is better debated—in its details, at least—between the expert bureaucrats who inform the minister and will have to apply the

[1] The term imperial parliament, as applied to the existing British parliament, is bound to become more and more an anachronism. From its cognizance are already in practice excluded the commercial relations of the great dominions; and the more British foreign policy is made a matter of common concern to British dominions, the less will be the control exerted over it by a parliament of the British Isles.

legislation, and the spokesmen of those who will suffer or profit from their administration.

Parliamentary government does not therefore involve government of everything by one parliamentary method or by a single parliament. The exigencies of the empire have long ago disposed of that sort of unity and uniformity; and the problem is how to preserve a common bond between the various methods and institutions, and to prevent the specialization of functions from developing independent species. In other words, is the British empire a state or a collection of states? The question was once asked of a British student who had spent some years in Canada whether he would describe the British empire as a state, and he said "Yes." He was then asked whether he would have given the same answer in Canada, and he said "No." Events are moving rapidly, but that dissonance remains a faithful reflex of the imperial situation; and with it remains the doubt how long it will be possible in different parts of the empire to give diametrically opposite answers to the same question. Our immediate concern is to consider whether, if at all, parliament will be the means of finding a solution.

It is not theoretically essential that parliament should be the bond of unity in an empire. It was not the reichstag which gave substance to the unity of Germany, nor did Roman unity owe aught to parliamentary institutions. Religion has sometimes formed a basis, and it was, perhaps unfortunately, the strongest tie between all the Russias of yesterday. But churches, inasmuch as their ultimate appeal is to the individual soul, tend to be fissiparous; and the amalgamation of churches has been of the rarest and most local occurrence. No church could provide a foundation of unity for the British realms. The crown has to be presbyterian in Scotland and anglican in England; and, had not the impossibility of identifying church and state been recognized in time, the crown might also have been roman catholic in Ireland and heaven knows what in other of its dominions. So long as unity was attempted by religion, the effect was rather to distract the crown than to unite the churches. Race has been a commoner bond than religion, but race breaks down as the link of British unity, and racialism is rather the bane than the basis of the empire. Language is in a somewhat better case; but the events of 1776 proved that language was no specific against disruption, and there are millions of white citizens in British realms who speak no English. Customs, again, traditions and history are as diverse as they could be in the British empire; indeed, in these respects there is no more unity in the empire than in the world. Where then is that differential basis to be found on which to build a British state of such divergent elements? Race, religion, history, and language stand for so much in men's culture that they leave but little room for the other foundations of community.

It is clear that those foundations can only be political, not racial or religious. The greatest political failure of any people in the world's history has been that of the Jews, and that wonderful race failed in politics because of its racial purity and its religious concentration. The jealousy of their God left no scope for the state; and it needed Christianity to find room for Cæsar in a Jew's allegiance. Ever a church, but never a state since the dispersion, the Jews owed their failure to their repulsion of gentile elements. A Jew can assimilate almost any quality, but he cannot draw gentiles into his fold. So, too, the German can transform himself into any other nationality, but he cannot make others German to any appreciable extent, and within the heart of Germany there are alien colonies which have resisted for generations the permeation of German culture. For this reason the German was driven to force as his panacea; the lack of political attractiveness made him a repellent militarist; and, however brilliant the triumph of military genius and organization, empires won by the sword have a habit of falling on their own weapon. Militarism, at any rate, is not the bond which binds the fabric of the British realms. They are only held together by consent, and that consent is based upon political considerations, some of them merely sentimental, some of them idealistic, and others severely practical in character.

It is only in the political sphere that the essential claims of the state are valid or will be admitted. So discordant is the voice of the state from those of the churches, that there is no longer an established church, outside England, in the whole of the British empire, and free churches mean everywhere a limitation of the state. The absolutism of the state, upon which Hobbes and Austin dilated, is, in fact, an ambiguous term. Within its sphere the state, whatever its form, must possess a final authority, but that authority, while absolute in degree, is not unlimited in extent. The state therefore can only be built on foundations that lie within its jurisdiction; and it is only by recognizing the limits of its sphere that the state can expect recognition of its authority within that sphere. Theology, if not religion, certainly lie outside; the state does not now dream of establishing truth and is even shy of creating legal fictions. The circumstance that Germany acted on Hobbes's maxim, " in the right governing of opinion consisteth the right government of man," indicated a fundamental distinction between British and German conceptions of the state. Attempts on the part of the state to determine language are also illegitimate, and constitute a manifold cause of friction. Social customs are an equally dangerous field of interference; and, in spite of recent appearances, there are grounds for maintaining that the absolutism of the state has been purchased by the limitation of its sphere, and that its theoretical omnicompetence depends upon the widening circle of things it does not attempt. It is at least perfectly clear that if the British realms are to be a state, the jurisdiction of that state will be severely restricted.

But again, the problem may be obscured by the inevitable use of the term " the state." It is easier to conceive of the British realms forming a community, or perhaps a commonwealth; and the absolutism of the community does not suggest the same perplexities as the absolutism of the state. For one thing, it does not imply antithesis to the church.

It does not, in fact, isolate one aspect of human activity and proclaim its supremacy over all the rest. Even those who hold that the state is man in the state, often lose sight of man in the state, just as others lose sight of man in the church. This veiling of humanity breeds a greater antithesis between church and state than there is between man as a political animal and man as a religious being; and the community or commonwealth embraces both, promoting concord in the place of conflict. Concord, however, is only possible in the British realms through the surrender of much that clings to the state, its uniformity and its omnicompetence, if not also its appearance of unity. The old French ideal of *une foi, une loi, un roi* is clearly unattainable; the British realms have one king, but they have many faiths and many legal systems, and only such unity is possible as is compatible with an infinite variety.

Underlying these varieties there is, however, room for one foundation. Indeed, it is no paradox to say that the greater is men's attachment to their particular culture, the greater is their need of the British empire. The self-sufficient independence and seclusion of small communities is in a parlous state to-day, when might is ever growing and the world is ever shrinking; and liberty within the British empire is a better security than independence beyond its pale. The case would be different if the purpose of the British empire were, as it has been alleged, to give each of its citizens an English mind. The idea of the British empire is, rather, to provide its citizens with the means of developing minds of their own, and no sane Briton wishes to make a French-Canadian indistinguishable from a South African Boer, or even a Welshman exactly like a Scot. There are many mansions in the British empire, and no one wants to build them all alike or fill them with a homogeneous population. For that and for other reasons, empire is not a happy term; it implies an unconstitutional authority, military domination, and rigid uniformity. The essence of the British realms is government by consent, liberty, and heterogeneity.

This freedom to develop along lines of their own is the quality in the empire which its dominions value most; and it might seem that here was substance enough without grasping at the shadow of an imperial sovereign state. Indeed, the imperative, exigent tone of the absolute claims of state sovereignty involve no little risk to the finer threads of feeling which really unite the British realms. It is not as a state which extorts, but as a community which grants, that a British commonwealth may develop a common organization. No British realm will merge itself in an absolute British commonwealth, after Hobbes's conception of a commonwealth by institution, when every man was supposed to have surrendered all his rights, including his rights of conscience and private judgement, to a common despot. The compact would necessarily be a combination of Hobbes's and Locke's ideas : it would be an agreement among the British realms to set up a single imperial government, but only for certain purposes, and the compact would be a treaty by which the imperial state would be bound. It could not be an absolute state. Even in that model union of 1707 Scotland reserved its religion, its law, and its justice, and required specific advantages. It will be long ere British realms consent to a uniform tariff policy, or to a common taxation. Indeed, a common taxation is impossible where conditions are so divergent : import duties on corn, which Canada would not feel, would ruin the English working classes. Land taxes which Australia and New Zealand bear with equanimity, would revolutionize English society. Neither the dominion of Canada nor the commonwealth of Australia has yet been able to impose direct taxation on its component provinces and states (*v*), and to imagine a central government in London imposing on the dominions what the dominions cannot impose on their provinces is a phantasmagoria of visionary enthusiasm.

Political unions which last are not made in a moment nor without the co-operation of deep-seated causes; and there is always danger in arbitrarily selecting one out of the many forms of union adopted in British realms and imposing that as a standard on others.   The Anglo-Scottish and the South African unions, even if we add New Zealand, do not constitute a rule.   Against the Scottish must be set the Irish union, by way of warning and not of example; and against the South African and New Zealand constitutions must be set the federation of Canada and the still looser combination of the states of Australia.   There remain the disunited West Indies, scores of other colonies, and the empire of India, with its hundreds of semi-independent principalities. They represent every stage of political development; and democratic expedients which suit Canada and Australia would be disastrous in other realms of the empire.   No common standard of self-government is applicable, and it is irrational to suppose that a central authority could rule these diverse dominions so well as the expert and specialized governments which control them at present.   The government of the empire is, in fact, only possible through a diversity of methods adapted to a diversity of needs; and only the elasticity of mind, which comes of political aptitude and experience, tolerates such diversity.   If the average British elector really determined such questions as the locality of an Indian capital or the careful adjustment of Indian self-government and the Indian civil service, he would decide them by the sort of criteria he applies to his own local environment, and the result would be chaos.

No doubt men are heedless of things for which they are not responsible, and the increase of responsibility is a potent factor in political education; but the imperfection of the result in matters for which the responsibility is immediate and direct, counsels caution in our expectations from a responsibility which cannot be felt.   It has often been said that a democracy cannot govern an empire; the truth is, that an empire such as the British cannot be governed on exclusively democratic principles, and democracy is apt to regard its principles as valid at all times and under all circumstances, and as matters of simple right and wrong which only original sin leads men to dispute.   It is easy to say that imperial questions should be decided by an imperial electorate; it is less easy to define that electorate, and still less so to create it. We doubt the expediency of giving a vote in Indian affairs to an Indian electorate which cannot read or write; to give them a vote on all the affairs of the British realms would be a fantastic form of imperial suicide. The problem of colour would be accentuated and not exorcised by a popularly-elected parliament representative of the empire; and no principle is sounder in practice than that which denies responsible self-government even to Englishmen who are a handful among a vast coloured population. The great dominions deservedly call for a greater share in the control of imperial policy, but we cannot, in reconstructing the empire, ignore our own West Indian history, or the practical limitations under which the United States pretends to combine democratic principle with the facts of the negro question.

Practically the problem of an imperial parliament which shall represent more than the British Isles resolves itself into a question of how to include Canada, Australia, New Zealand, South Africa, and Newfoundland; and thus limited, it is not entirely impracticable, provided that an enthusiasm as unhistorical in its outlook as that of the first French Revolution does not seek to solve it wholly at one gigantic *auto-de-fe*.[1] There are common foundations on which to work. Common politics, as the genesis of parliament has shown, are the outcome of common law, and English law is the groundwork of all colonial constitutions. A judicious admixture of Roman law and other systems is not inadmissible, as we know from Scotland and South Africa; but one of the most fruitful suggestions for empire-building was made by Lord Haldane, when he outlined a proposal that the judicial committee of the privy council should periodically appear in sessions throughout the British realms. By such judicial eyres Henry II had brought royal justice home to his subjects and, more important from our point of view, had made the same law common to

---

[1] *Auto-de-fe* is properly an " act of faith "; it came to mean a holocaust, and the *auto-de-fe* proposed in some quarters would involve a holocaust of the many constitutions in the empire.

all England. Thus he had done more perhaps than any one else to create an England out of a congeries of tribes. The diversities of law throughout the empire to-day are not more multifarious than those in the mother country in the eleventh century; and the court that could hammer out and apply a common law of the British realms would be doing as much to create a united empire as Henry II and his judges did to make England by creating its common law.

Without this common law parliament could not have grown; and, indeed, it was well that the common law was the plastic work of judges, and not the cast iron of a parliamentary statute. No one could have drafted it or put it into an act; it had to grow from case to case through centuries of judicial argument and experience, and various were the materials moulded together into the final product. It was but partly Anglo-Saxon; and an imperial common law would leave out a great deal that is English, particularly in the sphere of real property, and would incorporate some things that are not. So, too, it will not be made by statute or embodied in a code; it must needs be the outcome of judicial experience garnered by the highest legal minds in sessions throughout the empire. Statutes might come later: the judges of the king's court not only gathered experience on their eyres, discussed it in common sessions of the council, and applied it in Westminster Hall; they also drafted their deductions into statutes, which were promulgated in the high court of parliament. So our imperial justices-in-eyre might draft into statutes for submission to an imperial parliament the fruits of their imperial missions.

Their labours would be facilitated and their prospects improved by their restoration to something of their original status in the constitution. Their gradual degradation, as the king's council in parliament was perverted into a house of lords, was doubly unfortunate; it impaired the constitutional authority of the judges and the legislative skill of parliament; for, however expert may be the staff of our present drafting department, its members have not the experience of the judges who were wont to determine the form of legislation. It led also to the illogical growth of two supreme courts of appeal. The judicial committee of the privy council represents the king's council out of parliament; the law lords represent the king's council in parliament. But these two courts were not in earlier times co-ordinate; the medieval king's council in parliament was superior to the king's council out of parliament, could resolve its doubts, remedy its errors, and direct its action. It might have retained its superiority but for the reduction of the judges of the council in parliament to the status of assistants in a house of uninstructed peers. The intrusion of an hereditary caste into the technical sphere of appellate judicature was the cause of the disjunction; it was removed when the peers abstained from exercising the judicial functions they had assumed; and there seems no adequate reason why the two courts should not be united into a single supreme imperial court of justice. The *personnel* of the two courts has much in common; but the lords sit in some state to hear appeals from the British Isles, while the judicial committee shrouds itself in mean obscurity to hear those from great dominions overseas

The house of lords might possibly be used for further imperial purposes. No sane politician wantonly interferes with vigorous institutions, but the house of lords is moribund; it has, in any event, to undergo a radical reformation, and the peers' necessity is the statesman's opportunity. It is, at any rate, worth inquiry whether the house of lords could not be reconstituted to meet in some degree the desire for a more adequate representation at Westminster of our overseas dominions. An attempt at reform in this direction would necessarily involve the abandonment of the principles of heredity and primogeniture. None of the overseas dominions has tolerated the introduction of these principles into their councils or their legislatures; and an imperial chamber based upon them would have no attraction for the empire as a whole. Nor, as a matter of fact, would it receive much serious support within the British Isles.

The difficulty is to find some principle that does commend

B B

itself as the basis for a second chamber. Various expedients have been tried in different parts of the empire. Second chambers have been selected by nomination, sometimes for life, sometimes for a period of years. They have been constituted by election, sometimes on a restricted, and sometimes on a democratic franchise, sometimes by small constituencies, sometimes by provinces as a whole. The result has everywhere been much the same, and second chambers are the political failure of the British empire. It is not only in the British Isles that a second chamber is threatened with mending or ending : the cry is also heard in Canada, where the second chamber is filled by nomination, and in the states of Australia, where it is elected. The truth seems to be this : it is doubtful wisdom to set two bodies of men to do the same work ; but, admitting the wisdom, the two bodies should not be alike. The house of lords has probably given more whole-hearted satisfaction, albeit to a minority, than any other second chamber in the empire, because it is so unlike the house of commons. If the British realms are to be asked to abandon any part of their constitutions to the imperial melting-pot, they will one and all find it easier to sacrifice their second chamber than anything else ; and it is not at all impossible that something might be made of this refuse in the imperial crucible.

A hint might perhaps be borrowed from the United States. Its senate is not by any means an ideal body, though the recent change to the popular election of its members may make it more responsible ; but it is undeniably the strongest second chamber in any Anglo-Saxon community, and its strength is due to the fact that it is based on a clear principle, distinct from that of the house of representatives. The house represents the people of the United States as a whole ; the senate represents the states of which the union is formed, and it is the special guardian of their rights. The house is based on numerical population ; the senate contains two representatives, and no more, from every state, whatever its population. A house of lords, reconstituted so as to comprise representatives from every British realm and colony would not be more out of touch with the British electorate than it is at present; it would be vastly more capable, and its value as the king's imperial council in parliament would be far-reaching. The vast majority of electors in the British Isles would gladly see some such body substituted for their existing house of lords, and it is quite possible that the dominions would consent to a similar substitution. There would thus in the British empire be a variety of first chambers, but a single second chamber, constituted on a principle which would give it weight and independence. It would possess a qualification indispensable in an efficient second chamber, namely, a differential basis from the first. There would be no doubt about its strength; there might be some fear that its strength would impair the democratic self-government of the individual realms, but this danger would be met by differential work corresponding to its differential basis.

Politics stand in constant need of searching analysis, and nothing confuses political thought more seriously than the assumption that democracy means the determination of all political issues by popular vote. In practice democracy combines with it a strong admixture of monarchy and aristocracy; a British prime minister is more of a monarch than many who bear the title, and some have approached dictatorship; a cabinet is a genuine aristocracy, because cabinet rank is (as a rule) attained by merit and not by inheritance. Both institutions are essential to modern democracies. It has, moreover, already been pointed out that whole categories of public questions are decided without reference to the electorate. The dividing line between those which are, and those which are not determined by the ballot, is naturally and properly determined by the electors, not consciously, but through the influences to which their minds are subject. An issue on which many votes will be turned will infallibly be brought with prominence before the electors; an issue to which they are indifferent will be decided without a popular consultation. The foreign policy initiated by Lord Lansdowne in 1903–4 was an issue of supreme importance; but no one dreamt of fighting a general or even a by-election upon it. Even the sanction of the house of commons was not required for it, or for such a step as the grant of responsible self-government to the Boer colonies. On the other hand, no cabinet could sanction a religious catechism in elementary schools, limit the number of public-houses, or carry a scheme for national insurance without risking shipwreck on the rock of popular indignation. The line between the two categories of public questions is not, of course, hard and fast; but it is deep enough to provide a discrimination between the functions of a popularly-elected house of commons and an imperially-constituted second chamber. The latter would thus have differential work as well as a differential foundation.

The change would involve an act of imperial union, an expansion of sphere, and a specialization of function. The second chambers of the empire would be formed into one, the sphere of which would be expanded; and instead of each realm having two chambers performing similar functions, the imperial second chamber would specialize on imperial questions, and the first chambers on domestic questions. This, it may be objected, provides for two chambers, but not for the functions assigned by convention to a second chamber. Both would, so to speak, be courts of first instance, and there would be no court of appeal. The objection is not irrelevant; but the inadequacy with which second chambers have fulfilled their function as courts of appeal from the first, however they have been constituted, suggests the doubt whether it is a legitimate function. No second chamber, in fact, claims any right to decide the appeal, and a court of appeal which cannot decide seems somewhat superfluous. The real court of appeal from a first chamber is not the second chamber, but the electorate; and of recent years second chambers have generally confined their claims to a right of reference. The necessity for this safeguard clearly depends upon the period for which the first chamber is immune from a general election; and a shortening of that period might be a simpler method of bringing home responsibility than the somewhat spasmodic action of second chambers. If, however, this power of reference were retained, it would be exercised to more general satisfaction by an imperial chamber than it is by existing institutions. The universal complaint is that the power of reference is invariably used for party purposes, and the general demand is for its impartial exercise. Now impartiality can surely be expected with greater confidence from a chamber composed of members drawn from all parts of the empire, and mostly without party interest in the dispute, than from local chambers consisting almost exclusively of members belonging to the parties involved. Independence would accompany impartiality, and inasmuch as the issues are always between two political parties of which neither chamber is now independent, the question of reference to the electorate would better be left to a body containing at least a large external element.

A more fundamental problem would be the control by the lower chamber of the functions and powers of the upper. There is no escape from the tyranny of finance : he who pays the piper calls the tune, and the chamber which finds the revenue will determine its destination and define the objects upon which it shall be expended. The deduction will be drawn that there can be no imperial unity unless the single imperial second chamber controls imperial finance. If that deduction is valid, imperial unity is a distant prospect ; for a single taxing assembly for the whole empire is not yet possible, however complete its representative character might be. Taxes are things which electors feel, and upon which they really do vote at elections. The parts are not so lost in the whole that Australians and Canadians will pay taxes imposed by a chamber in which Australia and Canada would have a vote, but not a veto ; and Polish history tells the tale of assemblies in which individual delegates have a *liberum veto*. Whatever imperial revenue may be required will have to be granted by the individual representative chambers of the several realms. Those chambers would act like the estates of a medieval parliament : the financial needs of the empire would be laid before them, and each would make its own response in the form of a grant. Each, too, would be responsible for its methods of assessment, incidence, and collection. In one dominion the imperial contribution might be raised by a tariff, in another by income-tax; in one by a tax on land, in another by an excise duty on spirits. The essential condition would be that each would manage its own finance, for no British realm would tolerate intervention in so domestic a matter. The one source of revenue which might conceivably be at the disposal of an imperial second chamber would be an imperial tariff; but the reorganization of the empire will have some time to wait if it is postponed to the adoption of that proposal. No one can circumscribe the future, and the British realms may grow so close together that not merely an imperial tariff, but an imperial income-tax might be levied by a single imperial chamber. We are considering less distant possibilities.

It does not follow that even during this interim the imperial chamber would be impotent in finance because it could not levy taxation. A chancellor of the exchequer is not powerless because he cannot tax by edict, and it is quite possible to conceive the financial recommendations of an imperial council having as much weight with the voters of taxes as the proposals of a chancellor. The imperial council would frame estimates of the expenditure needed for imperial purposes; it would suggest the distribution of the burden; and from a body, in which all the realms were properly represented, it would not be unreasonable to expect an equitable allocation. Given these conditions, the individual chamber which refused to provide its share of supply would be incurring a grave responsibility and a serious risk of forfeiting the confidence of its constituents. Common feeling and public opinion is already keen enough throughout the empire to guarantee the readiness of each of the realms to shoulder a share in the common burden.

So far we have got, in our imaginary constitution, one crown and one imperial chamber, combined with a variety of houses of commons or representatives. The crucial point is the question of the executive. The anomaly of the existing constitution is the existence of an imperial executive without any regular relation or responsibility to an imperial chamber. It is responsible solely to the British house of commons, and other British realms have no formally re-organized constitutional right to any share of control over the foreign policy in which they are involved, or the declaration of wars in which they spend their lives and treasure. Tentative steps have, indeed, been taken to mitigate this anomaly : at the last imperial conference before the war, Sir Edward Grey admitted its members to the secrets of British foreign policy, and more recently the prime ministers of Canada, Australia, and South Africa have attended British cabinet meetings. It is well that the elasticity of our constitution should permit of such experiments and should oppose no bar to the growth of a really imperial cabinet. Much of the constitution has been erected in this tentative way without formal legislation; and it would be rash to abandon that method for the alternative plan of constitution spinning.

But even tentative steps must have a direction and goal; and we might have a clearer idea of direction if we could know what was said to and by Sir Robert Borden, Mr. Hughes, and General Botha during the cabinet meetings made famous by their presence. We might also gather some hints from Lord Kitchener's attitude during the cabinet deliberations on the Welsh church suspensory bill or the home rule act in September 1914. He was in the cabinet for the purposes of the war, and Sir Robert Borden, Mr. Hughes, and General Botha were asked to attend in the interests of the empire.[1] What would they have said on peaceful domestic topics like Mr. Lloyd George's budget of 1910 or insurance bill of 1912? The rôle of a sleeping partner would have been the most convenient attitude; and a cabinet of the empire would be atrophied for domestic

---

[1] From 1917 to 1919 General Smuts was a full member of the war cabinet; and the problem now is to adapt the temporary expedients of war to the permanent uses of peace.

purposes, just as a domestic British cabinet too nearly approaches atrophy for the purposes of the empire. The divergence leads straight towards two sets of executives : a single executive for imperial purposes responsible to the single imperial chamber, and a series of domestic executives for each self-governing realm responsible to their respective domestic legislatures. The control at present exercised by the British government over India and those colonies which do not possess responsible self-government would naturally be vested in the imperial cabinet and imperial chamber.

Such an arrangement would involve both a definition of functions and the provision of means to prevent a division of will. The evil to be avoided is the conflict of jurisdictions ; and two independent sets of executives and legislatures, one dealing with imperial and the other with domestic affairs, would be certain to come into conflict unless there were means of regulating their relations with one another. Here again finance would be the determining factor ; and the chambers, which controlled supply and the domestic executives, must also control, directly or indirectly, the imperial chamber and the imperial cabinet. The imperial cabinet would be immediately responsible to the imperial chamber, but the imperial chamber itself would be responsible to the dominions.[1] Its members might be selected by three alternative methods : they might be the nominees of the domestic dominion executives ; they might be chosen by the domestic dominion legislatures ; or they might be elected by the peoples of the dominions. The objection to the last method is that imperial issues do not, as a rule, evoke any wide and intelligent popular interest, and the local qualifications which commend candidates to so many constituencies are singularly out of place in an imperial election. The objection to the second is that indirect election usually fails of its object : the American college of electors, which was intended to collect the wisdom of the nation, consists of ciphers ; while the conduct of United States senators

---

[1] The word is intended to include Great Britain and Ireland.

has been explained on the ground that they were elected by legislatures, and not by the people, and election by legislatures has recently been abandoned in favour of popular choice. An American senator is, however, the special representative of local interests; the members of an imperial British chamber would be chosen for an exactly contrary purpose, and a different method might be more appropriate. They would resemble the agents-general of the dominions, and might be appointed by similar means. The superficial resemblance of such a chamber to the old bundesrath of the German empire may be enough to condemn it for the moment. But there would be two fundamental differences: firstly, the members of the bundesrath were appointed by governments which were not responsible to the people of the states they represented; and secondly, our imaginary chamber would not possess the extensive control which the bundesrath exercised over domestic legislation. It would, no doubt, be desirable to synchronize general elections throughout the empire, and the new dominion governments would thus simultaneously select their representatives to the imperial chamber. But this would hardly be possible; and a change of dominion government would not necessarily involve a recall of imperial representatives any more than it does a substitution of agents-general, or a change in the British government involves a re-appointment of ambassadors or of members of the imperial defence committee.

There remains the problem of delimiting the spheres and powers of the imperial chamber and the dominion houses of commons. It is thorny enough, but there is no reason to think it more insoluble than the kindred problem of defining the respective spheres of dominion and provincial parliaments in Canada or Australia. Most of the functions of government are sorted by nature into one or other category. Foreign affairs, imperial defence, issues of war and peace, belong obviously to imperial government; questions of religion, education, the franchise, social reform, labour problems, public health, insurance, appertain no less distinctly to the domestic sphere of the dominion parliaments. Between the two spheres there lies an important borderland, including the treatment of native races, commercial policy, naturalization, citizenship, and marriage; and it would be essential to leave its frontiers as elastic as possible. There might be concurrent rights of legislation, while the growth of unity would facilitate a gradual increase of imperial influence in this sphere. There would have to be a written constitution, but the less of it the better. The working of a constitution never really depends upon its form, but upon the spirit which informs it. If the peoples of the British realms want a united empire with a common government, they will get it and will work it, whatever the defects of its constitution. If they do not, no constitutional machinery, however artistic its construction, will attract them.

Nor is it of much use attempting to frighten them into political upheaval by logical dilemmas, after the fashion of Hobbes's idea of the social contract. According to him the life of man in the state of nature was " nasty, short, brutish and mean," so intolerable, in fact, that he was left no option but to submit himself to an absolute sovereign as protector. According to some of our modern imperialists, the British realms are in an equally parlous condition; there is no alternative to disruption but fusion in a single state. Such logical dilemmas have no terror for the historian, for history consists for the most part of solutions of logical impossibilities; *solvuntur ambulando*. The empire is not in the parlous condition depicted : it will not split into fragments because its parts decline to fuse. It lightly evades the horns of the dilemma, of being " either a phantom or the most intolerable of oppressions," because it is not " a democracy pretending to sovereignty over other democracies." Canadians and Australians are not our subjects, but our fellow-subjects, or rather partakers in the sovereignty which is the capital of the empire. The partnership is not perfect; but it is none the less real because its terms have not been stated in a written constitution.

Neither was it a phantom that the crucial test of the great war revealed. For, when all is said and done, political unity is a thing of the spirit, and not a bond of parchment; and Germany's challenge to all for which parliamentary government stands could not have met with a finer response from the British realms, had they all been merged in a single state. The heart and the head of the empire were sound. Its peoples grasped the fundamental issue of the war. The Germany, which provoked it, began with Bismarck's defeat of a parliament and its principles, and developed a natural alliance, first, with the Hapsburgs and then, by a logical consummation, with the Turk; and the conflict ended, as it was bound to end, in defeat at the hands of parliamentary peoples, after a struggle in which the one autocracy among them went to pieces.[1] Upon those parliamentary principles the British empire is based; it stands for the force of argument against the argument of force, for the rule of law against the rule of the sword, for popular consent against the will of monarchy or militarism masquerading as the state. If the Allies had failed, parliamentary government might have perished from the earth. Through their success peace will be placed on the broad foundation of common acceptance by the world of principles, dimly discerned in the middle ages and wrought out in hundreds of parleys, until the parleys themselves grew into a parliament and a mother of parliaments, and their reason supplanted force as the rule of human affairs.

[1] This passage, as originally written in August 1915, ran: " it will end in defeat at the hands of parliamentary peoples after a struggle which bids fair to convert the one autocracy among them to belief in responsible government."

APPENDIX I

THE illustrations herein reproduced refer exclusively to the development, in the " parliament chamber," of those " parliaments " of the king in council with other representative and non-representative elements of the nation, which in modern times became the house of lords. That development is historically the essential feature in the evolution of the English parliament, and it is the most difficult to grasp. The growth of the house of commons, from its original sessions in the refectory and chapter house of the abbey to its transference to St. Stephen's chapel in the palace and subsequent encroachment upon the neighbouring " parliament chamber," is another story, simpler in its details, subordinate in its historical, though not in its political importance, and lacking pictorial representation until we come to the seventeenth century. We are here dealing with the pictorial evidence for the earlier stages of our parliamentary history.

The first of our reproductions is the earliest which possesses much historical value. There are pictures of an older date representing the king in parley with some half a dozen or more councillors, which are correctly entitled " the king in parliament " and are valuable as illustrating the fact that the first parliaments were simply parleys of the king in council. But they represent only the germ, and are without exception centuries later than the parliamentary conditions which they profess to portray. Our first illustration, on the other hand, while it correctly contains traces and relics of earlier stages of parliamentary development, is an exact and contemporary representation of the parliament of 1523. Its date and provenance can be determined with some precision. It was first reproduced by Richard Fiddes (1671–1725) in his *Life of Cardinal Wolsey*, published in 1724 (p. 302); and the drawing, from which the reproduction was made, was sent to Fiddes from the Heralds' College by John Anstis, then Garter King of Arms—in whose house at Putney Fiddes died in 1725—with a long explanatory letter which is dated 2 Jan., 1722–3, and is printed by Fiddes (ib. *Collections*, pp. 108–14). In this letter Anstis remarks that "though this draught be meanly performed, yet it must be allowed to be of authority . . . since it was designed by the order of the then Garter King of Arms and preserved in a fair velom manuscript which hath his name and arms in several places and likewise represents him performing his duty at this parliament in his proper robe and place." The "then Garter King of Arms" was Sir Thomas Wriothesley (*d.* 1534), of whom Anstis gives an elaborate account in his *Order of the Garter* (i., 369–73). He had been created Garter in 1505 and confirmed in that office on Henry VIII's accession; he was father of Charles Wriothesley the chronicler, and uncle of Thomas Wriothesley, lord-chancellor and earl of Southampton.

The picture represents the opening of parliament on 15 April, 1523. The last parliament had been opened on 5 February, 1514–15, but Wolsey was not then a cardinal, while he is here represented as sitting above Warham, archbishop of Canterbury, and next to the throne, with a cardinal's hat over his head and above it the arms of the see of York impaling Wolsey's own; and it was only after 1515 that Wolsey took precedence of Warham. The figure standing behind the traverse, between Wolsey and the king, is Tunstall, bishop of London, who delivered the opening speech in 1523.[1] The other two figures behind the archbishop's seat are two priests bearing, according to Anstis, Wolsey's two crosses as cardinal and archbishop, and not one belonging to him and one to Warham (Fiddes,

---

[1] *Rot. Parl.* 14, Hen. VIII, prefixed to *Lords' Journals*, vol. i. p. lxxv; *Letters and Papers of Henry VIII*, iii. 2956. The *Lords' Journal* for 1523 is not extant. Wolsey, as *legatus a latere*, seems to have disdained the parliamentary functions of a chancellor; hence Tunstall's oration.

Collections, p. 110). On the front bench running down
from the right of the throne and of the cloth of state sit
the bishops in their order of precedence, and behind them
the abbots, the latter extending on to a cross-bench. Dimly
seen behind that cross-bench are the commons, standing at
the bar, with Sir Thomas More, their Speaker on this occasion,
in their midst. On the front bench stretching down from
the left of the throne sit the temporal peers. First comes
the duke of Norfolk, who holds in his hand the Lord High
Treasurer's staff; next to him is the duke of Suffolk.
There were only two dukes in England in 1523, and only
these two wear the four ducal bars of white miniver on
their robes. The earls, who come next,[1] have only three.
The barons begin on the cross-bench, and the first is the
" premier baron of England," namely the Prior of St.
John's, who, although reckoned a spiritual peer in earlier
times, is described as the " premier baron " in Edward IV's
and succeeding reigns down to 1540; he is indicated by
his different robe. The line of barons is continued from
the cross-bench to the bench behind the dukes and earls.

Returning to the cloth of state, we see three earls, one of
them, apparently Worcester, on the king's right, bearing
the cap of maintenance, and the other two, on the left, the
sword and the earl marshal's baton; the latter was borne
by a deputy for Norfolk, who was both earl marshal and
lord high treasurer. The two figures behind the traverse
on the king's left are non-episcopal and non-baronial councillors, and to their left is apparently a throng of eldest
sons of peers, preceded by Garter King of Arms. On the
highest of the four woolsacks, where usually sat the chancellor, are the two chief justices. Other judges sit on the
woolsack running down from the right of the throne, and
on the left, according to D'Ewes, who follows Glover, are
the master of the rolls, the chief baron of the exchequer,
the king's council learned in the law, and the masters in
chancery. But D'Ewes is writing a century later; and it

---

[1] D'Ewes, *Journals*, p. 11; the figure next to Suffolk might have
been Dorset, England's only marquis at that date; but he was serving
on the Scottish borders. Marquises had only three bars of miniver, like
earls, and viscounts only two, like barons.

is more probable that in this illustration the occupants of these two woolsacks are all judges, the fourth woolsack being occupied by masters in chancery and king's council, behind whom kneel the clerk of the parliaments and the clerk of the crown. The points of general interest are : (1) the pre-eminence of the crown, which Henry VIII further empha-sised in 1539 by enacting that no one not a member of the royal family should presume to sit on the cloth of state ; (2) the inner ring or square formed by the council in parlia-ment ; the specially summoned spiritual and temporal peers are accretions on that parliament of the council, which Maitland has called the core of every session ; (3) the presence of the commons, headed by the Speaker, who alone and for himself alone claims liberty of speech in these parliaments ; and (4) this scene is not laid at West-minster, but at Blackfriars, where the parliament of 1523 sat until its transference to Westminster in July. Parlia-mentary paraphernalia were still comparatively simple, and could be carted without difficulty from one meeting-place to another.

Our second illustration can be dated as precisely as the first. It is taken from Robert Glover's *De Nobilitate Politica vel Civili*, which was edited from his MS. and pub-lished by his nephew, Thomas Milles, in 1608, folio. Glover was Somerset herald, and both Camden and Dugdale owed a good deal to his antiquarian labours. He died in April 1588, and this picture illustrates his account of the opening of parliament on 22 November, 1584, which under the title of *Pompa Parliamentaris* forms part of the volume pub-lished by Milles in 1608. The text of that tract is the best commentary on the illustration, although some ad-ditional light is thrown by the account of Elizabethan parliamentary ceremonial which Sir Simonds D'Ewes in-corporates in his *Journals* (pp. 11–12).

There are notable changes since 1523. The abbots and prior of St. John's have disappeared ; there is no cardinal and no place for archbishops on the cloth of state ; and monarchy is still more aloof than it was in the early years of Henry VIII, while his statute of 1539 has given secretaries of state and other non-baronial councillors places on the woolsacks. The scene now is laid in the Painted Chamber, which ran east and west at right angles to the old house of lords (see plate 5); the throne was at the west end, which the queen approached through her majesty's robing-room; and, as the shadows indicate, the south side of the chamber was on her right. Immediately on her right stands the lord chancellor, then Sir Thomas Bromley, and on the left Lord Burghley as lord high treasurer. The two groups on either side are described as *procerum primogeniti*, though the first figure on Bromley's right is in ecclesiastical garb. The cap of maintenance is borne by the marquis of Winchester, the marshal's baton by the earl of Worcester *vice* the earl of Shrewsbury, who had been created earl marshal in 1573, and was present on this occasion, but was disabled by gout. On the queen's left was the earl of Kent, bearing the sword, and apparently the earl of Leicester, the lord steward, with Garter King of Arms to flank him. The upper woolsack has by this time been monopolised by the chancellor, and is called his seat, though when the queen is present he stands at her right hand. Glover does not specify the places on the two side woolsacks, beyond saying that on them sat the master of the rolls, the queen's secretaries, the judges, the barons of the exchequer, and the counsel learned in the law; but D'Ewes avers that on the woolsack to the right " of the Estate " (*i. e.* the throne), which he wrongly identifies with the north side of the chamber, sat the two chief justices and other judges, and on the left side the master of the rolls, lord chief baron, the queen's learned counsel and others. He then makes the confused and contradictory statement that " all these may properly be said to sit on the inner side of the woolsacks, and the queen's learned counsel on the outside next the earls. The masters of the chancery sat, two on the same side, and two on the other side, next the bishops." He only accounts for two occupants of the lower woolsack, the clerk of the parliaments and the clerk of the crown, and assumes that the kneeling figures, now increased to four, were all clerks to the clerk of the parliaments. He notes the table which now first makes its appearance. The Speaker on this occasion was Sir John Puckering.

Our third illustration is less satisfactory. It is the frontispiece to D'Ewes' *Journals of the Parliaments of Queen Elizabeth*, which were compiled in 1629–30, and published by his nephew, Paul Bowes, in 1680 (2nd ed. 1682). It professes to represent a parliament of Elizabeth's reign; but in spite of the queen on the throne and the entirely unauthorised location of Walsingham on her left, it illustrates a seventeenth- rather than a sixteenth-century parliament. Neither the picture nor the parliament can be precisely dated; but the costumes are those of the parliaments of Charles I, and it is probably a fair representation of a parliament of that reign. I am inclined to think that D'Ewes' frontispiece is more accurate than his text in identifying the four occupants of the lower woolsack with the masters in chancery, and in reducing all the clerks to the kneeling posture. The changes since Glover's time are : (1) the appearance of an official with the mace of the house of lords; (2) the increase in the number of barons, owing to James I's creations, and the consequent multiplication of the cross-benches and proportionate reduction of the conciliar element in parliament; and (3) the increase and growing emphasis of the attendant commons. The Speaker bulks larger than before; on his right is seen Black Rod, and on his left the serjeant-at-arms with the mace of the house of commons.

The fourth illustration is from the British Museum Print Room, and is a representation of the close of the session, after Walpole's fall, in February 1742; it was engraved and published in 1749 by John Pine, who had in 1743 been appointed Bluemantle pursuivant-at-arms, and had already published valuable engravings of the tapestries of the house of lords. It illustrates in a remarkable way the constitutional changes of the Revolution, and exhibits monarchy in tutelage : so far from no one being permitted on the cloth of state except the king, he is overshadowed by his magnates, and parliament is swamped with peers.

C C

The judges and other elements of the council have been reduced to a handful in a house of hundreds; but the peers themselves are threatened by the dominating figure of Speaker Onslow and the commons below the bar.

The last illustration is a reproduction of an undated and unsigned pencil plan in the library of the Society of Antiquaries.[1] On the back of it, however, is a reference to Capon's engraved plan, published in *Vetusta Monumenta* in 1828.[2] This led Mr. Somers Clarke to believe that the one was " in some respects at least " an original from which the other was produced; but, whereas the engraved plan shews the lowest level of the Palace, the one reproduced here illustrates the arrangement of the floor above (when such exists) where most of the important apartments were situated. However, the two certainly bear much evidence of a common authorship, and there is little doubt that both were drawn by Capon. The plan published by the Society of Antiquaries is definitely stated to have been drawn between 1793 and 1823. Other plans and drawings of the Painted Chamber by the same artist were made between 1795 and 1800;[3] and the one here reproduced is certainly near that period; for the house of Lord Thurlow, Teller of the Exchequer, is shewn, and he only obtained that office in 1786; while the placing of the House of Lords in its pre-1801 quarters, and the references to the houses of John Hatsell and Edward Delaval (see *D.N.B.* for both) indicate the same date.

[1] In the volume entitled " Houses of Parliament," No. 11.
[2] Vol. V. plate xlvii. It was purchased by the Society of Antiquaries in 1826 and engraved by Basire. See *D.N.B.* under Capon, William. For Mr. Somers Clarke's remarks see *Archaeologia*, vol. l. p. 10.
[3] There are two coloured drawings of the Painted Chamber in the Library of the Society of Antiquaries, " Houses of Parliament," Nos. 1 and 2, and a coloured Plan of the Painted Chamber, Crace Collection. Maps and Plans. Portfolio XI, No. 47. I have to thank Mr. H. S. Kingsford, of the Society of Antiquaries, for his kindness in shewing me the plans and drawings in the library.

As the original is a pencil plan, reproduction was difficult. The method adopted was to photograph the original and make a tracing of the photograph. Care has been taken to avoid error, but the drawing is very detailed, and the pencil faint. For other than purely minor details, however, the reproduction may be taken as accurate. There has been no attempt to reproduce the actual handwriting on the original. I have to thank Mr. J. Hill for his care in making the tracing. [I. M. C.]

APPENDIX II

THE suggestion on pp. 316–20 that the writs *de expensis*
may provide a more accurate indication of the actual
attendance at a medieval parliament than the sheriffs'
election returns has provoked some criticism, and it seems
desirable to discuss a little more fully the evidence on which
it is based. The main point, that election returns are no
evidence of actual attendance in parliament, is too obvious
to need much elaboration. A summons to serve on a jury
is no proof of actual service : many more jurors are summoned than are actually required. Some stay away,
relying on the chance of not being called in court, or preferring to pay their fine if they are called; others attend, but
produce an exemption from service; and even those who
are actually sworn serve for but a part of the business and
time of the court. Scores of summonses are issued in order
to ensure a jury of twelve for each particular case; and
even though it were proved that every member of parliament returned by the sheriff journeyed to Westminster, it
would prove nothing about the attendance when any
particular bill or tax was under discussion. Most of the
peers disregard to-day, as they did in the fourteenth century,
their special writs of summons, and in the house of commons
itself the test of attendance is the division-lists and not the
election returns. There would be no point in the clause of
the Act of 1918 confiscating the deposit of the successful
candidate who never attends, if his election return were
proof of his having taken his seat; and no penalties seem
to have been actually inflicted in the middle ages either

on boroughs which failed to make returns, on members who failed to put in an appearance, or on their manucaptors or sureties.

There is thus good reason for discounting the ' evidence ' of the election returns, quite apart from the writs *de expensis*. But these writs, while proof of the attendance of the members who obtained them, are not disproof of that of those who did not; and there is the further difficulty that, apart from stray copies of the writs themselves entered on borough records or preserved elsewhere, we have only enrolments on the close rolls, and the enrolments may be incomplete. Indeed, after 1414 they cease altogether, although writs *de expensis* undoubtedly continued to be issued down to the seventeenth century.[1] They are but one of the items on the close roll which appear and disappear without any obvious reason, and apparently the last enrolment of any kind of writ on the close roll dates from 24 Henry VIII. Conjecture might connect this particular disappearance of writs *de expensis* with a petition of members for their expenses in 1413 and a suggestion in answer on the part of the crown that the records should be searched for evidence of their claims.[2] This only referred to the payment of M.P.'s for attendance at a parliament dissolved by Henry IV's demise; but the reference to the records raised a delicate question. Some members, like those for London and York, were conscious of receiving double the rate which the enrolments prescribed; on the other hand, boroughs which were paying only 20*d.*, 18*d.*, 16*d.*, 15*d.*, and 12*d.* a day might not be pleased with members who established

---

[1] For some late references to writs *de expensis*, see Guilding, *Reading Records*, i. 80, 101 [1504]; *Hereford MSS.* (Hist. MSS. Comm.,13th Rep., App. iv. 306-7 [1514]); *Shrewsbury MSS.* (*ibid.*, 15th Rep., App. x. 22 [1568]); *Exeter MSS.* (*ibid.*, pp. 188-9 [1629]); and Prynne, *Briefe Register of Parl. Writs*, iv. 527-9, 535-50, 1187. Prynne mentions London, York, Bristol, Norwich, and Exeter as still [1662] paying expenses " voluntarily without writs," and notes that no more than 4*s.* and 2*s.* "can be legally demanded " (*ibid.*, iv. 610-11). Payment was prescribed for Wales and Cheshire in Henry VIII's statutes giving them parliamentary representation (27 Henry VIII, c. 26; 34 & 35 Henry VIII, c. 24; 35 Henry VIII, c. 11).

[2] *Rot. Parl.*, iv. 9.

their claim to 2s. There were many complications. Sheriffs were inclined to collect as much as they could in virtue of the writs, pay as little as might be thereof to members, and use the surplus to make up an account which it was never easy to balance.[1] The taxpayer's interest was to evade payment altogether or keep it as low as possible, while members desired at least the accustomed or official wage. It may be that magnates, who, like the Duke of Norfolk, desired the election of " such persons as longe unto him and be of his menyall servaunts,"[2] also wished them to look to their lords for recompense instead of depending upon kings' writs. Borough practice was more heterogeneous than that of the shires. " The agreement of the parties will prevail against the law,"[3] and boroughs were getting close by the time their records say much about paying M.P.'s. It was generally a matter of arrangement among twenty-four or forty-eight burgesses, most of whom might have been or might hope (or fear) to be members themselves; and the issue was a conflict between communal economy and individual desires, in which the growing lure of a seat in parliament tended at first to lower the demand for remuneration, was temporarily counteracted by the inflation of the currency, and finally caused the disappearance of wages altogether. Boroughs which had paid less than 2s. a day in the fourteenth and fifteenth centuries, found themselves paying 3s. 4d. in 1586, 5s. in 1604, 6s. 8d. in 1606, and nothing at all a hundred years later.[4]

The enrolment of writs may have ceased for some simpler or more technical reason. In 1515 it was made a statutory

[1] Prynne (*Briefe Register*, iv. 259–60) describes a case in which two deputies of the sheriff of Lancashire in 1362 elected themselves, did not attend, but levied their wages from the shire : cf. *ibid.*, iv. 532. As late as 1446 the commons petition against this abuse (Parry, *Parliaments*, p. 183).
[2] *Paston Letters*, i. 337 ; cf. *Rot. Parl.*, iv. 350.
[3] Holdsworth, *Hist. English Law*, 3rd ed. iii. 102.
[4] Whitley, *Parl. Repres. of Coventry*, pp. 61, 65. Some boroughs occasionally paid as much in the fifteenth century; Lynn's rate was 6s. 8d. in 1431 (*Archæologia*, xxiv. 320). Four London M.P.'s at the Cambridge parliament of 1388 ran up their bill for expenses to 14s. 4d. a day for each of them (*English Hist. Rev.*, xxxix. 521).

obligation on the second clerk of the parliaments *alias* the clerk of the house of commons to keep a book or register of attendance.[1]   Much of Henry VIII's legislation gave merely a statutory sanction to previous custom, and the ' roll-call ' of the commons, of which we first hear in the reign of Richard II, may have provided in time a register of attendance which superseded, as evidence for the writs, the entries on the Close Rolls.   That some record was kept is almost certain.   In 1462 the Reading town council resolved that the mayor should purchase a new writ *de expensis* in place of the one he had lost, or else pay the wages himself,[2] and it is difficult to see how a new writ could be issued unless some record had been kept.   Two things at least are clear : the cessation of the enrolments implies no cessation or diminution of the writs themselves ; it indicates an abrupt change in method of record, not a gradual decay in the payment of members or in their practice of suing out writs.[3]   There is ample evidence in local and other records of members suing their writs in the sixteenth and early seventeenth centuries : the commons themselves in 1430 petitioned for the continuance of their customary writs ;[4] parliament re-enacted the practice in the legislation it passed in the reign of Henry VIII for the extension of the parliamentary system to Wales and Cheshire; and on 18 March, 1580–1, the commons resolved that no writ *de expensis* should be issued without warrant from the clerk of the house.

So, too, the enrolments continue with no abatement until they suddenly stop in 2 Henry V.   Those for the knights of the shire are indeed more complete than they were a century earlier.   It may be hyperbole to ascribe regularity to the borough writs *de expensis* at any period,

[1] Henry VIII, c. 16.   I suspect that the early ' roll-calls ' were intended, not to ensure that the commons, who were called into the White chamber from that very public place, Westminster Hall, included all authorised persons, but excluded all who were not (*Rot. Parl.*, iii. 122).

[2] Guilding, *Reading Records*, i. 54.

[3] It may be a premonitory symptom that no writs are enrolled for the last three parliaments of Henry IV (Prynne, iv. 493, makes them into five).

[4] Parry, pp. 178–9.

but they were as regular and as numerous for the beginning of the Lancastrian period as in the time of the Edwards or Richard II, with the exception of the first decade of Edward III's reign and the period of the Good parliament; and the average for such Lancastrian enrolments as exist is precisely the same as the average for the fourteenth century.[1] If there are no borough writs enrolled for 20 Rich. II. and only six for 21 Rich. II and five for 6 Henry IV, there are also none for either 18 or 19 Ed. II, and only two for 17, four for 16, and five for 15 Ed. II, and no more for half a dozen parliaments of Edward III; and if the thirty-eight boroughs which received writs *de expensis* for the Northampton parliament of April 1328 marks the peak of enrolment, the Good parliament of 1376 with its twenty-two borough writs *de expensis* attains a higher figure than any of Edward I's or Edward II's, while the 16, 14, 15, and 16 of the first four parliaments of Henry IV maintain a steadier level than any other four consecutive parliaments can show. Whatever may have been the cause for the paucity of enrolments of writs for wages compared with the returns of members elected —whether neglect of members to sue for writs, negligence of clerks in enrolling them, private arrangement between members and their constituencies, or failure of members to attend the parliaments to which they had been elected—it is a cause which operates in the same way and with the same effect throughout medieval parliaments.

Prynne, whose vast and pioneer labours as keeper of the records in the Tower have not yet been quite superseded even by the *Calendar of Close Rolls*, suggested all these reasons in the first part of his *Briefe Register . . . of Parliamentary Writs*, which runs to 2,250 pages and consists mainly of statistics; but, as he went on with his work he slipped, with some efforts to avoid it, into the assumption that

---

[1] There are about 674 borough writs enrolled for 67 parliaments from 1327 to 1395, and 108 borough writs enrolled for eleven parliaments from 1397 to 1414. The average for the earlier period is just above 10 per cent., for the later it is just under 10 per cent. The fact that London, York, and Norwich have completely disappeared in the later period makes the difference. Most writs of course are for two members.

negligence of the recording clerks rather than the absentee-ism of members was to blame for the hiatus between the sheriffs' election returns and the record of wages paid for attendance.　He was a hero, as well as a giant, of historical research, but no one who has perused the results of his labours can fail to detect his bias as a parliamentarian not less zealous for its restoration in 1659-60 than he had been for its triumph in 1640-2.[1]　He was less unhistorical than nineteenth-century votaries of parliamentary legends, but his constant appeal to medieval precedent tended to dim his insight into the weakness of the parliaments he invoked; and his assumption that members necessarily attended parliaments because the sheriffs returned their names is not substantiated by any attempt at proof.

Proof is hardly, indeed, possible either of the attendance or absence of the great majority of members whose names were returned by the sheriffs.　If those returns create a presumption that members did attend, their failure to establish any record of their payment creates a presumption that they did not; otherwise we have to find some other explanation why some constituencies get their writs *de expensis* enrolled, and, if shires, get them enrolled with unfailing regularity, while others get them enrolled, if at all, in varying degrees of infrequency.　In view, however, of the general acceptance of the sheriffs' election returns as proof of actual attendance at parliament it may be well first of all to adduce specific evidence to rebut that presumption. On 12 Dec., 1382, Colchester, on account of its expense in repairing its walls, received from Richard II letters patent exempting it from sending members to parliament for a period of five years; [2] the exemption was renewed for another five years on 21 Sept., 1388, for three years on 3 March, 1394, for six years in 1404, and for twelve in 1410; and when Henry V confirmed it on 25 May, 1413, Colchester paid

---

[1] He claimed that the first two parts of his *Briefe Register*, published in 1659 and 1660, had been ' very instrumental ' in promoting Charles II's peaceful restoration (dedication of pt. iii. to the king, dated 24 Jan., 1661).

[2] *Rot. Parl.*, iii. 395-6; *Cal. Patent Rolls*, 1381-5, p. 214, 1385-9, p. 505, 1391-6, p. 379, 1401-5, p. 355, 1408-13, p. 199, 1413-16, p. 23.

40*s.* into the hanaper for the privilege. Yet the sheriffs of
Essex return two members to parliament for Colchester to
27 parliaments during the period of its exemption. There
is nothing inexplicable in this. The sheriff was instructed
in the writs he received " to cause to be elected " two
burgesses from the more capable boroughs in his shire.
They were to be elected in his county court, but there was as
yet nothing in his writs to say that they must be returned
by means of indenture between him and each particular
borough; nor was there anything about a poll. ' Election '
meant what is now called nomination : indeed, the word is
used in that sense in the Act of 1918, where (2nd Schedule,
pt. i.) it prescribes that the day fixed " for the *election* shall
be the eighth day " after the king's proclamation, and the
day appointed " for the *poll* shall be the ninth day after the
day fixed for the *election.*" Whether or no there were
burgesses present at the county court, it was the sheriff's
duty to " cause to be elected " there and then persons to
represent the chief boroughs within his jurisdiction, and to
return their names into chancery. It was no concern of his,
if higher authority dispensed with the attendance due, any
more than it is for the under-sheriff who summons our
modern jurors to determine whether they will be exempted
from service in court. Prynne[1] argues that Colchester's dispensation was invalid as being inconsistent with the statute of
1382 requiring sheriffs to make returns from their accustomed boroughs, and avers that Colchester " received no ease
or exemption at all." The sheriff in point of fact did make
his accustomed returns, but it was very much a seventeenth-
century mentality which concluded that Richard II could
not dispense with members' attendance merely because a

---

[1] *Brief Register,* iii. 241*b.* It may also be noted that, while the names
appear in the sheriff's returns, no dates of their election are given. None,
of course, occur until after the Act of 1406, but neither Colchester nor
Maldon have dates till 1453. Another point of interest is the gradual way
in which the different shires adopt the practice of giving different dates
for the different borough elections instead of dating them all the day of
the county court. This indicates the growing importance of the boroughs'
replies to the sheriffs' precept, compared with that of the sheriffs' returns
in the county court. Cornwall is the last to make the change, but all have
made it by the reign of Edward VI.

statute required their election; and, dealing with Close and not with Patent Rolls, his eye had not lit upon the repeated exemptions by Henry IV and Henry V nor upon the record that Colchester paid 40s. for the renewal of a privilege from which it " received no ease or exemption."

Colchester does not stand alone. Maldon, the only other parliamentary borough in Essex, obtained similar exemptions in 1388, 1392, and 1407;[1] yet the sheriff of Essex continues to make returns for it as well as for Colchester throughout the periods of exemption. There is, however, no return from Hull to the parliaments from which it was excused.[2] Torrington's familiar exemption[3] was not for a term of years but for ever. The less-known details of the story throw some light on our problem. The borough repeated in the parliament of 1368 a petition granted by the king in 1366 for relief from the burden of parliamentary representation; it averred that it had never sent members to parliament before 24 Ed. III, when the sheriff of Devon, in the words of the exemption granted, *dictam villam de Toriton burgum et duos homines pro eodem burgo ad veniendum ad parliamentum nostrum dicto anno vicesimo quarto tentum, summonitos fuisse malitiose in cancellaria nostra retornavit*; and *pretextu retorni prædicti* Torrington was burdened with labours and expenses to its *damnum non modicum et depressionem manifestam*. It is exonerated *in perpetuum* on 18 May, 1368. Nevertheless the sheriff returned two members for Torrington in 1369, and according to Prynne until 45 Edward III.

Again Prynne opines that the exemption was void in law, and ascribes to the realization of that fact the continuance of the sheriff's returns; but his explanation singularly fails to account for their discontinuance after 45 Edward III, if not earlier, and ignores the fact that the second exemption was granted *per petitionem parliamenti*. His ground for the

[1] *Cal. Pat. Rolls*, 1385-9, p. 508, 1391-6, p. 187 (2 Oct. 1392), 1405-8, p. 376; Prynne, iii. 200.
[2] *Ibid.*, 1381-5, p. 475.
[3] *Ibid.*, 1364-7, p. 246, 1367-70, p. 115; Rymer, *Fœdera*, new ed. III ii. 790; Prynne, iii. 196, 1239-41, iv. 946-7, 1175-6.

illegality is his discovery that the sheriff had made returns for Torrington to twenty-two parliaments before 24 Ed. III; Torrington was therefore an ' ancient ' borough which the king could not exempt from service,[1] and the scrutiny which Edward III said had been made of the rolls and memoranda in chancery must have been superficial. Torrington, however, does not deny that the sheriff had made returns for it before 24 Ed. III; it merely asserts that the borough had sent no members; and the clerks in chancery confirmed the assertion. It is also confirmed by the writs *de expensis*, and they likewise support the efficacy of the letters patent of exemption : none is enrolled before 1351 and none after 1363.[2] It seems fairly clear that in Torrington we have an instance of the sheriff returning, for 22 parliaments before 24 Ed. III and for at least one parliament after 42 Ed. III, the names of members who did not attend. Colchester and Maldon tell the same tale :[3] during the period of their exemption they get no writs *de expensis* in spite of the sheriff's continued returns.

The sheriff's returns are, in short, evidence of a *servitium* which he thought, for reasons which did not always bear scrutiny, was *debitum* from what he chose to consider the *potentiores burgos* in his shire. They do not express the views of the boroughs themselves on what they owed nor prove that the service was rendered.[4] The sheriff's writs

[1] Prynne is arguing throughout his *Briefe Register*, though not quite consistently, for a fixed parliamentary constituency, immune alike from royal dispensations and from frivolous creations at the sheriffs' whims.

[2] Torrington's grievance may have been enhanced by the exceptional number of writs *de expensis* it had to meet. It received seven during the twelve years, 1351–63, which is more than any other borough has enrolled for that period. How far that was due to the ' malice ' of the sheriff it is impossible to say; but a few years later Barnstaple complained that it was asked to pay wages for an M.P. who was not resident in and had not been elected by the borough.

[3] All of them received writs *de expensis* with at least average regularity until their exemption. Torrington's was perpetual and Colchester's extended until after the enrolments cease; but Maldon receives writs in 4 Henry IV, 5 Henry IV, and 1 Henry V (its seven years' exemption from 1407 having lapsed on the demise of Henry IV).

[4] Parliamentary representation was, as Prynne remarks (iv. 1182), " no franchise, but a service "; and it was never ' granted ' in a medieval charter of ' liberties ' (cf. Pasquet, *Essai*, pp. 183–9, 260; *Parl. Writs*, i. 44, 177, 187, ii. 337; Riess, *Gesch. des Wahlrechts*, pp. 18–21).

were generally worded; they never specified the boroughs to which he was to issue his precepts, and the latitude and inconsistency with which successive sheriffs exercised their discretion provided the boroughs with ample excuse for ignoring their precepts. Fifteen towns in Yorkshire had made returns to parliament before 1306 when the sheriff omitted all but two. The sheriff of Worcestershire returned six boroughs and the city of Worcester in 1295 but only the city in 1307, 1314, and 1319. In 1298 the sheriff of Buckinghamshire returned no boroughs as fit for or liable to representation. Two years later his successor returned Amersham, Wendover, and Wycombe. Two years later again another successor returned Wycombe but neither Amersham nor Wendover. In 1308 the sheriff returned all three and Marlow as well, but in 1311 made no return for any but Wycombe, which did not respond either then or in 1315. In 1353 a later sheriff sent a precept to Buckingham and entered it in his return, but neither then nor to any medieval parliament did Buckingham make any election. In spite of all these efforts to extract a *servitium debitum* out of boroughs in Buckinghamshire, Wycombe alone submitted to the burden. No boroughs were ever returned for Rutland, and the sheriff of Lancashire returned none after 1331, though both Lancaster and Preston had received precepts in earlier years. The sheriff of Hertfordshire declares there are none in his shire after 1336, though Hertford, St. Albans, and Bishop's Stortford had all elected to some previous parliaments, and Hertford reappears with a precept (and also a writ *de expensis*) in 1376. Sheriffs, says Prynne, "made and unmade, continued, discontinued, and revived" boroughs "at their wills."[1]

But boroughs frequently refused to make returns after as well as during the reigns of Edward I and II. Between 1327 and 1397 four boroughs in Yorkshire summoned to send members to parliament—Beverley, Hedon, Richmond, and Ripon—never responded, though Hedon appears four times in the sheriffs' returns. Hindon in Wiltshire,

[1] *Ibid.*, iii. 233.

summoned to nine parliaments, made no election to any.
Out of twelve boroughs summoned for that county in
1361, six make no return; out of 11 summoned in Sept.
1388, five make no return; out of seven summoned
in 1368, four make none; three make none in five parliaments, and two in five other parliaments. Bedwin and
Calne reply to less than a third of the precepts they receive;
and these figures are irrespective of the parliaments for which
no returns have been found. Of the 170 boroughs which
did make returns to some parliament or other between 26
Ed. I and 12 Ed. IV, Prynne reckons that 22 returned only
once, 8 but twice, 4 thrice, 4 four times, 4 five times, 4 six
times, and 5 seven times.[1] For at least a third of the so-
called 'parliamentary' boroughs a parliamentary return
was a rare, if refreshing, experience; and in the face of this
record of successful reluctance to go through the form of a
return, what presumption is there that the return itself,
not necessarily representing any choice by the borough and
sometimes a bare nomination by the sheriff, involved any
actual attendance at Westminster? Abstention was not
disobedience to a royal writ, because no boroughs, and still
less any persons, were specified by the king in those writs;
there is no hint of penalties before the vague and ineffective
statute of 5 Rich. II; and clearly it required no special
exemption to make an occasional return or no return at all.
"A much simpler way of evading the duty," says Stubbs,
"was to disregard the sheriff's precept." When a wealthy
borough like Coventry, which stood fourth among the English
boroughs in wealth and population,[2] could, after making two
returns to parliament in 1346 and 1353, escape representation
for a century, even in parliaments held within its walls,
there is no reason to wonder that insignificant boroughs
escaped with a casual and spasmodic attendance, even
though they appeared in sheriffs' returns. No law yet
required attendance, and, when in 1321 the mayor of Lincoln

[1] *Ibid.*, iv. 223.
[2] Subsidy Roll for 51 Ed. III printed in *Archæologia*, vii. 340–3 : Whitley,
Parl. Repres. of Coventry, p. 17.

reports that one of its burgesses—although he had consented to his election—*ne se deygne venir par riens que nous savoms faire*, he can only suggest another election.[1]

The problem is to ascertain the precise effect of this inertia and irregularity upon the actual composition of medieval parliaments. An analysis of the returns themselves is sufficient to show that their personnel was shifting and uncertain, though there was a solid residuum consisting of the knights of the shires and the representatives of London, York, and other boroughs, some of which rarely failed in their representation and others were fairly regular; and the enrolled writs *de expensis* serve for the most part to strengthen and to develop this impression. The number of boroughs appearing in the sheriffs' extant returns to a medieval parliament (from 1295) ranges from none to 114;[2] the number having enrolled writs *de expensis* ranges from none to 38. A model parliament, containing two members from each shire and two from all the 170 boroughs for which a return was ever made, would have had 414 members. The highest specific return before the sixteenth century was for 114 boroughs to the Model parliament of 1295; and these, with the shires, would have produced a ' house ' of 302 members. The average number of election returns to fourteenth-century parliaments gives about 135 borough members and 70 knights of the shires. The highest specific number of enrolled writs *de expensis* yields 76 borough members and 74 knights of the shires; but the average number of enrolled writs *de expensis* for boroughs is between 10 and 11 and gives about 21 burgesses, to whom must be added the 74 knights of the shires, about a dozen members from London and other cities or boroughs which dispensed with writs, and (after 1365) a similar number from the Cinque Ports, which also had no writs *de expensis* enrolled.

[1] *Parl. Writs*, II i. 252; Stubbs, iii. 435.
[2] The number has hitherto been given as 110, but the missing return of the sheriff of Norfolk and Suffolk has now been found and is printed in the *Bulletin* of the Institute of Historical Research (November 1925). He returns Norwich, Lynn, Ipswich, and Yarmouth, but reports that he has had no answer from Bury St. Edmunds, Dunwich, and Orford, to the steward and bailiffs of which he had sent his precepts.

This would give a house of about 120 members, the majority of whom would be knights of the shires. Which of these figures comes nearest to the truth and helps us best to understand the parliamentary insignificance of the boroughs in the fourteenth century? The ideal maximum of 414 can, of course, be ruled out. So can the actual maximum of 302 in 1295. Just as the number of specially summoned barons sank from more than a hundred to less than fifty, and the abbots from 72 to 27, so the number of boroughs returned by the sheriffs dwindled from 114 to an average of 65 or 70. Is it also true that, just as the special summons to spiritual and temporal peers was no proof of their presence in parliament, so the general summons through sheriffs was no proof of the actual attendance of burgesses?

Apart from personal references in the rolls of parliament and in the chronicles we have no specific evidence of the presence of particular members in parliament except in the enrolled writs *de expensis* and the scattered details provided by borough records, of which the former are much the more comprehensive and systematic. The hiatus between their figures and the sheriffs' returns can be explained in two ways: either the enrolments of the writs *de expensis* exclude many members who actually sat, or the sheriffs' returns include many who did not. But both statements are true to some extent. There is no doubt that some members returned by the sheriffs did not attend parliament; it is equally true that members sat for London and other constituencies whose wages are not recorded on the close rolls in chancery. But none of the great cities and boroughs, commonly thought to have dispensed with writs, is entirely absent from the rolls. Even London has writs enrolled down to 1336,[1] Norwich to 1335, York to 1352, and

---

[1] *Calendar of Close Rolls*, 1333-7, p. 707. The writ *de expensis* is only for two M.P.'s for 2s. a day each; the writs never require a higher rate for boroughs, not even when they are made counties. On the other hand, no objection was ever taken to boroughs paying either more money or more members. If London chose to send and pay four (or even more) members instead of two, it was welcome to do so. There was no known voting by division in a medieval house of commons; and if there was voting at all apart from the collective vote of estates, it was almost certainly by con-

Bristol till the last extant enrolment in 2 Henry V. Southampton also appears in that enrolment; and Lincoln, Nottingham, Leicester, Exeter, Salisbury, Winchester, Oxford and both the Newcastles figure in the Lancastrian close rolls. Uniform absence is limited to London, York, and Norwich after 1352; and irregular, arbitrary, and incalculable negligence on the part of the clerks seems to be the only explanation of the erratic entries on those rolls, unless their vagaries are due to a correspondingly casual attendance of members of parliament.

Official negligence is, however, a somewhat facile solution of archivistic problems. It is quite possible that the occasions, on which the enrolments break off without recording any writs for boroughs at all, are due to negligence; but these only amount to about half a dozen for over a hundred parliaments, and hardly affect the main obstacle to this explanation. For there is no negligence, either by the makers or keepers of records, so far as the writs for the shires go. Throughout the whole period the knights of the shires get writs for their wages enrolled with remarkable regularity, and the substance of these writs is no matter of common form. From the beginning of Edward III's reign they specify each member's name, the exact number of days he served, and the total sum to which he was entitled. If one knight only attended, one name only appears in the writ; if one serves for the whole parliament and another for but part of the time, the partial length of service is specified; if some members remain at the king's request after the first leave to depart is given, their names and days of additional service are recorded, and allowance is made for their extra expenses.[1] When clerks were so punctilious about the attendance of knights, why should they be so negligent in recording that of the burgesses?

The theory would be more plausible if we could establish a considerable category of boroughs to which writs *de expensis*

stituencies and not *per capita*. The London writs in Edward III's reign are for 1327, 1328, and 1336, the Norwich writs for 1328, 1334 *bis*, and 1335, the York writs for 1334 *bis*, 1337, and 1352. Bristol has eleven in all.

[1] *Ibid.*, 1337–9, p. 388.

were never issued or never enrolled; but, as we have seen, there were only three for which this rule was established, and then not until the middle of the fourteenth century. We could also more readily believe that boroughs found it easier than shires to dispense with the writs,[1] if it were not the *potentiores burgi* which most often get writs *de expensis* as well as sheriff's precepts, and if, having once realized this alleged advantage over the shires they had pursued it with some consistency. But why, for instance, should it have been easier for Leicester to dispense with a writ *de expensis* for the first, than for the second, parliament of 1332, and for the second, than for the first, parliament of 1380? Why so easy for a dozen boroughs to do without writs for a dozen parliaments before 1376 and then all at once to discover that an enrolled writ *de expensis* was necessary to secure payment for their signal attendance at the Good parliament, relapsing thereafter into their accustomed independence? Why, again, if the negligence of clerks or independence of boroughs be the explanation, do we find enrolled for the York parliament of February 1334 writs *de expensis* for both members from twenty-four boroughs and for single M.P.'s from ten others, and five out of fifteen boroughs receiving writs for only one member apiece in the next parliament six months later?[2] Is there not a reason, less arbitrary than neglect of the clerks to record them, for the facts that, out of thirty-four boroughs which sent members to a parliament at York in February, only thirteen should send members to a parliament at Westminster in September; that out of the thirteen eight should have two members apiece in one of the parliaments and only one in the other; and that only five boroughs should have two members apiece in both? Is it not also odd, for instance, that in the four successive parliaments of 1327–8, held at Lincoln, York, Northampton, and Salisbury, the clerks should happen to have enrolled writs for Leicester

---

[1] *English Hist. Rev.*, xxxix. 512.

[2] If writs were omitted from the enrolments in order to save the clerks trouble, it would have saved them so much more to omit a writ altogether than merely one member's name; the same writ served for both members for a constituency, whether it was a county or a borough.

DD

to the two nearer parliaments of Lincoln and Northampton, and to have neglected to enrol those for the more distant parliaments of Salisbury and York?

The argument that boroughs were independent of writs is, however, somewhat beside the point. There is no doubt of the value of writs, whether or not those writs were enrolled. There are repeated petitions from the commons that they should have their writs *de expensis* as usual; the chancellor or his deputy, in dismissing a parliament regularly enjoined it upon members that they should sue out their writs; and they continued to do so long after those writs had ceased to be enrolled.[1] The suggestion that is really arguable is not that burgesses were independent of writs, but indifferent to their enrolment. Even that argument has to ignore the fact that most boroughs returning M.P.'s have occasional writs enrolled so long as enrolment lasts. Some of course cease, but most of these also cease to appear in the election returns. The practical value of enrolment is illustrated by a letter on the close roll for 1341.[2] It recites that sheriffs of 'all' counties, bailiffs of boroughs, and others have levied excessive wages for members of parliament, and announces that the king has therefore sent down extracts from the rolls in chancery containing the names of knights, citizens, and burgesses and the specific sums assigned to them for wages in order that the justices may be able to adjudicate upon the complaints that have been made; and the judicial use to which the enrolments were thus put helps to explain the meticulous detail in which they abound.

So far as the knights of the shires are concerned, the theory of negligence on their part to sue out writs or on the part of the clerks to enrol them can be definitely rejected. With the exception of Cambridgeshire in the second parliament of 1383 there are enrolled writs *de expensis* for every shire for every one of the twenty-four parliaments held between 1376 and 1395 inclusive. For eight of these parliaments the writs are for two knights for every shire: for another

---

[1] See above, p. 388, *n.* 1.   [2] *Cal. Close Rolls*, 1341-3, p. 109.

eight of these parliaments there is only one absentee in one
shire; for three parliaments there is an absentee in two
shires; for one parliament there are two absentees in
one shire and one in another; for two parliaments there
is one absentee in three shires, and for another two parliaments there is one absentee in each of four shires. In
other words, the enrolments record the attendance of all the
74 knights throughout eight parliaments; of 73 throughout
another eight, of 72 throughout three, of 71 throughout
another three, and of 70 throughout the remaining two
parliaments. The total possible attendance of 74 knights
in twenty-four parliaments is 1776, the total attendance
recorded in the enrolments is 1745. If there was negligence,
it does not amount to much; and since the clerks took the
trouble to record those 1745 attendances, specifying not
only the names of the members but the exact sums to which
they were entitled and exact length of service for which they
were paid, even calculating the difference of time allowed for
travelling from each county, and making a fresh calculation
for each different place—Westminster, Gloucester, Northampton, Salisbury, Cambridge, Winchester, and Shrewsbury
—at which parliament was held, the inference is that the
thirty-one omissions were due, not to negligence on the part
of the clerks, but to a perfectly natural and amazingly
small proportion of absences on the part of members
themselves.

It was, however, only by degrees that the knights of the
shires worked up to this exemplary standard of attendance.
Early in Edward III's reign we may find in a single parliament as many absentees as in a dozen parliaments in
that of Richard II. For the parliament of March 1329–30
all the shire election returns except that for Northumberland
are extant, but eight shires get no writ *de expensis* and for
six [1] others the writs are for single members only. In
February 1339 nine shires have no writs *de expensis*, and in

---

[1] Prynne, iv. 107–9; the *Calendar of Close Rolls*, 1330–3, p. 137, omits
Leicestershire from Prynne's list, but the total, £4 4s., given for that county
for twenty-one days' service is the wage for one knight, not for two.

the July parliament of 1340 seventeen shires are omitted. That was the third parliament within six months,[1] and the bad attendance does not perhaps require any negligence of the recording clerks to explain it. The attendance of burgesses dwindles in the same way during that year. Nine boroughs get writs for two members each in February, four get writs in March (three of them for single members), and only one in July. It was immediately after this that the complaints of excessive levies for wages by the sheriffs, bailiffs, etc. led the king to provide the justices with extracts from the enrolments to guide them in their decisions. We can hardly afford to brush them aside on the bare suggestion that the election returns were sufficient proof of attendance. It is not the election returns but the enrolments *de expensis* that are cited as proof to the justices.[2]

All these records, nevertheless, exhibit a process of development which it is interesting to note, if only to show how much growth there was within a single century of the supposedly static middle ages.[3] This applies to the sheriff's returns as well as to the writs *de expensis*. At first, as we have seen, his discretion was almost unlimited : he was simply required to cause to be nominated two citizens or burgesses from the more capable cities and boroughs in his shire. But which those boroughs were (if any) and how the burgesses were to be 'elected' was left to his discretion, and parliament does not appear to impugn it until 5 Rich. II. Till, if not after, then he made his selection of boroughs with impunity. He also, on occasion, selected the burgesses.[4]   There was nothing

---

[1] The first was in January and the second in March; there had also been two parliaments in 1339.

[2] This is proved by the reference to the sums paid as wages.

[3] This, of course, makes it irrational to treat the reign of Richard II as though it were typical of the rest of the century. There was progress throughout the middle ages, and parliamentary development in the fourteenth century was fairly rapid. The statute of 1382 was followed in 1384 and 1385 by the earliest known petition (Shaftesbury) against false returns (Prynne, iii. 286; *Return of M.P.'s*, i. 220; cf. *ibid.*, i. 225); and the pluralism of returns declined (see below, p. 412).

[4] As late as 1410, 1437, and 1446 the commons assert in their petitions that sheriffs often return for cities and boroughs persons not 'elected' (Parry, *Parliaments*, pp. 168–9, 181, 183; Prynne, ii. 117–18, iii. 234–7, 241–3).

in his writs to say that they must be chosen by their respective boroughs. Even when the indenture system is developed, it is at first a simple indenture between him and casual suitors present in court, who may or may not include suitors from the particular boroughs whose members are there elected. It was not apparently until the fifteenth century that the practice [1] (there was no specific legislation on the point) became at all general of making the indenture. between the sheriff and a group of suitors containing four from each borough in the shire returning members. Thus in 2 Henry V the members for seven Dorset boroughs are returned by an indenture between the sheriff and twenty-eight nominators, four from each of the boroughs concerned, and the members for four Somerset boroughs are returned in the same way. But as late as 27 Henry VI the knights of the shire for Devon and burgesses for seven Devon boroughs are returned by an indenture with twenty-eight indiscriminate nominators.[2] Meanwhile parliament had in 1382 attempted to restrict the sheriffs' discretion by requiring them to send their precepts to ' ancient ' boroughs and no others, and to return only such members as were chosen by the boroughs themselves. But repeated parliamentary petitions in the next three reigns complain of extensive breaches of these principles; and so far as later constituencies are concerned, Prynne is full of invective against the " practice of sheriffs and ambition of private gentlemen," which down to his own day multiplied constituencies without any royal or legal warrant.[3] The practice seems, however, to have been temporarily checked at the end of the fourteenth century, and Prynne says no new constituencies were created in the reigns of Richard II and Henry IV and V; but it began again about 1445,[4] and while the number of constituencies became stable about the time of the Good parliament, that stability did not necessarily affect the attendance of their

---

[1] It existed much earlier in some shires; there is a separate indenture for Derby borough as early as 2 Ed. III, and others for Bedford (Prynne, iii. 262, 266).

[2] *Ibid.*, iii. 254–8.   [3] *Ibid.*, iii. 229.

[4] See above, p. 158.

representatives. Members of parliament were, in fact, much less anxious to go to parliament [1] than to get paid if they went; and the growth of specific precision was less marked in the sheriffs' writs and precepts than it was in the writs *de expensis*.

These, too, had been in the beginning vague and void. The earliest simply direct the sheriffs to pay members their ' reasonable expenses,' but by the accession of Edward II there is added *respectu habito ad loci distantiam*.[2] In 2 Ed. II the writs seek to restrain the sheriff from levying too much on the pretext of wages, and in 5 Ed. II they begin to specify the number of days that parliaments lasted. In 1315–16 the sheriffs are required so to levy wages as not to cause complaints to reach the king's ears, and in 1322 rates of payment are for the first time prescribed, 3s. a day for knights and 1s. 8d. for burgesses; a schedule of the number of days required for travelling, *eundo et redeundo*, from and to the different counties has been worked out and becomes stereotyped. All the boroughs in a shire are generally, but not always, reckoned as equi-distant from Westminster, and no allowance is made for the distance of private residences from the county-court where the election was held. At first some account seems to have been taken of slower travelling in the winter, and of such accidents as blizzards and floods, the breaking of bridges, and the laming of horses; but claims on such accounts were difficult to check and lent themselves to abuse; and eventually the travelling allowance becomes sterotyped for each county, except, of course, when parliament was held elsewhere than at Westminster. For the second parliament of 1322 the rates of pay are increased to 4s. and 2s., though knights of the shire who have not been knighted receive a lower rate than their colleagues and sometimes no more than burgesses. This distinction is soon ignored and the 4s. and 2s. rates are practically fixed from 1 Ed. III. From 4 Ed. III the clerks make the

[1] The total absence of references to contested elections before Richard II's reign seems in itself almost enough to negative the view that burgesses coveted election (cf. Stubbs, *Const. Hist.*, iii. 432).

[2] Prynne, *op. cit.*, iv. 2–3, 19, 24–8, 31, 49–51, 53, 66–8, 71, 84, 114.

writs still more specific by doing the necessary arithmetic and entering the precise sum to which each member is entitled *eundo, morando, et redeundo*. Generally the writs for knights of the shire state that wages are to be levied *tam infra libertates quam extra*; and when this clause was occasionally omitted, as in 28 Ed. III, it provoked a protest in parliament and was restored in subsequent issues. The object was to reach the tenants of lords who held franchises but were not specially summoned to parliament; but a prolonged dispute was apparently waged over the question whether boroughs which had ceased to make, or were irregular in, their returns could be made to contribute to the wages of knights of the shire. An occasional return by a borough of members of its own may have been some insurance against regular assessment to wages for knights of the shire. There may have been some connexion between this and the petitions in parliament, which were occasionally presented as late as Henry VI, that the writs *de expensis* for burgesses as well as for knights should be sent to the sheriffs.[1]

The obvious policy of the Crown to establish, so far as precision in writs could effect it, a uniform standard of parliamentary service and remuneration could not, however, be achieved at once. The knights of the shires rose to it more readily than the burgesses, and after the middle of the fourteenth century their attendance was as exemplary as their predominance in the house of commons was marked. It would not perhaps be fair to say that burgesses were more class-conscious than the knights, for the rolls of parliament bear ample witness to the fact that the knights regarded themselves as *la commune* and the law of the land as equivalent to the land laws. But burgesses were less confident of making their views and interests prevail at Westminster, and they were more locally- and economically-

[1] *Rot. Parl.*, iv. 350, 352; to both these petitions the government in 1430 refused the royal assent. As late as 17 Ed. III writs *de expensis* for Warwick borough and Shaftesbury had been addressed to the sheriffs of Warwickshire and Dorset respectively (Prynne, iv. 196; cf. *ibid.*, iv. 115.)

minded than the landed gentry. Two or four shillings a
day was a heavier burden for a single borough than four
or eight shillings for an entire county;[1] there was less chance
of evading or distributing its weight; and the increasing
length of parliamentary sessions was always magnifying
at least the appearance of the exaction. The wages bill for
the city of York for a single parliament mounted from
£3 4s. and £1 16s. in two parliaments of 1334 to £83 4s. for
one parliament in 1472,[2] and eventually the oligarchical
councillors had to shoulder the burden themselves.
" Although," resolves the Reading council in 1555, " the
charges thereof ought of right to be borne and paied by
th' enhabitantes of the borough," they reluctantly assess it
on themselves, 8d. for each " burgess of the bench " and 6d.
for each other burgess.[3]

The earliest writs *de expensis*, which had sanctioned lower
rates than 2s. a day, were themselves an obstacle to
acquiescence in the higher rate which became almost uniform
in the writs after 1330. There are occasional exceptions.
In 8 Ed. III, when all the other boroughs have writs for 2s.
a day, the two burgesses for Nottingham have one for only
40s. for twelve days, *i.e.*, 1s. 8d. a day, the original rate
of the writs; and as late as 1437 its council resolved that
its representatives should receive 1s. 4d. a day and no more.[4]
But in the other parliaments for which Nottingham receives
a writ *de expensis* its burgesses are allotted 2s. a day.[5]
Northampton provides another exception in 1361; after
receiving a number of writs for 2s. a day it then gets one for
one member only at 1s. 4d. a day.[6] But Northampton again

---

[1]   Stubbs, *Const. Hist.*, iii. 465–6.
[2]   Davies, *York Records*, p. 45; *Return of Members*, i. 362.
[3]   Guilding, *Reading Records*, i. 249–50.
[4]   *Nottingham Borough Records*, ii. 423–4; Prynne, iv. 132. In 1427
Cambridge made an arrangement to pay only 1s. a day (Cooper, *Annals*,
i. 178, 186).
[5]   In 1348 Prynne (iv. 208) gives them £4 4s. for fifteen days, but I
think he has omitted six days' travelling; the Notts knights for that
parliament get £8 8s. for twenty-one days. For the same parliament the
40s. assigned to two Reigate M.P.'s for fifteen days is apparently a mis-
print for 60s. All the other burgesses get 2s. a day.
[6]   *Cal. Close Rolls*, 1360–4, p. 252.

gets 2s. a day in the other writs it receives; and after 1330 that is the established rule for almost all burgesses who obtain writs *de expensis*. Another rule is that writs are available only for members who attend throughout the session. They were not issued until the last day, and no one who left without leave got his writ. Slight relaxations were occasionally made for late comers, especially from a distance. Helston, for instance, gets a writ at 2s. a day for thirty-two days in 25 Ed. III when it should have been for thirty-six; and in 10 Ed. III Tavistock is also four days short. In 17 Ed. III four shires have different attendances specified for the two knights who represented each of them; the difference between the two Bedfordshire knights is two days, between the Shropshire knights six, the Staffordshire knights seven, and the Hampshire knights eight days. This appears to be the maximum discrepancy in the writs except for the unique case of Cambridgeshire in the second parliament of 1340, where one of the knights, Rishton, was paid for fifteen days only, while Colville, his colleague, was paid for forty-eight (the session lasted for forty-five). Prynne suggests that Rishton was elected during the session to replace a dead predecessor, but his name appears with Colville's in the original return; more probably Rishton fell ill after the first fortnight, but was allowed his expenses for the time he attended.

There is one general concession made in the writs to the difficulty in securing a perfect attendance. No knight or burgess is penalized on account of his colleague's absence We have noted the rare occasions after 1376 on which a single knight for a shire obtains a writ *de expensis*. The occasions on which the same thing happens to a burgess are far more numerous,[1] amounting sometimes to three-quarters of the burgesses obtaining writs for a particular parliament, and at other times to three-quarters of the burgesses from a particular shire. Thus in March 1340 three out of the four boroughs receiving writs have them for single M.P.'s, and

---

[1] I have not, however, noted a single case in which one member for a borough gets one amount and the other a different sum.

in October 1362 three out of the four Devon boroughs receiving writs have them for only one member apiece.[1] For the rest it is clear that a member who wants a writ *de expensis* must attend throughout the session and be paid the standard rate. The rule was not a very effective means of compulsion, but the government ventured upon no other. It was weak in the middle ages, but chancery could at least refuse to give official sanction and aid to the breach of the rules it adopted in its writs *de expensis*. Richard II, indeed, threatened to amerce his burgesses and knights of the shire as he did his barons for non-attendance; but evidence is lacking for any effects of the threat, and the crown was of course interested principally in securing the attendance of some, rather than all, of the representatives of the various estates. The grant by some borough representatives of a tenth, and of some knights of a fifteenth, made it binding on all; there was no more need for all boroughs to participate in taxing themselves than for all peers to participate in the trial of one of their number. It met all the obligations of the law if the trial were by some peers and the taxation by some burgesses and knights.

The evolution of these rules of the writs does, however, help us a little in bridging the gulf between them and the sheriffs' returns. Members might, and did, attend parliament and yet fail to obtain writs for their wages, either because their attendance fell short of the requisite standard or because their constituencies refused to pay the wages prescribed in the writs. Obviously neither cause affected the shires, which all as a rule met both requirements. Nor is it probable that brevity of attendance deprived many burgesses of their writs, except possibly in constituencies near to Westminster. A member was not likely to spend sixteen days in travelling to and from London and then forfeit his writ for payment for those days, as well as for his actual attendance, by absence if he could avoid it. The rate of payment did not, however, depend upon him, and economical boroughs tried all sorts of expedients to

[1] *Cal. Close Rolls*, 1339–40, p. 468; 1360–4, p. 440.

evade or reduce their commitments in this respect. Again
and again boroughs bluntly refused to make any return at
all, and with many of them repeated refusals developed into
total abstinence from parliamentary representation. Some
of them bound their Recorders,[1] others their mayors or
bailiffs,[2] to serve *ex officio* ; occasionally representation was
thrust on a sheriff's clerk who had other business in town.[3]
In Wessex there flourished for a time the practice of making
one representative serve for several constituencies, even as
many as half a dozen.

This curious expedient deserves further investigation
than it has yet received.[4] It seems to have started in 1344,
when Robert de Bridport is returned both for Exeter and
Bridport. In 1346 Thomas de Trente is returned simultaneously for three Dorset boroughs, Bridport, Dorchester,
and Shaftesbury. In January 1347-8, Robert de Bridport
is returned for Bridport and Lyme, and again for those two
constituencies in the next parliament, to which also Roger
of Maningford is returned for three other Dorset boroughs,
Blandford, Shaftesbury, and Wareham. Bridport and Lyme
both chose one Robert Beyminster in 1351, and he was also
returned for Exeter, where his colleague was a more
notorious pluralist, Nicholas Whyting. Whyting had ousted
Robert de Bridport from Exeter in 1348, as Beyminster
ousted him from Bridport and Lyme in 1351; and Whyting
was now returned not only for Exeter, but for the county
of Devon and Dartmouth as well. He went further in
1352, when he was simultaneously returned for Devon,

---

[1] See, for instance, *Salisbury Corporation MSS.* (H.M.C. " Various
Collections "), iv. 240; *Shrewsbury MSS.* (H.M.C. XV. x. 5, 12, 13);
Nottingham Records, iii. 320. Shrewsbury in 1553 says membership of
parliament " is supposed to be incident to his office of Recordership."
At Reading the " Recorder or Steward " had the return of writs (Guilding,
i. 225, 226). Elsewhere it was more usually the mayor and (or) bailiff
who, failing others, might feel bound to return themselves.
[2] *E.g.* in 1382 Northampton resolved that the mayor should normally
be elected M.P. (Markham and Cox, *Borough Rec. of Northampton*, i. 248).
In 1555 the mayor of Reading was paid £1 instead of £5 as M.P. for the
borough (Guilding, i. 249-50. Cf. *Engl. Hist. Rev.*, xxxix. 517).
[3] In February 1333-4 Richard Foxton, " sheriff's clerk," was M.P. for
the borough of Leicester (Bateson, ii. 14; *Off. Ret.* i. 102).
[4] See above, p. 155 *n.* 2.

Dartmouth, Tavistock, Torrington, and Totnes. Henry Percehay, his colleague in the representation of the county, was also his colleague at Torrington, and John Mille, his colleague at Tavistock, was also returned for Barnstaple. The infection had spread to Cornwall; John Tremayne was returned for both Bodmin and Helston, and his son for Launceston. For the 1354 parliament there are only three Devon returns extant, but Whyting appears in two of them, Devon and Tavistock; and in Dorset Robert de Beyminster, senior, and Robert de Beyminster, junior, are both returned for both Bridport and Dorchester, the senior finding a third seat at Lyme. No Cornish boroughs appear in the returns for 1354, but in 1355 six gentlemen monopolize the fourteen seats in the duchy. Three of them modestly have but one apiece, but the other three members divide the remaining eleven seats between them. John Tremayne is returned for the shire, Bodmin, and Liskeard; John Caeron for Bodmin, Launceston, Lostwithiel, and Truro; and John Hamely for Helston, Liskeard, Lostwithiel, and Truro. Dorset has one pluralist, who is returned for Dorchester and Weymouth; and Somerset another, who sits for Bridgewater and Taunton.[1]

This record of pluralism in 1355 is not again equalled, although in 1362, to John Hill's six seats and John Wonard's four[2] must be added Cary's representation of Devon and Launceston, and Beyminster's continued occupation of Bridport and Lyme, which lasted till 1363. Wonard remains a pluralist till 1384, but is not returned for more than two constituencies in any one parliament. Dartmouth and Barnstaple return the same two M.P.'s in October 1377, and each of the two finds a third seat in the shire.[3] In Cornwall the same member continues occasionally to appear for three constituencies in the same return; but even Cornwall was by the end of the century able to find a different

---

[1] These details can all be found, under their respective dates, in Prynne's *Briefe Register* (part iv.), the *Official Return of M.P.'s* (pt. i.), and the *Calendar of Close Rolls*.
[2] See above, p. 155 *n.* 2.   [3] *Official Return*, i., App. p. xv.

member for each of its fourteen seats, and pluralism grew rare, if not extinct, elsewhere. Its significance is a matter of speculation. Was greed on the part of members or economy on that of constituencies the motive? In 1346 Thomas de Trente secured writs *de expensis* in respect of all his constituencies, in two of them for himself and a colleague, in the third for himself alone.[1] Similarly in 1348 Maningford gets writs for his three seats, involving, of course, treble pay not only for attendance but for travelling as well. Nicholas Whyting in 1351 gets half of £6 12s. for Exeter, the same sum for Dartmouth, and half of £13 4s. as knight of the shire. In 1352 he gets half of sixteen guineas as knight of the shire and half of eight guineas for each of his four borough constituencies. This would give him twenty-four guineas for his forty-two days' service as against the eight guineas to which a knight, and the four to which a burgess, was entitled for that parliament. Possibly he was a contractor for the Crécy and Calais campaigns.

His fellow-profiteers seem to have been equally grasping and successful down to 1362. But in that year Cary gets a writ *de expensis* for Devon, but not for Launceston; and Hill gets one for Exeter but not for any of the five other boroughs for which he was returned. The profiteering game was up. Members might get returned for various constituencies; they might even get some pay from more than one, but they would not get more than one writ giving them the full rate of remuneration. Pluralism was also discouraged by parliamentary protests against the return of non-resident members, and possibly by a growing local desire for self-expression, though we may be sure that, when Barnstaple protested against a stranger in 1385, it was the payment and not the person to which it objected; the protest was provoked by the writ *de expensis* and not by the sheriff's return. So Derbyshire had protested in 1324 against the sheriff's nomination of two knights of the shire, not because he had violated electoral rights, but because he

[1] This, at least, seems fairly conclusive evidence that his colleague in the third constituency did not attend.

levied £20 for the wages of his nominees when other members could have been procured for £10 or even 10 marks.[1]

Pluralism may have promoted economy in the matter of wages; but it was an arrangement which could only be manipulated successfully in the court of a county returning a number of borough members. Hence its prevalence in Cornwall, Devon, Dorset, and occasionally Wilts and Somerset, each with from half-a-dozen to a dozen parliamentary boroughs. A more regular method of reducing expenses was persistence in the older and lower rates of payment; and this undoubtedly accounts for the absence of many members' names from the enrolled writs *de expensis*. The boroughs were not, however, quite consistent in their cheese-paring policy. All, except those which rarely made a return, felt it desirable at more or less regular intervals to pay members at the full rate and get writs *de expensis*. Leicester is a case in point. It received four writs in the first seven years of Edward III, and then none in the next seventeen. The reason seems clear; the borough would not raise its rates of payment to the level now specified in the writs. Members continue to be paid for some parliaments, but the rate is usually 1s. 6d., and it falls to 1s. 3d. and to 1s. in 1340–1. We also have such entries in the borough records as the payment of £1 to R. Donnington for one parliament and 13s. 4d. for the next, and "W. Brid and John of Stafford for their expenses at parliament and for scrutinizing a tally, 10s." But from 1341 to 1350 the borough records fail to note, by any payment at all, the presence of members in parliament, in spite of sheriffs' returns for 1344, 1346, and twice in 1348.[2] But in 1351 Leicester comes fairly up to the mark, pays £4 16s. to its two burgesses, and has a

---

[1] *Official Return*, i. 225 n.; *Parl. Writs*, II, ii. 315.

[2] Bateson, *Leicester Borough Records*, ii. 14–15, 17, 40, 45, 47, 48; the payment (ii. 28) of £6 18s. 6¾d. to "persons" going to parliament "and to the king" in 1337 might be an exception, but the MS. is torn, no names and not even the number of persons are forthcoming, and the sum bears not the remotest relation to the wages paid for that parliament, which only sat eleven days and would therefore have entitled a Leicester burgess to 34s. Persons, of course, went to the king and to parliament for various purposes without being members of parliament. See below, p. 426.

writ. The writ, indeed, is for £5 8s., being 2s. a day for a twenty-one days' parliament and six days' travelling; the twelve shillings were perhaps deducted for incidental expenses paid by the borough, such as the cost of the writ —a deduction against which members sometimes protested.[1]

This level is not, however, maintained. In 1353 the two members are paid at 1s. 6d. and get no writ. In 1354 they get a writ for £5 12s., but are only paid £4 4s., the rate not being specified. In 1358 their rate is specified at 1s. 8d. a day and no writ is enrolled. There are, in fact, no more writs for Leicester till 1371, unless it received an unrecorded writ for the spring of 1360. The parliamentary history of that spring is anomalous,[2] no writs *de expensis* exist, and the names of the Leicester burgesses, returned by the sheriff, do not agree with those paid by the borough; the rate is 2s. a day, but only for six days. This may have been for that one of the five simultaneous provincial assemblies which was held at Leicester in March, in which case the absence of writs *de expensis* is easily understood; if it was for the May parliament at Westminster, the whole of the sum would have gone in travelling expenses. Apart from an omnibus sum of £11 6s. 8d. for parliaments which cannot be identified, the wages until 1371 are below the standard; one Leicester M.P. alone is paid as a rule, and he receives in 1362 £2 4s., when £4 10s. would have been his proper wage, and in 1363 has only 1s. 8d. a day for twenty-four days instead of 2s. for thirty. In 1369 two members are paid the sum due to one. In February 1371 we have a case which illustrates the defects and conflicts of our evidence. There are no sheriffs' returns for that parliament. Leicester, however, has a writ *de expensis* for its two members, Taillard and Knighton, who are allotted the proper amount of £8 4s. for the thirty-five days that parliament sat and six days' travelling. Taillard was one of the M.P.'s nominated by the crown to attend also the ' council ' held at Winchester in June, which sat for

---

[1] Some boroughs at least paid for the cost of their members' writs (cf. Bacon, *Annals of Ipswich*, p. 185).
[2] Stubbs, *Const. Hist.*, ii. 429, 433.

nine days. The borough records note his payment of 28s., apparently for this council, but say nothing about paying the heavier expenses for him and Knighton at the preceding parliament. By this time the borough clerk who kept the mayor's accounts seems almost to have decided that, if there was a writ *de expensis*, there was no need to enter M.P.s' wages in the borough accounts. Thus in 1372 and 1373 there are borough accounts of payments but no writs, in January 1375–6 (the Good parliament) there is a writ for full attendance, but no reference in the borough accounts, and for January 1376–7 no writ though full wages are [1] paid to two Leicester M.P.'s. But then the mayor's accounts cease " and the chamberlain's accounts, which should have supplied their place, have been lost." [2] However obscure and contradictory may be the conclusions they suggest, they agree with the writs *de expensis* in containing no record of payment for many members whose names appear in the sheriffs' election returns.

Reading is another borough whose published records [3] yield some information. It appears with almost unfailing regularity in the sheriff's election returns, and has nine enrolled writs *de expensis* between 1327 and 1351, then none till the Good parliament, and none after it except in 1403 and 1414. The borough records unfortunately do not give any details until the parliament of February 1357–8, when W. Warde, one of the members, *pro expensis suis versus parliamentum pro ix. diebus*, receives an unspecified or obliterated sum. But that parliament sat for nineteen days, and

---

[1] Or at least credit is claimed for the payment in the chamberlain's accounts a year later. The clerk originally wrote " R. Knighton and R. Gamston," who were M.P.'s in October, not January 1377, then crossed them out and substituted the correct names. Gamston or Gamelston, one of the M.P.'s in October, had been in January one of the chamberlains in whose account the entry occurs!

[2] Bateson, *Introd.*, vol. i. p. xvii.; the other references to Leicester M.P.'s (not specified in the index) are *ibid.*, ii. 80, 91, 106, 108, 110, 141, 147–8, 158.

[3] *Hist. MSS. Comm.*, 11th Rep., App. vii. 171 *sqq.* These are, of course, merely extracts, but my impression is that Dr. Macray extracted all the references to payment of M.P.'s that he noted. He certainly gives all those which occur before 1500 in Guilding's subsequent verbatim publication of the Reading *Diary* (4 vols., 1892–6). Unfortunately it does not begin till 1431.

neither Warde nor his unpaid colleague gets a writ. The next reference is to the parliament of May 1368, when two members received 50s. between them *pro parliamento.* Since that parliament sat for twenty-one days, they were obviously paid less than the proper rate [1] or attended but part of the session, and no writ was forthcoming. The borough records yield nothing more till the parliament of January 1379–80, when one of the members receives 4s. for four days' attendance, and the other 6s. for six days. That parliament sat for forty-eight days. There is, of course, no writ, but Reading pays an unspecified sum to Richard Budd, its mayor, who was not M.P., for his expenses *in eundo et redeundo London. et ibidem morando pro licencia habenda pro hominibus villae de parliamento.* For the Northampton parliament of November 1380, two Reading M.P.'s are paid 31s. 4d.; again there is no writ because parliament sat for thirty-three days, and Reading paid its two members less than half the wages due to one.[2] The next payment is one of 10s. each to the two M.P.'s in the parliament of October 1385, which sat for forty-eight days, and a full attendance at which would have entitled them to £5 apiece. The same paragraph assigns to Thomas Drovere *pro mora sua apud Westmonasterium in parliamento,* 40d., and to John Balet *pro consimili,* 15d.; neither was M.P., but both attended it for some business relating to the borough. Balet, however, is mentioned as M.P. with a colleague at the Cambridge parliament of 1388, but without any record of their wages, though 3s. 4d. was then paid to a third person *pro licencia petenda de parliamento.* From 1393 to 1413 the account rolls are wanting; but in 1403 two Reading M.P.'s have a writ for £14 4s. for seventy-one days, and in 1414 for £7 for thirty-five days.[3]

Details are abnormally scanty elsewhere than at Reading

---

[1] Reading was only allowed one day's travelling expenses each way; its proper wage for a twenty-one days' parliament was therefore 46s. for each M.P.

[2] For a parliament meeting at Northampton the Berkshire travelling allowance was two days each way; a single burgess's proper wage was therefore £3 14s.

[3] Prynne, *op. cit.,* iv. 468, 505.

EE

Appleby, which, apart from its distance from London, was sometimes laid waste by the Scots, that Newcastle and the whole of Northumberland should on occasion reply that they could spare no men to send to Parliament,[1] and that 27 out of 170 boroughs summoned at one time or other during the period should receive no writs *de expensis* at all.   The summons may have sometimes been due to malice; it was occasionally thoughtless.   Exmouth replies in 1337 that there is no " villa de Exmouth, set aqua quædam . . . pertinens ad villam Exon." [2]   Of the 27 boroughs which never receive a writ *de expensis*, 13 are summoned but once, and of those 13 three are recorded to have made no return, and from two others no returns have been found.   Of the 14 which are summoned more than once, two made no return, four made but two, and six others responded to less than a third of their summonses.   The only constituency which makes fairly frequent returns, yet has no writ *de expensis* enrolled is the twin-borough of Bramber and Steyning.[3]   Whatever may be the reason for the absence of these 27 boroughs from the enrolments, it cannot be that, like London, Norwich, and York,[4] they systematically paid their members without asking for writs; for boroughs which never or rarely sent members to parliament cannot have paid them on any system at all.

Regularity in making returns is in fact accompanied by comparative regularity in having enrolled writs *de expensis*. Although the figures are bound to be imperfect, it may be worth while putting side by side the approximate numbers

---

[1] *Return of Members of Parl.*, i. 77, 99, 236, 239.

[2] *Ibid.*, i. 113; a representative from Exmouth is, however, paid £5 2s. for fifty-one days' attendance at a conference in 1341 (Prynne, iv. 187).

[3] Conceivably it regarded itself as one, sharing the expenses, but was regarded as two by chancery, and so neither got writs.

[4] Bristol got writs, after its creation as a county in 1372, sometimes with the shires and sometimes with the boroughs; there was considerable dispute whether it should pay 4s. or 2s. (Prynne, iv. 506).

The other borough-counties were York (created 1397), Newcastle-on-Tyne (1401), Norwich (1403), Lincoln (1413), Hull (1442), Nottingham and Southampton (1449), Coventry (1455), and Canterbury (1463).   See Parry, *Parliaments*, under the respective dates.   Being counties had nothing to do with making private arrangements about wages.   Gloucester and Poole were made counties later (Prynne, iii. 295).

of sheriffs' returns and writs *de expensis*. The former come
from Prynne, and would have to be supplemented to make
them complete; they deal with the period 26 Ed. I–12 Ed. IV,
to which his *Briefe Register* is restricted. The enrolments
of writs *de expensis* cease in 1414, and the following figures
exclude the enrolments before 1327, as lacking in regular
detail. The returns, therefore, cover a period just twice as
long as that covered by the enrolled writs *de expensis*. We
cannot infer that the enrolments would have been twice as
numerous had the two periods been co-extensive, but
assuredly there would have been a nearer correspondence in
numbers. Prynne, then, calculates that the highest number
of returns extant in his day and actually made by or on
behalf of any borough during those 174 years is 91.[1] Three
boroughs, Northampton, Oxford, and Worcester, reach this
figure; forty-three have between 90 and 80 returns apiece,
fifteen between 80 and 70, eleven between 70 and 60, ten
between 60 and 50, five between 50 and 40, and the remainder
between 40 and a solitary unit. The highest number of
writs *de expensis*[2] (for the half-period 1327–1414) is Oxford's
40. Bedford has 32, seven boroughs between 30 and 20,
twenty-one between 20 and 10, and the remainder between
10 and a single writ. London, York, and Norwich would
no doubt have come high in the list, if not at its head, had
their writs been issued and enrolled; and no account has
been taken of the Cinque Ports, which (except in 1265 and
1302) were not summoned till 1322, made no extant returns
till 1366, and have no enrolled writs *de expensis*.[3] With these
exceptions there seems no good reason to suppose that the
enrolments do not give a fairly accurate indication of the
number of borough (as they admittedly do of the shire)

[1] *Brief Register*, iii. 188–220.
[2] Calculated from the *Calendar of Close Rolls* and Prynne, pt. iv.
[3] No account has been taken either of the singular parliament of January
1336–7, to which certain towns were directed to send three or four men each.
Of the 17 whose returns are recorded (*Return of M.P.'s*, i, 113), four—
Faversham, Leamington, Porchester, and Teignmouth—do not otherwise
occur in the *Return* during the middle ages. Teignmouth (which Prynne,
iv. 1136, identifies with Tynemouth), Exmouth, and some others, however,
appear in Prynne (iv. 187), where he gives the wages paid to a similar
assembly in January 1341.

members who attended parliaments throughout the sessions and were paid the prescribed rate of wages.

Another feature of interest appears from a comparison of these writs. Insufficient meaning has sometimes been attached to Stubbs's remark that the medieval house of commons was a concentration of county-courts. We have noted the fact that the elections for the boroughs as well as the shires were made there. The shires are the units which supply the respective quotas of suitors to the king's high court at Westminster; the sheriff makes all the returns (except those of the Cinque Ports after 1366)[1]; and it is from his jurisdiction that a few boroughs escape when they are made into shires themselves. Now, grouping the burgesses' writs *de expensis* under the various shires, as the sheriffs grouped the returns, the writs indicate far more equality in actual representation in parliament between different shires than the number of boroughs would suggest. Devon, with its seven boroughs, does indeed get 54, the largest number of borough writs *de expensis*, but Oxfordshire, with its single borough, comes next with 40; Kent and Lincolnshire, with two boroughs each, get 39, the same number as Sussex with seven boroughs; Herefordshire, with two boroughs, gets 38; Surrey, with four, but 36; Dorset, with seven, but 35; and Wilts, with nine, but 33. On the other hand, Bedfordshire with one borough gets 32 writs; Shropshire and Cornwall each get 29, though Cornwall has six boroughs and Shropshire only two. Somerset with seven boroughs has 28 writs, but Worcestershire with only one gets 25. It seems also natural that, when there is only one parliamentary borough in a county and that is the county borough, it should get far more than the average number of borough writs *de expensis*. Thus Oxford comes highest with 40 and Bedford next with 32. Even where there is a second borough in the county, the county borough remains high and generally has more writs than the other. Thus Hereford has 29 to

---

[1] Even when merchants alone are summoned, they are summoned by the sheriffs *del corps du countie* (*Rot. Parl.*, ii. 120; this, however, was not always the case; see *Return of M.P.'s*, i. 113 and 115 n.).

Leominster's 8, Lincoln 27 to Grimsby's 8, Reading 12 to Wallingford's 6, and Ipswich 11 to the 3 of Dunwich. Where there are several boroughs in a shire, the number of writs is equally discrepant. Thus Exeter has 24, but no other Devon borough more than 8; Chichester has 24, no other Sussex borough more than 4; Salisbury (including Old Sarum) has 18, no other Wiltshire borough more than 3. On the other hand, Rochester with 19 is nearly equal to Canterbury with 20, Bridgnorth with 14 to Shrewsbury with 15, Southwark with 13 to Guildford with 17; while Shaftesbury with 11 outdoes Dorchester with 8; Maldon with 9, Colchester with 8; Bristol with 11, Gloucester with 5. In Cornwall Helston has 7, Launceston 6, Truro and Bodmin 5 each, Liskeard 4, and Lostwithiel 2. In Buckinghamshire Wycombe has 9, while Buckingham never makes a return.[1] The effect of distance from London is also marked; in spite of parliaments held in the north, no borough north of the Trent gets any great number of writs; Newcastle has 13, Hull 8, Carlisle 6.

Oxford's record suggests one further comment. Between 1376 and the end of Richard II's reign it obtained writs *de expensis* for 23 out of 24 parliaments. Yet from Oxford [2] comes the suggestion that boroughs get few writs enrolled, compared with the shires, because it was so much easier for them to collect their wages without any writs at all. Why then these enrolments for Oxford? Is not exemplary attendance on the part of members a better explanation of the enrolments than an imaginary surcease of an imaginary independence of writs, which, whether enrolled or not, continued to be issued down to the seventeenth century? We might look for light from the local records, but if the accounts exist at Oxford they have apparently escaped attention.[3]

---

[1] It has a solitary summons in 1353, but no return to it has been found (*Return of Members*, i. 153).

[2] *English Hist. Rev.*, xxxix. 512.

[3] Andrew Clark's edition of Wood's *City of Oxford* (Oxf. Hist. Soc.) merely copies the names of its M.P.'s from the official *Return*, and Thorold Rogers' *Oxford City Documents*, while it contains a good deal about payment of taxes, says nothing about the payment of members. No other of the Society's 36 volumes appears to deal with the subject. One of the

It is only from local sources that the problem of the actual attendance in medieval parliaments can be solved; and, so far, few of those borough records have been edited or examined in such a way as to give much help. Generally editors print an extract or two as samples without attempting to determine whether the extracts are examples or excep-

most recent volumes on borough records (Farley's *Winchester Records*, 1923) illustrates the information required but not provided for our purpose. Little more than a page is devoted to the subject (pp. 110–11), though even that supplies evidence of irregularity in parliamentary attendance from a constituency where we should hardly expect it. Only eight parliaments are instanced. In 26 Ed. III " only one burgess was sent," and he received but 20s.; the parliament lasted thirty days, and a single member was entitled to £3 and his travelling expenses. In 27 Ed. III two members attend and receive £3 15s.; this was pretty full payment at 2s. a day each for a parliament which sat for eighteen days, though it leaves only 3s. instead of 12s. for travelling expenses. The names of these three members are given that they do not agree with those returned by the sheriff. For the Winchester ' parliament ' of June 1371 there is no item for payment in the borough records, though Stephen Haym was nominated by the king to attend. He is said, however, to receive 2s. a day for the parliament of 2 Rich. II and £3 0s. 4d. for divers business in London. But we are not told for how many days he was paid; there were two parliaments in 2 Rich. II, Haym's name does not appear in the sheriff's returns for the first, and there is no return for the second. In 1394 we are told that the " parliament at York " cost Winchester £10 15s. in members' wages. No parliament was held at York in Richard II's reign: one was summoned there in 1392, but was prorogued *sine die* before it met. The members' names are not given; if the parliament was that held at Westminster in January 1394, they were well paid, for it sat for thirty-nine days and the normal wage for two Winchester citizens would have been £7 16s., excluding travelling expenses. But in 21 Rich. II two burgesses, whose names again are not given but can be found in the official return, were only paid £3 instead of £5 10s. for a parliament which sat for twenty-five days, not counting travelling expenses to and from Shrewsbury, to which it was adjourned after twelve days' session at Westminster: possibly the Winchester members did not go (the travelling expenses for this parliament are apparently calculated on the singular assumption that it had sat all along at Shrewsbury and for twenty-five days; Prynne, iv. 442–6). A parliament of 8 Henry IV cost Winchester, we are told, £13 16s. 8d.: the members' names are again not given, but this may be the parliament which had three sessions, two of them in 7, and one in 8 Henry IV (Parry, *Parliaments*, pp. 164–5), and sat the unprecedented length of 171 days. If so, the Winchester members received a writ for £36 12s. (Prynne, iv. 481) for the whole session and six days' travelling, and the extract from the borough records may refer only to the last session. Otherwise the members were scandalously under-paid. In 9 Henry IV, for which parliament no extract is given from the borough records, two other Winchester M.P.'s received a writ for £10 for fifty days. These writs, of course, were at the standard rate of 2s. a day each, but Winchester may not have paid it. The last extract states that in 1422 the two burgesses (whose names are once more given and agree with the official return) were only paid a shilling a day for twenty-four days, with 15s. to one and 2s. to the other for uncovenanted services.

tions. The records themselves are often defective, and, even when printed *in extenso* like Stevenson's *Nottingham Records* or Guilding's *Reading Records*, they contain very meagre references to the payment of M.P.'s in the middle ages. There is no more promising soil for the activities of branches of the Historical Association, or for historical students anxious to write a thesis but debarred by distance from regular access to the Public Record Office. The above figures will many of them need correction in detail, and the conclusions which they seem to indicate might even be completely overthrown. Unrevealed borough accounts might conceivably show that boroughs, especially boroughs on the ancient demesne, were amerced for not sending members to parliament.

But before pursuing detailed investigations it is well to acquire some knowledge of what a medieval parliament was like and to avoid such assumptions as that litigation in parliament involved the election of the litigants to the house of commons, or that " it is impossible to believe " [1] that bodies were not represented in the parliaments to which they presented petitions. The petitions mentioned above [2] show what a curiously comprehensive and ill-assorted assembly a parliament under Edward I must have been, if its petitions from foreign potentates and prisoners in gaol, paupers, friars, and Jews prove that petitioners were present or represented there. Are we really to believe that Oxford University sent members to parliament in 1305 because it presented a dozen petitions to that parliament; [3] that Ireland, Wales, Scotland, Gascony, " and other lands beyond the sea, and the isles "

[1] *Engl. Hist. Rev.*, xxxix. 514, 520.
[2] Pp. 38, 42, 52. The receivers and triers of petitions appointed at every parliament were not appointed to receive and try the petitions of the house of commons; and their report on many a petition is *non est petitio de parliamento*.
[3] Printed in Maitland's *Memoranda*, pp. 44–7; other Oxford petitions (mainly city) are collected by Miss L. Toulmin Smith in the Oxf. Hist. Soc.'s *Collectanea*, iii. (1896), pp. 79–161. Cambridge as well as Oxford university and the four mendicant orders complained in 1366 *par lour petitions mis devant le roi en parlement* (*Rot. Parl.*, ii. 290; cf. *ibid.*, ii. 310). For petitions from Ireland and Calais, see *ibid.*, iii. 66, 85–6.

were represented because at the beginning of every medieval parliament persons were appointed to receive and to try their petitions; and that Manchester and Birmingham in 1831 and the Chartists in 1848 were represented in parliament because they petitioned for representation? This is the old fallacy of Haxey's case; Haxey was not a member of parliament, but chief clerk of the court of common pleas, and Richard II was naturally indignant at his *trahison*. Parliament was, of course, a body to which everyone was from its beginning invited by proclamation to present all sorts of petitions; and, in the form of private bills, they still come from all sorts of bodies and companies which have, as such, no representation. It should also be remembered that then, as now, all sorts of persons who were not members of parliament had business at Westminster. Lobbying, though not by that name, was well enough known in the middle ages, and even parliamentary boroughs sent other persons 'to parliament' than their members. When Leicester pays its steward "for carrying bills to parliament for obtaining pontage" and " other jurats and honest men before parliament at London," it was not paying the wages of members.[1] Salisbury in 1305 sent four citizens to parliament to plead against its bishop's right to tallage, and two of them only to do the king's business as 'members.' One of the duties of a mayor, whether an M.P. or not, was to run on errands to London for his borough. 'Members' were not, indeed, summoned to parliament by the king to present petitions at all; they could do that without being 'members.' It was powers and not petitions with which the king insisted that 'members' should be armed, and they were summoned by the king *ad faciendum quod de communi consilio ordinabitur in præmissis*, which in practice meant consenting to taxation; a handful were all that were legally required or were anxious to come.[2]

[1] Bateson, *Leicester Borough Record*, i. 345, ii. 77; cf. *ibid.*, ii. 42, 108.
[2] Maitland, *Memoranda*, pp. lxxviii. 265–79. 'Member of parliament' is not, of course, fourteenth-century terminology, and to modern ears it conveys a mass of false analogies, due to the consolidation of innumerable

The difficulty of securing attendance at county-courts is familiar enough to students of the thirteenth century. It would have been a miracle had Edward I encountered less difficulty in his far harder task of securing a full attendance at his more distant high court at Westminster. His sheriffs issued precepts to about 150 boroughs, just as he summoned over a hundred temporal peers and over 70 abbots. All estates fell short of his vision, and the writs of summons sank to half. But even they prove nothing in the way of attendance. The writs *de expensis* prove the full attendance of a solid and fully-paid phalanx of knights of the shire and of a nucleus of borough members. Borough records further testify to the presence and payment of burgesses who receive no writs *de expensis*, either because they attend but part of the session or because they are underpaid. The numbers in this category can only be ascertained from borough records. If many of them were like the Reading M.P.'s in 1380, who put in but ten days' attendance between them instead of a hundred, they would not increase the size of the house very much. It is, however, unlikely that members from any constituencies except those near London fell into this habit. On the other hand, members from distant boroughs would be more likely to shirk attendance altogether, and no penalty, save the loss of wages, appears to have been imposed on them or their manucaptors.[1] The most probable reinforcements of the

---

brief colloquies into an almost continuous unity. Cf. Pasquet, *Essai*, p. 80; early parl aments were summoned *ad hoc*, to assent to one thing only, and medieval parliamentary history consists mainly in the development of a custom into an institution.

[1] Manucaptors were not always appointed (Prynne, ii. 50–1, iii. 182–4), and they seem to have been little more than a form; sometimes the knights of the shire and burgesses have the same manucaptors, clearly nominated in the county court (Riess, *Wahlrecht*, pp. 104–5); the M.P.'s returned by the sheriff for Colchester during its exemption have manucaptors (*ibid.*, iii. 241*b*). The old story of the *Modus Tenendi Parliamentum* that boroughs were amerced for failing to send representatives was severely criticised by Prynne (*ibid.*, iv. 571–92; cf. ii. 52, and Pasquet, p. 192 *n.*) : "there is no president in history, Parliament rolls, or Fine rolls to warrant it " (Prynne, iv. 575), and there appears to be no record of such amercements in the Public Record Office. The statute of 1382 was merely *quoad terrorem populi*, and the passages cited to prove its effect will not bear the interpretation put upon them. No specific absences are recorded

M.P.'s who receive writs *de expensis* are the members for boroughs which paid less than the standard rate.

Pending the extensive and co-operative research which alone can answer that specific question, the general indications lead us to the conclusion that, while some additions have to be made to the numbers named in the writs *de expensis*, parliament fell shorter of Edward I's ideal (if, indeed, he really expected all those his sheriffs summoned to attend) than even the diminished returns of the fourteenth century suggest. The shrinkage was mainly due to reaction against Edward's attempts to ignore feudal liberties and treat all boroughs like those on the king's demesne; and most of the refusals to act on the sheriff's precepts came from franchises where his writs did not run. Edward's real policy was expressed not so much in *pactum serva* or in Justinian's *quod omnes tangit ab omnibus approbetur* as in his own curt phrase *rex non vult aliquem medium;* and feudal liberty consisted largely in freedom from parliaments which helped to curb whatever impeded the course of common law.[1] It is not till 1529 that the sheriffs' returns to the Reformation parliament rise again to the level of Edward's Model parliament of 1295.

There is nothing surprising in this. Government, and particularly self-government, depends upon the mentality of the governed; and Edward I could not by some magic stroke create in one generation a national out of a local consciousness. Even his writs were vague and lacked that specific detail which subsequent experience showed to be necessary before they would be obeyed. Medieval government lived from hand to mouth in its struggle for existence. Many an

---

after the " roll-calls "; and if the lack of such mention proves that all were present, then we must make the absurd assumption that thereafter every single peer, prelate, councillor, knight, and burgess summoned to parliament actually attended. The act, like a good deal else in Richard II's policy, was a hasty effort to anticipate the discipline of Tudor times. Henry VIII was more skilful and successful in the matter than Richard II (see my *Henry VIII*, p. 265). But the discipline was not really effective until it was exerted by the commons themselves (see their resolutions of 18 March, 1580–1, *Commons' Journals*, i. 135–6); even then they had a good deal of absence to correct.

[1] See Pasquet and his references, pp. 244–50.

effort broke like a wave against the rocks of local inertia and the strongholds of sectional privilege. Kings got what service they could in the field, in court, and in parliament; but they could not get all they wanted nor assemble all whom they summoned. Their one great success was with the knights of the shires; but boroughs, as Prynne re- marks,[1] " rather reputed " parliamentary service " a charge, burthen, and oppression than an honour." Their inadequate representation, concludes Bishop Stubbs, " will account in great measure for their insignificance in action and their obscurity in history." [2]

[1] *Briefe Register*, iii. 233*b*.
[2] *Const. Hist.*, iii. 613; cf. *ibid.*, ii. 643. 548; iii. 428–9, 432, 466, 577.

APPENDIX III

ADDITIONAL NOTES AND REFERENCES

Page 5 (*a*). "*Post conquestum* forms no part of the style of any king of England before Edward III, and its insertion is due to the fact that two Edwards reigned before the conquest" (C. G. Crump in *History*, April 1921, p. 46).

Page 14 (*b*). This requires some modification. See Prof. Rait's *The Parliaments of Scotland*, 1924, and *The Times Lit. Suppl.*, 25 Nov., 1920; also Dr. Tait in *English Hist. Rev.*, April 1921, p. 255, and Principal Barker in *Edinburgh Rev.*, July 1921, pp. 64–5.

Page 21 (*c*). The phrase "high court of parliament" is not of sixteenth nor even fifteenth, but fourteenth-century origin. The rolls of parliament have it under Henry VII (1489) and Edward IV (1472), but the earliest reference I have found is its use by Chief-justice Thirning in pronouncing judgement upon the Lords Appellant on 3 Nov., 1399 (*Rot. Parl.*, iii. 451, v. 6, vi. 422). The mental process by which it was reached is indicated in an earlier passage of 11 Richard II relating to the Appellants (*ibid.*, iii. 244), where it is recorded that "in this parliament the lords, spiritual as well as temporal, then present claimed as their liberty and franchise that the great matters moved in this parliament, and to be moved in other parliaments in time to come, touching peers of the land, should be handled, judged, and discussed by the course of parliament and not by the civil law, nor by the common law of the land, practised in other and lower courts of the realm ; which claim, liberty, and franchise the king graciously admitted and accorded in open parliament."

Page 32 (*d*). Prynne (*Briefe Register of Parl. Writs*, iv. 567) says the earliest record he had found of the word *parliamentum* is on the dorse of membrane 12 of the close roll for 28 Henry III, referring to the *parleamentum de Rumened'* [sic] between John and his barons; there is, he says, another reference on the dorse of membrane 13 of the close roll for 32 Henry III. Both Prynne's references are correct (*Cal. Close Rolls*, 1242–7, p. 242; 1247–51, p. 107).

Page 33 (*e*). " I am sure," writes Prof. Rait, " that in Scotland *plenum parliamentum* = open parliament " (cf. his *Parliaments of Scotland*, pp. 420–1). Professor W. A. Morris has also shown that *plenus comitatus* means ' open ' rather than ' full ' county-court (*English Hist. Rev.*, July 1924).

Page 39 (*f*). Professor McIlwain (*Amer. Pol. Sci. Rev.*, 1921, p. 296) demurs to this interpretation of the distinction between ' original ' writs and writs *de cursu ;* but cf. Holdsworth, *Hist. of English Law*, 3rd ed., i. 398 : " the barons did not wish to leave the chancellor an uncontrolled power to issue original writs—a power which was equivalent to a power to make new law." See also my references on p. 248, and Stubbs, *Charters*, ed. 1900, pp. 389, 393, where the chancellor swears " he will seal no writ, excepting writs of course," without direction. In vol. ii. 193 Dr. Holdsworth, referring to " the distinction between original and judicial writs," says, " Some writs, *e.g.* the writ of right, are original, that is they originate an action. Others are only issued in the course of the proceedings." But " among the domestic and more especially legal duties of the clerks of the chancery was the issue of original writs " (ii. 228), and " there were indeed a growing number of writs of course which could not be changed without the consent of the common council of the realm " (ii. 245). In 1347 the fee for an original writ was 6*d.* and for a judicial writ 7*d.* (*Rot. Parl.*, ii. 170*a*).

Page 47 (*g*). The statement about the " Rolls of Parliament " beginning in 1278 refers to the printed volumes entitled *Rotuli Parliamentorum ut et petitiones et placita.* They have petitions and pleas from 1278, but nothing the editor calls a *rotulus* till 1290; even then the word is wrongly used.   This chapter should be compared with and checked by M. Pasquet's third chapter on *Les Parlements de Edouard Ier*.

Page 66 (*h*).   The identification of knights or *milites* with *barones minores* is not, of course, complete.   Usually knights of the shire were smaller military tenants-in-chief; but in the first place even a greater baron was not necessarily a knight in the fourteenth century; secondly, many *barones minores* were not knights of the shire; and thirdly, men who had not been knighted were occasionally, if not frequently, elected knights of the shire (see p. 114): some of Edward II's writs *de expensis* prescribe a lower wage than a knight's for their parliamentary service.   The discrimination between *miles* and *chivaler* is simply due, as Mr. Crump says, to the fact that " when the editor of the *Official Return of Members of Parliament* described a man as *miles et chivaler*, he did so because he found the same man called *miles* in one part of the return and *chivaler* in another " (*History*, April 1921, p. 46).   Professor McIlwain, in referring (*Amer. Pol. Sci. Rev.*, 1921, p. 296) to my " identification of knights and *barones minores*," has, I think, overlooked my remark in the same note : " nor must we identify *milites* with *barones minores*."

Page 68 (*i*).   An adequate edition of the *Modus Tenendi Parliamentum* is yet to seek, and the need of it may be inferred from the comments of a reputable critic (*London Mercury*, April 1921, p. 681), who, after remarking that it has for nearly a generation " been an ordinary subject of undergraduate teaching at one English university at least," proceeds to confuse it with Maitland's *Memoranda de Parliamento*.   Pending that edition all its statements must be received with a caution which Dr. Tait suggests that I have ignored when he refers to my accepting it " without reserve " (*Engl. Hist. Rev.*, loc. cit.).   He has, I think, overlooked my reservations (p. 73) that the " Rolls of Parliament do not support " the theory of the *Modus* " in its entirety " (p. 74), that " if the picture drawn in the *Modus* ever represented actual practice, that practice was

greatly modified during the fourteenth century," and
(p. 95) that an inference from it " would not be safe." I
doubt if the *Modus* is more scientific than Tacitus' *Germania*,
though the author's opportunities of observation must have
been far closer, and an earlier MS. than that quoted by
Dr. Tait says, not that "two knights of any shire have a
greater voice in parliament than the greatest earl in England,"
but that *habent plus vocis in concedendo vel negando pro
comitatu suo quam comes ejusdem comitatus*, which no one
could deny. Its original draft probably dates from the
latter half of Edward II's reign, the considerable dis-
crepancies between the two extant MSS. of Richard II's
reign suggesting a common origin a good deal earlier. It
seems to have emanated from Lancaster's entourage; it
is undoubtedly tendencious, and I am not aware that I
have accepted any statement in it that is not corroborated
by other and better authority. Still, it is undeniably a
tract contemporary with fourteenth-century parliaments;
and a pamphleteer, however reckless, does not deliberately
make himself unintelligible to his readers. Mr. Hilaire
Belloc does not, for instance, in his strictures on Parliament ignore the two houses, and the *Modus* could not
have talked a lot about " six grades " and said not a word
about three estates, if three estates had been the essence
of the parliaments he was describing. Even a revolutionary
says something about the things he wants to eradicate.

The ' authority ' of the *Modus* does not, moreover,
depend merely upon its anonymous author, nor on the
suggested desire in 1509 of a clerk of the parliaments and
of chancery (who sat in the house of lords and was also
clerk of convocation) to emphasise " the superiority of the
commons over the lords." We have also to account for
the transmission of a version of it in 1418 under the great
seal of Henry V to the Lord-deputy of Ireland, and its
attestation by two obscure but identifiable clerks of the
Irish hanaper (see Steele, *Tudor and Stuart Proclamations*,
vol. i. pp. clxxxviii–cxcii). Nor does the text quite justify
the charge of inconsistency in asserting that " there can be

FF

no parliament without the presence of the *communitates*"
while admitting that if any of the "sex gradus" is absent
a parliament is none the less valid.   The *Modus* does not
say that all the *communitates* must be present.   That
would, indeed, be a hard saying in the fourteenth century,
when there were many parliaments from which some shire
or other was absent, and never a one in which all boroughs
were represented.   The absence of any one individual or
communitas, if properly summoned, always gave consent;
and the *Modus* does not hedge in its six grades with the
sanctity with which we have sometimes invested the Three
Estates : [1] it admits that one (possibly more) may be absent
without holding up the crown in parliament; and no one
can say, in view of the absence of clerical proctors from the
English house of commons and of the protests of prelates
in the lords, that consent on the part of each of the three
estates was essential to legislation.

The "validity of a parliament" is a question to which
I cannot propound an answer, because I cannot find a
definition of *parliamentum* which fits all the assemblies
called by that name in the fourteenth century.   There
are, I believe, in the city records of London early indications of the view that no one but a king or his deputy can
hold a parliament; but there were exceptions in abbeys
and inns of court, and even this does not carry us very
far in the way of definition.   The vagueness of the word
is perhaps most conveniently illustrated in Parry's sum-
maries of the writs in his *Parliaments and Councils of England*,
but the ambiguity of his title saved him the task of discrimination.   The *Official Return of Members of Parliament*
attempts to discriminate by means of a list of parliaments.
But it has refined the meaning of *parliamentum* and has
relegated to notes a good many summonses which Prynne
regarded as parliamentary writs.   Still, even it will include
among 'parliaments' as late as June 1371 an assembly
consisting of "certain specified knights, citizens, and

[1] The *sex gradus* are simply ranks, and the best MSS. have *gradus
parium parliamenti* (see *Engl. Hist. Rev.*, xxxiv. 209–25).

burgesses " all nominated by the king. When does a
parley with the king cease to be a valid *parliamentum ?*
We have indeed many invalid *parliamenta* on our hands
if we apply any one definition to them all; and we need
not quarrel overmuch with the author of the *Modus*,
especially if he lived in Edward II's reign, for describing
the way in which ought to be held what he thinks a parliament ought to be. He does not think that all the *communitates* nor even all his *gradus* need be present; he
might even have hesitated to deny—in Edward II's reign
—the word *parliamentum* to a conference between the king
and a single estate, or legal validity to an agreement reached
between them. It is not until Richard II's reign that the
other *communitates* attempt to deny the binding character
of petitions from the clergy granted by the king. When
and how do we get, out of *communitates*, a *communitas
communitatum ?*

There is, it seems to me, a substantial grain of truth in
the idea of the *Modus* that the essential element in a parliament is the conjunction of the king with one, more, or all
of the *communitates*. Every *parliamentum* was a *tractatus ;*
and like the ' treaty ' at Runnymede (also called a *parliamentum* by Henry III in 1244) it was a matter of give and
take between parties which had the power to give. In
1215 the parties were substantially the barons and the
king, but in the fourteenth century they are substantially
the king and the *communitates*. The greater barons have
been inveigled into accepting, and indeed claiming, the
position of *consiliarii*, and the peers reduced to born advisers
of the crown. The judges may have manœuvred them into
it; but I doubt if there is any sanction for the view that
counsellors had any legal right of treaty with the crown.
In strict modern theory no one has; but there was a good
deal in the fourteenth century to give colour to the view
of the *Modus* that a *parliamentum* was essentially a means
of treaty, mainly about supplies, between the king and the
communities. The *communitates* were outside the council,
and parliaments grew out of the need of treating with them

(cf. Pasquet, *Essai*, pp. 82–3, 156). This was a theory which succumbed in England to the doctrine of sovereignty, but the American view of English history, essential to the logical justification of American independence, is that Magna Carta was a treaty, compact, or social contract, and parliament a Congress of estates (see my *Factors in American History*, 1925, pp. 32–48, 302–6).

Page 71 (*j*). A few further illustrations of the use of the words ' estates ' and ' states ' may be added. In 1533 the Constable, Marshal, and Steward are termed " the three high estates " at the coronation of Anne Boleyn (*Letters and Papers of Henry VIII*, vi. 396). On 16 Jan., 1594–5, an " ordinance or decree made by the commissioners of the office of Earl Marshal of England " fixes " the precedency of all estates, according to their birth and calling " (*Hist. MSS. Comm.*, 11th Rep., App. vii. 273). The first of the political questions which William Thomas propounded to the young Edward VI runs : " Whereof hath growen th' aucthoritie of Astates, and howe many kindes of Astates there be ? " (Ellis, *Original Letters*, 2nd series, ii. 189; Strype, *Eccles. Mem.*, ii. 100). The Authorised Version of the Bible has " the chief estates of Galilee " (Mark vi. 21), and Milton " the bold design, Pleas'd highly those infernal states " (*Paradise Lost*, ii. 386). Even Burke says that the English people at the Revolution of 1688 " acted by the ancient organized states in the shape of their old organization " (*Reflections on the French Rev.*, ed. Payne, p. 25). Each American colony claimed to be a " perfect state " because it had a " complete legislature within itself " (*Factors in American History*, p. 43). The most familiar use of ' states ' for ' estates ' is in " States-General " of the Netherlands.

The modern idea of the three estates appears in the " Rolls of Parliament " (vi. 39, 98, " Dominus Rex ac Tres Status Regni," 1473; and more fully in English " the thre Estates of this Reame of Englond, that is to wite, of the Lords Spiritualls and Temporalls, and of the Commons " in 1483, *ib.*, vi. 240); and in 1581 the commons refer to "the Common House or Third Estate of the Parliament," *Journals*, i. 126).

Page 72 (*k*). See Fuller, *Church History* (1656), Bk. vi. p. 352 : "Such priests as have the addition *Sir* before their Christian name, were men not graduated in the University, being in *Orders*, but not in *Degrees*." In the account of the opening of Henry VIII's first parliament in 1510 the style of the chancellor has been corrected in the MS. from "doctor William Warham" to "lord William Warham" (*Letters and Papers*, new ed., I. i. 342). Wolsey appears as "Sir Thomas," and other priests likewise (*ib.*, No. 1046).

Page 75 (*l*). Dr. Tait demurs (*Engl. Hist. Rev.*, April 1921, p. 255) to the importance here attached to the sub-ordination of the 'estates' to the 'high court of parliament,' as a means of avoiding revolutions in English history, on two grounds : firstly, that the cortes of Castille and estates of Scotland, which resembled the English parliament in receiving petitions and in other respects, nevertheless collapsed; and secondly, that Scottish legislation without a majority in each of the estates shows that such a requirement was "not inherent in the system." No one, of course, would contend that the character of the English parliament as a high court was the sole reason for the avoidance of revolutions in English history; the causes go deeper than that, but it was assuredly an indispensable element in orderly constitutional development, and the Scottish and Spanish analogies support that conclusion. It is no doubt true that Scottish kings could override a recalcitrant majority in a Scottish estate, and James VI said he "ruled Scotland with a pen." He could not have made that "no idle boast" (Rait, *Parl. of Scotland*, p. 60) had Scottish estates been fused into a parliament like the English; and that failure to fuse made Scottish constitutional history anything but an orderly development. The requirement of assent from each several estate may not have been "inherent in the system," but it was the way in which estates developed wherever they developed fully—in France, in Germany, and in Poland. The theory was put forward in England in Elizabeth's reign and has been used ever since as an argument to prove the unconstitutional character of her ecclesiastical settlement; and only the reserve power in the crown to override the claim of two ' estates,' the lords spiritual and the lords temporal, to veto legislation saved England from revolution in 1832, if not later. There may be " no necessary divorce between a high court of parliament and a division of estates on class lines "; but where estates are so divided, the division precludes that predominance in the high court which fusion promoted in England. It was the absence of fundamental distinctions between an indefinite number of estates, and their association in and with the high court of parliament which gave that composite entity the elasticity and strength it developed in England alone. The collapse of the cortes of Castille is surely not to the point. Castille became one with half-a-dozen other monarchies in which its system did not prevail; and it is very doubtful whether the English parliamentary system would have survived if Henry V's policy of union with France had succeeded, let alone other realms.

Page 130 (*m*). The famous discussions in the house of commons in 1601 and 1628 whether it should proceed by way of petition or bill have stamped on the minds of historians the almost indelible impression that parliamentary bills and petitions had always been fundamentally different methods of procedure; and the most recent historian of the law refers to " the change in procedure from legislation by way of petition to legislation by way of bill " as " gradually solving " constitutional difficulties (Holdsworth, ii. 429, 438). It is necessary, therefore, (i) to point out that in the fifteenth and early sixteenth centuries there was no difference between a parliamentary petition and a parliamentary bill, and (ii) to suggest some explanation of the fact that a century later men drew a distinction between them. It should be remembered that the earliest legislative records are simply narratives; the roll records, but does not make the act, and the narrative form persists from the *fet a remembre* of Henry III and Edward I,[1] through the *memoranda* of his successors down to " the king remembreth" of Henry VII. But these 'remembrances' gradually subside into our preambles, and, with the growth of positive law, the substantive part of an act ceases to be its narrative and becomes an expression of will, " Be it enacted," the *nuances* of which varied from time to time. It might imply a petition from the commons; it often meant an injunction from the crown. There is not much doubt of its meaning in most of the acts of the Yorkists and first two Tudors; what it meant under the Lancastrians has never been ascertained. The meaning was not affected by calling its formal expression a 'bill' or a 'petition.' Both words often occur in the same document.[2] In these cases it is more usual for the clerk to call it a *petitio* at the beginning, and a *billa* when he is recording the royal assent, but in at least one instance in Henry VII's reign that order is reversed.[3] Moreover, a *petitio* is described as *formam actus in se continens* almost as often as a *billa ;* and the bills which are turned into so-called 'public acts' are always entered on the rolls as *communes petitiones.* As late as 1530 an act for the Duke of Norfolk is called a *petitio* throughout, and is immediately followed on the roll by *quædam alia billa* concerning John Roper's will.[4] Neither in form, substance, nor procedure is there yet any difference between a petition and a bill.[5]

But there is a difference between one bill and one petition and another; and that difference is marked by the careful insertion of the words *formam actus in se continens.* They mark that change in procedure which has been wrongly

[1] *E.g.* in the Provisions of Oxford and Confirmation of the Charters (Stubbs, *Charters*, ed. 1900, pp. 390, 392, 496).

[2] *Rot. Parl.*, vi. 478, 488–9, 492–3, 530.

[3] *Ibid.*, vi. 452–3.

[4] *Ibid.*, Supplement [bound up with vol. i. of *Lords' Journals*], pp. cliii.–clvi.

[5] The student in search of a basis of discrimination between *le roy le veult* and *soit fait comme il est desiré* would do well to begin with the answers recorded, *ibid.*, pp. ccxliii.–ccl.

ascribed to the alleged substitution of *billa* for *petitio*. What happened was that *billa* gradually came to be more and more restricted to parliamentary requests drafted in the form of acts, leaving *petitio* to such as merely made the request without prescribing the remedy.　There was political subtlety underlying the change in parliamentary ritual. It may be suspected that even over-mighty subjects of the Lancastrians found it convenient to represent their petitions to the crown as emanating from the commons; many a great lord adopted the practice, and then the new monarchy took a leaf out of their book.　If lords could inspire and inform petitions to the crown, why should not the crown suggest and even draft petitions to itself?　The idea grew very attractive when Henry VIII after 1529 found the commons inclined to support him but more than half the lords in opposition.　" Be it enacted " was imperious enough to cast no slur on the king's most excellent majesty; *le roy le veult* expressed most of the facts better than *soit fait comme il est desiré ;* and the king's grace which granted suits might be left out of matters of state, and omitted from *petitiones rempublicam concernentes.*[1]

So bills *formam actus in se continentes* became the order of the day and the conveyance of positive law.　The Tudor Frankenstein died before his leviathan came to maturity. But substance grew into the form of parliamentary participation, and " Be it enacted " began under Elizabeth to sound less like an order from, than an order to, her majesty.　The commons themselves shrank from its reverberations in 1601 and even in 1628, and fell back on petitions rather than bills.　It was the ' form of an act ' at which they shied.

Page 144 (*n*).　Some of the obscurity in the law about taxation is due to reading back more modern ideas into the fourteenth century.　Taxation then was not so much an act of parliament as a series of gifts made in parliament by representatives of those who would have to pay.　No estate could tax or veto the grant of any other estate.

[1] *Ibid.*, p. lxxiii.

Even tonnage and poundage came under this rubric: in 1372 the knights of the shires were dismissed while the citizens and burgesses were retained to vote it.[1] Similarly a fifteenth was granted " by earls, barons, freemen, and the communities of all the counties of the realm," a tenth by " all the cities, boroughs, and ancient demesnes of the king," [2] and a clerical tenth by the clergy. Such external advice as was given was given by peers and others, not as estates of parliament but as members of the king's council, great or small. There might be differences of opinion between peers and knights of the shire over a fifteenth because both classes voted and paid it; but peers as such had nothing to do with tenths granted by the clergy or by cities and boroughs. Neither had the latter anything to say when in 1400 the lords spiritual and temporal, " in order to avoid the summoning of a parliament and the consequent imposition of a tax or tallage upon the common people," made in council a grant to be paid by themselves.[3] As late as 1523 the burgesses voted their own taxation, leaving the knights of the shires to vote theirs; and only the laborious persuasions of the Speaker, Sir Thomas More, brought them to agree on a compromise.[4]

By that time the fusion of estates was fusing taxation, and the growth of a common authority to deal with common taxation was creating the modern problem of predominance in the partnership. The point was discussed by the judges in connexion with tonnage and poundage as early as 1454. It was then held that the lords could reduce but could not increase a grant made by the commons; for the greater included the less, and the commons' grant of tonnage and poundage for four years would imply their assent if the lords reduced it to two.[5] The lords' assent was now required because grants were taking the form of bills and being " enacted." The sanction was no longer the

---

[1] *Rot. Parl.*, ii. 310.
[2] *Ibid.*, ii. 447.
[3] Nicolas, *Proceedings of the Privy Council*, i. 104.
[4] Hall, *Chronicle*, p. 657.
[5] *Year-Books*, ed. Tottell, 33 Henry VI, fol. xvii.

gift from the representatives of those who would have to pay, but the act of a parliament feeling its way to sovereign power. Counsel who argued the case in 1480 were harking back to the past, but the argument is clear enough if we remember that by *communitas* is meant the knights of the shire and that a fifteenth is the tax referred to; counsel goes on to remark that a clerical tenth is granted by the clergy. Presumably a fifteenth granted by the *communitas* would not be paid by peers and their tenants, any more than the knights and theirs would pay the lords' taxation in 1400; and in spite of Professor Holdsworth's remarks,[1] it is by no means clear that counsel was not right in assuming that the lords had no more control over the grant of fifteenths by knights of the shire than knights had over the self-taxation of peers. The Year-book case of 33 Henry VI does not refer to fifteenths but to tonnage and poundage.

Page 155 (*o*). Stubbs, *Const. Hist.*, iii. 465-6: " The most influential cause of this diminution was undoubtedly the desire of the country towns to be taxed with their country neighbours, to be rated to the fifteenth with the shires and not to the tenth with the boroughs. Whilst avoiding the heavier rate, they were also relieved in a perceptible degree in the matter of the members' wages. It was much cheaper for a town to pay its fifteenth and contribute to the payment of the knights than to pay the tenth and remunerate its own burgesses." The criticism of this view,[2] on the ground that it ignores the stereotyping of tenths and fifteenths after 1334, cannot apply to the seventy boroughs or so which Stubbs calculates to have escaped making returns by that date, and the whole question is complex. Tenths were supposed to take the place of tallage, and it was natural that boroughs should pay them. But what was a borough for the purposes of taxation and representation? It was from *villæ* that representatives were summoned in 1213 to what has been called the first

---

[1] *Hist. English Law*, ii. 440. Cf. the passage from the *Modus* quoted above, p. 433.   [2] *Engl. Hist. Rev.*, Oct. 1924, p. 514.

real national council. When Exmouth excused itself in 1337, it was on the ground that it was not a *villa* and had no bailiffs.[1] How much negligence on the part of sheriffs or of boroughs themselves was required to enable seventy or so to escape, between 1295 and 1334, from the category of tenth-paying boroughs into the more privileged class which only paid fifteenths with the shires? In the fourteenth century the argument was that boroughs paid tenths because they were boroughs; in 1628 the house of commons argued that boroughs were boroughs because they paid tenths, and on that ground restored their parliamentary representation.[2] But neither age attempted a definition, and Prynne, revising his former opinion, came to the conclusion that parliamentary boroughs were made neither by custom, prescription, nor charter, but by the whim or discretion of sheriffs.[3] No need was felt in the fourteenth century for a precise definition of a parliamentary borough. It was enough to get samples together in parliament to make an ' estate ' and bind the rest. The idea of defining a category and summoning all who came within the definition was limited in the middle ages to bishops; custom determined the rest.

Nor was there any hard-and-fast rule about tenths and fifteenths. In 1346 parliament granted two fifteenths to be *levez en citees, burghs, et aunciens demeignes auxi come des communes des countees*.[4] London had secured the lower rate in 1327 and it was confirmed by Edward III in 1335.[5] In 1357 Leicester was pardoned certain fines in return for the grant of " a certain yearly fifteenth." [6] Bridgewater refers to the £26 it paid whenever a fifteenth was granted.[7]

---

[1] Pasquet, *Essai*, pp. 47–52; *Off. Return of M.P.'s*, i. 113. Parliamentary boroughs are often called *villæ*, e.g. Ipswich, Bridgewater, Newcastle-on-Tyne, Bodmin, Arundel, Dunwich, Scarborough, Southampton, Nottingham, and Yarmouth (*Rot. Parl.*, ii. 147, 178, 180, 185, 210, 221, 346, 350, 352); cities and boroughs are briefly called " villes " in 1377 (*ibid.*, iii. 7).

[2] *Commons' Journals*, 1 May, 1628.

[3] *Briefe Register*, iii. 230–1.

[4] *Rot. Parl.*, ii. 159b.

[5] *Finance and Trade under Edward III*, ed. Unwin, pp. 36–7.

[6] Bateson, *Records*, ii. 106.

[7] *Rot. Parl.*, ii. 189.

From 1389 to 1496 Oxford was petitioning for the exemption of inhabitants from fifteenths,[1] and other boroughs were doing likewise.[2] The fact that boroughs paid " tenths " clearly does not mean that no inhabitants paid fifteenths. Various towns were gradually exempted, and their exemptions amounted to £6,000 out of a total of about £39,000, and to twice that sum when two tenths and fifteenths were granted. The development of poll-taxes and subsidies, levied on persons and not on communities, further diminished, by ignoring, the difference between borough and shire taxation ; and the same may be said of the increase of customs, the cost of which was passed on by the merchants to all consumers alike, and of unparliamentary taxation such as forced loans, benevolences, and monopolies. In boroughs which were prospering, the fixed assessment based on a tenth in 1334 must have become much less than a real fifteenth before the end of the century. On the whole it seems that the effect of the difference between tenths and fifteenths upon borough representation has been exaggerated, certainly after 1334 ; if may even be doubted whether a borough ever escaped the higher rate by evading parliamentary representation.[3] If it could show good cause, it could even, while sending members to parliament and after being made a shire, get exemption from tenths and fifteenths altogether.[4]

Page 158 (*p*). An unofficial list for 1491 has been found in Brit. Mus. Harleian MS. 2252, f. 28.

Page 248 (*q*). Dr. Tait (*English Historical Review*, April 1921, p. 253 *n*.) points out " the resemblance of the four

[1] Oxford City Documents (Oxf. Hist. Soc.), pp. 98–129 ; *Parl. Petitions* (Oxf. Hist. Soc.'s *Collectanea*, iii.), pp. 87, 152, 156, 158 ; Stat. 12 Henry VII, c. 13.

[2] Cf. Whitley, *Parl. Repres. of Coventry*, p. 20 ; Chanter and Wainewright, *Barnstaple Records*, i. 128–9, 245 ; ii. 88.

[3] Cf. Riess, *Gesch. des Wahlrechts*, pp. 25–6 ; Pasquet, *Essai*, p. 197.

[4] In 1497 the statutory exemptions were for the laity " within the shire of the city of Lincoln," Yarmouth and New Shoreham, while Cambridge had confirmed its limitation to £20 for each tenth and fifteenth enacted by 3 Ed. IV. These statutory exemptions account for a very small fraction of the £6,000 allowable. The universities of Oxford and Cambridge and colleges of Eton and Winchester were also exempted from the subsidy of that year (12 Henry VII, cc. 12, 13).

woolsacks arranged in a square . . . to the four benches
(*scamna*) which were a feature common to English shire
courts and the courts of German towns." In each case
the arrangement indicates confidential discussion rather
than formal debate and, so far as the shires courts are
concerned, a much smaller gathering than a meeting of
four men from each vill and twelve from each borough
whom the sheriff summoned (Pasquet, *Essai*, 1914,
p. 18).

Page 304 (*r*). The number of peerages is considerably
larger because (i) there have to be added the Scottish and
Irish peerages which do not entitle their holders to sit in
the house of lords, and (ii) a number of peers hold more
than one peerage. Whereas two centuries ago the house
of commons was two and half times as large as the house
of lords, the latter now outnumbers the former by more
than a hundred. So far as the peers by inheritance are
concerned, they are now a public meeting which does not
meet.

Page 331 (*s*). I cannot agree with Dr. Holdsworth
(*Hist. Engl. Law*, i. 364, *n.* 7) that the case to which I refer
" is merely an inquiry without any reference to strictly
judicial proceedings," unless " strictly judicial " excludes
all proceedings in the house of commons and therefore
begs the question. " The bill against Benet Smyth for
the murder of Giles Rufford " was read first on 6 Nov.,
1555; on the 18th the house ordered " that Smyth be
brought hither from the Tower," and desired two of the
council to move the queen " that Smyth and his accusers
may be brought personally to this house." On the 20th
the council ordered the lieutenant of the Tower to conduct
him " there to be examined "; and on the 22nd we have
" the bill against Benet Smyth—*judicium*." It became law
that session (2 and 3 Phil. and Mary, c. 17). It merely
deprived him of his benefit of clergy, but without that
he could not have been hanged; and the examination
of the accused and his accusers and *judicium* by the
house of commons, if not " strictly judicial proceedings,"

were more than " merely an inquiry " and had a very strict reference to the judicial proceedings at the assizes.[1]

Page 343 (*t*). F. S. Oliver, *Alexander Hamilton*, 1906, p. 476. The remark was used with some effect by Prof. McIlwain in his *High Court of Parliament*, and appears to be reminiscent of Machiavelli's *di tutte le servitu dure quella e durissima che ti sottomette ad una Republica* (see my *Factors in American History*, 1925, p. 32).

Page 347 (*u*). With the possible exception of the Reform Act of 1832.

Page 365 (*v*). During the war the Dominion of Canada imposed an income-tax which is probably permanent, and there have been many other illustrations of the growth of unity within the several Dominions.

---

[1] *Commons' Journals*, i. 43*a*, 44*b*, 45*a*; *Acts of the Privy Council*, 1554–6, pp. 195, 231, 243 ; Machyn, *Diary*, pp. 102, 349.   For other references to more judicial proceedings see my *Henry VIII*, p. 259, *n.* 2.

INDEX

Guildford, 423
Guilds, 174–5, 227, 351, 353

Hakewill, W., 68, 163, 231, 270, 323
Haldane, Lord, 367
Hale, Sir Matthew, 31, 308
Halifax, 174
Hallam, H., 64, 144, 163
Hamely, John, 412
Hamilton, Alexander, 236
Hampden, John, 146, 163
Hampshire, 53, 162–3, 409
Hanover, house of, 303
Hardy, Sir T. Duffus, 68, 138, 168
Harold, King, 137
Hatton, Sir Christopher, 23
Haxey, Thomas, 74, 426
Hedon, 396
Helston, 409, 412, 423
Henry I, 42, 54, 86, 109
—— II, 5, 14, 26, 32, 36, 45, 54,
65, 89–92, 111, 127, 135, 192,
195–6, 225, 244, 359, 367–8
—— III, 9, 28–9, 32, 36, 49, 90,
101, 135, 143, 285, 335, 435
—— IV, 70, 206, 281, 308, 335, 391
—— V, 68, 70, 104, 330, 392, 438
—— VI, 22, 72, 133, 155, 158, 171,
217, 245, 283, 285, 294, 316,
320, 418, 433
—— VII, 33–4, 61, 71, 76, 100, 113,
130, 132, 142, 145–6, 158, 162,
173, 188, 252, 259, 263–5, 273,
276, 284, 293, 301, 323, 331, 335,
439
—— VIII, 11, 14, 34, 76, 104, 117,
126, 161–3, 173, 176, 191, 193,
198, 203, 207, 212, 214–15, 225,
230–2, 261, 264, 266–72, 276,
283–5, 294, 301–3, 309, 321–3,
331, 336, 342, 383–4, 390, 440
Heraldry, 104
Hereditary right, 78–9, 82–5, 87,
94, 99–100, 102–5, 141, 178, 220,
232, 274, 299, 300, 304, 306–7,
310–12, 314, 369
Herefordshire, 422
Heresy statutes, 210, 243, 267, 275
Hertfordshire, 163, 396
Hildebrand, 189, 192, 207, 221
Hill, John, 155 n. 2, 412–13
Hindon, 396
Hobbes, Thomas, 151–2, 185, 226,
343, 347, 363, 365, 378
Hohenzollerns, 341
Holdsworth, W. S., x, 431, 438,
442, 445
Holland, 213
Holles, Denzil, 163

Honours, 6, 89, 146
" Houses " of Parliament, 20, 34,
52, 59, 61, 74, 79, 117, 122–4,
246, 272, 310, 322–4, 334, 375
Hull, 394, 420 n. 4, 423
Humber, R., 136–7, 200
Hundreds, 89, 109, 152
Hunne, Richard, 270, 301

Impeachment, 78–9, 93, 112, 147,
239, 247, 249, 253, 309
Indenture, nomination of M.P.'s by,
405, 418
Independence, 180, 191–2, 194, 208,
213, 215, 227, 351
—— War of American, 181, 237,
436
India, 10, 137, 366–7, 376
Individualism, 143–4, 166, 174–6,
183, 217, 219–20, 342, 353–4, 356
Infallibility, papal, 193
—— parliamentary, 14, 177, 231–2
Innocent III, 211
Inquest, grand, 79, 97, 309
Ipswich, 318, 398 n. 2, 415 n. 1
Ireland, 68–9, 71, 167, 250, 304, 342,
344, 361, 367, 423, 425, 433
Ireton, General, 182
Italy, 4, 46, 108, 189–90, 213

James I, 71, 106, 157, 163, 177–8,
214, 230, 251–2, 273, 299, 303,
308, 335, 342, 385, 437
—— II, 191, 316, 337
Jews, 38, 42, 49, 169, 362
John, King, 8, 39, 86, 90, 108, 135,
168–9, 187, 299
Journals, Lords', 24, 35, 68, 100,
104, 125, 287, 330, 332, 336
—— Commons', 24, 35, 113–14,
125, 159, 263, 322, 325–6, 329,
332
Judges, 86–7, 110–11, 195, 238–9,
244–5, 252, 259, 293–5, 301, 368
—— in parliament, 24, 31–2, 37–
42, 69, 79, 97, 112, 120, 123–4,
129–31, 141, 143, 178–9, 240, 248,
250, 292, 300, 307–10, 386
Judicium parium, 91–3, 96–7
Juries and jurors, 29, 38, 109,
134, 153–4, 173, 185, 387
Jury, trial by, 27, 147
Justices, lords, 250
—— of the peace. *See* Peace.

Keighley, Henry of, 115
Kent, 163, 174, 422
—— Henry Grey, Earl of, 384
—— Thomas, 285

PRINTED IN GREAT BRITAIN BY
RICHARD CLAY & SONS, LIMITED,
BUNGAY, SUFFOLK.